COLORS *of the* ROBE

Studies in Comparative Religion
Frederick M. Denny, *Series Editor*

COLORS *of the* ROBE
Religion, Identity, and Difference

Ananda Abeysekara

University of South Carolina Press

© 2002 University of South Carolina

Published in Columbia, South Carolina, by the
University of South Carolina Press

Manufactured in the United States of America

06 05 04 03 02   5 4 3 2 1

Library of Congress Cataloging-in-Publication Data

Abeysekara, Ananda, 1968-
  Colors of the robe : religion, identity, and difference / Ananda
Abeysekara.
    p. cm. — (Studies in comparative religion)
Includes bibliographical references and index.
  ISBN 1-57003-467-2 (alk. paper)
  1. Religion and culture—Sri Lanka. 2. Buddhism—Social aspects—Sri Lanka. I. Title.
II. Studies in comparative religion (Columbia, S.C.)
BL65.C8 A24 2002
306.6'943'095493—dc21   2002005687

Portions of the book have appeared in slightly different form in the *Journal of the International Association of Buddhist Studies* 22, no. 2 (1999): 251–80, and *Numen* 48, no. 1 (2001): 1–48.

For my late grandfather L. D. L. Abeysekara
and my late parents, Herbert and Ariyawati Abeysekara

After Bandung, after the dissolution of the project of the anti-imperialist sovereignty, after Michael Manley, we do not inhabit the same political horizons as before; nor do we inhabit the same intellectual and ideological context of options. That dream is over. Therefore, we have to ask ourselves (postcolonial intellectuals and critics, and critics and intellectuals of the postcolonial) whether we want to continue to pursue this line of preoccupation opened up by postcoloniality on the very eve of Bandung's decline. We have to ask ourselves what the yield will be of continuing to deepen our understanding of a conceptual space whose contours we have now become so familiar with, and whose insights are rapidly on their way to becoming a new orthodoxy. We have to ask ourselves whether it might not be more useful to try to expand the conceptual boundaries themselves by altering the target of our criticism. *This,* it seems to me, is the challenge of our present.

—David Scott, *Refashioning Futures*

I seek to diagnose, to carry out a diagnosis of the present: to say what we are today and what it means, today, to say what we do say. This work of excavation beneath our feet has characterized contemporary thought since Nietzsche.

—Michel Foucault, "Who Are You, Professor Foucault?"

CONTENTS

SERIES EDITOR'S PREFACE

The study of Buddhism in the West has undergone significant developments since the nineteenth century, when the subject was energetically engaged by orientalists, Christian missionaries, Eastern wisdom enthusiasts, and others whose primary focus was the tradition's central doctrinal teachings and meditative practices, whether its Mahayana or Theravada expressions. The post–World War II period witnessed a diverse proliferation of Buddhist studies in both humanistic and social scientific directions. Anthropological studies based on fieldwork and informed by local knowledge have considerably broadened and enriched our understanding of Buddhist peoples and their social, cultural, and political identities beyond the classical doctrines and practices of the tradition, however vital and compelling they continue to be.

One of the most appealing and challenging Buddhist regions for study, whether by historians of religion or anthropologists, has been Sri Lanka. Two earlier books in this series have meaningfully captured for our understanding key elements of Theravada Buddhism in Sri Lanka and beyond: George D. Bond's *The Buddhist Revival in Sri Lanka: Religious Tradition, Reinterpretation and Response* (1988) and Donald K. Swearer and Russell F. Sizemore's *Ethics, Wealth and Salvation: A Study in Buddhist Social Ethics* (1990).

Ananda Abeysekara's *Colors of the Robe: Religion, Identity, and Difference* ventures beyond most other studies to date in tracking, identifying, and locating Sri Lankan Buddhism in its sectarian, ethnic, cultural, social, and political dimensions by means of a detailed, assertive, and illuminating postmodern analysis and critique. The book is enormously well informed both about Sri Lankan Buddhist traditions and modern scholarship on them. It addresses the most difficult and challenging dimensions of contemporary Sri Lanka, including the roles played by various factions in that country's competing constructions of religion and politics. There are, as the author argues, various "colors of the robe" in the postcolonial heritage of Sri Lankan identity and difference where the very definition of Buddhism is problematic. And although the author forthrightly criticizes what he perceives to be serious errors, limiting biases, and fundamental misunderstandings in previous scholarship, he does so in a balanced and judicious manner. This book will be read, debated, and cited worldwide, both for the light it sheds on Sri Lankan Buddhist affairs and for the theoretical implications it carries for new approaches to the study of religion, culture, politics, and violence in other global regions.

FREDERICK M. DENNY

ACKNOWLEDGMENTS

I owe thanks to many who shared in the labor that went into making this work possible. The field research for the book was carried out in Sri Lanka at different times spanning roughly four years from 1994 to 1997. I spent countless hours conversing with and learning from an innumerable number of people from all walks of life—monks, laymen and women, university lecturers and students, journalists, three-wheel drivers, hotel owners, waiters, politicians, and others—in various villages, towns, and cities of the Sri Lankan geopolitical universe. First and foremost, without wanting to relegate them to a mere footnote, I wish to record my deepest gratitude to these people for accommodating my intrusive and obtrusive questions about the domains of their public/private and moral/political lives of struggle, pain, suffering, and indeed death that inform the contents of this book.

I have incurred enormous intellectual debts. To George Bond, under whose direction and council I conceived and completed the dissertation project on which this book is based, I remain forever indebted. I feel truly privileged and honored to have worked with an *āchārya* of his caliber and can never adequately acknowledge the kind of intellectual support and friendship he has extended to me over the years. As what I will call my second adviser, Robert Launay read and reread several versions of this work with unrivaled patience and offered penetrating criticisms that salvaged it from many theoretical mishaps. As a graduate student, I came to impose on his time and intellectual space to such an extent that I find myself ever in his debt. His wisdom, wit, and irony guided and guarded me through numerous stages of mapping out the contours of this project.

That my greatest intellectual debt remains to David Scott should be glaringly visible to any reader of the book. The spirit of his profound thinking; his radical, (perhaps) unconventional approach to interrogating and impeaching yesterday's disciplinary claims; his critical vision to reimagine today's intellectual horizons and refashion for tomorrow new ways of thinking about and inhabiting our postcolonial world of identity and difference; and, in a nutshell, his sustained commitment to refashioning postcolonial criticism, animates, I think, every page of this work. His comments on a couple of later drafts enabled me to pass through major theoretical barriers and give the book its current shape and coherence.

Another ardent and vigilant critic whose works I have found indispensable to reconfiguring the disciplinary productions of knowledges about culture and identity is Pradeep Jeganathan. He read an early draft and posed crucial questions about delimiting the field of politics. The detailed suggestions by the anonymous readers for the University of South Carolina Press have been helpful to reshaping the final version of the manuscript. One reader who later cast off his anonymity, Charles Hallisey, deserves special mention for offering meticulous readings of several drafts. He raised hard questions, challenging me to scrutinize my own assumptions as I scrutinize those of others. Indeed, some of the substantive final revisions that have made this a better book owe to the diligence and interest with which he engaged the text. I value Joseph Walser's instructive feedback on several versions of the draft and thank him for lending me an ear whenever I needed a question clarified or a statement thought out loud. Gananath Obeyesekere, in the midst of completing his own work in Sri Lanka, took time and care to read the introduction and offer some critical suggestions, and I am grateful to him. The vast body of his phenomenal and pioneering work has deeply inspired me in laboring to conceive many of the ideas pivotal to the book. Others who have commented on specific chapters of the book during different phases of its making and remaking are Gunjan Bakshi Pant, Brook Zyporin, C. R. and Daya de Silva, Rachelle Jacobs, Caitrin Lynch, Jim Laine, Brian Britt, Elizabeth Struthers Malbon, Carol Ryzack, and the late Edmund F. Perry. I give them all my sincere thanks.

I presented aspects of this work at the University of Minnesota, the University of Chicago, the University of Wisconsin at Madison, the University of Florida, Virginia Polytechnic Institute and State University, and the American Academy of Religion; I thank those who participated on these occasions for their comments and queries. In particular, I would like to mention the two-day conference "Disciplines, Location, and Politics" held in May 2001 at the Department of Anthropology and Global Studies, University of Minnesota. This proved a signal forum: a cast of scholars from several disciplines, with particular stakes in Sri Lanka, engaged each other's work by way of sustaining an ongoing conversation to part company with the dominant representations of Sri Lanka as an empirical archive in which ready-made knowledges about its violence, terrorism, difference, and division await disciplinary explanation and authorization. I thank those who participated in the conference and commented on my work: Malathi de Alwis, Qadri Ismail, Pradeep Jeganathan, David Scott, Vasuki Nesiah, Vyjayanthi Rao, Antony Anghie, and Niveditha Menon. One of the demands of our meeting was to begin conceptualizing Sri Lanka as a site of particular moral-political debates central to reordering the terms of democracy and pluralism in the postcolonial world. Indeed, this work, in some small measure, aspires if not contributes to this kind of urgent task, insofar as the book is not simply about Sri Lanka but about such moral-political debates. It is not about Sri Lanka as a culture of difference in some far-off corner of South Asia, but about the ways in which differences as such are contingently fashioned, debated, and subverted. Another demand of our meeting was to explore the possibilities of becoming part of, inserting ourselves into, such debates. This book does not, of course, address that specific concern in explicit terms, but I believe that the very exercise of demonstrating the emergence and submergence of debates, their centrality to constructing organized spaces in which different kinds of subjects can come to voice different kinds of argument, discord, and disagreement so as to eventually enable differing forms of democratic, pluralizing being, constitutes an attempt. I wish to take up these issues in detail in a future study. I have also put to test key theoretical concepts in the book in two of my upper-level courses at Virginia Tech—namely, "Violence in Religion and Culture" and "Colonialism, Religion, and Nationalism in India"—and thank my students for their patient indulgence and probing questions.

Antonio Chiareli, Niran Weerasinghe, Nirmala Salgado, Stacy Floyd-Thomas, Bardwell Smith, and Mahinda Degalle have afforded me much support and encouragement. Among many others who have assisted me in all too numerous ways, in both Sri Lanka and the United States, are Kakkapalliye Anuruddha, Warakawe Dhammaloka, Dewalegama Medhananda, Kehelulle Pannasoma, J. B. Disanayaka, Niran Weerasinghe, Sadagomi Koperahewa, Michael Roberts, H. L. and Indrani Seneviratne, Hema and Vernon Weerasinghe, Joy and Dale Batchelor, and Chandrika and Abey Bandara. I can never repay the debt to my sisters Deepa, Nilmini, and Lakmali, and my brother, Priyantha, who graciously hosted me and generously gave me of their time and energy to nurture my venture. Gunjan Pant endured the agony of reading, rereading, listening to me read, and reread every word of this work at the most inconvenient times and places. My indebtedness to her is inestimable. My late grandfather prepared me for the daunting task of arriving at this juncture in ways he could never realize. I do not know how to thank him sufficiently. As a small token of gratitude, I dedicate this book to his memory and to that of my late parents.

I also wish to thank my editors, Fred Denny and Barry Blose, for their support of this project, their enthusiasm, and their counsel. The research for the book was conducted with financial assistance from Northwestern University, the Center for International and Comparative Studies, and the Rocky Foundation. I would be remiss if I did not thank my copyeditor, Dennis Marshall, for his fine work on the manuscript, and Barbara A. Brannon and Karen Beidel at the University of South Carolina Press for their counsel at final stages of producing this book.

CHAPTER ONE

Limits of Disciplinary Claims on Religion and Culture

Today "culture" and "religion" have become the objects of a specific kind of disciplinary inquiry. "Culture," as the familiar, if not the dominant, argument in the social sciences goes, is not unitary, reified, solid, fixed, and essential, but is unbounded, nonunitary, fluid, changing, and so on. On this view, the very concept of culture or religion (and the instances of their plurals, like "Indian culture" or "Hinduism") appears suspect—and indeed dangerous—in that such labels, whose formation can be located in specific historical, ideological contexts, reify complex plural practices and discourses that supposedly constitute unbounded and hybrid identities.[1] Consider, for example, Arjun Appadurai's recent attempt at rethinking the concept of culture in the postcolonial context of what is being called globalization:

> Culture is not usefully regarded as a substance but is better regarded as a dimension of phenomena, a dimension that attends to situated and embodied difference. Stressing the dimensionality of culture rather than its substantiality permits our thinking of culture less as a property of individuals and groups and more as a heuristic device that we can use to talk about difference.[2]

Appadurai's suggestion is an important one because it wants to question the normalization of the relation between culture and difference. In other words, Appadurai, as I read him, wants to divest "culture" of any essential,

1. Of course, as early as the 1960s, Wilfred Cantwell Smith made a similar argument for religion. He went so far as to propose that the word *religion* was so "distorting" that the concept be "dropped"; see Smith, *The Meaning and End of Religion: A New Approach to the Religious Traditions of Mankind* (1962; reprint, New York: Macmillan, 1963), 50. In a masterly reading of this work, Talal Asad has shown that Smith, who undoubtedly broke new ground by rejecting an essence of religion, eventually fell prey to an essentialism (Asad, "Reading a Modern Classic: W. C. Smith's *The Meaning and End of Religion,*" *History of Religions* 1 [2001]: 205–22).

2. Arjun Appadurai, *Modernity at Large: Cultural Dimensions of Globalization* (Minneapolis: University of Minnesota Press, 1996), 12–13.

homogenous "identity" that would preclude "differences" from it.[3] However, this argument about what culture is or is not is not wholly unproblematic. As David Scott has suggested, one critical question that we need to pose is, "For *whom* is 'culture' unbounded [or essenceless]? For the anthropologist [and the like-minded scholar] or the native? That is, for (Western) theory or for the (local) discourse which theory is endeavoring to engage, inquire upon?"[4] Scott states that we need to be cautious with this unboundedness-of-culture argument because some native discourses "do in fact 'establish' authoritative 'traditions,' discrete temporal and spatial parameters in which it is made singularly clear to cultural subjects *and their others* what is (and who are) to belong within it, and what (and who) do not."[5] He goes on to argue that "the idea that 'culture' is unbounded" is problematic because it is grounded in a set of assumptions about "what culture is or is not."[6] (In a different context, Akhil Gupta and James Ferguson have reminded us that even the so-called "deterritorialization" does not simply create "subjects who are free-floating

---

3. Important in this regard is also Lila Abu-Lughod's famous attempt at "writing against culture" as a way of dismantling the normalization of culture and identity: Abu-Lughod, "Writing against Culture," in *Recapturing Anthropology*, ed. Richard Fox (Santa Fe, N.M.: School of American Research Press, 1991).

4. David Scott, *Formations of Ritual: Colonial and Anthropological Discourses on the Sinhala Yaktovil* (Minneapolis: University of Minnesota Press, 1994), xvii–xviii. Scott's work has yet to be sufficiently appreciated; it is one of the most significant disciplinary interventions in interrogating the colonial assumptions that have gone into the uncritical anthropological and anthropologically minded production and deployment of categories such as Buddhism, demonism, religion, culture, ritual, and so forth. I am astounded by the lack of any reference to Scott's work in Frank E. Reynolds's "Coming of Age: Buddhist Studies in the United States from 1972–1997," *Journal of the International Association of Buddhist Studies* 22, no. 2 (1999): 459–83.

5. Scott, *Formations of Ritual*, xvii–xviii (emphasis and wording are true to the original). Here Scott has in mind James Clifford, who argues that "'cultures' do not hold still for their portraits"; see his "Partial Truths," the introduction to *Writing Culture: Politics and Poetics of Ethnography*, ed. James Clifford and George E. Marcus (Berkeley: University of California, 1986), 10. For Clifford's more recent attempts at rethinking ideas of culture/identity in terms of what he calls "everyday practices of dwelling and traveling: traveling-in-dwelling and dwelling-in-travel," see "Traveling Cultures," in *Routes: Travel and Translation in the Late Twentieth Century* (Cambridge: Harvard University Press, 1997), 36. Scott has detailed the argument about the inadequacy of the antiessentialist claims in his "Criticism and Culture: Theory and Post-Colonial Claims on Anthropological Disciplinarity," *Critique of Anthropology* 12, no. 4 (1992): 283–300. Also see Scott's "Criticism after Postcoloniality," in his *Refashioning Futures: Criticism after Postcoloniality* (Princeton: Princeton University Press, 1999), esp. 9–10.

6. Scott, *Formations of Ritual*, xvii–xviii.

monads, despite what is sometimes implied by those eager to celebrate the freedom and playfulness of the postmodern condition.")[7]

I find Scott's remarks penetrating. They unmask some unquestioned essentialist assumptions that remain seemingly authorized in an antiessentialist (Western) scholarly theory. However, I want to point out that—as Scott himself seems to recognize—we cannot simply stop at the point where we just identify the formations of authoritative "traditions." It seems to me that if we are to resist the obviously problematic antiessentialist argument—without, at the same time, falling back on an earlier but problematic essentialist view of culture—and continue to interrogate the often normalized unity of culture and difference,[8] we need to do something else. My purpose in this book is to propose such an alternative.[9]

I want to demonstrate modestly some of the ways in which the relations between what can and cannot count as Buddhism, culture, and difference, alter within specific "native" debates. That is, to demonstrate the ways in which what I call "minute contingent conjunctures" make possible and *centrally* visible the emergence and submergence, the centering and marginalizing, the privileging and subordinating of what and who can and cannot constitute "Buddhism" and "difference" (in this case, in Sri Lanka). To be more precise, what concerns me are the ways in which diverse persons, practices, discourses, and institutions conjoin to foreground competing definitions about "Buddhism" and its "others" within a period of a few years, if not months or days. Those competing discourses that seek to foreground such definitions often do so in order to take precedence over formerly authoritative discourses defining the terms and parameters of religion and difference. This, as I will theorize it in depth below, is what I mean by *contingent*

7. Gupta and Ferguson, "Beyond 'Culture': Space, Identity, and the Politics of Difference," in *Culture, Power, Place: Explorations in Critical Anthropology*, ed. Akhil Gupta and James Ferguson (1997; reprint, Durham: Duke University Press, 1999), 50.

8. Gupta and Ferguson suggest that to problematize the essential "unity of 'us' and the otherness of the 'other' . . . [and] the radical separation" between culture and difference, we explore the "the processes of the *production* of difference"; ibid., 43. My interest, of course, is in the contingent, altering formations of the relation between identity and difference.

9. Valentine Daniel seeks to move beyond the constructedness-of-culture argument, claiming that what needs to be shown is not how a "reality . . . is historically and culturally constructed, but how deeply so"; Daniel, *Charged Lullabies: Chapters in an Athropography of Violence* (Princeton: Princeton University Press, 1996), 14. But Daniel and I do not share the same concern.

conjunctures.[10] More generally, this is a study of the formations and deformations of contingent relations between "religious" identity and difference. Here I take *difference* to mean that which is *made* to differ from, oppose, or contrast with (religious) identity by particular competing discourses. We see this, for example, when falsehood is contrasted with truth, where violence is made to differ from Buddhism, terror from civilization, or politics from religion. I do not, of course, claim that something called "religious identity" remains essentially and permanently opposed to difference, nor vice versa; I seek to show how the relation between what comes to count as religion or difference alters in varying conjunctures.

Now at the risk of restating the obvious, I should note that my interest here is not to tell in complicated ways the now-familiar Western progressivist story of secularism, about how religion changes or how politics play a role in religion.[11] Indeed, my labor is to think against the grain of such assumptions and provide alternatives to conceptualizing altering definitions of religion and difference, which is often referred to as "religious change." What I want to point out is that if we are to produce a different kind of understanding of the shifting relation between religion and difference, we need to locate the *central visibility* of the emergence and submergence, authorization and unauthorization of specific knowledges about what does and does not count as "Buddhism" in conjunctures of debates. I want to approach this task by problematizing a particular set of arguments embedded within a genre of important "postcolonial" literature busily "decolonizing" the supposed "colonial" knowledges of religion, culture, and difference in South Asia.

Something of the general significance of the emergence of these decolonizing projects can be captured in the words of Bernard S. Cohn, one of the most provocative and fruitful thinkers in the field. Writing in the mid-1980s about the British rule in India, Cohn argued: "The conquest of India was a

---

10. To be absolutely clear, I will repeat what I mean by contingent conjunctures: I mean a period of a few years, if not months or days, in which competing narratives and debates conjoin (and converge) to make centrally visible particular authoritative knowledges about what can and cannot count as Buddhism. Henceforward, the phrases *contingent conjunctures* and *conjunctures of contingent discourses and debates* are used to mean just that.

11. For a fascinating discussion of the problematic of secularism, see William Connolly, "Conceits of Secularism," in his *Why I Am Not a Secularist* (Minneapolis: University of Minnesota Press, 1999); also see Talal Asad, "Religion, Nation-State, and Secularism," in *Nation and Religion: Perspectives on Europe and Asia,* ed. Peter van der Veer and Hartmut Lehmann (Princeton: Princeton University Press, 1999).

conquest of knowledge."[12] Cohn's remarks point to, if not precede,[13] the now familiar argument that in "determining, codifying, controlling, and representing the [Indian] past,"[14] the colonial empire, followed by its baggage of Christian missionaries, orientalists, philologists, et al., produced particular authoritative knowledges of what India's culture, religion, and history were/ are all about. Stated differently, the conditions of colonialism/orientalism made possible the authorization of an "India" of essences; that is, that India was a "village" community, its religion centered around "caste," and so on (in particular, I here think of Ronald Inden's influential book *Imagining India* as one of many examples of this kind of argument.)[15] Since Cohn, a number of scholars have argued that our postcolonial disciplinary representations of South Asia continue to disseminate those essentialist knowledges, for they are more often than not informed by colonial categories and objects of knowledge such as "Hinduism," "Buddhism," "demonism."[16] What I seek to point out is that, stretched beyond a particular limit, the logic

12. Bernard S. Cohn, "The Command of Language and the Language of Command," in his seminal *Colonialism and Its Forms of Knowledge: The British in India* (Princeton: Princeton University Press, 1996), 16; originally published in *Subaltern Studies IV: Writings on South Asian History and Society*, ed. Ranajit Guha (Delhi: Oxford University Press, 1985), 276.

13. As Nicholas Dirks notes in his foreword to *Colonialism and Its Forms of Knowledge*, (ix), Cohn began to write about the colonial constructions of knowledge "long before . . . Foucault made 'knowledge' a term that seemed irrevocably linked to power, and before Edward Said so provocatively opened up discussions between power and knowledge in colonial discourses and Orientalist scholarship." For Cohn's writings between the early 1950s and the 1980s, see his *An Anthropologist Among the Historians and Other Essays* (Delhi: Oxford University Press, 1985).

14. Cohn, *Colonialism and Its Forms*, 3.

15. Ronald Inden, *Imagining India* (London: Basil Blackwell, 1990). The major premise of Inden's book is that orientalist discourses created essential knowledges about India, displacing the Indian "human agency." Inden is concerned with locating and restoring that agency to Indians. I am in sympathy with this concern, but skeptical of its theoretical value because I do not think that there is some supposed "Indian" agency to be restored. For an empirical criticism of Inden's work, see David Kopf, review of *Imagining India*, by Ronald Inden, *Journal of the American Oriental Society* 112, no. 4 (1992): 674–77. This kind of concern with locating Indian agency bears some relation to the work of the Subaltern Studies Collective, inaugurated by Ranajit Guha, Partha Chatterjee, and others. Gayatri Spivak's important question "Can the Subaltern Speak?" (in *Marxism and the Interpretation of Culture*, ed. Gary Nelson and Lawrence Grossberg [Urbana: University of Illinois Press, 1988]), is now well known. For a critical reflection on this question, see Teresa Hubel, *Whose India? The Independence Struggle in British and Indian Fiction and History* (Durham, N.C.: Duke University Press, 1996), 119–26.

16. For unmasking colonial constructions of Buddhism, see Philip Almond, *The British Discovery of Buddhism* (New York: Cambridge University Press, 1988). For such labors in the area of Theravada Buddhism, see David Scott, *Formations of Ritual*; Pradeep Jeganathan, "Authorizing

of this argument shatters, running the risk of reproducing the very problematic that it sets out to displace.

As a way of pointing to the place where this decolonizing/deconstructing problematic begins to emerge, let me turn to the general argument of the important volume *Orientalism and the Postcolonial Predicament*, edited by Carol Breckenridge and Peter van der Veer.[17] Clearly inspired by the now familiar Saidian critique of "Orientalism"[18] and Foucauldian concepts of power/knowledge (more on this later), the book is concerned with exploring the relations between colonialism, knowledge, and difference. The book is not, however, just another attempt at making visible the dynamics of the production of orientalist knowledges about India within the context of the colonial past; nor is it about the reproduction of such knowledges by some present-day disciplinary texts. Though both concerns inform it, the "common theme" (as they call it) that pervades the overall theoretical organization of the book is the claim that there is a direct relation between orientalist discourses and contemporary Indian identity. Take, for example, the following eloquent statement:

> It is very difficult for both Indians and outsiders to think outside of orientalist habits and categories. The consequence is not a sort of lag, where political independence runs ahead of intellectual dependence. Rather, *the very cultural basis of public life has been affected (and infected) by ideas of difference and division that have colonial and orientalist roots* [my emphasis]. Whether it is a matter of language and literature, communalism and the census, or caste and social science, orientalist theory casts its shadow over cultural politics in postcolonial India even though the specific politics of colonial domination are no longer relevant. This irony is at the heart of the "postcolonial predicament," namely that a theory of difference that was

---

History, Ordering Land: The Conquest of Anuradhapura," in *Unmaking the Nation: The Politics of Identity and History in Modern Sri Lanka*, ed. P. Jeganathan and Qadri Ismail (Colombo: Social Scientists' Association, 1996); Charles Hallisey, "Roads Taken and Not Taken in the Study of Theravada Buddhism," in *Curators of the Buddha: The Study of Buddhism under Colonialism*, ed. S. Donald Lopez Jr. (Chicago: University of Chicago Press, 1995): the entire collection of papers in this volume is concerned with the relation between colonialism/orientalism and Buddhism in general.

17. Carol Breckenridge and Peter van der Veer, eds., *Orientalism and the Postcolonial Predicament* (Philadelphia: University of Pennsylvania Press, 1993).

18. See Edward W. Said, *Orientalism* (New York: Vintage, 1978).

deeply interwoven with the practices of colonial control lives on in the absence of foreign rule.[19]

What Breckenridge and van der Veer seek to do, interested as they are in conceptualizing the relation between culture and difference, is to understand contemporary India as suffering from the *infection* of colonial influences, for the very terms *India, Hindu,* and even *Muslim* are, as they claim, themselves to a large extent colonial constructs.[20] For Breckenridge and van der Veer, the point where the infection of colonialism/orientalism becomes most apparent is contemporary Indian "nationalism." "By casting its master questions in terms of what made Indians different qua Indians, and also what made differences among Indians so much more pervasive than differences elsewhere (that is, the specter of caste), orientalist discourse gave a peculiar essentialist twist to nationalist discourse."[21] Or, as the editors so eloquently put it, "nationalism is the avatar [incarnation] of orientalism."[22] (Note here that for them "nationalism"—colonial or contemporary—is a transparently identifiable category as such; that is, what counts as nationalism always remains the same.)[23]

Breckenridge and van der Veer go on to state that "one of the most lasting and fundamental of the orientalist contributions to knowledge about India was the essentialization of the Hindu-Muslim opposition."[24] On this view, "Indians," particularly those classified as nationalists, are ambassadors of orientalist discourses living in a culture of orientalism.[25] Van der Veer, in his contribution to the volume, speaking of the supposed dissemination of Hindu "nationalist discourse" beyond the confines of India, for example, argues that "in an ironic twist of history, orientalism is now brought by Indians to Indians

19. Breckenridge and van der Veer, eds., *Orientalism and the Postcolonial Predicament,* 11.
20. Ibid., 17.
21. Ibid., 11.
22. Ibid., 12.
23. Here I would even accept (with some reservation) Chatterjee's claim that nationalism that emerged in the context of colonialism was a "derivative discourse"; see Chatterjee, *Nationalist Thought and the Colonial World: A Derivative Discourse?* (1983; reprint, Minneapolis: University of Minnesota Press, 1998). Critics like Veena Das have rejected this argument; see Das, "Language and Body: Transactions in the Construction of Pain," in *Social Suffering,* ed. Veena Das et al. (Berkeley: University of California Press, 1997), 90n. But my suspicions pertain to the relation between the colonial and postcolonial nationalism(s). For my perspective on the postcolonial constructions of nationalist discourses, see chapter 5.
24. Breckenridge and van der Veer, eds., *Orientalism and the Postcolonial Predicament,* 12.
25. Ibid. For a similar argument, see van der Veer, *Religious Nationalism: Hindus and Muslims in India* (Berkeley: University of California Press, 1994).

living in the West."[26] It is in light of such a verdict that the editors contend that "moving beyond orientalism is one of the most pressing needs of contemporary scholarly investigations."[27] "Thus, one way out of the orientalist dilemma," they go on to write, "is to remain steadfastly focused on the present, seen as a historical movement that owes itself at least in part to the very heritage of colonialism that we seek to undo."[28]

Now anyone who possesses a modicum of familiarity with the world-conquering project of colonialism can easily see some insight in these remarks. Today it has become almost an orthodoxy that colonialism, as Scott notes, "was involved in disabling old forms of life by systematically breaking down their conditions, and with constructing in their place new conditions so as to enable—indeed, so as to *oblige*—new forms of life to come into being."[29] I can accept this argument. But what I find problematic is the postcolonial labor to decolonize colonial knowledges of "Indian" religion, culture, and difference; that is, "the very heritage of colonialism" supposedly embedded in contemporary Indian discourses.[30] I worry that this labor reproduces the very *colonial distinction* between the "colonial" and the "native," the "oriental" and the "Western."[31] If colonialism/orientalism, among other things, classified, categorized, defined, and even created an "India"—producing, as van der Veer

26. See van der Veer, "The Foreign Hand: Orientalist Discourse in Sociology and Communalism," in *Orientalism and the Postcolonial Predicament*, 43.

27. Ibid., 17.

28. Ibid., 18.

29. Scott, "Colonial Governmentality," *Social Text* 43 (summer 1995): 193. For a similar argument, see Talal Asad, "Conscripts of Western Civilization," in *Dialectical Anthropology: Essays in Honor of Stanley Diamond*, ed. Christine Ward Gailey (Gainesville: University Press of Florida, 1992), 337–40. Note that what Scott and Asad argue is not the same as saying, as does van der Veer, that "the orientalist impact on the way Indians perceive themselves is also far-reaching"; see van der Veer, *Religious Nationalism*, 20. Van der Veer further maintains, "I do believe that Colonialism brought about a major transformation of Indian society" (61). In my view, these kinds of remarks run the risk of suggesting a normative concept of a *break* with *the Indian past*, and they contradict van der Veer's own argument that religious boundaries are "subject to negotiation, revision, and reinterpretation" (11). Further discussing Islamic practices in precolonial times, van der Veer takes care to note that "there has been constant debate about 'orthodoxy' throughout Islamic History," an argument I can easily endorse. But he goes on to say that "*the shape of that debate* was transformed in the nineteenth century" (43) (my emphasis). This, as will seen later, is not my understanding of culture as a debate or an embodied argument.

30. Breckenridge and van der Veer, eds., *Orientalism and the Postcolonial Predicament*, 18.

31. On how some of these distinctions were made to be visible, if not produced, in the context of the "orientalization" of clothes during the British rule in India, see Cohn, "Cloth, Clothes, and Colonialism," in his *Colonialism and Its Forms*, esp. 121–27.

says, a "picture of Indian society as being static, timeless, and spaceless,"[32]—
the postcolonial argument that a colonial "theory of difference that lives on"
in India, a difference that has remained *unchanged* over the years for disciplinary identification and classification as "colonial" or "orientalist," indeed
assumes a timeless and static conception of Indian identity. Breckenridge
and van der Veer take for granted that a *specific* colonial view of "India"
and "Hindu," "Muslim" and "difference," which has "affected (and infected)"
"the very cultural basis of [Indian] public life," have remained as ahistorical,
nondiscursive categories. In my view, this labor that seeks to "undo" the heritage of colonialism fails to recognize and appreciate sufficiently that categories such as "Hindu" and "Muslim," "Indian" identity and difference, were
not just colonial/European constructs[33] but were products of complex relations between the "colonizers" and the "colonized."[34] (Here I am reminded of
Homi Bhabha's conceptualization of the attitude of the colonized toward the
colonizer in terms of the practices of "mimicry," which Bhabha calls, "not
quite/not white," as a significant attempt to bypass that problematic distinction.)[35] More important, such constructs are often fought out by "Indians"
themselves in varying debates, and in such debates the questions and terms

32. Van der Veer, "Foreign Hand," 26.

33. We know that well before the European colonial powers arrived, discursive distinctions
between "Muslim" and "Hindu" had become visible. For example, eleventh-century Ghaznavid
Muslim scholar al-Biruni's writings, as Ernst has pointed out, constitute "the first statement that
clearly puts the Hindu in opposition to the Muslim in religious terms"; see Ernst, "Historiagra-
phies of Islam in India," in his *Eternal Garden: Mysticism, History, and Politics at a South Asian
Sufi Center* (New York: State University of New York Press, 1992), 23–24. For al-Biruni's writings,
see A. T. Embree, ed., *Alberuni's India* (New York: Norton Library, 1971). David Lorenzen,
based on the writings of al-Buruni, Eknath, Jesuit priests, and others, argues that the British did
not invent Hinduism and that the references to the differences between Hindus and Muslims
existed prior to British colonialism; see David Lorenzen, "Who Invented Hinduism?" *Comparative Studies in Society and History* 41, no. 4 (1999): 630–59. Insightful though it is, Lorenzen's
argument seems to undermine the significance of the emergence of "Hinduism" as a *conceptual
label* when he says that he is prepared to accept the fact that "simply the English word [*Hinduism*] itself" was invented by the British. In my view, the colonial context did give birth to certain epistemic conditions in which distinctions such as Hindu and Muslims came to be invested
with "new meanings."

34. I must, in all fairness, note that in his *Religious Nationalism*, van der Veer states that the
relation between Western and Indian discourses should be seen as an "intricate interplay." But
his claim that "orientalist discourse found its way easily into religious reform movements and
religious nationalism" fails to capture the dynamics of that interplay.

35. Homi Bhabha, "Of Mimicry and Man: The Ambivalence of Colonial Discourse," in
The Location of Culture (1994; reprint, New York: Routledge, 1997); Hallisey's ideas of "local

of what it means to be Hindu or Muslim shift. So this antiessentialist, anticolonialist argument does not yield any new insight into understanding culture, identity, religion, and difference as nonessential and unfixed categories.

Lest I be misunderstood, let me point out that what I am suggesting here is not that *specific* kinds of authoritative "colonial" knowledges about identity and difference cannot be located within the discursive economy of the colonial context in which they were produced. Nor am I implying that, for example, concepts such as "demonism" (or "demonic"), as David Scott has shown in the case of Sri Lanka, if taken uncritically, without an awareness of the specific colonial discursive arsenal in which they were constructed, cannot reinscribe those specific colonial meanings in contemporary disciplinary texts that employ such terms as ready-made theoretical categories to represent Sinhala Buddhist practices like *yaktovil* in Sinhala society.[36] On the contrary, I am arguing that disciplinary efforts to locate and deconstruct the colonial infection of "native" discourses (that is, "nationalism") take native discourses at face value. They assume that, despite the shifting social conditions in which they are debated and battled out, something called nationalism or communalism, with particular "colonial roots," have awaited unchanged as specific objects of disciplinary knowledge.[37] So, in my view, they are unable to theorize critically the altering relations between identity and difference, religion and violence, in a way that does not depend upon the colonial notions of secularism and culture.

Here I have alluded to the limitations of these dominant postcolonial claims on colonialism and culture not to pretend to speak for "India" or South Asia, but to raise some doubts about pervasive disciplinary assumptions about

---

production of knowledge" and "elective affinity" are other important attempts at coming to terms with the dynamics of colonial/native relations in South Asia; see his, "Roads Taken and Not Taken in the Study of Theravada Buddhism," in *Curators of the Buddha*.

36. See David Scott, "Exorcisms and Demonic Experience, Anthropology and Yaktovil," in *Formations of Rituals*, 111–36. In further thinking about concepts of colonialism/postcolonialism, I have found David Scott's later work very instructive; see his "Colonial Governmentality"; "The Aftermaths of Sovereignty: Postcolonial Criticism and the Claims of Political Modernity," *Social Text* 48, no. 3 (1996): 1–26; and "Colonialism," *International Social Science Journal* 49, no. 4 (1997): 517–27.

37. Pandey's argument—that "quests" for defining the "national" identity of India "are never quite finished, for new contests, new visions, and new perceptions of earlier visions arise even before the older visions are fully played out"—I find convincing; see his *The Construction of Communalism in Colonial North India* (Delhi: Oxford University Press, 1990), 22.

categories like identity, religion, nationalism, and violence. To explore further some of these doubts, let me navigate beyond India and provide some examples from a few prominent (both Western and non-Western) "academic" studies of Buddhism in Sri Lanka that advocate a similar mission of disarming supposed (colonial) Sri Lankan nationalist claims about the "Buddhist nation."

In one of his influential texts, *Sri Lanka: Ethnic Fratricide and the Dismantling of Democracy*, S. J. Tambiah, seeking to explain the "causes" of the famous riots of July 1983 in Sri Lanka, argued that the urgent task awaiting "imaginative" and "liberated" scholars of Sri Lankan history and Buddhism is to find archaeological and other forms of evidence and "deconstruct" the Sinhalese claims that they are a pure, unmixed Aryan (Buddhist) race.[38] Tambiah made this suggestion by claiming that, as he began to write his book (self-labeled as "an engaged political tract" as opposed to "a distanced academic treatise"), "I became increasingly confident that I was correctly comprehending, both theoretically and scientifically, the historical movement of Sinhalese-Tamil relations as a whole, and that this understanding necessarily led to certain conclusions that have to be acted upon if the conflict in question [that between the Tamils and the Sinhalese] is to be resolved."[39] Anthropologist Bruce Kapferer, trying to explain the "culture of violence" in Sri Lanka, readily endorsed Tambiah's suggestions and saw his own work as a "modest beginning" of such a deconstructive project.[40] Several other scholars, whether or not explicitly following Tambiah and Kapferer, have made similar claims.

In his work on the "the history" of the famous Kelaniya temple, the historical site popularly believed to have been visited and consecrated by the Buddha himself, Jonathan Walters argued that the Sinhalese Buddhist claim that they are a "distinct ethnic group" is "curious (and untrue)"[41]—strong words of conviction, indeed![42] Walters went on to state that the modern

38. S. J. Tambiah, *Sri Lanka: Ethnic Fratricide and the Dismantling of Democracy* (Bombay: Oxford University Press, 1986), 6–7.

39. Ibid., ix.

40. Bruce Kapferer, *Legends of People, Myths of State: Violence, Intolerance, and Political Culture in Sri Lanka* (Washington, D.C.: Smithsonian Institute Press, 1988), 22. I discuss the category of violence in chapter 7 in relation to an archive of literature on the subject.

41. Jonathan Walters, *The History of Kelaniya* (Colombo: Social Scientists' Association, 1996), 120.

42. The text is replete with other problematic vocabularies such as "oppressive perspectives" (6), "a decidedly ugly turn" (15), "unBuddhistic roots" (96n),"capitalist exploitation" (105), and

history of the Kelaniya temple, "produced originally by British imperialists rather than by pious Buddhists," a history that informs the "standard" native Sinhala narrative about the temple, perpetuates such a false view and so fosters "division rather than unity" and "participates in forms of oppression" of other ethnic groups in Sri Lanka.[43] (Walters does not think here that the idea of "unity" itself is a problematic discourse that nationalism often constructs in order to erase differences in the interest of the hegemonic identity of the nation.) Walters stated that such a history of the Kelaniya temple, a center of contemporary Buddhist "piety," is "less inspiring to reverence." The history of the temple that he has uncovered, Walters claimed, "provides a foundation upon which a multiethnic nation might be constructed."[44] In my view, these kinds of claims as to whether a given Buddhist place/practice is more or less inspiring to reverence are, unfortunately, more orientalist and colonial than the colonialist "standard" Sri Lankan view of the Kelaniya temple that Walters wants to deconstruct. The assumption here is that what is and is not "inspiring to reverence" are not historically and discursively produced;[45] that is, a specific colonial history of Kelaniya has remained static, and, as Walters says, "until that history is recovered, its reproduction . . . is guaranteed. Whether conducting extensive field interviews or poring over ancient documents, the result will be the same: 'the history of Kelaniya' is made real by a

---

"Colombo's urban evils" (105). My point is that these concepts are not in and of themselves theoretically invalid, but that their genealogical locations are never questioned by Walters to produce a sound, nonessential criticism of nationalism that would be less susceptible to moral polemics (see note 45 below). Put differently, had Walters shown that the configurations of questions about what counts as "unBuddhist" or "evil" must be found in fluctuating moral debates among Sri Lankan Buddhists, he could have argued that nationalism's hegemomic discourses cannot decide how they (that is, such questions) should be framed. For an attempt at problematizing concepts like "evil" in the aftermath of postmodernism, see Jennifer L. Geddess, ed., *Evil after Postmodernism: Histories, Narratives, and Ethics* (New York: Routledge, 2001).

43. Walters, *History of Kelaniya*, 121–22.

44. Ibid., 121.

45. Walters's text generated some controversy in Sri Lanka. In a review of the book in the Sinhala press, K. N. O. Dharmadasa argued that Walters "distorted" the history of Kelaniya and questioned "what right he ('the foreigner') had to denigrate Buddhists in Sri Lanka"; see Dharmadasa's series of newspaper articles entitled "Bedumvādīn Vikurta Kala Kālaniyēitihāsaya" ("The history of Kelaniya distorted by the separatists"), *Divayina*, June 1997. As the title of the article indicates, Dharmadasa has placed Walters in the camp of those "minority" forces now seeking and supporting a separate state in Sri Lanka. Needless to say, my comments on the theoretical unsoundness of Walters's argument do not participate in Dharmadasa's normative critique of Walters's *The History of Kelaniya*.

particular way of thinking about history, which happens now to be the way
the 'natives' also think about history."[46] In other words, the natives, helpless
and hapless as they are, have never thought and talked about Kelaniya any differently than the colonialists, and so they remain mired in a colonial history
that repeats itself.

Decentering "the erroneous perception" that the "Sinhala race has pre-
served its religiocultural [Buddhist] purity" is also central to Tessa Bartholomeusz's recent study of "Buddhist Burghers and Sinhala-Buddhist
Fundamentalism."[47] In a similar vein, John Holt, whose idea of "the inclusive
nature" of Sinhala Buddhist culture Bartholomeusz supports, maintains that
in order to "resurrect" the "lost multiethnic, multireligious" society of Sri
Lanka, Sinhalese Buddhists should "transcend the sacred canopy of nationalist discourse" and "marginalize fundamentalistic and totalistic persuasions."[48]
In short, then, for these scholars Sri Lanka has become, to borrow a word
from Jeganathan, a "curative project."[49]

Now I want to say that I am sympathetic to these disciplinary attempts that
aim to disarticulate and disarm the hegemony of nationalist claims about
nation, religion, identity, and difference, but I suspect the theoretical soundness of such exercises that seek to excavate the foundation of a supposedly
authentic (precolonial) cultural past upon which a contemporary multicultural society can be reconstructed. The crucial question that I want to pose is
this: What are the conditions of the authorization of these disciplinary decon-
structions of the supposedly "untrue" (colonial), "pseudo-historical ideology"
of "Sinhala Buddhist culture" (I am using Walters's terms)?[50] My answer is
that they are authorized by and rooted in the assumptions of what is itself a
colonial and ideological project. These disciplinary enterprises that seek to
disarm problematic ideologies of Sinhala culture and urge upon Sri Lanka
the need for a "multiethnic society" subscribe, perhaps unconsciously, to an
equally problematic ideology of party-based political interests, for such a

46. Walters, *History of Kelaniya*, 122.
47. Tessa Bartholomeusz, "Buddhist Burghers and Sinhala-Buddhist Fundamentalism," in
Buddhist Fundamentalism and Minority Identities in Sri Lanka, ed. Tessa Bartholomeusz and
C. R. de Silva (New York: State University of New York Press, 1998), 168.
48. John Holt, "The Persistence of Political Buddhism," in *Buddhist Fundamentalism*, 194.
49. Pradeep Jeganathan, "Sri Lanka as a Curative Project: Ordering and Authorizing a Post-
Colonial Scholarship" (forthcoming).
50. Walters, *History of Kelaniya*, 120–21.

concept carries a "genealogy," a history of its production and contestation authorized by debates in Sri Lanka and other parts of the world. My point here is that, be they "postcolonial" or "politically engaged" tracts, authored by scholars teaching at academic institutions, these kinds of works that propose ideologies to cure the supposed (colonial) ideological problems of culture and difference end up simply constituting a normative, if not a (post) colonial-civilizing, project.[51] The problem as I see it is that, in assuming the availability of colonial knowledges for deconstruction in the present, Walters and company fail to examine critically the discursively constituted and shifting relation between Buddhism and difference, religion and politics, violence and civilization. As I have noted elsewhere, one way to fashion and sustain a criticism of the hegemony of nationalism is to demonstrate that the

51. A body of scholarship by such thinkers as William Connolly, John Gray, David Scott, and Chantal Mouffe today attempts to reconfigure the politics of democracy, liberalism, identity, and difference in important ways that seek to bypass these colonial moral problematics; see William Connolly's works for some of the most productive attempts to offer viable (post-Nietzschean and post-Foucauldian) alternatives for the practice of a "politics of difference" that no longer privileges the hegemony of identity or nationalism; for example, The Augustinian Imperative: A Reflection on the Politics of Morality (London: Sage: 1993), esp. chapter 5, "Beyond the Moral Imperative." Connolly seeks to understand, among other things, the possibilities of moving from "relations of antagonism," in which, obviously, identity and difference are fought out, to "agonistic respect" for "difference" (155). For an elaboration on "agonism versus antagonism" from a Foucauldian viewpoint, see Beatrice Hanssen, "Power/Force/War," in her Critique of Violence: Between Poststructuralism and Critical Theory (New York: Routledge, 2000), 148–57. For other useful ways of thinking about agonistic liberalism/democracy, see John Gray, "Agonistic Liberalism," in Isaiah Berlin (Princeton: Princeton University Press, 1996), 141–68; Chantal Mouffe, "For an Agonistic Model of Democracy," in her The Democratic Paradox (London: Verso, 2000), 80–107. As Mouffe says, agonistic liberalism is about "constructing 'them' in such a way that it is no longer perceived as an enemy to be destroyed but an adversary . . . somebody whose ideas we combat but whose right to defend those ideas we do not put into question" (102). I do not, however, share Mouffe's division between the "ethical" and the "political," and by extension the division between the secular and the sacred, the private and the public, as the condition for agonistic liberalism: Democratic Paradox, 107. For a helpful way of thinking about pluralism that does not depend upon such a binary, see Dipesh Chakrabarty, "Modernity and Ethnicity in India," in Multicultural States: Rethinking Difference and Identity, ed. David Bennett (New York: Routledge, 1998). One does not have to agree with Chakrabarty's claims about the relation between modern ethnicity and British colonialism to appreciate his argument. David Scott's Refashioning Futures, esp. chapter 8, "Fanonian Futures?" is important in this regard: Scott wants to "read Fanon with [final] Foucault" to reconfigure the narrative of postcolonial liberation. On rethinking the ideas of pluralism and difference in relation to the demand of a new kind of postcolonial conjuncture, see idem, "The Permanence of Pluralism," in Without Guarantees: In Honor of Stuart Hall, ed. Paul Gilroy et al. (New York: Verso, 2000).

authoritative discourses that seek to totalize and essentialize *the* identity of religion, tradition, nation, and so forth are contingently and differently authorized.[52] Disciplinary projects interested in making available religion, nation, and difference as historically constituted, nonessential objects of knowledge must inquire into ways in which questions about them are contingently posed, battled out, and subverted in those conjunctures of debates. Such projects can contribute to opening up new spaces for thinking about democracy and difference in that, as political critics like Ernesto Laclau have pointed out, a "democratic society is one which permanently shows the contingency of its foundations."[53] In thinking about identity, difference, and contingency in the way I propose to do in this work, we can, as Slavoj Zizek has recommended, "thoroughly reject the standard multiculturalist idea [the idea that Walters, Holt, Tambiah, and others so eagerly endorse] that, against ethnic intolerance, one should learn to respect and live with the Otherness of the Other, to develop a tolerance for different lifestyles, and so on."[54]

Note here that my seeking to understand the contingent formations of identity and difference is far from simply suggesting that we locate multiple local narratives and practices and recover some supposed native "agency" before or after colonialism. To state this point differently, what I have in mind here is not what Richard King proposes in his provocative *Orientalism and Religion*. King, as a way of rethinking Gayatri Spivak's claim that colonialism "wholeheartedly eradicated" "non-western forms of knowledges" (the words are King's), urges us to look "back with renewed vigor at the legacy of pre-colonial forms of indigenous knowledge. To fail to do so is to concede defeat to colonialism and to accept as unproblematic Western-derived notions of 'modernity,' thereby cutting ourselves off from our disparate pasts."[55] Rather, my point is that particular conjunctures, removed from those

52. See my review of *The Work of Kings: The New Buddhism in Sri Lanka*, by H. L. Seneviratne, *American Ethnologist* 28, no. 2 (2001): 499–501.

53. Laclau, "Identity and Hegemony," in Judith Butler, Ernesto Laclau, and Slavoj Zizek, *Contingency, Hegemony, Universality: Contemporary Dialogue on the Left* (New York: Verso 2000), 86.

54. Slavoj Zizek, *The Fragile Absolute—or, Why Is the Christian Legacy Worth Fighting For?* (New York: Verso, 2000), 11. I do not, however, endorse all of Zizek's claims and propositions about the self-evident availability of fundamentalism for deconstruction.

55. Richard King, *Orientalism and Religion: Postcolonial Theory, India, and 'The Mystic East'* (New York: Routledge, 1999), 213; King is thinking of Gayatri Spivak's "Rani of Sirmur," *History and Theory* 24, no. 3 (1985): 128–51.

of (pre)colonialism and (pre)orientalism, make possible and centrally visible the emergence and submergence of specific knowledges of what can and cannot constitute religion, identity, and difference, and it is the examination of such contingent conjunctures that should form the basis for disciplinary works seeking to understand religion, identity, and difference as historically varying ideas.

Organizing Arguments: Discourse and Knowledge, Identity and Difference

In this study, I have set myself the task outlined above. Constituting Sinhala Buddhist monastic "identity" as my primary subject of inquiry, I explore some of the ways in which divergent questions about what it means to be "Buddhist" came to be fought out within the conjunctures of a few years—primarily between 1980 and 1990. Today there are, by some estimates, more than forty thousand Buddhist monks in Sri Lanka,[56] and the robes of different colors that they wear—saffron, ochre, maroon, burgundy, and so on—are some of the most visible representations of the island's Theravada Buddhist "tradition." The Buddhist monks (as members of the Sangha) are seen as one of the Three Jewels—the other two being the Buddha and the Dhamma—that constitute an important part of the identity of Buddhism, and, therefore, the questions of what it means to be "Buddhist" are often framed and argued in relation to the questions of what it means to be a Buddhist monk. Some of the questions central to this book are these: What kinds of discourses, practices, and persons make possible and centrally visible the relation between Buddhism, identity, and difference? What kinds of claims, debates, and arguments authorize what kinds of "Buddhist" subjects to demarcate and define what kinds of relation between "Buddhism" and "politics," or monks and the state? How are the parameters and borders between "Buddhism," "nation," and "state" established, stylized, articulated, and contested? What kinds of statements enable what forms of configurations of the relation between "Buddhism" and "violence" to come into central view and fade from view? It is important to note that, in employing conceptual oppositions like Buddhism and difference or religion and difference, I take the term *difference* to mean that which gets authorized and positioned so as to be opposed to, to be

---

56. This estimate is according to the Ministry of Buddhist Affairs, Colombo: interviews conducted with ministry staff in 1996 and 1997.

different from, "Buddhism." This, as noted earlier, does not imply even remotely that there always remains a monolithic, static entity called Buddhism against which difference is constructed. So when I argue, as I do often, that the relation between Buddhism and difference, religion and violence, does not remain available for disciplinary apprehension as self-evident objects of knowledge, I mean that the questions of what it means to be Buddhist and the answers to them are made possible and centrally visible by altering conjunctures of discourses and debates.

The reader, even after a cursory glance at the preceding questions, may detect a parallel between my preoccupations with the discursively produced knowledges of religion, identity, and difference and the nexus among "discourse," "power," and "knowledge" that Michel Foucault has labored to bring to light in an oeuvre of literature. I recognize some noteworthy similarities but want to insist on a crucial difference that enables me to think of that nexus in a way pivotal to this book, particularly in terms of spelling out the ways in which I seek to conceptualize religious identity and difference in contingent conjunctures.

For Foucault, especially in light of his three-volume *History of Sexuality* (the second and third volumes of it are sometimes thought to constitute "final Foucault"),[57] discourse is intimately linked to power in that it can be both an instrument and effect of power.[58] From the *History of Sexuality* (vol. 1), I take the following quotation to be presenting some of his most important ways of conceiving the relation between discourse, power, and knowledge:

> Indeed it is in discourse that power and knowledge are joined together. . . .
> We must conceive discourse as a series of discontinuous segments whose tactical function is neither uniform nor stable. To be more precise, we must not imagine a world of discourse divided between accepted discourse and excluded discourse, or between the dominant discourse and the dominated one; but as a multiplicity of discursive elements that can come into play in various strategies. It is this distribution that we must construct, with the

---

57. For a recent discussion of some aspects of "final Foucault," see Ivan Strenski, "Religion, Power, and Final Foucault," *Journal of the American Academy of Religion* 66, no. 2 (1998): 345–67.

58. Michel Foucault, *The History of Sexuality*, vol. 1 (1976; reprint, New York: Vintage, 1990), 100–101.

things said and those concealed, the enunciations required and those forbidden, that it comprises; with the variants and different effects — according to who is speaking, his position of power, and the institutional context in which he happens to be situated—that it implies; and with the shifts and reutilization of identical formulas for contrary objectives that it also includes. Discourses are not once and for all subservient to power or raised up against it, any more than silences are. We must allow for the complex and unstable processes whereby discourse can be both an instrument and effect of power, but also a hindrance, a stumbling-block, a point of resistance and a starting point for an opposing strategy. Discourse transmits power and produces power; it reinforces it, but also undermines and exposes it, renders it fragile and makes it possible to thwart it.[59]

Here, as he already began to do in his previous work *Discipline and Punish*, Foucault is seeking to avoid a "negative" or "repressive" conception of power and to think of it in what he calls "productive" terms. Writing about power in *Discipline and Punish*, Foucault suggested that we abandon "once and for all" the idea that it "excludes, it represses, it censors, it abstracts, it masks, it conceals." Rather he argued that "in fact power produces, it produces reality, it produces domains of objects and rituals of truth."[60] Foucault admits (elsewhere) that in his early works like *Madness and Civilization*, he himself sought to conceptualize power in terms of "repression" and noted that repression failed to grasp the "productive aspects of power,"[61] later noting that even in his study of prisons he "insisted . . . too much on the techniques of domination" and repression.[62] To think of power in negative terms of repression, Foucault states, is to think of it in "judicial" terms; that is, to associate power with "a law which says no" and to assume that power just carries "the force of prohibition." He considers this problematic and asks, "If power were never anything but repressive, if it never did anything but say, no, do you

59. Ibid.

60. Michel Foucault, *Discipline and Punish: The Birth of the Prison* (1977; reprint, New York: Vintage, 1995), 194.

61. Michel Foucault, *Power/Knowledge: Selected Interviews and Other Writings, 1972–1977* (New York: Pantheon, 1980), 118–19. More on his attempt to demonstrate the irreducibility of power/discourse simply to the concept of repression, see idem, "The Repressive Hypothesis," in *History of Sexuality* 1, esp. 10–12.

62. Michel Foucault, "About the Beginning of the Hermeneutics of the Self," in his *Religion and Culture*, ed. Jeremy R. Carrette (New York: Routledge, 1999), 162.

really think one would be brought to obey it?" Foucault contends that "what makes power hold good, what makes it accepted, is . . . that it does not weigh on us as a force that says no, but that it traverses and produces things, it induces pleasure, forms knowledge, it produces discourse."[63]

What Foucault is attempting here, it is important to note, is a subtle move from a theory of "techniques of domination" to a theory of "techniques or a technology of the Self"; that is, from techniques of "pure violence or strict coercion" to techniques of the construction, authorization, modification of identity/subject. In 1980, in a lecture entitled "About the Beginning of the Hermeneutics of the Self"—where he discusses the emergence of the early Christian notions of penance—Foucault spells out what he means by techniques of the self: They are those "that permit individuals to effect, by their own means, a certain number of operations on their own bodies, on their own souls, on their own thoughts, on their own conduct, and this is in a manner so as to transform themselves, modify themselves, and to attain a state of perfection, of happiness, of purity, of supernatural power, and so on."[64] Though Foucault is clearly interested in the productive conception of power/discourse, he does not want to abandon—at least not entirely—thinking about power in terms of domination or coercion. It is the *emphasizing* of domination over authorization, negation over affirmation, concealing over unmasking that he is worried about. What Foucault wants is to locate the ways in which an "interaction between these two techniques" not only produces subjects and subjectivities, selves and identities, but enables, authorizes, and obliges those selves/identities to "act upon themselves"; that is, not only to know the "truth" about themselves, about who and what they are and are not, but to tell it, to "publish" it.[65] In terms of publishing or being obliged to publish the truth about oneself, Foucault has in mind the techniques of the "care of the self," from "an entire activity of speaking and writing" about oneself to

63. Foucault, *Power/Knowledge*, 119.

64. Foucault, "Hermeneutics," 162–63. These techniques are further elaborated upon in a 1982 lecture, "Technologies of the Self," in Michel Foucault, *Ethics, Subjectivity, and Truth*, ed. Paul Rainbow and trans. Robert Hurley et al. (New York: New Press, 1994), 223–25. Foucault also uses the phrase *arts of existence* to mean "those voluntary and intentional actions by which men not only set themselves rules of conduct but also seek to transform themselves, to change themselves in their singular being, and to make their life into an *oeuvre* that carries certain aesthetic values and meets certain stylistic criteria"; see *The Use of Pleasure: The History of Sexuality*, vol. 2, trans. Robert Hurley (1985; reprint, New York: Vintage 1990), 10–11

65. Foucault, "Hermeneutics," 162.

others (which is evident in the works of Seneca, Plutarch, and others in the first two centuries of our era—works he detailed in *The Care of the Self*) to the Christian obligations of verbalizing the truth about oneself, particularly in terms of both monastic and nonmonastic forms of Christian confession.[66] As Foucault puts it, publishing the truth is how one is obliged "not only to believe in certain things but also to show that one believes in them."[67] This is what he calls "government." "Governing people, at least in the broad meaning of that word . . . is not a way to force people to do what the governor wants; it is always a versatile equilibrium, with complimentarity and conflicts between techniques which assure coercion and processes through which self is constructed or modified by oneself."[68]

What involves the techniques and processes through which power/discourse produces self/identity is identity's inevitable counterpart, other/difference. That is, knowledges about what constitutes the self, the "truth" of its identity, are produced in relation to, measured against the other—against the difference, the "untruth" of "other" selves, persons, practices, and institutions. This is, of course, not such a controversial, unorthodox point of view. As William Connolly has put it nicely, "Identity requires difference to be: differences provide it with the shadings and contrasts that animate it."[69] Or as Judith Butler says, "no particular identity can emerge without presuming and enacting the exclusion of others, and this constitutive exclusion or antagonism is the equal and shared condition of all identity-constitution."[70] However, in seeking to understand the complex shifting configurations of the relation between religious identity and difference, Buddhism and violence, I want to suggest, by way of extending the above Foucauldian analysis of power/discourse, that it is then no longer theoretically sound to think that identity *only*

66. *History of Sexuality*, vol. 3, trans. Robert Hurley (1986; reprint, New York: Vintage, 1988), 39–68. For a summary of these ideas, see Foucault, "Hermeneutics," and "Technologies."

67. Foucault, "Hermeneutics," 169, n. 28; 171–73. In other words, Foucault is interested in how obligation, "obedience," gets imposed in terms of "the relation of the individual to himself and to his city in the form of respect or shame, honor or glory—not the relation to the other person." *Use of Pleasure*, 169.

68. Foucault, "Hermeneutics," 162. More on this complex relationship between the ruler and the ruled, see *Use of Pleasure*, 172–74.

69. Connolly, *Why I Am Not a Secularist*, 144. Also more on his conceptualization of identity and difference, see Connolly, *Identity/Difference: Democratic Negotiations of Political Paradox* (Ithaca, N.Y.: Cornell University Press, 1991).

70. Judith Butler, "Restaging the Universal: Hegemony and the Limits of Formalism," in *Contingency, Hegemony, Universality*, Butler et al., 31.

denies (or excludes) difference. Rather, identity produces difference so as to deny it. It unmasks it so as to mask it, to conceal it. Identity makes difference emerge so as to submerge it, to make it subordinate. It authorizes it for debate, discussion—within its own authorized bounds—so as to unauthorize it for debate, to render difference not up for discussion, to censor it. This is the kind of formulation that governs this book.

"Religious" Discourse/Knowledge, Contingent Conjunctures

The problem for me, as for Foucault, is not to assume that the relation between identity and difference is self-evidently available for disciplinary apprehension, but to locate the conditions that alter it in different contexts. For Foucault, broadly speaking, the configurations of identity\difference relations—that is, the ways in which what constitute as madness and sanity, sickness and health, criminality and humanity, and so forth became objects of knowledge, how they came to be "put into discourse,"[71] classified, named, and canonized in terms of their supposed opposition to each other—are to be located in the (macro)context of one or several centuries. Foucault argued that there is, of course, no homogenous, constant, permanent domain of discourses, statements, rules, knowledges, but "an interplay" of discourses that "make possible the appearance of objects [like madness] in a given period of time."[72] He recognized the possibility of the transformation of such discourses and knowledges precisely because they operate, come into being, within conditions that carry "no means of guaranteeing . . . that [they] will remain stable or autonomous."[73] As he said, "I have not denied—far from it— the possibility of changing discourse. I have deprived the sovereignty of the subject of exclusive and instantaneous right to it."[74] But, for Foucault, that changing discourse is to be located in a broad economy of power encom-

71. Foucault, *History of Sexuality*, vol. 1, 11.

72. Michel Foucault, *The Archaeology of Knowledge and the Discourse on Language* (1969; reprint, New York: Pantheon, 1972), 32–33. It is important to note that, for Foucault, an *episteme* is "not a form of knowledge" but "the total set of relations that unite, at a given period of time, the discursive practices that give rise to epistemological figures" (191); see also his *The Order of Things: An Archaeology of Human Sciences* (1966; reprint, New York: Vintage, 1990), xxii. Elsewhere Foucault wanted to think of the *episteme* as a *"discursive apparatus"* that consists of "strategies of relations of forces supporting, and supported by, types of knowledge" (Foucault, *Power/Knowledge*, 196–97).

73. Foucault, *Archaeology of Knowledge*, 207–8.

74. Ibid., 209.

passing a period of one or several centuries. My concern, however, is to conceptualize the appearance and disappearance of knowledges about religious identity and difference within a period of just a few years, if not months and days.

Now I do not want to suggest that it is theoretically unproductive to examine the macrodiscursive domains that made possible the emergence of particular objects of knowledge, to locate the "genealogies" of their formations. Foucault, obviously following Nietzsche, thinks of genealogy as a form of "historical contextualization [that] needed to be something more than the simple relativisation of the phenomenological subject."[75] Hence for Foucault genealogy is

[not about] historicizing the subject as posited by phenomenologists, fabricating a subject that evolves through the course of history. One has to dispense with the constituent subject, to get rid of the subject itself, that's to say, to arrive at an analysis which can account for the constitution of the subject within a historical framework. And this is what I call genealogy, that is, a form of history which can account for the constitution of knowledges, discourses, domains of subjects etc., without having to make reference to a subject which is either transcendental in relation to the field of events or runs in its empty sameness throughout the course of history.[76]

I can think of categories like "religion(s)," "Buddhism," and "Hinduism" as good examples of objects of knowledge with such genealogies. In this regard, I can readily see the value of sophisticated works (such as Philip Almond's *The British Discovery of Buddhism*, Peter Harrison's *"Religion" and the Religions in the English Enlightenment*, and Talal Asad's *Genealogies of Religion*) that show in different ways how concepts like "Buddhism," "religion," and "religions," which are, more often than not, taken at face value, are in fact categories produced within discursive economies such as the

75. Foucault, *Power/Knowledge*, 117.
76. Ibid., 117. On Foucault's rethinking of genealogy in relation to Nietzsche's ideas of Entstehung ("emergence") and Herkunft ("descent"), see his "Nietzsche, Genealogy, History," in *Aesthetics, Method, and Epistemology*, ed. Paul Rabinow and trans. Robert Hurley (New York: New Press, 1988), esp. 373–75. For a fine discussion of the history of the phenomenological argument, see Gavin Flood, "Limits of Phenomenology," in his *Beyond Phenomenology: Rethinking the Study of Religion* (New York: Cassell, 1999).

Enlightenment, the Reformation, and colonization.[77] My point is that given that knowledges about such categories are discursively produced and so cannot simply transcend history unchanged, cannot "run in [their] empty sameness throughout the course of history," our claims about the historicity of such concepts need to be carefully qualified. In other words, it is not conceptually adequate to say that categories like religion and Buddhism became formulated as objects of knowledge in those macrodiscursive fields alone. For example, Peter Harrison began his excellent *"Religion" and the Religions* by contending that "the concept of 'religion' and 'religions,' *as we presently understand them* [my emphasis], emerged quite late in Western thought, during the Enlightenment."[78] This claim clearly hangs on the assumption that there exists a particular set of knowledges—which have passed through history since its formation—that constitute the identity of religion. This kind of assumption, I noted earlier, is central to many postcolonial works that seek to unmask the supposed colonial knowledges about South Asian identities. I want to question this assumption, at least part of that assumption. How precisely do "we" (the adherents of a given religion) understand religion at present? One could, of course, simply assert that a set of particular definitions of the word *religion* can be found in the dictionary. But, as Mikhail Bakhtin has reminded us, "the word does not exist in a neutral and impersonal language (it is not, after all, out of a dictionary that the speaker gets his words!), but rather it exists in other people's mouths, in other people's contexts, serving other people's intentions."[79]

So since a concept like religion is inevitably "dialogical," since the questions of what kinds of persons and practices can and cannot be included in it are always subject to discourse and debate, we will need to renounce the assumption about how we presently understand religion and ask different kinds of questions about the relation between discourse and knowledge. To do so we will have to think more critically about religion and difference as discursive concepts whose fleeting knowledges/meanings are authorized to

---

77. Almond, *British Discovery of Buddhism*; Peter Harrison, *"Religion" and the Religions in the English Enlightenment* (New York: Cambridge University Press, 1990); Talal Asad, *Genealogies of Religion: Discipline and Reasons of Power in Christianity and Islam* (Baltimore: Johns Hopkins University Press, 1993).

78. Harrison, *"Religion" and the Religions*, 1.

79. M. Bakhtin, *The Dialogic Imagination*, ed. Michael Holquist and trans. Caryl Emerson and Michael Holquist (Austin: University of Texas Press, 1981), 294.

24

come into central view and fade from view in contingent conjunctures that are not available for disciplinary canonization. The point I want to stress is that (continuing Foucauldian) disciplinary labors of mapping those large discursive domains cannot help us theorize such conjunctures of contingent "religious" knowledges.

Recent thinkers such as Alasdair MacIntyre and David Scott have proposed some provocative ways of conceiving religious identity and difference, discourse and knowledge that do not, I think, depend upon the old secularist distinction of tradition\modernity or upon postcolonial assumptions about the hybridity and the substancelessness of culture. MacIntyre and Scott (who follows Talal Asad and Michael Walzer) suggest that we understand concepts like tradition, religion, and Buddhism, as "embodied arguments,"[80] or as "traditions of moral argument."[81] What interests me in thinking about religion as an embodied, moral argument is that questions about knowledges, virtues, parameters, and boundaries that should and should not embody its identity are debated, argued, and fought out in terms of "the standards internal to that tradition"—standards that are "revised and extended in a variety of ways" in opposition to rival and competing claims operating "within and without" that tradition.[82] My task is to delineate the processes and techniques of revising, arguing, and debating those standards, borders, and questions about religious identity and difference, Buddhism and violence, civilization and terror. In seeking to do so, it may be obvious, I find helpful the final Foucauldian formulation of the nexus among discourse, power, and knowledge in terms of an interaction between techniques of authorization and domination. Authoritative discourses and arguments make possible and centrally visible what knowledges can and cannot count as religion and difference. But the difference is

---

80. See Alasdair MacIntyre, *After Virtue: A Study in Moral Theory* (1981; reprint, Notre Dame, Ind.: University of Notre Dame Press, 1984), esp. chapter 15, 222. For an interesting collection on the history of moral theory, see Christopher W. Gowans, ed., *Moral Disagreements: Classic and Contemporary Readings* (New York: Routledge, 2000); included in it is a piece by MacIntyre, "Rationality of Tradition," taken from his *Whose Justice? Which Rationality?* (Notre Dame, Ind.: University of Notre Dame Press, 1988).

81. Scott, *Refashioning Futures*, 122–27. Scott has in mind Talal Asad's "Limits of Religious Criticism in the Middle East: Notes on Islamic Public Argument," in his *Genealogies of Religion*, and Michael Walzer's *Interpretation and Social Criticism* (Cambridge: Cambridge University Press, 1987).

82. MacIntyre, *After Virtue*, 277.

that I locate them in minute conjunctures. What I want to show in this book is that if we can have no a priori epistemological guarantee of, a privileged access to, the altering relation between religious identity and difference, we must explore those conjunctures of debates in which authoritative persons, practices, and institutions that counted as religious identity yesterday become vulnerable to being thwarted, deauthorized, as difference today.

Chapter 2 seeks to understand Sinhala Buddhism and monastic identity as categories of shifting meanings within strategic relations between monks and lay Buddhists in contemporary Sri Lanka. First it briefly sketches the history of the constructions of Buddhism and monasticism as objects of disciplinary knowledge and interrogates the assumptions that govern several key texts on religion and change, Buddhist identity and difference, by distinguished scholars like S. J. Tambiah, Sarath Amunugama, Richard Gombrich, Gananath Obeyesekere, and John Holt. This exercise, I plead, is critical to the conceptualization of Buddhism, identity, and difference as discursive concepts or embodied arguments. Second it locates the altering images of Buddhist monasticism by offering a critical reading of a Sinhala novel authored by a Buddhist monk named Orukmankulame Chandana in Sri Lanka. Though a fictionalized representation set against the political landscape of the late 1980s, the novel unfolds configurations of shifting relations between Buddhism and difference debated in varying contexts.

In the second part of the chapter, complementing the novel's representation of the differing images of the Buddhist monkhood, I present an "ethnographic" study of altering formations of questions about who and what can and cannot count as Buddhism among the Sinhalese Buddhists within a cluster of closely knit villages in the area of Sigiriya in the northern part of Sri Lanka. Here my aim is to point out that such questions are rendered possible and centrally visible by contingent fields of competing moral arguments and debates and hence they do not license us any permanent disciplinary purchase on the relation between Buddhism and difference. My argument here, it must be noted, is not simply that concepts like religion and culture are impossible to produce as objects of disciplinary analysis because our ethnographic knowledges are *constructed*. Rather, my point is a different one; namely, that particular authoritative narratives that contend to represent Buddhism cannot be taken as readily available ethnographic examples of the relation between religion and society because they are to be found in those altering ideological conjunctures.

In chapter 3 I am concerned with reconceptualizing the concepts of "religion and politics" that have become the subject of numerous studies that seek to construct the relation between them (in both the East and the West) as specific objects of disciplinary knowledge. Again, as in chapter 2, I seek to think against the grain of dominant disciplinary assumptions about these categories and offer a novel way of reflecting on the discursive production of the relation between religion and politics. It would be easy to see that I find inadequate the continuing disciplinary arguments—advanced in various ways by scholars like Chantal Mouffe, Richard King, Peter van der Veer, Donald Smith, Heinz Bechert, Donald Swearer, S. J. Tambiah, and Michael Carrithers—about the supposed link between religion and politics for the critical task of conceiving them as concepts operating within a tradition of moral arguments. I do not, however, make the obviously inverse argument, either; that is, religion and politics are separate. These arguments, from my point of view, are theoretically unsound because they hang on a priori notions about what do and do not constitute religion or politics, identity or difference. Rather what preoccupies me are the ways in which particular discourses come to authorize and contest the "proper" boundary between religion and politics in particular conjunctures.

Central to this preoccupation is locating the emergence of the discourse of "Buddhism and politics" in Sri Lanka. My argument here is that prior to its formation as an object of academic inquiry, the discourse of Buddhism and politics emerged in the space of a landmark monastic/lay dispute in the 1940s. Facilitated by particular party-based ideological interests, the debate gave birth to competing and contesting narratives about what and who should and should not be part of "Buddhism" or "politics." Disciplinary works that canonized the subject, however, failed to inquire into the dynamics of the debates at the time and uncritically reproduced the ideological and political interests of particular discourses.

The remainder of chapter 3 demonstrates that such debates do not stand still forever, in that other debates emerge, altering the formerly authorized terms of the line between religion and politics. This is what I do by examining the Jayewardene government's construction of the Buddhist and Pali University (BPU) for monks in 1982. Seemingly an expression of the government's commitment to the "development" of Buddhism and Pali, the construction of the BPU worked as a strategy, enabling the state to authorize and make visible a hegemonic conception of an "apolitical" Buddhism. This state discourse of Buddhism was, however, contested by the BPU monastic students, who competed for the representation of themselves as "ordinary university monks" and supported the Janata Vimukti Peramuna (JVP) that struggled to overthrow the state. Today, as a symbol of that contestation, if not subversion, of the Jayewardene state's definitions of apolitical Buddhism, a new "national" BPU university, constructed by the People's Alliance government, with a new act, stands in a different location. My argument is that the story of the BPU is a significant example of a debate about who and what can and cannot define the relation between Buddhism and the state, monks and politics—a debate whose characters, forms, contents, and logics changed, making it possible for other debates to come into prominence.

Chapter 4 demonstrates the ways in which questions about Buddhism, monasticism, and difference became the subject of argument in the context of Sri Lanka's new economic and political interests in the 1980s. My contention here is that, inaugurated by the Jayewardene government, and further fostered by the Premadasa administration, Sri Lanka's new economic and foreign-policy relations, particularly with Japan, enabled the construction of a "new economy" of persons, practices, discourses, and knowledges that came to authorize a particular image of Buddhism and the monkhood. The idea of a new economy is not an attempt to advance (the Western secularist/Enlightenment) argument about how "religion" has undergone transformations or how innovations are taking place in "religion" in Sri Lanka. Rather, I am after locating the dynamics of a particular epistemic space in which a seminal debate about the relations between Buddhism and society, religion and nation, came into central view and faded from view.

Chapters 5 and 6 advance this exploration of the discursive formations of the relations between religion and nation, tradition and difference. In chapter 5, I detail the configurations of the relations among Buddhism, nation, and difference during Ranasinghe Premadasa's lengthy political career as prime minister and second executive president of Sri Lanka. What I seek to point out is that within the context in which Premadasa came to perform some unprecedented acts of "religious" patronage—like the construction of a Golden Canopy for one of Sri Lanka's most visible symbols of its "Buddhist" heritage, the Tooth Temple—a particular kind of relation among religion, nation, and state came to be authorized. But what interests me here are the discourses that made possible the submergence of such relations. The submergence of such formerly authorized relations tells us something very complex about the configurations of the altering relation among religion, nation-state, and difference that cannot be conceptualized in terms of "religious nationalism."

In chapter 6 we see similar questions unfolding about tradition, identity, and difference within the tradition of caste-based monastic ordination in Sri Lanka. While I show how this supposed "age-old" tradition is itself an embodied argument, constituted by a history of varying interpretations, the main discussion revolves around the emergence of a new movement that claims to challenge this tradition. It presents a crucial instance of how questions about tradition and difference are constructed and battled out. Here, seeking inspiration from Alasdair MacIntyre, David Scott, Friedrich Nietzsche, and Pierre Bourdieu, I am interested in understanding tradition not as something that existed prior to modernity, but as a particular discursive concept, as an embodied moral argument about religious identity and difference. I show that a moral tradition like the caste-based ordination occupies sites of competing narratives that confirm or contest the supposed "unity" of its tradition.

In chapter 7, I propose radically alternative approaches to theorizing "religion" and "violence." An important body of disciplinary texts by several leading scholars (for example, Bruce Kapferer, S. J. Tambiah, Gananath Obeyesekere, Peter van der Veer, Rene Gerard, and Mark Juergensmeyer) seek to theorize religion and violence in terms of their supposed opposition or interrelation, while chronically failing to appreciate them as discursive categories. Following the instructive works of Pradeep Jeganathan, David Scott, and Michel Foucault, the chapter contends that the relation between religion and violence is not available for disciplinary canonization in the now familiar vocabularies of "Buddhism Betrayed?" "religious violence," and "religious terrorism."

Part of my labor here is to intervene in the disciplinary space in which terms like *religious violence* now stand authorized as universally applicable objects of knowledge. I examine the conjuncture of (especially) the mid- and late-1980s in which competing Buddhist discourses began to authorize to come into central sight a "Buddhist" identity of a "fearless" monk, who was prepared to lay down his life and march to the battlefield in order to save the country and the nation from the *adharmista* ("unBuddhist") Jayewardene state. While delineating in detail different kinds of practices and persons that authorized the making of this fearless monkhood, I show how those same practices became contested and subverted as "terror" (*bhīshanaya*) and unBuddhist in a different conjuncture. To do so I trace out, in a somewhat Foucauldian fashion, a partial genealogy of "terror" that has today become the dominant local discourse for identifying the period of nationwide sporadic bloodshed from the mid-1980s to the early 1990s between the state and the JVP. It is crucial that we exercise caution in employing ideologically invested and deployed discourses like "terror" to represent "violence" as opposed to "religion." The scholarly failure to do so produces ideological and normative texts competing against or endorsing the interests of one political party or another. To bypass such pitfalls, we must dispense with a priori assumptions about what is "religion" or "violence" and cultivate a critical awareness of the discursive conjunctures that offer competing, altering definitions of the line between them, rendering it unavailable for disciplinary canonization.

A final word of caution. Throughout this work, as must be clear now, when referring to specific persons, practices, and discourses that seek to foreground competing definitions of Buddhism, I use phrases like *coming into central view, fading from view, central visibility,* and *emergence and submergence.* I want to emphasize that seeking to understand what and who became, for example, centrally visible is not to ask empirical questions about whether *everybody* knew, talked about, favored, or rejected a given event, practice, person, or discourse; rather I am interested in the ways in which *particular* narratives, persons, practices, and institutions come into central view at particular times and places, marginalizing other competing discourses. What is centrally visible today may not be so tomorrow.

CHAPTER TWO

Shifting Configurations of Religious Identity and Difference

säbä bhikshūn vahansē silvatva gunavatva vesena samājaya yahapatata haravanna vehesena unmattakayeki. mevan utuman händinvena arahat nama bōdhisat-vayeki yannai. mevan gaurava sammānayak tavat ädda?

A real Buddhist monk who lives a moral and virtuous life and strives to steer society in the right direction is an insane man. The honorable name that identifies such an enlightened monk is Bodhisatva (a Buddha in the making). Is there an honor higher than this?

These seemingly paradoxical words, written on a piece of paper in large, curvaceous Sinhalese, hang on the wall behind a desk in a Buddhist monk's room at Sangaramaya, the monastic dormitory at Peradeniya University in the highlands of Kandy, Sri Lanka. I asked the monk what the words meant. He said: "Yes, it is the ideal, the proper monastic life [*niyama bhikshu jīvite*]. We should all strive for it. But what monk can do it?"[1]

This chapter inaugurates a critical inquiry into the shifting configurations of the relation between Buddhism and difference, discourse and "religious" knowledge, in contemporary Sri Lanka. It begins with a partial but crucial examination of scholarly literature that constructed the relation between Buddhism, monkhood, and society as objects of disciplinary knowledge. It seeks to challenge, on both empirical and analytical grounds, the assumptions that animate the conventional conceptualizations of that relation by demonstrating the ways in which concepts like Buddhism come to be invested with and divested of authoritative meanings and knowledges in conjunctures of contingent moral arguments and debates.

First, this chapter tells a story of a Buddhist monk in Sri Lanka from the perspective of a Sinhala novel authored by a monk himself. Though a

1. Interview, Aug. 3, 1996.

fictionalized representation, the novel unravels the complex fashioning of the relation between Buddhist identity and difference, monasticism and society. Second, as a way of elaborating the novel's representations of Buddhist identity and difference, the chapter reports on my ethnographic fieldwork carried out among Sinhalese Buddhists in a cluster of villages located near Sigiriya in the northern part of Sri Lanka. My purpose is to demonstrate the conjunctures of competing moral debates and arguments that seek to authorize and unauthorize specific persons and practices as "Buddhism" and "non-Buddhism," religious identity and difference, orthodoxy and unorthodoxy. These moral debates are not self-evident examples of ethnography that guarantee us any authoritative epistemological purchase on Buddhism and society. Rather, they are products of specific debates that render possible and centrally visible the differing demarcations between what can and cannot count as Buddhism. I contend that by locating disciplinary questions about Buddhism, monkhood, identity, and difference in these debates, we can bypass the problematic assumptions through which an archive of scholarship constructed such categories as readily canonizable forms of knowledge and can think of radically new alternatives to understanding Buddhism as a tradition of fleeting moral arguments and debates in contingent conjunctures.

Buddhism and Monkhood, Disciplines and Knowledge Productions

Almost two decades after Ceylon's independence in 1948, a number of important anthropological studies of Theravada Buddhism emerged. They constructed Buddhism, as David Scott has pointed out, as a theoretical problem, "the problem of Buddhism and society."[2] The anthropological construction of this problem "was something of a conceptual intervention in a field virtually constituted by Indology."[3] These studies, partly influenced by the then current (Western) academic interest in the studies of the South and Southeast Asian "village," sought to understand and explain the relation between "text and context."[4] The analyses they provided revolved around the popular binary categories such as "the great tradition" and "the little tradition," "worldly" and "otherworldly," "sacred" and "secular," "orthodox" and

2. David Scott, *Formations of Ritual*, 176.
3. Ibid., 177.
4. Ibid.

"syncretistic," "Buddhist" and "animistic."[5] Yet these studies included little or no substantial discussion of Sinhala Buddhist monasticism that undoubtedly formed a crucial aspect of this anthropologically constituted relationship between "Buddhism and society."

A few years later, however, the academic debate took a different turn. A significant number of mostly Western anthropological studies of the Sinhala monastic universe appeared.[6] One can but conjecture that the island's political climate at that time had some impact on the emergence of these postcolonial studies. A watershed in this political climate was the election of S. W. R. D. Bandaranaike as prime minister in 1956, for which many monks actively campaigned. Equally important, perhaps, was the assassination of

5. Some of the early anthropological studies that labored to conceptualize the relation between Buddhism and society, using structural approaches, are Michael Ames, "Magical Animism and Buddhism: A Structural Analysis of Sinhalese Buddhism," *Journal of Asian Studies* 23 (1964): 21–52; Nur Yalman, "The Structure of Sinhalese Healing Rituals," *Journal of Asian Studies* 23 (1964): 115–50; idem, "Dual Organization in Central Ceylon," in *Anthropological Studies of Theravada Buddhism*, ed. Manning Nash (New Haven: Yale University South Asian Studies, 1966). More recent additions to the list are Martin Southwold, *Buddhism in Life: The Anthropological Study of Religion and the Sinhalese Practice of Buddhism* (Manchester, U.K.: Manchester University Press, 1983); idem, "True Buddhism and Village Buddhism in Sri Lanka," in *Religious Organization and Religious Experience*, ed. J. Davis (London: Academic Press, 1984). This is with the exception of Gananath Obeyesekere's felicitous essay "Great Tradition and the Little in the Perspective of Sinhalese Buddhism," *Journal of Asian Studies* 22, no. 2 (1963): 139–53. In order to avoid these problematics, Obeyesekere argued that Sinhala Buddhism should be understood as a "whole." But recently David Scott has argued that in constructing Buddhism as an object of scholarly inquiry, both early and recent anthropological works on Sinhala Buddhist society (an example of the latter being Richard Gombrich and Gananath Obeyesekere, *Buddhism Transformed* [Princeton: Princeton University Press, 1988]) retain a colonial preoccupation with identifying authentic parts of Buddhism. As a corrective, Scott suggests that Buddhism be understood not as a whole but as a "discursive tradition"; see David Scott, "Historicizing Tradition: Buddhism and the Discourse of Yakku," in his *Formations of Rituals*, 173–203.

6. Some of the postindependence anthropological, sociological, and historical studies of Sinhala monks are Hans-Dieter Evers, "Monastic Landlordism in Ceylon," *Journal of Asian Studies* 28, no. 4 (1969): 685–92; Heinz Bechert, "The Theravāda Buddhist Sangha: Some General Observations on Historical and Political Factors in Its Development," *Journal of Asian Studies* 29, no. 4 (1970): 761–78; Gananath Obeyesekere, "Religious Symbolism and Political Change in Ceylon," in *The Two Wheels of the Dhamma*, ed. Bardwell Smith (Chambersburg, Pa.: American Academy of Religion, 1972); Hans-Dieter Evers, *Monks, Priests, and Peasants* (Leiden: E. J. Brill, 1972); Steven Kemper, "The Social Order of the Sinhalese Buddhist Sangha," Ph.D. diss., University of Chicago, 1973; idem, "Buddhism without Bhikkhus: The Sri Lanka Vinaya Vardhana Society," in *Religion and the Legitimation of Power in Sri Lanka*, ed. Bardwell Smith (Chambersburg, Pa.: Anima, 1978); Kitsiri Malalgoda, *Buddhism in Sinhalese Society* (Berkeley: University of California Press, 1976); Michael Carrithers, "The Modern Ascetics of Lanka and the Pattern of Change in

Bandaranaike three years later, masterminded by a Buddhist monk.[7] The subsequent anthropological studies of Sinhala Buddhist society constructed a new theoretical problem in terms of "religion and politics" in Sri Lanka, and the analysis of that theoretical problem forms the basis for the next chapter. Here I want to examine critically but briefly a few recent works by several distinguished scholars of Buddhism and unmask the kinds of problematic ideological assumptions that have gone into their conceptualizations of the relations between Buddhism and difference, monasticism and society, in Sri Lanka. This task, I insist, is crucial to the kind of critical theoretical perspective that this work seeks to sustain on understanding Buddhism, monkhood, politics, and difference as categories whose authoritative meanings alter in conjunctures of moral debates and discourses.

S. J. Tambiah's *Buddhism Betrayed?* is particularly notable because one of its preoccupations is to conceptualize the relation between Buddhist identity and difference in terms of what he calls "the changing or the changed shape" of Buddhism in the context of "politics and violence" within the last decade in Sri Lanka.[8] Tambiah begins his account by writing: "The main question I

Buddhism," *Man* 14, no. 2 (1979): 294–310; idem, "The Social Organization of the Sinhalese Sangha in an Historical Perspective," in *Contributions to South Asian Studies*, vol. 1, ed. Gopal Krishna (Delhi: Oxford University Press, 1979); idem, *The Forest Monks of Sri Lanka: An Anthropological and Historical Study* (New Delhi: Oxford University Press, 1983). For some of the recent studies that attempt to discuss and evaluate the monastic role in relation to "violence," "ethnicity," and so forth, also see H. L. Seneviratne, "The Buddhist Monkhood and Social Concern," *Lanka Guardian* 19, no. 9 (1996): 17–19; idem, "The Sangha's Role Reassessed," *Lanka Guardian*, Mar. 15, 1997, 11–12. On similar themes, see C. R. de Silva, "The Plurality of Buddhist Fundamentalism," in Bartholomeusz and de Silva, *Buddhist Fundamentalism*; idem, "The Monks and the Pontiff: Reflections on Religious Tensions in Contemporary Politics in Sri Lanka," *South Asia* 19 (1996): 233–44; Josine van der Horst, "With Regard to the Sangha during Premadasa's Presidency," in her *Who Is He, What Is He Doing? The Religious Rhetoric and Performances in Sri Lanka during R. Premadasa's Presidency* (Amsterdam: VU University Press, 1995). The most recent account of Buddhism and monkhood is H. L. Seneviratne's *The Work of Kings: The New Buddhism in Sri Lanka* (Chicago: University of Chicago Press, 1999). It will be easy to see that this work, which is written from the provocative standpoint of a "native anthropologist" who seeks to question and evaluate the ideological formations of Buddhist identity, is grounded in a theoretical project radically different from mine. Seneviratne's book became available to me too late to do more here than refer readers to my review of *The Work of Kings* in the *American Ethnologist*.

7. On Bandaranaike's biography, see James Manor, *The Expedient Utopian: Bandaranaike and Ceylon* (Cambridge: Cambridge University Press, 1989).

8. S. J. Tambiah, *Buddhism Betrayed? Religion, Politics, and Violence in Sri Lanka* (Chicago: University of Chicago Press, 1992). The categories of Buddhism and violence are the subject of my chapter 7.

shall probe is the extent to which, and the manner in which, Buddhism as a religion espoused by Sri Lankans of the late nineteenth and twentieth centuries, has contributed to the current ethnic conflict and collective violence in Sri Lanka." If it has, Tambiah asks, "were these changes in the nature of that contribution over time? If there have been changes, how are we to describe the changing or the changed shape of Buddhism itself as a lived reality."[9] After several chapters of briefly tracing the history of politics and Buddhism from 1860 to 1960, Tambiah goes on to identify the emergence of a "political Buddhism" and equates it with things like "Buddhist nationalism," "chauvinism," "violence," and "fundamentalism." He obviously does not think of them as categories but as particular modalities of Sinhala practice, and he argues that they "could . . . have little links [sic] with the major tenets of canonical Buddhist ethics."[10] This political Buddhism, which, among other things, "envisages a central role as advisors and counselors for activist monks at all levels of the national polity,"[11] is not a continuity but a transformation of an earlier model.[12]

Tambiah bases this argument on a distinction he makes between "religion as a moral practice" and "religion as a cultural and political possession," or between "religiousness" and "religious-mindedness."[13] For Tambiah, a gradual "shift" from the former to the latter has "weakened, displaced, and distorted . . . the substantively soteriological, ethical, and normative components of doctrinal Buddhism";[14] this shift, for him, symbolizes change or transformation. The implicit question that pervades Tambiah's analysis is whether that change is "religious" (Buddhist) and, hence, whether the Sinhalese monks and lay Buddhists whose behavior brings about that change are really Buddhist—at least, in light of certain canonical Buddhist concepts. It is this question that Tambiah frames in terms of the question in his title *Buddhism Betrayed?*

The problem with Tambiah's argument is that the distinction between two kinds of religion—"Buddhism as a moral practice" and "Buddhism as a

---

9. Tambiah, *Buddhism Betrayed?* 2.

10. Ibid., 59.

11. Ibid., 60.

12. Ibid., 59.

13. Ibid., 59. Tambiah does not mention sources, but as far I know the distinction between "religiousness" and "religious-mindedness" was first propounded by Clifford Geertz in his *Islam Observed: Religious Development in Morocco and Indonesia* (Chicago: University of Chicago Press, 1973), 106.

14. Tambiah, *Buddhism Betrayed?* 58.

political possession"—is taken to be self-evident and hence unproblematic. Given the recent anthropological calls for the critical examination of the "genealogies" of Western (and very often colonial) concepts that we deploy to represent non-Western cultural practices, we may question the ideological/epistemic location of such a distinction.[15] As David Scott has shown so meticulously for Sri Lanka, the construction of the religious world of Sinhalese Buddhists in terms of "two systems"—canonical Buddhism as "authentic" Buddhism and other noncanonical ritual practices like *yaktovil* as "demonism"—can be traced to the British colonial economy of representing Buddhist identity.[16] Though Tambiah insists on not trying to find "something reified as Buddhism,"[17] his distinction between two religions, alas, produces a similar colonial problematic of identifying a "true," authentic Buddhism because the very question *Buddhism Betrayed?* hinges on the assumption of an abstract, essential Buddhism that can be betrayed.

My point here is not that Sinhalese Buddhists do not debate what does and does not constitute "true" Buddhism.[18] My point is that such debates, as we will see throughout this book, are rendered possible and centrally visible by specific ideological-epistemic conjunctures, and it is to such debates that scholars interested in understanding and representing religious change should devote careful attention. Any scholarly attempt to understand, explain, and evaluate the "changing or the changed shape" of Sinhala Buddhist culture in terms of a "shift" from Buddhism as a "morality" to Buddhism as a "political possession" is an exercise that does not yield productive analytical insights; it takes that distinction as given and fixed and so fails to inquire critically into

15. Two recent anthropologists of religion who have made such forceful arguments are Asad, in *Genealogies of Religion*, and Scott, in *Formations of Ritual*. On the concept of genealogy, see the introduction to this book.

16. See David Scott, "Colonial Christian Discourse, Demonism, and Sinhala Religion," in *Formations of Ritual*, 137–69.

17. Tambiah charges, without mentioning sources, that "all too often a certain kind of scholarship . . . has essentialized Buddhism in terms of its 'pristine' teachings and has viewed all subsequent historical developments, especially those of a political kind, as deviations and distortions from the canonical form": Tambiah, *Buddhism Betrayed?* 3, 101.

18. One may object that Tambiah's question in the title of his *Buddhism Betrayed?* is an allusion to a local discourse in that "the Betrayal of Buddhism" was a "local" discourse in postcolonial Sri Lanka. But he frames the whole question in relation to an international interlocutor, who asks him how has a religion like Buddhism, which preaches nonviolence, produced monks and lay Buddhists who advocate violence; see *Buddhism Betrayed?* 1. I owe this point to Pradeep Jeganathan.

and understand fleeting debates that authorize such distinctions. Put differently, an account that wants to conceptualize the "changed shape of Buddhism" based on a dichotomy that regards one Buddhism as "ethical" (authentic) inevitably sees any supposed change in it as an (ethical) opposition to that Buddhism.

Such a position is clearly evident in the following statement that Tambiah makes. Concluding a brief discussion about the relation between violence and Buddhist monastic identity, he writes that "many Buddhists among the ranks of the laity as well as the sectarian community of monks must necessarily feel a profound misgiving, even consternation, when monks get caught up in political violence. . . . There is an inescapable dilemma here which surely must tug at the moral sensibilities of all Buddhists."[19] It should be obvious that my quarrel here is not so much with the ethnographic accuracy of these remarks as with the theoretical soundness, and indeed the very possibility, of such assertions.[20] For me, they are predicated upon moral, not to mention colonial, assumptions about Buddhism; they hence fail to consider different conjunctures of discursively shifting knowledges about Buddhism and difference.

Tambiah's questionable conception of religious change, it seems to me, stems from taking "identity" itself as a readily identifiable object of anthropological inquiry. Consider, for instance, these varying labels that Tambiah employs frequently and randomly to identify monks of different periods: "reformist," "activist," "political," "orthodox," "modern," "conservative," "radical," "chauvinist," "ideological," and, yes, even "thoughtful." Tambiah's analysis makes explicit contrasts between "modern-educated young monks" and "old conservative monks," thereby portraying a community of monks polarized into two groups: "conservative" vs. "modern" or "radical."[21] These should

19. Tambiah, *Buddhism Betrayed?* 101.

20. For such questions about the inadequacy of the book's "ethnographic material," see the exchange between Tambiah and Sasanka Perera: Perera, review of *Buddhism Betrayed? Religion, Politics, and Violence in Sri Lanka*, by S. J. Tambiah, in *American Ethnologist* 23, no. 4 (1996): 905–6; and Tambiah, "On the Subject of Buddhism Betrayed? A Rejoinder," *American Ethnologist* 24, no. 2 (1997): 457–59; Perera, "Some Comments on Tambiah's Response," *American Ethnologist* 24, no. 3 (1988): 492–94.

21. Following Tambiah, Peter Schalk makes a similar ahistorical, dichotomous argument: "The political monk of the twentieth century thus deviates from his predecessor by questioning the very basis of his existence, the Vinaya [the monastic rules]" (Schalk, review of *Buddhism Betrayed?*, in *Temenos* 29 [1993]: 183–89).

not be dismissed as mere adjectives; these terms carry ideologically deployed meanings, and they reveal one's own (Western) political orientations far more than the (non-Western) persons and practices that one seeks to represent. For instance, as David Scott has cautioned, a distinction like "conservative\radical," which has "so shaped and guided our modern/modernist ways of affiliating politically . . . hangs on buying an Enlightenment story about progress, reason, and emancipation."[22]

While concurring with Scott, I would argue that such fashionable terms of caricaturing non-Western identities are names for the disciplinary incomprehensibility of the contingent conjunctures in which the relation between religious identity and difference gets authorized, argued, and battled out in ways that anthropology cannot canonize. But the use of such distinctions assumes a sense of privileged anthropological knowledge of what culture/identity is all about. Consider the following statement that Tambiah makes, continuing his discussion of the changing shape of Sinhala monastic practice:

> Have we in Sri Lanka today arrived at a critical turning point? Large numbers of young monks, more widely than before drawn from the lower reaches of rural society, are recruited into the *sangha* and find themselves on the upward path of education in monastic colleges and at higher levels of education, including the national universities. Being in much the same situation as the young men and women who joined the JVP [the Marxist-oriented youth movement that tried to capture state power by a bloody armed revolution (1987–89)], they are alienated more than ever before from the system of politics and the politicians who participate in it and are frustrated by their inability to create a political economy and a public culture in which they can participate. At the same time, they are more fully involved in public politics in larger numbers than at any other time in the history of the *sangha*, and *this involvement makes them less distinguishable from the laity participating in politics* [my emphasis]. The questions that we are compelled to pose but can not answer are: Will the *sangha* renew and reproduce itself, and what might its possibly transformed shape be, when the present generation of more 'orthodox' monk-elders and the *mahanayakes* [chief monks] pass away? What would be the structure of the *sangha*, its public representation of itself, and the substance of the monk's

22. David Scott, "A Note on the Demand of Criticism," *Public Culture* 8 (fall 1995): 48.

vocation? What would be the activities and the pattern of transactions between monks and laity?[23]

There is much one can contest in this sweeping statement that seeks to explain the present state of the monastic community by asking questions about its future. My concern here, however, is with two of Tambiah's notable points about contemporary relations between Buddhist identity and difference, religious orthodoxy and unorthodoxy. First, the concept of a "critical turning point" assumes that (Buddhist monastic) identity has remained unvaried until a *certain point* in history; it was only very recently, Tambiah says, that young monks began to take part in "politics" in increasing numbers, a practice that he thinks "makes them less distinguishable from the laity." Second, Tambiah's concern as to what the "transformed shape" of Buddhist monasticism will be after the elderly, "more orthodox" monks pass away presupposes the existence of a uniformly "orthodox" elderly monastic community. Tambiah does not pause to tell us who these "more orthodox" monks might be, much less what kinds of discourse, uttered by whom, under what circumstances, authorize what kind of monk is more or less orthodox.

These assumptions about Buddhist identity and difference have animated other writings.[24] In an essay entitled "Dilemmas of Modern Sinhala Buddhist Monks in Relation to Ethnic and Political Conflict," where he discusses the complex political landscape in the late 1980s in Sri Lanka, Sarath Amunugama states that the ethnic conflict has caused serious "dilemmas" for Buddhist monks.[25] Speaking of the relation between monks and the JVP movement, Amunugama writes:

> The intrusion of monks into the arena of revolutionary politics has resulted in a loss of their charisma. Monks are arrested, stripped of their robes, publicly humiliated and even killed by armed Sinhala Buddhists. . . . This dwindling of social esteem of and for Buddhist monks may have long term implications for recruitment, education, influence and the religious vocation of the Sinhala Sangha.[26]

23. Tambiah, *Buddhism Betrayed?* 99–100.

24. Borrowing one of Tambiah's questions, Tessa Bartholomeusz wonders (optimistically, I think) about the future status of lay nuns after the "orthodox monks pass away"; see *Women under the Bō Tree: Buddhist Nuns in Sri Lanka* (Cambridge: Cambridge University Press, 1994), 190.

25. Sarath Amunugama, "Buddhaputra or Bhumiputra? Dilemmas of Modern Sinhala Buddhist Monks in Relation to Ethnic and Political Conflict," *Religion* 21 (1991): 115–39.

26. Ibid., 138.

What is important to note here is that Amunugama assumes that monks have supposedly remained "charismatic" in the past and that their "Buddhist" identity is now teetering on the brink of extinction. Amunugama grossly over-simplifies that "charisma" and "social esteem," by which he seems to think the Sinhalse Buddhist society determines monastic identity, are historically, discursively constituted. Differently put, Amunugama takes for granted that there is a universally and essentially unvarying relation between charisma and (proper) "Buddhist" monkhood in Sri Lankan society.

The late Newton Gunasinghe, writing about Buddhism, monkhood, and modernity in mid-1980 Sri Lanka, echoes similar views:

> With the accelerated commercialization within the previous decade or so, traditional Sinhala society had undergone far-reaching changes not devoid of tensions and strife. The social status of and the power of the monk, who essentially used to be a member of the traditional authority hierarchy, was bound to decline with these changes.[27]

The idea that the monk in contemporary Sri Lanka has lost his "social sta-tus" and "power" owing to the "accelerated commercialization" is rooted in the assumption about an ahistorical, homogenous past in which existed a determinate, causal link between monastic power and a particular Buddhist virtue; namely, the ideal of attaining nirvana. As Gunasinghe further argues, "Although in classical Indian Buddhism, the sangha seems to have taken an intensively salvation-oriented direction . . . it is not so in contemporary Sin-hala Buddhism. Except for the small communities of the forest-dwelling monks who are not actors in the political field, the bulk of the Buddhist monkhood resident at the temples have lost their [*sic*] *moksha* [nirvana] ori-entation long ago."[28] For Gunasinghe, as for some other prominent scholars, to understand the relation between Buddhism and change (that is, the sup-posed loss of the monk's power and charisma) is to speak of how Buddhists (monks) have gradually "deviated" from the "pristine" Buddhist path.[29] My

27. Newton Gunasinghe, "The Symbolic Role of the Sangha," *Lanka Guardian*, Oct. 1, 1986.

28. Ibid.

29. The story of how monks have over the course of time deviated from the "pristine" Buddhist path has become part of textbooks on Theravada Buddhism; for example, Richard Gombrich, *Theravada Buddhism: A Social History from Ancient Benares to Modern Colombo* (London: Routledge, 1988), speaking of the Sinhalese Buddhist sangha after 1753, says that the "Sangha's life as landowners in peasant communities led to further deviation from the pristine

point here should be obvious: The so-called social status and power of the monk—the relation between identity and difference—is not determined by, or dependent upon, a timeless Buddhist "orientation," but one that is historically and discursively conditioned and contingent.

It is clear that these works that seek to theorize Buddhism and difference rest on a particular normative (Enlightenment) conception of religion and secularism, modernity and tradition.[30] They assume that religion/Buddhism is prior to the secular/the modern and so see them as readily apprehensible, nondiscursive objects of knowledge. My point is that we cannot conceptualize the relation between Buddhism and difference, religion and change, in terms of a "shift" or "deviation" from some supposed essential "religious" life, or in terms of a "clash" between religious tradition and modernity, because such views are grounded in ideas about the availability of that relation at face value. For example, in a recent study that seeks to understand the place of monastic identity in the "changing world," Ananda Wickremeratne argued that previous studies of the relation between Buddhism and society have overemphasized the dichotomy between "tradition and modernization" and instead proposed a different approach:

> The real issue is a dichotomy of another sort. It rests on a clash between two views. The lay view of what the Sangha ought to be and must necessarily be in terms of role fulfillment and the Sangha's own perceptions of their role and their relations with the laity. Here one feels lies the real tension (dramatically highlighted recently in political and ethnic issues), modernizing often providing merely the stage on which the drama is enacted.[31]

This is precisely the kind of approach I suggest we reevaluate if Buddhism is to be understood as a historically contingent moral argument. The idea of a clash, "a real tension," between monks and lay society is not an analytically

---

ideal." Gombrich characterizes this "deviation" in somber, if not nostalgic, colonial, terms: "catastrophic decline," "sad state of affairs," and "corruption" (166–67). More recently, other Western scholars have argued in a similar fashion; for example, "Traditional Buddhist culture, greatly distorted by the twentieth century urban-based reformers, already may be irrevocably imperiled": John Holt, *Buddha in the Crown: Avalōkiteśvara in the Buddhist Traditions of Sri Lanka* (Oxford: Oxford University Press, 1991), 223.

30. Again, on the assumptions of the secularist/modernity theory, see Connolly, *Why I Am Not a Secularist*; Scott, *Refashioning Futures*; and Asad, *Genealogies of Religion*.

31. Ananda Wickremeratne, "The Sangha in a Changing World," in his *Buddhism and Ethnicity in Sri Lanka: A Historical Analysis* (New Delhi: Vikas, 1995), 262.

useful one. The relation between Buddhism and difference—a "real tension" between what the laity expect from monks and vice versa—is not an aspect of a social reality that remains readily available for disciplinary identification. I argue that questions about what kinds of "Buddhist" practice should be performed by whom are made possible by fleeting debates.

My proposition is that our disciplinary preoccupations with understanding the differing relation—"tension," if you will—between Buddhism and difference, religion and change, must be located in what I call strategic discourses (discursive strategies). The concept of strategic discourses denotes specific conjunctures of competing moral arguments, disagreements, and debates that make possible and centrally visible the terms and parameters of who and what can or cannot count as religion or difference. Such strategic discourses, as Talal Asad has pointed out, consist "of antagonistic wills, struggling for supremacy over a terrain that may always not be delimited, with forces that are not always constant, in conditions whose changing significance cannot always be anticipated."[32] In other words, these antagonistic wills or arguments compete to stake out in centrally visible ways authoritative moral claims about what do and do not constitute Buddhism, seeking to preempt the space of other opposing narratives.

What I want to suggest is that the critical examination of the emergence and submergence of competing narratives about Buddhism\difference in different conjunctures helps us dispense with the continuing disciplinary concerns with identifying what religion (or "the genius of Sinhala Bud-dhist culture") was all about in a given historical period.[33] For example, in a recent study of Buddhist temple wall paintings sponsored by King Kirti Sri

32. Asad, "Discipline and Humility in Medieval Christian Monasticism," in his *Genealogies of Religion*, 139. Asad's is a rethinking of the idea of strategy that Bourdieu made famous; see Pierre Bourdieu, *Outline of a Theory of Practice* (Cambridge: Cambridge University Press, 1977). Scott, following Asad and Foucault, speaks of strategy as operating "in a domain of confrontation of socially constituted [opposing] forces" in which "the outcome—failure or success, loss or victory—is not given in advance": Scott, *Formations of Rituals*, 209. Foucault's seminal essay where he speaks of strategy is "Subject and Power," the afterword in Herbert L. Dreyfus and Paul Rabinow, *Michel Foucault: Beyond Structuralism and Hermeneutics* (Chicago: University of Chicago Press, 1983).

33. Holt, "Persistence of Political Buddhism," 194. Holt claims that "for centuries . . . the genius of Sinhala-Buddhist culture was expressed through its remarkable inclusivity and assimi-lations." He goes so far as to call for the "resurrection of that same spirit of inclusivity" as a solution to the contemporary political crisis in Sri Lanka. Similar claims are made in Holt's earlier *Buddha in the Crown*.

Rajasimha in eighteenth-century Kandy, Sri Lanka, John Holt concluded: "More than any other form of cultic religious expression, these paintings clearly illustrate . . . not only the fundamental mythic history of the Theravda Buddhist tradition but also the basic behavioral actions and cognitive tenets that explain what it meant to be Buddhist during this time."[34] One may, on an empirical level, question how Holt could so confidently ascertain what "Buddhism" meant for the entire "general and nominally Sinhalese Buddhist populace" in late medieval Sri Lanka based simply on some wall paintings done by one king's decree.[35] But mine is not such an empirical question. Rather, my point is that such patently problematic (generalizing) claims like Holt's arise from the misguided exercise of attempting to *explain* how certain kinds of discourses count as "unmistakably Buddhist" because they "do not stand in marked contrast to the sacred texts or the mythic literature of the Pali tradition, but summarily incorporate them."[36]

For Holt, while such paintings are unmistakably Buddhist, other practices (that is, "political ideology") of Buddhists, as he has argued elsewhere, are "not *primarily* religious" because their "avowed aims are not ultimately soteriological in nature."[37] These assumptions, in my view, spring from the chronic disciplinary failure to theorize Buddhism as a discursive concept whose meanings are made to emerge and submerge, to become centered and marginalized in differing conjunctures of native debates. Seeking to apprehend some practice as "primarily religious" does not help us understand the shifting configurations of competing discourses that render variable and veritable the terms and parameters of "Buddhism" but perpetuates colonial notions of religion and secularism, tradition and modernity.

Buddhism and Difference in a Novel

Guided by doubts regarding these kinds of disciplinary claims about Buddhist identity and difference, in this section I undertake a reading of the Sinhalese

---

34. John Holt, *The Religious World of Kīrti Śri: Buddhism, Art, and Politics in Late Medieval Sri Lanka* (New York: Oxford University Press, 1996), 93.

35. Ibid.

36. Ibid., 39, 93.

37. Holt, "Persistence of Political Buddhism," 189. Holt calls some Sinhalese "misguided Buddhist zealots" because they rationalize certain practices (such as violence) that he assumes do not accord with Buddhism. Holt, *Religious World*, 104. For further comments on this, see chapter 7.

novel *Buddhaputrayekugē Dēshanāva* (A sermon by a son of the Buddha), by Orukmankulame Chandana,[38] which deals with the complex fashioning of the relations between Buddhist identity and difference in Sri Lanka. One may object to the novel's representations of Buddhist identity: it is a "fiction," an imagined account, not an "ethnography." Here I do not wish to contribute to the well-rehearsed debate about the relation between fictions and ethnographies;[39] my reading of this novel is not to provide more ethnographic "facts" about the nature of Buddhism and society in Sri Lanka. Rather it intends to point out, in a preliminary fashion, particular ways in which questions about what persons and practices constitute Buddhism and monkhood are fashioned and debated.

The novel is a fictionalized biography of a young Buddhist monk named Sudhira.[40] The first part of the novel unravels the social dynamics of Sudhira's poverty-stricken life as a young boy, then named Madduma Bandara, in Orukmankulame, a village near Anuradhapura, an ancient capital of Sri Lanka.[41] Madduma Bandara comes from a single-parent family and dreams of attending a big school in a city. In the midst of a scandal that ensues after he commits a theft, the boy, fearing ridicule, refuses to attend the village school. The head monk of the village temple, who seems to learn about the problem from the boy's mother, Yasawati, intervenes to assist the family. He takes the boy to a temple in Kandy where he can stay and attend a nearby school.

The head monk of the Kandyan temple, however, engineers different plans for the boy. Refusing to send him to school, the monk seeks to convince Madduma that he can receive a better education as a monk. Initially, the boy, having confronted within a few weeks of his stay at the temple some harsh realities of the monastic life, balks at the suggestion. One day, for instance, he witnesses the head monk severely whipping a young monk who has violated

---

38. Orukmankulame Chandana, *Buddhaputrayekugē Dēshanāva* (Ratmalana: Petikada, 1995). There are, of course, other relevant novels. For a lay Buddhist perspective on Buddhist monasticism, see Jayakodi Senaviratna, *Podi Hāmuduruwō* [Junior monk] (Colombo: Dayawamsa Jayakody, 1995).

39. For a debate on this issue, see Michael Carrithers, "Is Anthropology Art or Science?" *Current Anthropology* 3 (1990): 263–81; also see *Writing Culture: The Poetics and Politics of Ethnography*, ed. James Clifford and George Marcus (Berkeley: University of California Press, 1986), esp. James Clifford's "Partial Truths"; Marilyn Strathern, "Out of Context: The Persuasive Fictions of Anthropology," *Current Anthropology* 28, no. 3 (1987): 251–82.

40. The names of places and institutions the novel refers to are all actual.

41. The author of the novel comes from the same village.

the rule of eating at night (that is, any time after twelve noon). The head monk's irate words about the monk's infraction echo in his mind:

> You monks must remember well: The food that people offer, having worshipped you, is fire. You are eating fire [*kanne gindara*]. If you want to put out that fire you must observe the rules [*pilivet puranda ōnä*]. Those monks who did not observe the rules are the bulls that draw carts. This behavior [eating at night] does not suit monks. Moreover, what if a lay patron came to the temple? Is it not a bad name for the temple? Would I not be blamed?

The future Sudhira acquiesces to the suggestion as the head monk threatens to send him back to the village unless he enters the monastic order. Seeing no prospect of education in his poor village, he convinces himself that being a monk is the only path out of the suffering of his family's poverty. He gradually becomes accustomed to life at the temple. He mingles closely with monks. On occasion he wraps himself playfully in bedsheets and parades in front of a mirror, picturing what he would look like as a monk in a real robe. Before long this playing becomes a reality: he finds himself undergoing ordination in front of a large audience of monks and lay people.

Immediately following the conclusion of the ordination ceremony, Sudhira—as he is now called—remains overwhelmed by the transformation of his identity. People, including his mother, kneel and worship him. This transformation becomes more acutely visible to him when his little sister approaches and innocently questions him: "Brother [*ayye*], when are you coming back home?" Sudhira looks at his sister dumbfounded. The head monk overhears the conversation and rushes to Sudhira's rescue: "Ha, Ha, your brother is not here. From now on, you must call him *podi hāmuduruwō* (junior monk)."

Debating Buddhist Identity and Difference

Years pass, and Sudhira, now an adult, visits his village in Anuradhapura. On the footpath to his house, Sudhira meets his former best friend and learns that he is already taking the university entrance exams. Sudhira, envious, returns to the temple in Kandy and cuts his classes at the *pirivena* (monastic school) to study for the ordinary-level exam (SSE) and enter university. He knows that the head monk does not approve of his students' attending universities. But one day, expecting the worst, Sudhira informs the head monk of his decision to study for the exam during the break from the pirivena. The head monk flies into a rage. "What SSE? SSE? This has become a fashion [*mōstarayak velā*] for monks these days. They do not want to study how to preach a sermon and chant *pirit*. [They think] taking SSE will make everything all right. Do you not understand that we live on food that people give. We must learn [to do] something beneficial for people [*minisunta vädak vena*]." This yelling ends the conversation. But Sudhira begins to ruminate that he can "no longer live in fear" (*biyata yatatva*) and decides to take the exam. He knows that no other monk at the temple has ever disobeyed the head monk. He keeps his plans a secret. He skillfully maneuvers other monks and lay friends into assisting him in finding books and notes for the exam as well as money to pay for the exam registration. During months of preparation for the exam, Sudhira neglects his monastic duties at the temple, such as preaching (*bana*), pirit chanting, and attending alms-giving ceremonies and funeral rituals (*pānsakūla*).

The head monk finds out about Sudhira's underhanded activities. One day Sudhira receives the letter of his exam results from the postman. He tries to bury the letter under his robe, but the head monk, seated in the foyer, sees it and lashes out at Sudhira: "Sudhira, you must remember well that it is either Don or Siman [*don nan don siman nan siman*]. You cannot be both Don and Siman here.[42] . . . I know what you want. But do not call me the villain [*naraka minihayi kiyanda epā*]. That is all I have to say." Sudhira disregards the warning of the head monk and continues his activities, refusing to perform his share of the duties at the temple.

Some of the monks at the temple also begin to disapprove of Sudhira's behavior and accuse him of neglecting his monastic responsibilities. They fling caustic remarks at Sudhira as he walks past them: "Two years have passed since his higher ordination. But he cannot preach a word of bana [*bana padayak*]. They say he passed great big [*mahaloku*] exams. He [thinks he] is a 'great' person [*loku minissune*]. That is why he does whatever he likes." Sudhira screams back: "My faults seem to hurt everyone. Yes, everybody will not mind it if I gulp down free food and sleep [*dan gagahā budiya budiya innavanam*]. The talk is as if I am the only one who commits faults." The recurrent exchange of antagonistic words renders the environment hostile at the temple, and Sudhira contemplates giving up his robes. Yet the horrifying vision of returning to his indigent home and facing the people in his

42. This is a Sinhalese slang expression.

village dissuades him. He rebels against the situation. He disappears for days without a trace and refuses to shave his hair and beard, a rule that monks at the temple should observe once every two weeks.[43]

Sudhira even begins to comb his hair in front of a mirror, now envisioning what he might look like as a lay person. One day, weeks after avoiding direct contact with his teacher, Sudhira, with his long hair and beard, comes face to face with the head monk. The enraged teacher spits out:

> I am not telling you again. This is the last time. If you are going to conduct yourself in this manner I will have to make a decision immediately. But do not call me the villain later. It seems you have forgotten that this is a temple. You do not know who the teacher is and who the pupil is. You can't be a monk like this. It is either the monkhood or the lay life. You can do only one of the two. You cannot do both at the same time. . . . Monks who grow up these days have no propriety [*vārayak nä*]. You must think that you are attractive when you grow your hair and beard. So long as one wears the robe, whether he grows hair or ties it at the back, people know that bloke [*ēkā*] is a monk. Morality is not in your hair or beard [*sīlaya tiyenne kondevat rävulevat novē*]. I know that. But people respect [*minissu pähädenne*] the clean-cut, shaven monk. You must remember that the honor of the Buddha sāsana also depends on that.

Sudhira realizes that he can no longer reside at the temple and decides to give up his robes and find employment. He eagerly awaits a letter from one of his monk friends who promises him lodging at his temple in Colombo. One day he departs from the temple at the crack of dawn, leaving only a brief note of farewell for the head monk:

> Pardon me! [*avasara*] I am leaving the temple tomorrow. This journey had to take place one day. It happened so soon because I know I will receive no latitude from you to study for the advanced-level exam. My staying at this

---

43. The growing of hair by monks is a highly controversial subject that Buddhists often debate, even in the press; see "Should Buddhist Monks Grow Their Hair," *Observer*, May 8, 1994. In the mid-1930s, there was a public debate (*rävulu vādaya*) among monks and lay Buddhists about whether a monk should shave his upper head while retaining his beard; see Talpawala Silawamsa, *Vāda Dekak: Mahana Rāvulu Vādaya, Pävidi Kula Vādaya* (Colombo: Ratna Mudranalaya, 1960), 7–62. The most famous monk who often appeared in full beard and spiky hair in recent years was Yakkaduwe Paññarama, head of the Vidyalankara Pirivena; on Paññarama, see chapter 3.

temple will no longer do either the temple or you any service. I will need to look after my mother and sister. That is why I was forced to make this decision. But I am not going home. I implore that you not come looking for me.

Learning "Buddhism" in the City

With almost full-grown hair and a beard, Sudhira arrives at his friend's temple in the bustling capital of Sri Lanka. Excited yet ambivalent, he thinks he will adapt himself better to the monastic life in the city. But he soon realizes that city people are not so welcoming of him. They eye his hair and beard with suspicion. Immediately after seeing Sudhira, his monk friend tactfully remarks that Sudhira has to alter his appearance if he wishes to live at the temple. The friend also suggests that until Sudhira finds employment, he attend a pirivena and study for the advanced-level exam. He promises to help Sudhira gain admission to Sri Lanka Vidyalaya Pirivena, where he teaches, on the condition that Sudhira shave his hair and beard and begin to behave "properly" (*pilivelakata*). Sudhira thinks that going to a pirivena is another trap and doesn't want to get rid of the hair and beard that he "grew so passionately" (*āsāven vavā sitina*). But he knows that he cannot burden his friend with his problems and agrees to register at the pirivena and take classes until he finds a job. He shaves off his hair and beard hoping that he can at least move about in the city without "hesitation and fear" (*cakitiyakin biyakin torava*) of people staring at him.

Within a few months, Sudhira moves into a residence hall at the pirivena and rooms with another monk. At the pirivena, Sudhira finds himself bound by an even stricter monastic regimen than the one he encountered at his village temple. Here Sudhira learns for the first time the art of "taking food from the alms bowl" (*pāttarayē dānaya väldīmata*), a practice with which he has little familiarity. The novel describes the monastic regimen at the pirivena: "No monk is allowed to eat from a plate. They all use begging bowls. At the first toll of the bell, monks take their begging bowls to the dining room and place them where they usually sit. The second toll of the bell indicates that it is time to eat. Following the meal, every monk should wash his begging bowl and take it back to his room."

Gradually Sudhira begins to part with his plan to give up the robes. The first term of the pirivena draws to a close and, as is usual, many students return to their home temples to spend the vacation. Sudhira confronts the dilemma of being "homeless": He has no place to go. But as other monks question whether he will return to his temple, Sudhira replies, "Yes, I should go." Yet he ponders, "How can I return to the temple? The head monk? Sumana? Nalaka? Wimala? I have now no relation with any of them." The novel dramatically portrays Sudhira as being helpless, with no one to give him shelter or refuge. Even the option of spending the vacation at the pirivena does not at first seem available. (The novel itself states no reason for this; however, my research indicates that the administrators of many pirivenas demand that all students vacate the dormitories during breaks because of an insufficiency of state funds. This controversial issue has generated rioting among monks at numerous pirivenas. Some student-monks claim that the pirivena officials pocket portions of grants that the government allocates for the upkeep and maintenance of the pirivenas.)

Sudhira, as though cognizant of the situation, hesitantly asks the principal-monk for permission to spend the vacation at the pirivena. The monk acquiesces on the condition that Sudhira perform monastic duties such as delivering sermons, a practice he abhorred as a young monk at his temple. He learns and practices assiduously the art of bana preaching. Before the vacation ends, Sudhira has become an eloquent, highly-sought-after preacher, frequenting some of the wealthiest Buddhist homes in Colombo. He makes money by selling back gifts (pirikara), such as robes, umbrellas, packets of powdered milk, sugar, and tea, that he receives from his patrons (a common monastic practice at most temples; people called pirikara kārayō often call on monks at temples to buy and resell monastic gifts).

Negotiating Multiple Buddhist Identities

After passing the advanced-level exam and gaining admission to university, Sudhira visits his village. The news about Sudhira's acceptance to the university circulates fast among the villagers. They gossip crudely about it.

> It does not matter whether he becomes a monk or the Buddha. Yasawati's son is Yasawati's son. . . . Ov [yes]! Once he goes to the university he will strip himself of the robes and bring home a woman on his shoulder. . . . No question about it! He'll leave his robes on a lime tree branch [dehi attak] for sure and will come home without telling even his sleeping mat.[44]

44. "Leaving the robe on a tree" (sivura gahak uda tiyalā yanavā) is a common expression that the Sinhalese use to satirize disrobing. The expression "to leave the robe on a lime tree

By showing how the villagers forecast the future course of Sudhira's life at the university, the novel attempts to undermine these general conceptions about monks attending universities in the city. Sudhira, for instance, tries to explain to his mother the difficulty of finding lodging for a monk studying at university, a fact she does not understand since she thinks that a monk should be welcome at any Buddhist temple. Sudhira points out that some temples prefer not to keep university monks. "Housing such monks is of no benefit to temples. University monks leave in the morning and return in the evening. Temples therefore cannot expect religious service [*āgamika sēvayak*] from them."

The four years that Sudhira spends at the university unmasks some complex dimensions of Buddhist monastic identity on campus. It tells us about the monks' acute awareness of the Sri Lankan social universe beyond the confines of the monastic life. During his first year at the university, for example, Sudhira learns about his sister having being raped by a married man and her consequent pregnancy. At this traumatic time, Sudhira borrows money from his friends and travels frequently to the village to appease both his sister and mother. The mother remains on the brink of insanity as her enemies in the village begin to spread gossip about the rape incident and sully the family's reputation. In this moment of crisis, Sudhira oscillates between giving up the robes to aid the family and remaining in the monkhood to complete his education and find employment.

We also read about the political life of monks on campus. Struggling to cope with the crises of his sister's rape, his mother's insanity, and the family's financial hardships, Sudhira begins to find the revolutionary environment of the university appealing. The novel sets its narrative against the background of the mid-1980s and describes the state of affairs on campus:

> New students took to these protests and struggles [*aragala*] as little children who were mesmerized by something enticing that they saw. They behaved as they pleased [*hituvakkāra ayurini*]. The protest that began without a specific agenda developed into a cohesive program. One of the main goals of the protest was to demand an increase in student financial aid. The second part of the agenda was to topple the existing government and create a

---

branch" (*dehi attak uda tiyalā yanavā*) is uncommon; if there is any significance in the difference, it is not known to me.

socialist state. Preventing the officials from burying the free-education system was also a theme of this struggle. Stones, trees, walls, and bulletin boards all carried slogans.

In this highly volatile atmosphere at the university, Sudhira positions himself as a curious onlooker, listening to other monks shouting words of incitement:

> We must eradicate the sovereign rule of the wealthy [*danakuvērayangē pālanaya*] and build a righteous society. The most intelligent people of a nation are the university students. We must be united to educate the country. We must gain our rights without any conditions. . . . Victory to the public student!

Sudhira gravitates toward the message gradually. At first, by way of supporting the students, Sudhira marches in the middle of these rallies. Later he finds himself leading the rallies and crying out slogans at the top of his lungs. The novel does not record other details about the above episode but moralizes about the relation between monks and riots:

> Those who come to the front of riots are the new students who think that the university is the only oasis [*kshēma bhūmiya*]. They do so because they do not know what the university is about, and they express openly the innocence of their naive ideas. The junior and senior monks never walk in front at these rallies; they always lag behind. They only pretend to take part. The seniors are only interested in getting out of the university with a degree. . . . Sudhira, who took part in these rallies, believed [naively] that the whole world had joined hands with him against a capitalist form of government.

This passage does not represent all monks as agents of protest but as inexperienced young people who are drawn into the action. The novel satirizes the naiveté of the new students attracted to these university demonstrations, and subsequently, it points out how monks like Sudhira, resorting to various strategies, "betray" their seemingly credible commitment to such political causes. It allows for different discursive spaces in which these monks perform shifting, multiple roles as they spend their three or four years at university. For example, while Sudhira is taking part in these antigovernment, pro-Marxist uprisings, he is also teaching private classes and preaching to wealthy Buddhists to earn money and support his family. Outside the university, Sudhira's behavior undermines the political causes that he seems to espouse inside the university. As time elapses, Sudhira finds himself less interested in such politics on campus and more concerned with earning a living.

Following his graduation from the university, Sudhira becomes popular for his weekly sermons on the radio in Sri Lanka. Once a monk with a Marxist outlook on life, revolting against the capitalist form of government, Sudhira now ministers to the rich and the famous in Colombo. The narrative ends with the wish: "May all people be rich." It satirizes the popular Sinhala Buddhist wish, "May all people attain Nibbana," which accompanies the conclusion of almost all Buddhist rituals (*pinkamas*).

The Novel and the Ethnography

In presenting my reading of the novel, what I have wanted is not to produce a correlation between its plot and the present state of the Sri Lankan Buddhist universe but to point out the complexity of the narratives about the altering configurations of the relation between Buddhist identity and difference. My purpose is to show not that there exist multiple Buddhist identities in the novel, but to present the practices and persons that are supposed to define Buddhism and difference and to show that they are made possible by particular kinds of arguments and debates fashioned in particular conjunctures. Seen from this perspective, we will understand the relation between the bana preacher and the JVP revolutionist, monkhood and politics, Buddhism and difference, not as a "tension" or a "turning point" but as something that is authorized by contingent debates.

Broadly speaking, I read the novel against the kind of normalization—indeed the moralization—of the relation between religious identity and difference that governs the theoretical frameworks of many disciplinary works. This normalization hinges on the Western story of secularization that has left a deep imprint on the disciplinary studies of "Buddhism and society" in terms of a particular distinction: the image of "ideal" Buddhism set forth in the Pali texts, which is often referred to as "traditional," and contemporary society, which is referred to as "modern." It is within the framework of these two overarching distinctions that many writings attempt to account for "continuities" and "discontinuities" (transformations) of Buddhist identity. A good example of this kind of work is Gananath Obeyesekere and Richard Gombrich's massive account in *Buddhism Transformed*, which seeks to explain how contemporary Buddhist society has deviated from "the rational and human tradition of Buddhism."[45] We know now something of the problem of this theory.

In the remainder of this chapter I take a different theoretical route to suggest some new alternatives to thinking about the relations between Buddhism and difference, identity and change. I do so by examining a series of competing debates and disputes that remained, at the time of my interviews in 1995 and 1996, central to the definition of the relation between Buddhism, monkhood, and society in the ethnographic landscape of Pidurangala and the surrounding cluster of villages in the northern part of Sri Lanka.[46] In unpacking these debates about controversial subjects like monks, women, sex, and celibacy, my labor—I want to insist upon this—is not to excavate different narratives to show how Buddhism, monkhood, and society work in a rustic, "traditional" village located far away from the "modern" capital of Colombo. On the contrary, I want to demonstrate that, competing as they are to define Buddhism, struggling to subvert and triumph over opposing narratives, these disputes are examples of the ways in which questions of Buddhism and difference are constituted by contingent conjunctures of local/national disputes.

Shifting Relations, Differing Discourses, Altering Definitions of Buddhism

Pidurangala is a small village situated in the neighborhood of the Sigiriya rock, the fifth-century stronghold of King Kashyapa, the famous parricide king of Sinhala Buddhist history. The village is named after its Buddhist temple, the *pidurangala*, which means either the "golden rock that was offered [to the monks]" or the "rock that was offered as a hermitage." While their opinions vary about the meaning of the temple's name, some villagers hold that it was King Kashyapa himself who offered it as a place of meditation to monks who first occupied Sigiriya. Several people claimed that this temple rock, which rises as high as the Sigiriya itself (about six hundred feet), was home to many arhats (the enlightened disciples of the Buddha) in the "distant past." Some villagers maintain that the god Vishnu—who is revered as the preserver of the Buddhasāsana in Sri Lanka and who inhabits the sacred grounds of the temple—is the guardian deity of the village, a belief that

45. Gombrich and Obeyesekere, *Buddhism Transformed*, 290–91.
46. Author interviews conducted from July 1 to 9, 1995, and Oct. 8 to 15 and Nov. 4 to 6, 1996.

enhances the temple's historical significance. The only access to the temple, situated several miles away from the village, is a gravel path that runs through a dense forest where wild elephants roam at night. Both the distance and the fear of elephants hinder the villagers from maintaining regular, close contact with their monks. It is in such a locale that an elderly monk, Buddharakkhita, had lived for several decades at the Pidurangala temple as its incumbent chief monk.

Buddharakkhita, a highly regarded physician (*veda hāmuduruwō*) of the Ayurvedic tradition, ordained eighteen students. All of his students fell away over time: seventeen gave up their robes; one (Dhammananda, whom we will come across soon) left Buddharakkhita owing to a dispute over the ownership of the temple. Buddharakkhita, deserted and forced to take care of the temple alone, came to associate with a married woman who had claimed to be interested in learning the skills of Ayurvedic medicine from the monk. Before long, the woman, along with her husband and two children, moved into the temple because of the difficulty of the daily commute from the village to the temple. In return, the woman offered to look after the monk (*balāganda*) and take care of temple chores. One of the villagers who accepted this living arrangement said the circumstances demanded it. "Some people, of course, were concerned; but I did not think anything about it [*ē gāna mama mokavat hituve nä*]. No one could say anything because the monk was alone in the middle of that forest. Who would go and take care of him?" In the course of time, it became common knowledge among villagers that Buddharakkhita's relationship with the woman included sexual intimacy. Some villagers also claim that the woman became pregnant while she was at the temple and that Buddharakkhita is the father of her youngest daughter.

Twelve years after the supposed relationship had begun, Buddharakkhita became blind and handed over the temple to the present incumbent, moving into the woman's former house. While Buddharakkhita continued to receive patients at her home, he reportedly imparted to the woman all his knowledge of medicine before passing away. Today the woman is the village's physician and claims to carry on the tradition of Buddharakkhita's Ayurvedic service. She keeps a picture of Buddharakkhita on the table over which she dispenses medicine to her patients. To me she recalled Buddharakkhita as "my god" (*mage deyyo*) and characterized the relationship with the monk in short, cryptic terms: "We all make mistakes" (*api kāge atinut väradi siddavenavā*).

What interested me were the narratives that the villagers used to come to terms with the saga—which, to put it mildly, may seem rather "unconventional"—and gaining understanding of the relation between Buddhism, orthodoxy, and difference. These narratives, I repeat, are not evidence of how a given community practices "Buddhism," but, located as they were in a complex web of disputes among the villagers at the time, they compel us to decenter our conventional approaches to the conceptualization of Buddhism and society. My argument is that the case of Buddharakkhita is not simply a matter about an individual monk whose supposed infraction of the vow of celibacy gave birth to different interpretations; these interpretations, as I read them, come to be important when viewed in relation to those of another saga—one that surrounded Buddharakkhita's student, the monk Dhammananda.

At the beginning of my inquiry into the case of Buddharakkhita, I suspected that the villagers would be averse to talking about the controversy due to the sensitive nature of its subject. The unrestrained candor with which some spoke about the monk and his "affair" with the woman surprised me. One of the informants was Deniyagama Ananda, the present incumbent of Buddharakkhita's temple. He tried to put the case in perspective:

> It is clear that Buddharakkhita's affair with the woman violated an important principle that constitutes the identity of a monk. But we cannot ignore the fact that the environment in which he lived had an impact on his behavior. He lived alone. So he needed some kind of protection [ārakshāvak], either good or bad [honda hō naraka]. Even I might do the same thing if I was in his position. People did not come to the temple often. Moreover, none of his students showed any interest in him or his skills as a physician. So he might have thought that the woman was the last hope. Moreover, the villagers knew that he had resurrected [goda gattā] many dying people. If a villager felt ill, Buddharakkhita would race to his house in the middle of the night. He would not care about the time. The villagers knew this. But that certainly does not validate the act [the affair].

Deniyagama stated that he was astounded by the massive crowd of people that had turned out for Buddharakkhita's funeral. People knew well "what kind of monk he was." The funeral was one of a kind; it was an event in which people eulogized Buddharakkhita's life as a physician while speaking openly about how he had "unfortunately drifted away from the monastic practice [of celibacy]." But what is interesting is that monks as well as lay people paid their last respects to Buddharakkhita "as a Buddhist monk" (*bhikkshūn vahansē kenek hātiyata*).

So what, after the scandal of the affair, were (are) the narratives through which the villagers came (and come) to terms with Buddharakkhita's identity as a "Buddhist monk"? Armed with a palm-fitting tape recorder and accompanied by my assistant from the village, Mr. Gunasekara, I spoke to more than fifty people. As they shed varying perspectives on the controversy, I began to realize that the villagers were more opposed to the monk's living with a woman than to the alleged affair itself. One devoted Buddhist patron (*dāyakayā*), whom I met at the temple, indicated that he had never failed to take alms to the temple on the day of the month allocated to his house, even when Buddharakkhita was living there with the woman. Commenting on how some people stopped taking alms to the temple, he said, "It was not the monk's fault [*varadak novē*]." One elderly woman noted, "Yes, those things are not appropriate [*sudusu dēval novē*] for monks. But it is a sin [*pav*] to find fault [*vāradi hoyanda*] with monks." Another opined that "though we stopped going to the temple, there was no difference [*venasak nä*] in our respect for the monk. Whenever we met him on the road or anywhere, we worshipped him. That was no problem. The problem was the woman living at the temple." When I asked why this woman had continued to revere a monk whom she knew had violated the monastic rules, she responded: "Whatever he may have done, the robe of the Buddha [that Buddharakkhita wore] is more noble than anything."

My conversation with a man in his late seventies, whom most villagers addressed as Upasakamahattaya ("Pious man"), is particularly noteworthy. Gunasekara and I went to see him at his home in Pidurangala. Upasakamahattaya asked me about the purpose of my visit to the village. I had been formerly warned by Gunasekara about the possibility of Upasakamahattaya's refusing to speak about the matter and said something to the effect that I had come to study the history of Pidurangala temple. He shocked me by blurting out:

> It is not our business [*vädak nä*] to investigate monks. What we need to do is to give alms to monks hoping for the protection of the triple gem [Buddha, Dhamma, and Sangha]. Yes, some people may prattle: "That monk is good and that monk is bad" [*ē hāmuduruwō hondai ē hāmuduruwō narakai*].

Those are differences of opinion [*mata bhēda*], and it is something we don't need. "We" is plural; I should say, "I" do not care about those things. For me all monks are good [*matanan hāma hāmuduru kenekma hondai*]. Monks descend from the lineage of Buddha's disciples such as Säriyut and Mugalan. When we respect a monk we respect the Buddha's disciples. I give alms to monks on the first day of the month.

What is important about these remarks are the discursive strategies through which Upasakamahattaya wants to produce a certain kind of authoritative understanding about Buddhism and monastic identity. Note that they are not an answer to an explicit question about Buddharakkhita or his alleged affair with the woman. It was a general statement directed towards my self-claimed interest in the "history of the temple," of which Buddharakkhita was clearly an important part. The statement seeks to authorize certain kinds of knowledges about monastic identity and its relation to society; and in so doing it seeks to preempt the space of other possible (even remotely challenging) questions about that relation, to make it not up for discussion. Put differently, the statement seeks to establish a set of "moral" standards by which it judges what should constitute the relation between monasticism and society, admitting yet ignoring the "differences of opinion" about that relation. Later, as our conversation proceeded, Upasakamahattaya did become explicit about Buddharakkhita, noting, in discussing the monk's service to the village, that "Buddharakkhita was a good monk; he developed the temple."

During my initial ethnographic encounter with these narratives, I labored to conceptualize—quite inadequately, I might add—the "reasons" for Upasakamahattaya and his comrades to represent Buddharakkhita, who had supposedly breached one of the most serious canonical rules that constituted monastic identity, as a "good monk." I thought that if we took those representations as readily visible knowledges about Buddhism in the village (that is, how the villagers understand Buddhism), we could question if people in Pidurangala embrace a different concept of Buddhism as they seemingly ignore the authoritative textual (vinaya) position(s) on the "centrality" of celibacy to monastic identity. Or we could ask if they have just wittingly compromised the canonical standards for the "invaluable service" that Buddharakkhita rendered as a physician. Now if we decide to settle on these questions—following, of course, in the footsteps of some of the distinguished scholars cited earlier—we can easily and logically deduce that

Buddharakkhita's case presents an illustrative example of "Buddhism transformed," at least in one locality in Sri Lanka. But I doubt the logic of this kind of argument. I doubt, in other words, that the "standards" by which the Pidurangala villagers understand Buddhism and monasticism (for want of a better term, call them *terms of orthodoxy*) have been and will be the same. There remains, I suspect, a particular kind of "other/difference" against which Buddharakkhita's "self/identity" as a "good" Buddhist monk gets measured. I want to explore this suspicion by turning to a field of debates and arguments about the identity of Dhammananda, a student-monk of Buddharakkhita's.

Dhammananda is the only remaining monk of Buddharakkhita's eighteen students. He lives at his own temple in Kashyapa, a village on the outskirts of Pidurangala. Although Dhammananda was Buddharakkhita's nephew, a few years before his death, Buddharakkhita signed over Pidurangala temple to another monk, named Inamaluwe Sumangala,[47] claiming that Dhammananda had neglected to look after him.[48] Since Dhammananda was the only pupil of Buddharakkhita and so was the legitimate heir to Pidurangala temple, he quarreled with Buddharakkhita over this impetuous decision and left Pidurangala in early 1990, assuming the incumbency of the Pabbataramaya temple in the neighboring village of Sigiriya. Pabbataramaya, a dilapidated branch-temple under the jurisdiction of Pidurangala temple, is located near the Sigiriya rock.

A few years after Dhammananda settled in the temple, the Cultural Triangle, a Sri Lankan archaeological project under the direction of Roland de Silva, officially declared that Pabbataramaya temple stood in the way of excavation works that the project was carrying out in Sigiriya. The Triangle suggested that the temple be removed—a suggestion that outraged village patrons of the temple like my assistant Gunasekara. As Gunasekara and others informed me, their forefathers built Pabbataramaya in the 1920s, with small donations solicited from many people, because they could not walk the long distance to Pidurangala temple. So Gunasekara and others set about challenging the Cultural Triangle's claim. They argued that the late renowned archaeologist Senarath Paranavitana had pointed out in the 1940s

47. Sumangala appears again in chapter 6.
48. This is what Dhammananda's accusers claim. But Dhammananda argues to the contrary, saying that Buddharakkhita handed over the temple to Dambulla after Dhammananda objected to the woman and her family living at Pidurangala temple.

that the temple would be no obstruction to the excavation works of the Sigiriya rock. However, after Buddharakkhita passed away, Dhammananda made a secret deal with de Silva and handed over the temple to the Cultural Triangle in exchange for a brand-new temple with seven acres of land and all modern facilities in Kashyapa village, situated a few miles away from Sigiriya village.

Sometime in the early 1990s, in the dead of the night, a crew from the Cultural Triangle began to bulldoze the buildings of the Pabbataramaya temple. By the time the villagers, awakened by the sound of bulldozers, hurried to the scene, it was too late; the temple had been almost totally razed. The villagers vehemently protested the demolition—one man even threatened self-immolation, dousing himself with kerosene, but today only a part of the front wall of the temple's shrine room stands—a mute survivor. The villagers filed criminal charges against Dhammananda, demanding the complete restoration of the temple—a temple, they argued, Dhammananda did not own—in its "exact location." Other villagers warned Dhammananda never to set foot in Sigiriya again. Until the case is resolved, the Pabbataramaya remains off-limits to the Cultural Triangle.

The significance of this controversy for my discussion of Buddhism, monkhood, and difference lies in the emergence of a litany of (now proverbial) "gossip and rumors" about Dhammananda following the demolition of the temple. Today, some of his most outspoken critics, including Gunasekara, my assistant from the village, have charged Dhammananda with flouting various Buddhist Vinaya norms; they seriously question the credibility of his monastic identity. Some accuse Dhammananda of drinking *kasippu*, a locally distilled illegal liquor. Still others castigate him for frequenting the house of a village woman notorious already for living with a monk who had practiced "black magic." It is even claimed that, one night, some villagers spotted Dhammananda sneaking into a house and attempting to force himself on a woman asleep. Others maintain that Dhammananda even gave one of his "woman-friends" the temple's *sānghika* items—an expensive piece of gold necklace—that a wealthy Buddhist woman donated to be enshrined in the newly built *cetiya* (pagoda) at the Kashyapa village temple (the donor herself is said to have encountered the woman wearing the necklace). Several others claim that they saw Dhammananda fondling a woman and bathing with her in a river. So goes the list of accusations. Dhammananda's allies, whom we meet below, simply dismiss these accusations as rumors and gossip (*katakatā*). But Gunasekara, Dhammananda's most formidable critic, egged on by a few other villagers, has vowed to catch him and his "mistress" in the act and "tether them to a tree [*gahaka bandinavā*] so that the whole village will know Dhammananda's character."

What is interesting to note is that before the dispute, people like Gunasekara remained close confidants and patrons of Dhammananda. In fact, Gunasekara mentioned that Dhammananda engaged in similar "indecent acts" (*käta väda*) even when he was the incumbent of Pabbataramaya, in Sigiriya. But Gunasekara, like many other villagers in Sigiriya, "did not care much" (*vädiya ganan gatte nä*) about such behavior because Dhammananda was "our monk" (*apē hāmuduruwō*) and so advised (*avavāda kalā*) him to give up his behavior. The demolition of Pabbataramaya, it may appear at first sight, altered such friendly relations of yesterday and have made Gunasekara and many other Sigiriya villagers Dhammananda's arch-enemies. But for Gunasekara, as for several other villagers, there is more at stake here. The Cultural Triangle's contention that the area of Pabbataramaya impeded the excavation works posed a future threat to properties of villagers who, like Gunasekara, live near Sigiriya.

Gunasekara, who has, more or less, financed the court case against Dhammananda and the Cultural Triangle single-handedly, owns a small restaurant/tourist lodge, situated by the side of Sigiriya's main road, only a few yards away from Pabbataramaya. Within walking distance of the bustling village of Sigiriya (its frescoes are a tourist attraction), it is in a prime location. Reported for its cleanliness and good food in international tourist handbooks on Sri Lanka, this family-owned, two-bedroom guesthouse accommodates mostly foreign tourists. It offers the most competitive rates of any hotel in the area and on most days is fully occupied. Encouraged by a recent increase in tourist preference for the experience of staying with a local family and enjoying home-cooked meals, Gunasekara has laid foundations for more guestrooms. To lose this lodge to the future excavation works at Sigiriya, for Gunasekara would mean losing the sole income for his family and his home's ever-increasing real-estate value. To win the court case by proving Dhammananda and the Cultural Triangle guilty of committing an "unBuddhist act" (*abavudda vädak*)—in other words, to persuade the court to order the restoration of Pabbataramaya temple—would be to lessen that possibility. The legal reconstruction of Pabbataramaya on its original site would render the area where Gunasekara's home is located completely off-limits to the Cultural Triangle.

The threat of excavation looms large for Gunasekara: one of his friends, Karunasena, has already lost some thirty acres of paddy-field land to the project. The Triangle promised Karunasena full restitution several years ago, but has not yet compensated him. Furious about the loss of his land and the broken promise, Karunasena, another former patron of Dhammananda, has supported the court case against Dhammananda and the Triangle; for him, winning the case would mean receiving several lakhs of rupees, with interest. The Triangle's threat to this area became so serious that recently Gunasekara, Karunasena, and several others disrupted a public meeting held by the Cultural Triangle and swore in front of the public to kill Roland de Silva if he did not rebuild the temple and withdraw his "false" (*boru*) and "destructive" (*vināsakāri*) plans to expand the excavation works. My point here is that the negative narratives about Dhammananda's character as a monk and the rhetoric about the rebuilding of the temple must be seen in relation to the dynamics of the controversy. The controversy, however, does not stop there. There are in Kashyapa village many Buddhists who support Dhammananda, assaying to counteract, if not subvert, Gunasekara's and his friends' portrayal of the monk.

I took the issue to Dhammananda himself. Dhammananda maintains that he is the rightful owner of Pabbataramaya. He argues that by turning over an "old temple" to the Cultural Triangle, he did a "noble thing" (*utum deyak*) to promote the discovery of the "hidden history" of Sigiriya, which "belongs not just to Sri Lanka but to the whole world." He feels sure that the court will rule in his favor and exonerate him from all charges, granting him the ownership of Pidurangala temple. Dhammananda then went on to speak frankly about the allegations against him, offering an exposition of the relation between Buddhism, monkhood, and society.

> We [*api*; monks] do not expect to attain nirvana after we die. We cannot do it in this life [*me jivitēdi karanna bä*]. But we can be truly happy about what we do. For instance, I have delivered more than a thousand sermons in Buddhist homes. If you count the days I have stayed up all night chanting pirit for people, you would count three hundred days. I have officiated at more than one thousand funerals. If a monk can make another person

kneel and listen to one word of bana and shout "*sādu*," that is a great service, an act of merit. What we do largely is social service. . . . Therefore, just because a small mistake happened, no one can chase a monk away [*elavala dānda bä*]. If they do that, it is a great injustice [*aparādayak*]. . . . No one can strip a monk of his robes and expel him from the order just because he touched a woman's hand [*gäniyekuge atin alluvā kiyalā*] or kissed a woman's face a little bit [*mūna poddak imbā kiyalā*]. I do not see the philosophy that other people see. People may say some are not virtuous. I do not say a monk can be virtuous one hundred percent. On a certain level we can be disciplined [*sanvara*]. Ordinary people in society may drink and behave like outcasts [*sakkili vage*] at bars. Monks do not do that. Now you see we keep the temple on a level at which you [referring to me] can come and talk. If a man wants me to chant some pirit, I will run to his home. That is a great thing. Is it not? When people come to talk to us, we are ready to speak to them. That is what people expect from us. I do not know how to practice morality in any other way [*venat vidiyakin sil rakinda*]. I can keep this temple and render a certain service to people.

Dhammananda's case provides a spectacular example of the complex ways in which particular debates authorize and alter the relation between Buddhism and difference, rendering theoretically questionable any effort to make simple sense of those debates. Let me give several examples. One man I spoke to about Dhammananda did not mince words: he called him "a son of a bitch" (*bällige putā*) and a *valattayek* (something like "womanizer"). I did not find these remarks surprising: I had heard other villagers level similar accusations at Dhammmananda. But I was astounded when I learned that the same man was one of Dhammananda's regular patrons. The man continued: "I do not even consider him a good monk" (*honda hāmudurukenek*). I asked him the obvious question: "Why then do you give alms to such a monk?" The answer: "That is the question [*ēka tamayi prashne*]. We need him. Who will come to a funeral in the village? He is the only monk who lives close to us."

More than twenty other people maintained that they support Dhammananda, turning a deaf ear to rumors that would expose his "bad character." One man said, "Dhammananda is our village monk. He comes to our funerals and other occasions. No other monk from a different village will come to this village [to perform such Buddhist rituals] when there is already a temple in it." A woman averred, "No matter what wrongs he has committed [*mona väradi kalat*], he takes leadership [*idiriyata yanavā*] when it comes to village affairs." A man named Karunaratna, who seemed torn amid the various sides of the debates, asserted that if he did not patronize Dhammananda's temple, he, Karunaratna, "will be cornered [*konvenavā*] [by other villagers], and there will be lots of trouble [*karadara*] for him." Karunaratna elaborated:

> I know that we should investigate [*hoyala balanda ōna*] monks because they live at our temples. But we just do not have time to do that. If we need merit, we would feed a beggar and give him a few rupees [because] we cannot trust about ninety-five percent of the monks nowadays. I worked in Tissamaharamaya. Even there people gossiped about monks. . . . Any monk is like that. What we need to do is to protect the temple. We do not need to protect monks. What I am saying is that we cannot protect [*ārakshā karanava*] monks. People, I think, whether they like it or not, give to monks like Dhammananda even when they know that monks are not that good. The reason is this. There are many ways in which we are related to him. We have known Dhammananda as a person for a long time. Our parents knew him. So we cannot just cut him off [*kapanna bä*]. As a person, he is good to associate with. But sometimes I think that he is not fit for the robe.

Such comments obviously hint that some serious issues of power animate this debate about Buddhism and monkhood among these villagers. The line that the man draws between the temple and the monk alludes, ironically, I think, to the inseparability of the two. Obviously, a temple without a monk has little to offer people, and this I found precisely to be the case in Kalundewa village, where I spent time doing research. To talk about protecting the temple as opposed to protecting the monk points to complex discursive strategies that people employ to authorize a particular relation between Buddhism and difference. These strategies are products of a volatile conjuncture that mark the destruction of Pabbataramaya and the court case that spawned a welter of polarized viewpoints about the identity of Dhammananda.

For me, the point here is that this type of polarization that animates the Dhammananda scenario is virtually absent in the case of Buddharakkhita, though both are alleged to have committed, in more or less complicated ways, similar offenses. What is crucial to note is that some of the same people who accuse Dhammananda of wanton practices, including Gunasekara, recalled Buddharakkhita in more than honorable terms. In fact, for Dhammananda's adversaries, the positive recalling of the history of Buddharakkhita's life and his memorable Ayurvedic service to the village inevitably involved some kind of a story of Dhammananda as a greedy, selfish monk who abandoned his blind teacher to control and eventually "sell" Pabbataramaya. Undoubtedly at work in such narratives is the formation of a particular opposition between identity and difference. Put differently, the "Buddhist identity" of the late Buddharakkhita as one who broke the vow of celibacy yet remained a "good monk" exists in opposition to the "difference" and "otherness" of Dhammananda. However, it is this otherness that rival voices seek to undo—to construct, instead, a particular "Buddhist" identity of Dhammananda. Now I want to point to the conditions of the possibility of these rival views.

In Dhammananda's village, I met an older man named Arachchilamahattaya. The villagers esteemed this man as the head of the community. He is the main patron of Dhammananda's temple. He has stood by Dhammananda throughout the scandal and raved about him:

> Don't you know [*dan nädda*]. Dhammananda is young [*tarunaya*]. But he has done many mature things. He went to Colombo city and won 'trophies' [*kap gahala āva*] for chanting pirit. Not even great Pandit monks can chant with him. He is a skilled monk [*dakshyā*], and he is good at preaching [*banata hondai*]. That is why we always invite him to preach in our homes. We never invite other monks to preach.

There are, of course, no Buddhist contests of preaching and chanting in which monks can win "trophies." The reference to trophies points to the discursive strategies by which these villagers battle out questions about Buddhism and identity at a particular time that saw the transformations of the conditions of the Kashyapa village. I will illustrate this further.

A number of Buddhists like Arachchilamahattaya, Karunaratna, and the man who reproached Dhammananda as a womanizer but patronized him belong to Kashyapa village. Before Dhammananda arrived in Kashyapa village, many of its families lived in harsh conditions. Situated several miles off the main road to Sigiriya, the village lacked many basic amenities (for example, transportation, grocery stores, and even an adequate supply of water). After building the new temple for Dhammananda, the Cultural Triangle transformed the conditions of the village. In an effort to attract more people and enhance material support for Dhammananda's temple, the Triangle, it is rumored, even offered financial assistance to build and rebuild houses in the village. The Triangle equipped the village with, among other things, water

pumps, a new road, a bus service, and grocery shops. More significantly, perhaps, it introduced an element of tourism to the village. Every day, hundreds
of visitors, local and foreign, visit the Sigiriya rock and its historic paintings.
Formerly, they purchased their admission tickets at the base of the rock; after
the Cultural Triangle built Dhammananda's new temple in Kashyapa village,
it moved the ticket counter there, diverting traffic through the village. Some
villagers informed me that part of the revenue from the sale of admission tickets also goes toward the "development" of the village. Many in the village
remain grateful to Dhammananda, maintaining that the Cultural Triangle
developed the village after Dhammananda accepted its offer to live in it.
Today others seek to purchase land in Kashyapa village because of its increasing real-estate value. Plans for further development are reported: there are
rumors that tourist hotels will soon be built.

It is in these conditions—Dhammananda having turned over Pabbataramaya temple to the Cultural Triangle for demolition and having accepted
the new temple in Sigiriya—that we must locate the furious dispute about
the monastic identity of Dhammananda. The demolition of Pabbataramaya
angered many people in Sigiriya and turned them against Dhammananda;
but, at the same time, Dhammananda's acceptance of the new temple, which
enabled the transformations of the conditions of the Kashyapa village, made
many Kashyapa villagers defend Dhammananda, admiring what he has done
for them. In fact, several women I interviewed took offense at my questions
about allegations against Dhammananda and stated angrily that all I was
doing was helping Dhammananda's enemies propagate wrong views about
him. Two women pointed out that "there is nothing wrong we can see [with
him]" (apitanam pēnda varadak nä), and "people can say anything about him
but we have not seen any fault" (varadak däkala nä). A man went so far as to
say that "even if there is some [tibunat] wrong we support him because it is
our village temple." Another woman turned a deaf ear to my questions, but
remarked that I should not find fault with monks.

What has been central to this chapter, especially to its second part, is the
demonstration that debates and disputes are not self-evident ethnographic
examples that enable us any privileged disciplinary access to Buddhism,
monasticism, and difference. Previous studies, oblivious of the dynamics of
such debates, have viewed categories like monkhood and society as readily
identifiable objects of anthropological knowledge. Take, for example, the
following statement by British anthropologist Michael Carrithers, whose

work on the sangha occupies an esteemed space within the archive of the anthropology of Buddhism in Sri Lanka: "The sangha . . . has a structure; and in fact the sangha is so conservative, and the conditions of its agrarian environment so enduring, that this structure is discernible throughout its 2,500–year history."[49] The case of Dhammananda, seen in relation to that of Buddharakkhita, is a modest instance that casts doubt on these conceptions of "discernible" structures of Buddhism and difference, monasticism and society. The dynamics of both cases, I believe, show the shifting terrains of ethnographic "evidence" on which we stake our claims about the relations between Buddhist identity and society. Thus I view what I have presented in the preceding pages not as "first-hand evidence"—evidence that enables us to secure new sophisticated claims about how Buddhism and society operate or operated in Sri Lanka—but as instances that debunk the kind of certainty that scholarly conceptualizations of religion ascribe to ethnographic evidence. So this chapter may be seen as a labor to render "Buddhism" unavailable as it has been conventionally constructed in the now dominant anthropological terms.

This is not, however, to advance the familiar argument that the ethnographic representations of what knowledges and truths are supposed to constitute the identity of Buddhism and difference remain impossible for us to know because "ethnographic truths," as James Clifford contends, "are . . . inherently partial—committed and incomplete."[50] Rather, the emergence and submergence of authoritative claims that define the relation between Buddhism and difference, truth and untruth, have to be sought within the fleeting conjunctures of discourses and debates. Recall, for example, the varying terms of discord about Dhammananda. Some villagers who admired Buddharakkhita as a good monk castigated Dhammananda as one not morally fit to wear the robe, although both had supposedly violated similar monastic norms that constitute (from a canonical, textual viewpoint) the identity of monkhood. Some of Dhammananda's avowed detractors today remained his steadfast allies yesterday! I have argued that these debates are important examples of the shifting formations of the opposition between identity and difference. Narratives about Buddharakkhita's "Buddhist identity" (recently widely authorized at his funeral) do not exist in a vacuum. They are told in opposition to the difference and otherness of Dhammananda.

---

49. Carrithers, "Modern Ascetics," 298.
50. Clifford, "Partial Truths," 7.

And today, new, rival, narratives about Dhammananda have emerged. Differently flavored and differently positioned, they compete to dismantle the dominant representations of Dhammananda as "other/difference." These new narratives seek to secure a space in which Dhammananda remains authorized as a "Buddhist" monk who can speak for and about Buddhism and monkhood to the villagers in centrally visible ways, especially in public spaces like funerals and pirit-chanting and bana-preaching *pinkama* (merit making) ceremonies. My point here is not that these new narratives about Dhammananda simply exemplify the existence of multiple discourses about religion and society, but that their possibility and central visibility are to be found in specific conjunctures of debates. So if we are to understand more critically what we mean by concepts like Buddhism, monkhood, identity, and difference, we must investigate those specific debates within which terms and parameters always remain subject to scrutiny and alteration. In the next chapter, I examine the relation between Buddhism and difference in terms of the theoretical problem of Buddhism and politics.

CHAPTER THREE

Formations of Religion and Politics

The disciplinary understanding that governs the discourse of "religion and politics" is that they are interrelated.[1] Indeed, I think it safe to say that this understanding has become canonized (and canonical) today. A good example of this is *The Encyclopedia of Politics and Religion*, published in 1998. As the editor of the volume, Robert Wuthnow, described it, the project, which consists of "256 original articles," was an attempt to understand the "continuing interaction between religion and politics."[2] The project's main interest, the editor went on to explain, was to solicit "articles that focus on all major regions of the world and on particular countries where the relationships between politics and religion have been problematic or where the relationships have had an impact on the wide world."[3] This kind of argument, now framed in different conceptual registers—the "politicization of religion," the "role of religion in politics," "religious fundamentalism," and so on[4]—has been central to an archive of literature on the subject in the context of South Asia. South Asia, as we will see below, has for decades functioned, mostly for the West, as a palpable (non-Western) example of the "problem" of the link between religion and politics.[5]

1. My concern in this chapter is primarily with the category of "religion and politics." One may, of course, want to think of "religion and violence," and, to use the popular disciplinary terms, *religious violence* and *religious terrorism* as similar categories. I turn to that subject and a critical engagement with the literature on it in chapter 7.

2. Robert Wuthnow, ed., *The Encyclopedia of Politics and Religion* (Washington, D.C.: Congressional Quarterly, 1998), xxv.

3. Ibid. The article on Buddhism is by Charles Keys.

4. The Fundamentalism Project, a series published by the University of Chicago, can be seen as one, if not the most, dominant recent statement on this subject; see Martin E. Marty and Scott Appleby, eds., *Fundamentalisms Observed* (Chicago: University of Chicago Press, 1991). For other accounts of the politicization of religion, see Patricia Jeffery and Amrita Basu, eds., *Appropriating Gender: Women's Activism and Politicized Religion in South Asia* (New York: Routledge, 1998).

5. For such a grand thesis in the context of South(east) Asia, see S. J. Tambiah's *World Conqueror and World Renouncer: A Study of Buddhism and Polity in Thailand against a Historical Background* (Cambridge: Cambridge University Press, 1976). Tambiah understands Buddhism

But this argument has been made not just for South Asia. More recently, some (postcolonial) critics have made similar claims about the West, which has formally disavowed any connection between religion and politics, church and state. These critics inform us, in more or less sophisticated ways, that the idea of the separation between religion and politics is an "Enlightenment [colonial] assumption"; the West deployed this idea to make privileged claims about its self/identity and the non-West other/difference.[6] Hence, contrary to that Western assumption, they have set about demonstrating that religion and politics are linked in complex ways in the West as well. As Gyan Prakash puts it, "the intermixture of religion and politics has characterized not only the 'backward' Third World but also the 'advanced' First World."[7] Yet other scholars, who remain convinced of the supposed problem of this interrelation in both the West and the East, from Northern Ireland to Sri Lanka, and of its propensity for violence, go so far as to endorse "[re]separating religion from politics."[8] Take, for example, this (obviously problematic) statement that the erudite political theorist Chantal Mouffe makes, following a discussion of how "a democracy requires the affirmation of a certain number of 'values,'" which, like equality and freedom, constitutes its 'political principles'":

> It establishes a form of human coexistence which requires a distinction between the public and the private, the separation of church and state, and

---

and polity, sangha and kingship, not in terms of an altering discursive relation but in terms of an "integral yoking," "coupling," and "indissolubly linked" (515–30). For a statement on how Buddhism has been instrumental in the legitimation of political power within the context of Sri Lanka, see the collection of articles in Bardwell Smith, ed., *Religion and Legitimation of Power in Sri Lanka.* For a statement that reconsiders this thesis, arguing that "politics did not exist as an autonomous sphere in the ideology but was contained within it as an integral component," see H. L. Seneviratne, "A Critique of Religion and Power in the Sociological Sciences," *Social Compass*, 32, no. 1 (1985): 36. Determining whether or not "Buddhism" played a "role" in the politics of the Sri Lankan "ethnic conflict" is central to Holt's discussion "Ethnic Identity and Alienation [in Sri Lanka]"; see his *Religious World*, 98–99. Holt accuses (unnamed) "scholars or journalists" who have supposedly "partly misunderstood" "the role of Buddhism in the contemporary ethnic conflict" (99).

6. See Richard King, *Orientalism and Religion*, 14. For a similar argument that seeks to correct supposed Western assumptions about the separation between religion and politics, see Peter van der Veer and Hartmut Lehmann, eds., *Nation and Religion: Perspective on Europe and Asia* (Princeton: Princeton University Press, 1999), esp. the introduction.

7. Prakash, jacket description of *Nation and Religion.*

8. See, for example, Mark Juergensmeyer, *Terror in the Mind of God: The Global Rise of Religious Violence* (Berkeley: University of California Press, 1999), 235–43.

of civil and religious law. These are some of the basic achievements of the democratic revolution and they are what make the existence of pluralism possible. One cannot therefore call these distinctions into question in the name of pluralism. Hence the problem posed by the integration of a religion like Islam, which does not accept these distinctions. . . . The relegation of religion to the private sphere, which we now have to make Muslims accept, was only imposed with great difficulty upon the Christian Church and is still not completely accomplished.[9]

In seeking to problematize this kind of view, in this chapter I am not, of course, concerned with constructing an alternative history of the relation between religion and politics in the West or the East. My concern is with the general claim about the supposed intermixture of religion and politics. I must say at the outset that I find this general claim theoretically wanting and that I wish to conceptualize the relation between religion and politics anew. To do so, I want to show how a significant body of scholarship has constructed a similar understanding about Buddhism and politics in Sri Lanka. In so doing, I will not seek to make the opposite argument; that is, that religion and politics are separate domains. On the contrary, I want to suggest that continuing theoretical questions about whether or not religion and politics are (or should be) interrelated cannot produce the kind of critical insights necessary to understand the altering discursive formations of the relation between religion and politics.

The subject of religion and politics in Sri Lanka has been both a disciplinary and native Sinhala Buddhist discourse. In fact, in the 1940s, long before it became an object of disciplinary inquiry, the discourse of "Buddhism and politics" was part of a seminal lay and monastic debate in Sri Lanka. It operates, in other words, within a tradition of moral argument and discord. Hence, one of the central tasks of this chapter is to present a brief genealogy of the formations of the relation between Buddhism and politics in disciplinary and native discourses. What interests me, first, is how (largely Western) disciplinary projects conceptualized the relation between Buddhism and politics as a "problem." This conceptualization rested on an argument about the supposed original separation, and the historically produced interrelation, between Buddhism and politics. The chapter inquires into some unquestioned

9. Chantal Mouffe, *The Return of the Political* (London: Verso, 1993), 132. I thank Kim Shapiro for drawing my attention to this passage in the book.

assumptions that have animated this argument for several decades by demonstrating some of the ways in which authoritative native debates configure and alter the relation between Buddhism and politics.

The discourse "Buddhism and politics" first emerged in an article that J. R. Jayewardene (then minister of Kelaniya and later the first executive president of Sri Lanka) authored in the mid-1930s. Jayewardene there argued that Buddhism and politics were separate modalities of practice. A few years later, this discourse became the subject of a polemical debate between Jayewardene and the Buddhist monks of the esteemed monastic college Vidyalankara Pirivena and drew into the controversy numerous other monks and lay Buddhists. During this acrimonious debate, Jayewardene, along with the other members of the newly formed United National Party (UNP), called for the divorcing of Buddhist monks from politics and for "cleansing the order" ("reform") of "political monks." Jayewardene's call for an apolitical Buddhism was a particular kind of narrative fashioned in opposition to other contending narratives. The scholars who later began to theorize the relation between Buddhism and politics failed to examine sufficiently the dynamics of the competing voices that made possible this historical debate, thereby accepting "reform" as an "authentic" Buddhist practice. "Reform," I want to argue, is not a feature of a readily visible reality, but rather a feature of a discourse. By accepting reform as a real Buddhist practice that would rid "Buddhism" of its political influences, scholars did not break new analytical ground but uncritically reproduced one authoritative ideological discourse among others.

After locating the 1940 debate, I examine the ways in which questions about the relation between monks and politics again became, in the early 1980s, the subject of public argument in the context of the construction of a university exclusively for monks—the Buddhist and Pali University (BPU). Ostensibly an expression of the Jayewardene government's commitment to preserving and promoting the study of Pali ("the words of the Buddha"), the BPU can be read as a strategic practice that enabled the state to authorize a particular form of an "apolitical" Buddhist monkhood favorable to the state. Central to the construction of a separate university for monks (in addition to other national universities where monks study) was the argument that Jayewardene's government, unlike previous political parties, sought to restore the "ancient" link between Buddhism and the state. Restoring this link did not imply that Buddhism and politics were inseparably linked; it was, rather, that the Jayewardene's "Buddhist" government was committed to keeping Buddhism "pristine" (separate from politics) by helping to teach and propagate "the meaning of Buddhism."

In fact, Jayewardene claimed that Buddhist monks should support the government and fulfill their "Buddhist" task by staying away from "politics." For Jayewardene, monks' political neutrality meant that they would neither support other political parties nor oppose his government. The student-monks of the BPU, however, began to contest the Jayewardene regime's definition of the relation between Buddhism and politics and sought to unseat the government by joining the JVP—the government's worst nightmare. One of my points is that the construction and reconstruction of the BPU were made possible by particular conjunctures of authoritative debates about who and what should and should not constitute Buddhism or politics.

Disciplinary Constructions of "Religion and Politics"

The emergence of Buddhism and politics in Sri Lanka as an object of specific disciplinary inquiry can be traced to the publication in 1966 of *South Asian Politics and Religion*, edited by Donald Eugene Smith, professor of political science at the University of Pennsylvania.[10] A collaboration of twenty-four essays, representing disciplines such as comparative religion, anthropology, history, political science, and comparative law, the volume was one of the earliest of several academic interventions that sought to conceptualize the relation between religion and politics in India, Pakistan, and Ceylon specifically in terms of a "problem" that had "until very recently, received little attention."[11] It becomes clear from Smith's preface to the volume that this conceptualization was based on the argument that "religion," or "religious communalism," played "the fundamental role in bringing about the present shape of South Asia." As an example of that role of religion in

10. Donald Eugene Smith, ed., *South Asian Politics and Religion* (Princeton: Princeton University Press, 1966).

11. In the 1960s and 1970s, Heinz Bechert published the three-volume *Buddhismus, Staat, und Gesellschaft in den Ländern des Theravāda-Buddhismus* (Frankfurt: A. Metzner, Wiesbaden; O. Harrossowitz; 1960, 1967, 1973). I do not read German; however, below I discuss Bechert's ideas about the subject in his English publications. Earlier attempts at sweeping comparative surveys of this subject in relation to Asia can be found in Richard Gard, "Buddhism and Political Authority," in *The Ethic of Power: The Interplay of Religion, Philosophy, and Politics*, ed. Harold Lasswell and Harlan Cleveland (New York: Harper & Brothers, 1962); Joseph Kitagawa, "Buddhism and Asian Politics," *Asian Survey* 2, no. 5 (1962): 1–11.

politics, it readily pointed to the partition of India and the founding of Pakistan as a separate Islamic country in the mid-twentieth century. This political landscape, Smith observed, provided a "near-perfect" case for the "comparative" study of "the emerging relationships between religion and politics in these countries since independence." Smith stated boldly that the essays in the volume "accurately reflect the real problems which are being faced in the three countries," and that some "significant parallels" between the countries can be found in areas such as "religious reform."[12]

The section on Sri Lanka, consisting of four chapters, two of which are authored by the editor himself,[13] seeks to explain the "dramatic developments by which *Buddhism has become deeply involved in the politics of the country*" (my emphasis).[14] What emerges from the pages of these chapters is a narrative of how Buddhism, "a vital component of traditional Sinhalese nationalism," "lost" its connection with the state ("place in society") during the colonial administrations.[15] But a few years after Sri Lanka gained independence in 1948, the "impaired"[16] Buddhism was identified with the new Sri Lankan government, particularly within the context of the Buddha Jayanti period (the nationwide celebration of the 2,500th anniversary of the Buddha's passing away).[17] This process of the postindependence "[re]identification of Buddhism with the state"[18] gave birth to forces that enabled the "making of a political monk."[19]

Here I wish not to review these chapters but to unmask certain assumptions that are central to the conceptualization of the relation between Buddhism (the sangha) and politics as a "problem," assumptions that linger unquestioned in many contemporary academic works on the subject. In his chapter "Political Monks and Monastic Reforms," for example, Smith

12. Smith, *South Asian Politics and Religion*, preface.

13. Donald Eugene Smith, "Sinhalese Buddhist Revolution"; idem, "Political Monks and Monastic Reform"; Jeyaratnam Wilson, "Buddhism in Ceylon Politics, 1960–1965"; C. D. S. Siriwardene, "Buddhist Reorganization in Ceylon," all in Smith, *South Asian Politics and Religion*.

14. *South Asian Politics and Religion*, vii–viii.

15. Ibid., 453.

16. Ibid., 531.

17. A discussion of some aspects of the Buddha Jayanti period can be found in George Bond, *The Buddhist Revival: Religious Tradition, Reinterpretation, and Response* (Columbia: University of South Carolina Press, 1988), 75–129.

18. *South Asian Politics and Religion*, 460.

19. Ibid., 490.

discusses the monastic career of Mapitigama Buddharakkhita, who helped to elect, and later assassinate, Prime Minister S. W. R. D. Bandaranaike in the late 1950s.[20] Writing about the transition of Ceylon/Sri Lanka from a "traditional" to "modern" (postindependence) society, Smith argues that Buddhism is "in the throes of revolutionary change":

> Modern society has deprived the monk of his traditional functions . . . , a capitalistic economy undermines his adherence to the Vinaya [disciplinary] rule against touching money, urban life allures him with worldly temptation, and the university education provides him with secular alternatives to the life in the Sangha. The tendency for monks to leave the order has reportedly increased alarmingly, and in 1962 the All Ceylon Buddhist Congress appointed a committee to investigate *the whole problem* [my emphasis].[21]

Apparently Smith saw a marked difference between religion and modernity, tradition and secularism, and by extension he considers the link between Buddhism and modern politics a "serious" problem. He goes on:

> It seems likely that the forces of modernization will continue to take a heavy toll on the ranks of the Sangha. It is difficult to see how the monastic order will fit into the modern society which is now emerging. This is an extremely serious situation because of the centrality of the Sangha in Buddhist doctrine, ritual and practice. It is quite possible for Hinduism to flourish without priests or for Islam to prosper without Ulama, but in Buddhism the believer venerates the three jewels: Buddha, Dhamma [teaching] and the Sangha.[22]

According to Smith, this conflicting relation between Buddhism and modernity "stem[s] from the nature of Buddhism itself as a monastic religion"; that is, "from the natural conservatism of a venerated institution, the Sangha . . . which is sufficiently well organized to resist change with great

20. It is interesting that John Strong's *The Experience of Buddhism: Sources and Interpretation* (California: Wadsworth, 1995), a rare, if not the only, introductory text book on Buddhism that includes a separate heading for "Buddhism and Politics," replicates word for word Smith's account of Buddharakkhita's monastic career as *the* illustrative example of the subject; see *South Asian Politics and Religion*, 247–50.

21. Smith, "Political Monks," 509.

22. Ibid.

effectiveness." The sangha overcame change and safeguarded its Buddhist "monastic" identity because it was the "chief object of reformist efforts" by "autocratic Buddhist kings" in the past. Since kingship is a thing of the past and the "Sangha has never reformed itself," and, moreover, since "democratically elected parliaments" are not "likely" to initiate monastic reforms,[23] the interaction between Buddhism and modern politics is inevitable.[24] This is how, then, Buddhism and politics are conceptualized as a problem.

For Smith, as for many other scholars, the supposed interrelation between religion and politics represented a crisis (that is, "decay") of "religious" identity in Sri Lanka. Take, for example, the esteemed 1970 essay by leading German Indologist Heinz Bechert titled "Theravāda Buddhist Sangha: Some General Observations on Historical and Political Factors in Its Development." Speaking of what is called "the political implications of Resurgent Theravda Buddhism," Bechert argued:

> Students of canonical Buddhism have always emphasized the nonpolitical nature of the Buddha's teaching. Max Weber has described Buddhism as a "specifically non-political, and anti-political religion of a social class." No doubt that there are many characteristic elements in early Buddhism to support this statement. However . . . the Sangha was incorporated into the structure of the traditional Buddhist states. Similarly, the religious factor as an important force within the political and social upheaval in the Buddhist countries of South and Southeast Asia in the recent past is too obvious to be overlooked and disregarded. *However, the question remains how far the religious movements in this development can be described as genuinely religious or else religious on its face only* [my emphasis].[25]

For Bechert, though Max Weber may be accurate that early Buddhism was "non-political," that assertion does not hold true for Buddhism in Sri Lanka because Buddhism was *later* "incorporated" into politics. So it is this supposed incorporation of religion into politics or the tie between the two that gives religion its "political" identity. (One can argue that the now-fashionable concept of "the politicization of religion" rests on similar assumptions.) Here, clearly, Bechert assumes that religion is prior to politics and so questions "how

---

23. I return to the issue of "reform" below.

24. Ibid., 508. Such concerns are also central to Smith's other essay in the section on Buddhism; see "Sinhalese Buddhist Revolution," 477.

25. Bechert, "Theravāda Buddhist Sangha," 774.

genuinely religious" this *politicized* religious identity is.[26] Seen from Bechert's viewpoint, the identity of Buddhism is not historically produced but remains unalterably defined because "Buddhism" lies outside the framework of politics. It is this Buddhism that elsewhere he calls "canonical Buddhism," which included "a coherent system of religious and philosophical teachings" to regulate the behavior of "early" Buddhist monks who had no "direct involvement in the affairs of state and society."[27] So the interrelation between Buddhism and politics, the sangha and the state, posed a crisis of religious identity as it was measured against the image of a supposed *apolitical* (and hence authentic) canonical Buddhism.[28]

These views about the relation between Buddhism and politics dominated literature on the subject. In 1970, speaking of the role of lay Buddhists in the "Buddhist revival" and of the relation between monks and society, Donald Swearer wrote:

> One of the early turning points in this revival was presented by Olcott and Dharmapala, both working as laymen outside the *Sangha*. A second major turning point was signaled by the election of a political party led by

---

26. In a different essay, Bechert argues that the "establishment of formalized state-Sangha relations" occurred during the reign of King Asoka in the third century B.C.E. He further argues that "The integration of Sangha in the structure of the state completely changed the original function and position of the Sangha"; see his "Sangha, State, Society, 'Nation': Persistence of Traditions in 'Post-Traditional' Societies," *Daedalus* 102, no. 1 (1973): 87. Elsewhere, in a German publication, Bechert claims that he has shown that the "union" between religion and nationalism in Sri Lanka can be traced back to the first century C.E.; see his "Zum Ursprung der Geschichtsscheibung im indischin Kulturbereich"; cited in his "Contradictions in Sinhalese Buddhism," in *Religion and Legitimation of Power in Sri Lanka*, 194, 198. It is based on this understanding of Buddhism as an entity prior to politics that Bechert calls "Sinhalese-Buddhist nationalism" a "contradiction" (198). It is important to note that early orientalist scholars of Buddhist studies such as Rhys David, the founder of the Pali Text Society in England, considered the Asokan era as the dawn of decline in pristine Buddhism; see his "Buddhism," *North American Review* 171 (1900): 522; cited in Kevin Trainor, *Relics, Ritual, and Representation in Buddhism: Rematerializing the Theravada Tradition* (Cambridge: Cambridge University Press, 1997), 9–10.

27. See Bechert, "Sangha, State, Society," 85. At the outset of the essay, Bechert made a distinction between three kinds of Buddhism: "canonical," "traditional," and "modern" (85).

28. For Smith, the relation between "modern" Buddhist society and the "ideal of renunciation" was "unclear"; he wrote, "The development of a Buddhist social ethic, and the organizational means to apply it to contemporary problems, are the pressing requirements of the times. But it is still not clear how this social gospel is to be reconciled with the ideal of renunciation, nor what place is to be accorded the Sangha within the framework of a modern Buddhist organization." Smith, "Political Monks," 509.

a convert to Buddhism from the Anglican Church. In a real sense it was Bandaranaike who provided the opportunity for unleashing the long-latent power of Buddhism in Ceylon, a power which has manifested itself in both noble and ignoble forms in the Sangha as well as in the laity. . . . Certainly, however, the progress of Buddhism in Ceylon will depend largely on the Buddhist laymen to bring about reforms within the *Sangha* and help formulate appropriate ways for Buddhism to engage the contemporary world. The Order must also play a role, of course; but due to long ingrained customs and vested interests in the *Sangha*, such as ownership of property and caste restrictions, the initiative for broadly based change rests with the laity.[29]

It is easy to see that Swearer's conception of what should and should not constitute the proper relation between Buddhism and difference, religion and politics, hangs on the Western Enlightenment idea of "progress." In his view, the progress of Buddhism depends upon the reform of the sangha; that is, of the relation between Buddhism and modern politics. Almost two decades later Swearer made a similar argument. In his contribution to the impressive volume *Fundamentalisms Observed*, Swearer contended that "fundamentalistic movements in Theravda Buddhism" are not "religious in the classical sense of the term."[30] (This is as if there remains a universally unvarying meaning of the term *religion* that one can identify.)[31]

Swearer concluded the section on Buddhism in Sri Lanka[32] by stating: "Shorn of these contemporary [fundamentalistic] influences, Buddhism may well continue to shape Sinhalese conscience toward the building of a truly

29. Donald Swearer, "Lay Buddhism and Buddhist Revival in Ceylon," *Journal of the American Academy of Religion* 68, no. 3 (1970): 259.

30. To be fair to Swearer, I must give the full quotation: "The absolutism of fundamentalism stems from this basic transformation of the religious world view. The narrowly ideological nature of fundamentalism means that it is not religious in the classical sense of the term but rather a variant of a secular faith couched in religious language and elevating traditional religious symbols stripped of their symbolic power to evoke a multiplicity of meanings": Donald Swearer, "Fundamentalistic Movements in Theravda Buddhism," in *Fundamentalisms Observed*, ed. Marty and Appleby, 650.

31. For a provocative criticism of unceasing anthropological attempts to define religion in terms of universal essences, see Asad's well-known "The Construction of Religion as an Anthropological Category," in his *Genealogies of Religion*, 27–54. This brilliant essay is primarily a critical reconsideration of Clifford Geertz's famous definition of religion found in "Religion as a Cultural System," in his *The Interpretation of Cultures* (New York: Basic, 1973), 87–125.

32. The other section of Swearer's chapter deals with Thai Buddhism.

universal and inclusive Buddhist state of righteousness, justice, and peace envisioned by many non-fundamentalistic Buddhists."[33] The assumption here is that Buddhism can be recovered by *depoliticizing* it, by divesting it of its *politicized* influences, that is, by reforming it. Only then can Buddhism do its work of creating a "truly" "inclusive" Buddhist society in Sri Lanka. "Reform" then is the disciplinary name for the depoliticization of the supposed political identity of Buddhism. Reform, in other words, is the name for the separation of religion from politics.[34]

The problem with these kinds of argument, informative as they are, is that they take not only Buddhism and politics but also reform as some kind of an authentic Buddhist practice. Reform, I contend, should be viewed as any other native discourse, and it must be located in specific debates that render its emergence (that is, talking about it) possible. By taking reform as an authentic Buddhist practice and recommending it as a viable means to depoliticize and recover an apolitical Buddhism, some scholars have, perhaps unconsciously, simply reproduced another dominant ideological native discourse. The uncritical reproduction of such native discourses fail to take into account other opposing native narratives that compete to outline and define the terms of what should constitute Buddhism, politics, and reform.

Surely a genealogy of the disciplinary discourse of reform remains to be written, but I will not undertake such a task here.[35] But before delineating the native Sinhala debates that make possible diverging conceptions of the relation between Buddhism and politics and the discourses of reform, let me

33. Swearer, "Fundamentalistic Movements," 651.

34. This line of thinking has become typical of many other recent disciplinary studies of Buddhism, culture, politics, and nationalism in Sri Lanka. Here I have in mind some of the works already engaged: Tambiah; *Buddhism Betrayed?* and Holt, "Persistence of Political Buddhism"; also, idem, "Postscript: Ethnic Identity and Alienation," in *Religious World*; and idem, *Buddha in the Crown*, 223; Walters, *History of Kelaniya*.

35. Here I do not wish to provide an extensive bibliography. But the standard postindependence scholarship on Theravada Buddhism in Sri Lanka says that it was king Asoka who initiated monastic reforms "to expel monks who were not willing to live and act according to the rules of Vinaya"; see Bechert, "Sangha, State, Society," 86. The other famous exponent of this argument is Tambiah, "Asokan and Sinhalese Traditions Concerning the Purification of the Sangha," in his *World Conqueror*, 159–78. This disciplinary notion of the purification of sangha is found in the dominant monastic version of the history of sangha/state relations recorded by the "great chronicle of Sri Lanka," the *Mahāvamsa*. Now, of course, reform is a particular kind of Western, Enlightenment, Reformation discourse. On the ways in which the rhetoric of reform came to condemn the "atrocity" of torture and dictate the terms of "humane" punishment and imprisonment, see Foucault, *Discipline and Punish*, esp. chapter 2.

briefly discuss and problematize the ways in which Michael Carrithers recently used reform as a concept to explore the relation between Buddhist monasticism and society as a visible arena of specifically anthropological knowledge.

Carrithers introduced his influential book *The Forest Monks of Sri Lanka: An Anthropological and Historical Study* as a study of "monks' various attempts to act by their precepts, embody their ideals." It is a study, he wrote, "of rediscovery, revival and reform" of the Buddhism of asceticism.[36] Note the titles of a few chapters in the book: "The Reform of Oneself and a Few Others"; "The Total Reform and the Unification of the Sangha"; "Starting a Successful Reform." The questions that pervade the central theme of the book are: "What would be the criteria of success [of reform]?" "Why did some [reform movements] succeed and some fail?"[37] Identifying Sri Lankan forest monks as a reform movement, Carrithers argued that "the modern hermitage movement can be regarded—and was so regarded by the forest monks—as an example of a recurring theme in Buddhist history, the reform of an increasingly worldly, that is, a *decayed* Sangha."[38] Thus, then, this anthropological identification and categorization of forest monks as a "reform" movement stands *authorized* by the native monks' supposed representation of themselves as those who seek to eliminate that decay. The decay of the sangha, as Carrithers estimates, is a product of "the failure [on the part of some monks] to follow the letter and the spirit of scriptures on account of conflicting circumstances, or even simple ignorance." (The idea of native Buddhists' "ignorance" of the Buddha's teachings is a specific colonial discourse.)[39] It is based on this supposed anthropologically privileged knowledge about the "letter and the spirit" of Buddhism, and monks' "ignorance" of them—the phrase *letter and spirit* is obviously a reference to one of the letters of Paul in the New Testament[40]—that Carrithers argues: "Most [forest] monks . . . eventually

36. Carrithers, *Forest Monks*, 4. Carrithers's book has received considerable praise in academia. In his review of the book, Gananath Obeyesekere claimed that it "superbly captures what might be called 'the spirit of Buddhism.'" He noted further that "now when I am asked by friends to recommend a book on Buddhism, I refer them to this work"; see Obeyesekere, reviews of *Forest Monks*, by Michael Carrithers, and *The Buddhist Saints of the Forest and the Cult of the Amulets*, by S. J. Tambiah, *American Ethnologist* 12, no. 4 (1985): 791.

37. Carrithers, *Forest Monks*, 4.

38. Ibid., 14.

39. See Almond, *British Discovery of Buddhism*, 98.

40. See 2 Cor. 3:6; Rom. 2:29. I thank Joseph Walser for these references.

seem to have had considerable success in achieving the way of life they set out to achieve."[41]

My point is that the characterization of a particular "religious" movement as "reform" is analytically problematic. When Carrithers argues that forest monks represent reform or a "rediscovery" of the Buddhism of asceticism, he assumes an apolitical Buddhism that existed and remains to be recovered.[42] This assumption is clearer when he states, elsewhere: "The preservation of the ideals of asceticism has ensured that reforms have continually occurred and it is the play between ascetic reform and domestication which creates the pattern of the Sangha history."[43] While forest monks represent a rediscovery— a reform of a monastic Buddhism—the "majority of monks" who do not live in forests represent "domestication," which, as he says, is the "inevitable" process of monks' "abandonment of ascetic values and the adoption of lay values" as they settle in permanent locations.[44]

The idea of domestication, it is easy to see, is simply another synonym for the "decay"—the politicization or secularization—of monastic identity,[45] and reform is the process that holds that decay in check, so to speak. According to Carrithers, this decay and secularism of the monastic identity is most visible in the ancient sangha-politics-king relations:

41. Carrithers, *Forest Monks*, 4.7.

42. In his review article, though generally favorable to *The Forest Monks*, Jonathan Spencer noted that Carrithers implies that "forest monks" lead the *authentic* monastic way of life "based on his own understanding of the ascetic ideal"; see Spencer, "Tradition and Transformation: Recent Writings on the Anthropology of Buddhism in Sri Lanka," *Journal of the Anthropological Society of Oxford* 21, no. 2 (1990): 132. However, Spencer's own understanding of reform comes close to that of Carrithers and others; for example, Spencer says that "the loss of kingship" in Sri Lanka "prized loose the Sangha from its place in a close symbiotic relationship with the ruler; in the long run it allowed more and more room for lay initiatives in Buddhist affairs" (130).

43. Carrithers, "Modern Ascetics," 294.

44. Ibid., 294–97. The idea of "domestication" has become a subject of debate; see Steven Kemper, "Radical Asceticism and the Sinhalese Case," and Carrithers's response to Kemper's comments, *Man*, n.s. 15, no. 1 (1980), 195–97; Ivan Strenski, "On Generalized Exchange and the Domestication of the Sangha," *Man*, n.s. 18, no. 3, pp. 463–77; and Michael Carrithers, "The Domestication of the Sangha." *Man*, n.s. 19, no. 2 (1984), 321–22.

45. This idea of the "decay" of religion is part of the Western story of the "secularization" of culture; that is to say, the "story of the decline of religion and of the efficacy of the supernatural in the face of the progress of scientific reason." It is also the Western story of the separation of church and state; see David Scott, "Religion in Colonial Civil Society," in his *Refashioning Futures*, 58–61; also published in *Cultural Dynamics* 8, no. 1 (1996): 7–23, for a revised notion of "secularization" in the context of rethinking the familiar academic story of the relation between

the conditions underlying the Sangha life, which produce the dynamic of reform, are logically and temporarily prior to the role of king as reformer. The need and inspiration for reform springs from within the Sangha itself, and the king merely exerts his power to weigh, more or less decisively, on the side of one party or the other. Only the most powerful kings—such as Parakkamabahu I of Ceylon . . . were able to carry out thorough reforms. On the other hand, many kings have squashed reform movements . . . or have created conditions such as large gifts of land to the Sangha, which encourage its decay.[46]

These, then, are the kinds of (colonial) assumptions that govern disciplinary understandings of religion and politics in Sri Lanka. The story of Buddhism and politics that these scholars tell is about the decay of Buddhism. My argument is that this notion of decay (now expressed in various subtle anthropological terms like *Buddhism betrayed, Buddhism transformed, domestication, political Buddhism, Buddhist fundamentalism, chauvinism, Buddhist nationalism*) depends as much on a Western (colonial) story of secularism and progress as on an uncritical acceptance of some native discourses that corresponded to scholars' own ideological orientations about certain values (for example, the concepts of inclusion, righteousness, tolerance, and peace) that are supposed to constitute the "real" identity of Buddhism.

To propose an alternative understanding of religion and politics, I want to explore the Sinhala native configurations of narratives about Buddhism and politics, locating arguments and counterarguments about them. My point is not that Buddhism and politics are inseparable, and vice versa, but that the emergence and submergence of questions about what should and should not constitute the identity of Buddhism or politics are made possible by particular shifting debates, and the theorization of them can never make them available for canonization.

---

religion, colonialism, and modernity told in terms of "disestablishment," "revival,""resistance," and eventual "survival" of Buddhism in the wake of colonialism in Sri Lanka; also see Asad, "Religion, Nation-State, Secularism," in *Nation and Religion.*

46. Carrithers, "Social Organization," 134. The questions of whether or not royal donations to the sangha created the conditions for the sangha's periodic reform are also found in Steven Kemper's "Wealth and Reformation in Sinhalese Buddhist Monasticism," in *Ethics, Wealth, and Salvation,* ed. Russell Sizemore and Donald Swearer (Columbia: University of South Carolina Press, 1990), 152–89. He writes that "the primary impulse of reformation has been to put corrupt monks on the right course by taking wealth away from them as individuals" (160).

Formations of "Buddhism and Politics"

The political context of the 1940s witnessed the emergence of one of the most important, if not the first, public debates about the relation between Buddhism and politics.[47] The debate was spearheaded by monks of the Vidyalankara Pirivena, one of the most prestigious monastic colleges in Sri Lanka.[48] Following the universal adult franchise in Sri Lanka in 1931, some Buddhist monks became vocal supporters of the leftist Lanka Samasamaja Party (LSSP), formed in 1936. As Urmila Phadnis points out, these supposedly "left-inclined" monks came from a "common" background: In some way, they were all affiliated with the Vidyalankara Pirivena; they had traveled and studied in India; they had witnessed the then-current tide of "nationalist" movements in India.[49]

The United National Party (UNP), founded by D. S. Senanayake, remained the dominant political party in the 1940s.[50] Senanayake, popularly known as the "Father of the Nation," became the first prime minister of independent Ceylon, and J. R. Jayewardene, the future leader of the UNP, became an important figure of Senanayake's elite political circle. Neither Senanayake nor Jayewardene took lightly the Vidyalankara monks' public support for the emerging leftist party. As early as 1934, Jayewardene published an article entitled "Buddhism and Politics" and sought to authorize an unequivocal definition of them:

47. I provide an account of this debate in order to locate the emergence of the discourse of Buddhism and politics in Sri Lanka. A conventional narrative and analysis of other aspects of this debate in terms of an "interplay between the religious and the political systems" can be found in Phadnis, *Religion and Politics in Sri Lanka* (New Delhi: Monohar, 1976), 158–73. For a holistic reading of the Vidyalankara monks' role in this controversy, see K. M. de Silva, "Buddhism, Nationalism, and Politics in Modern Sri Lanka," unpublished paper.

48. Vidyalankara Pirivena, founded in 1875 by Ratmalane Sri Dhammaloka, and Vidyodaya Pirivena, founded in 1873 by Hikkaduwe Sri Sumangala, are two of the most important Buddhist monastic colleges created to "revive" the Buddhist monastic education in the context of British colonial rule. Hikkaduwe Sumangala and Ratmalane Dhammaloka were both students of Walane Sri Siddharta, the founder of the Parama Dhamma Cetiya Pirivena in Ratmalane (1860). On some aspects of the Vidyodaya Pirivena and its monks, see Seneviratne, *Work of Kings*, 56–129.

49. Phadnis, *Religion and Politics*, 162–63. Phadnis identifies some of these monks: Walpola Rahula, Udakandawela Saranankara, Babarende Sirisivali, Narawila Dhammaratana, Kalalle Anandasagara. For more on these well-known facts about this period, see Seneviratne, *Work of Kings*, 130–35.

50. On the formation of this party, see Howard Wriggins, *Ceylon: The Dilemmas of a New Nation* (Princeton: Princeton University Press, 1960), 106–19.

Buddhism and politics are terms which refer to two different systems of human thought and activity. It is said that the Buddha advised members of the Buddhist Sangha not to take part in politics. No one can say, however, that he exhorted politicians not to study or follow his teaching, and politicians who rule nations and attempt to mold the lives of their fellowmen.[51]

Jayewardene further stated that the "ideal man, the pure citizen" does not get attached to wealth and power, and the "ideal state" should consist of such men. The "politician in power" could teach that ideal to society and . . . he must ensure that "there exists nothing inimical to the accomplishment of the ideal [of Buddhism]."[52] Jayewardene implicitly called into question the position of the Vidyalankara monks who had already begun to support the LSSP and who would later argue that taking part in "politics" is every monk's duty to the country.

The Vidyalankara Pirivena's claim about the monks' duty to take part in politics emerged in the space of a polemical debate between them and the members of the UNP. The debate originated in 1946, when, in a meeting held at the Vidyalankara Pirivena, D. S. Senanayake, who was formerly a member of the Vidyalankara Laymen's Board, castigated monks supporting the LSSP.

> The present movement for monks to take part in politics is a subversive activity [*kapati kriyā vak*] by the communists and the people of the Samasamaja [left-parties]. They have used the support of this [Vidyalankara] pirivena and its staff monks. If we do not guard against this, the pirivena and the Buddhasasana [monastic order] will be in jeopardy. They have started this movement to destroy our [UNP] lineage [*varige nätikarananyi*]. However I will protect our lineage. But I am sad that this movement will destroy [*nätivena ekata*] both the pirivena and the Buddhasasana.[53]

51. J. R. Jayewardene, "Buddhism and Politics," *Daily News Wesak Number,* May 19, 1934; reprinted in J. R. Jayewardene, *Buddhist Essays* (1942; reprint, Colombo: Government Press, 1982).

52. Ibid.

53. Cited in Yakkaduwe Paññarama, *Pävid Vaga Hā Sasun Maga: Kotahēnē Paññkitti Upahāraya, Apē Gaman Maga* (Monastic lineage and monastic order: Kotahene Paññakitti felicitation volume, Our Path) (Kelaniya, Sri Lanka: Vidyalankara Sabhava, 1970), xix. On March 13, 1946, addressing a prizegiving ceremony at the Dharmaraja Pirivena in Matale, D. S. Senanayake went so far as to say that by supporting political parties, Vidyalankara "monks have

Among those convened for this meeting was the director of the Vidyalankara Pirivena, Yakkaduwe Paññarama. Having listened to Senanayake's speech, Yakkaduwe Paññarama rose from his seat and stated sarcastically: "Well, Sir, you protect your lineage; the chief monks [the UNP supporting monks] will protect Buddhism [*mahānāyaka hāmuduruvaru buddasāsanaya räkaganīvi*]; we will protect the Vidyalankara Pirivena. Then, nobody will be wronged by this movement."[54]

The context of the debate witnessed at least two noteworthy developments within the Vidyalankara Pirivena: In 1946, one of the associate monks of Vidyalankara, the Venerable Walpola Rahula, authored a best-seller entitled *Bhikishuwage Urumaya*—it was later translated and published in the United States as *The Heritage of the Bhikkhu*.[55] The main thrust of the text, to put it in a nutshell, was that, beginning with the Buddha himself, the Sinhala Buddhist monks played an active role in various social and political spheres and that that role was the "heritage of the monk" in Sri Lanka.[56] In the same year, the Vidyalankara monks started a weekly newspaper, *Kālaya* (Time), and competed to render visible their authoritative perspectives on the subject of Buddhism and politics.[57]

The editorial of the first issue of *Kālaya* pointed out that it was time that monks communicate to the public the "timely question" (*kālōchita prashnaya*) about "Buddhist monks and politics" (*bhikshūn hā dēshapālanaya*), a question that they claimed would "determine the fate [*iranama visadana*] of

---

expressed willingness to transcend the boundary of monastic discipline" (*vinaya sīmāva ullanganaya kirīmata*). *Dinamina*, Jan. 17, 1946; cited in Welamitiyave Dhammarakkhita and Kakkapalliye Anuruddha, eds., *Vidyalankāra Pirivena: Satasanvassaraya, 1875–1975* (Colombo: Sri Lanka Rajaye Departumentuwa, 1975), 60.

54. Paññarama, *Pävidi Vaga*, xix–xx.

55. Walpola Rahula, *The Heritage of the Bhikkhu: A Short History of the Bhikkhu in Educational, Cultural, Social, and Political Life* (New York: Grove Press, 1974). Rahula earned a Ph.D. for *The History of Buddhism in Ceylon* (Colombo: Gunasena, 1956). The book that earned him international fame is *What the Buddha Taught* (Bedford: Gorden Fraser, 1959).

56. For a provocative reading of Rahula's *The Heritage of a Bhikkhu*, a reading that is interested in adjudicating between the truth and untruth of the ideological claims in the text, see Seneviratne's *Work of Kings*, 168–88. Seneviratne reads *The Heritage* in relation to an obscure(d) response to it by Henpitagedara Ñanavasa. Seneviratne says that Ñanavasa's text "is genuinely concerned about Buddhist goals and values, and saving the true path from the threat of destruction posed by socialism. Here we have a glimpse into the genuine core belief of the best Buddhists" (167–68).

57. *Kālaya* began Mar. 14, 1946; it ended Dec. 24, 1947.

the [Sinhalese] nation."[58] The issue included the famous article "Bhikkhus and Politics: The Declaration of the Vidyalankara Pirivena," written by Kirivattuduwe Paññasara, the principal of the Vidyalankara Pirivena. Describing how monks have played multiple roles in the past, Paññasara contended that the monastic life had changed, and the changes should be accepted as inevitable even though the rules of [textual monastic] discipline were not altered.[59] Paññasara, contrary to Jayewardene, defined politics as "whatever leads to the happiness of the citizens" and insisted that monks take part in such politics. To participate in "social programs such as rural development, education, crime prevention, temperance work" is indeed to participate in politics. "We do not accept that it is at all wrong [*varadakāyi api nopiliganimu*] for monks to engage in these kinds of activity. . . . To [keep monks away from politics] is to do a tremendous injustice [*barapatala aparādayak*] to the country, nation, religion."[60]

The subsequent issues of *Kālaya* carried a series of articles by Yakkaduwe Paññarama on "The Monk, Discipline, and Politics" (*bhikshuva, vinaya, dēshapālanya*). Paññarama claimed that major newspapers had misrepresented the controversy about Buddhism and politics. He castigated pro-UNP monks such as Yagirala Paññananda who had branded "political monks" (*dēshapālana bhikshūn*) as "impostors" and "sinners" (*pāpīhu*), insisting that such monks should be expelled from the order.[61] Paññarama claimed that Paññananda did not know the vinaya of the Buddha's teaching because the Buddha laid down no injunction that monks who participate in politics should be expelled from the order.[62] Paññarama demanded that Yagirala Paññananda give up his robes because he had accepted a gold medal, violating one of the ten basic monastic precepts.[63] Another monk, Baddegama Piyaratana, criticized Vidyalankara monks and requested "noble Buddhists" (*prabhū bauddhayan*) in the country to "punish" the monks trying to engage in "public service." These criticisms met head-on opposition. Some lay Buddhist supporters of the Vidyalankara Pirivena reproved Piyaratana as an "elite

58. *Kālaya*, Mar. 14, 1946.

59. Ibid.

60. Ibid.

61. *Sinhala Bauddhayā*, Mar. 9, 1946; *Kālaya*, Mar. 14, 1946; *Kālaya*, Apr. 4, 1946, respectively.

62. *Kālaya*, Apr. 4, 1946.

63. Ibid.

monk" who kowtows to the UNP government, warning him not to throw stones at other monks while "living in a glass house."[64]

In the wake of this polemic, seeing the monks' primary "Buddhist" duty as one of social and political service that would bring "happiness" to the citizens of the country, Vidyalankara monks identified "incumbents of temples" (*vihārādhipativaru*), who supposedly claim to take no part in politics, and the [UNP] politicians as enemies working against the principles of Buddhism. A good example of this kind of critical moral rhetoric is Paññarama's book *Vanakatā*.[65] Later banned on account of its attack on the government, the book popularized a particular verse lampooning the UNP and its monk supporters, a verse that even today some monks cite by heart in discussing the relation between Buddhism and politics in Sri Lanka:

> apāyata yanda ōnānam numbata
> karapan maha āmatikama eka davasakata
> nätinam pansalaka dēvālayaka sita
> adhipati kama karapan tun davasakata

> If you want to go to hell,
> Become a minister for a day.
> Or, of a Buddhist temple or of a gods' shrine,
> Become an incumbent for three days.[66]

This naming of hell as the place where the incumbents of temples and the supporter monks of the UNP would end up must be seen against the background in which Vidyalankara monks vied to authorize its support for the Samasamaja party, a theme to which I return below.

J. R. Jayewardene played a notable role in this debate. By 1946 Jayewardene had joined D. S. Senanayake's United National Party and had won the Kelaniya seat. By then, D. S. Senanayake had already requested, if not demanded, the monks of the Vidyalankara Pirivena to withdraw the Vidyalankara Declaration. Needless to say, the demand fell on deaf ears. Challenging the Vidyalankara monks' refusal to withdraw the declaration, on March 31, 1946, J. R. Jayewardene, D. S. Senanayake, and D. S. Wijewardene

64. *Kālaya*, Jan. 9, 1947.
65. *Yakkaduwe Paññarama, Vanakatā: Mituran Ketavīma* (Kelaniya, Sri Lanka: Sirisena Saha Mitrayo, 1947); cited in *Dinakara*, Mar. 6, 1986.
66. Ibid.

(J. R. Jayewardene's uncle), in association with the All Ceylon Buddhist Congress, organized a council, the Sāsana Sōdhana (cleansing of the Buddhist order). As the sponsors claimed boldly, the council was designed to empower some of the (progovernment) Mahanayaka monks to "remove political monks from their robe[s]" (*sivuren ivat kirīmata*) and even subject them to imprisonment.[67] The council, convened at the Kelaniya temple (it is sometimes called the Kelani Temple Conference), proposed the implementation of six guidelines for Buddhist monks:

1. It is absolutely improper for a monk to seek membership or become a member of any agency of the government, including parliament, senate, urban councils, rural councils, provincial councils, municipal councils, or to join any political party
2. It is improper for any monk to register as a voter or to vote
3. Monks should not play any role in electing ministers of the above-mentioned councils
4. It is improper for lay people to cause monks to deviate from the above guidelines
5. Any monk disrespectful of these guidelines should be expelled from his monastic fraternity, and lay people should not pay any obeisance to such a monk
6. A rule must be laid down in conjunction with the government to discipline the monks who disregard the demands of their respective monastic fraternities[68]

Satirically, the organizers of the Sāsana Sōdhana council sent an invitation to the Vidyalankara monks to attend its inaugural meeting. The monks responded by stating that they were ambivalent as to whether the "cleansing of the order" should be conducted in accordance with the Buddha's times or the contemporary times.[69] They insisted that "changes in the monastic life are

---

67. Yakkaduwe Paññarama, "Apē Gaman Maga," in *Pävidi Vaga*, 106. This, of course, is Pññarama's account of it.

68. See "Upa Grantaya," in *Vidyālankāra Pirivena*, 123.

69. *Kālaya*, Apr. 4, 1946; see also Yakkaduwe Paññarama, "Kälaniyē Sāsana Sōdhana?" *Kālaya*, June 26, 1946. Elsewhere Paññarama says that it was in this context in 1946 the Eksat Bhikshu Mandalaya (United Monks' Council) was established; Paññarama, *Pävidi Vaga*, 106. The council announced four objectives: (1) to assist in gaining independence for Sri Lanka; (2) to ensure that independent Sri Lanka would work in unison with independent India; (3) to safe

as visible as the sun and the moon" (*ira handa vage*) and refused to attend a meeting organized by "those who think that the monastic life should never change."[70]

It is no accident the Jayewardene party decided to hold the first meeting of the council at the Kelaniya temple, a few miles from the Vidyalankara Pirivena. The Kelaniya temple, an important site of Buddhist pilgrimage said to have been visited by the Buddha himself, is located within the (then-Jayewardene) electoral district of Kelaniya. Since British times, the temple had remained in a deteriorated condition, but it was restored at great expense in the late 1880s by Jayewardene's grandmother, Helena Dep Wijewardene.[71] Jayewardene used his family's relationship with the temple to pursue his political agenda. During elections in 1943, Jayewardene claimed that since "it was his grandmother . . . who was responsible for the restoration of the temple, it was obligatory for them [the Kelaniya people] to support Mr. Jayewardene's candidature."[72] Jayewardene made such statements over a loud-speaker on the grounds of the Kelaniya temple. Some Buddhists, appalled at Jayewardene's message, wrote to newspapers: "No true or intelligent Buddhist can remain undisturbed when his religion or the holy places of his creed are desecrated in this fashion."[73]

Jayewardene's relationship with the Kelaniya temple changed significantly during the later phase of the debate. In 1947, the head of the Kelaniya temple, the Venerable Dhammarakkhita, died, leaving two student monks, one, Sangharakkhita, senior, the other, Buddharakkhita, junior. Contrary to the conventional practice, Dhammarakkhita had signed over the temple's incumbency to the junior monk. This generated a prolonged process of bitter litigation between the two monks, involving, if not creating factions within, the Jayewardene family itself. As the disagreements about the legitimacy of the Kelaniya incumbency raged, Jayewardene sided with Sangharakkhita;

guard the political rights of all Sri Lankans; (4) to improve the economic and social conditions of the country and create a righteous society; see *Kālaya*, Sept. 26, 1946.

70. *Kālaya*, Apr. 4, 1946; see also Yakkaduwe Paññarama, "Kälaniyē Sāsana Sōdhana?" *Kālaya*, June 26, 1946.

71. My knowledge of these events comes from interviews I conducted with monks at Kelaniya temple and Vidyalankara Pirivena on Sept. 4 and 6, 1997.

72. "Religion and Politics: Electioneering in Kelaniya Temple," *Times of Ceylon*, Apr. 22, 1943.

73. Ibid.

his uncle, D. S. Wijewardene, joined forces with Buddharakkhita.[74] Buddharakkhita was not a supporter of the Jayewardene party, to say the least. In fact, Buddharakkhita, a close associate of Vidyalankara Pirivena, became a sought-after ally of Jayewardene's main opponent, the former prime minister, S. W. R. D. Bandaranaike, who in 1951 founded the Sri Lanka Freedom Party (SLFP).[75] Jayewardene used his political clout to challenge the authority of Buddharakkhita's claim to the temple's incumbency, disrupting the activities of the temple. As Kelaniya's minister, Jayewardene once tried to stop the temple's annual procession by blocking off the main route. In defiance of Jayewardene's political power, Buddharakkhita, along with the help of some Vidyalankara monks, cut a new road for the procession to proceed.[76]

As the next general election approached in 1947, the Vidyalankara monks began to challenge Jayewardene and his political party in a direct way: In 1947 they nominated their own Samasamaja candidate, Dr. Bodhipala, for the Kelaniya seat and campaigned vigorously to unseat Jayewardene. An Ayurvedic physician by profession, Bodhipala was a prominent member of the Vidyalankara Laymen's Board. This campaign would prove to be a fiercely polemical and bloody physical battle.

A few months prior to the election in 1947, the *Kālaya* newspaper published a number of articles about "the exploitation of the monks by the wealthy." The articles pointed out that the very same politicians who had demanded earlier that Buddhists should stop giving alms to monks taking part in politics were seeking the support of several major Buddhist monks.[77] As examples of such monks, *Kālaya* named Henpitagedara Ñanasiha, Hapuwalane Ñanaloka, and Hancapola Wimalwansa,[78] the chief monks of the Malwatte and Asgiriya chapters, and Yagiral Paññananda.[79] Some of these monks went on national radio and endorsed the UNP political agenda. Among them, Henpitagedara Ñanasiha stands out. He actively campaigned for the UNP leader, D. S. Senanayake, who had promised to build a Buddhist

74. Telephone interview with the late Hevanpola Ratanasara, Apr. 4, 1998.

75. Prime Minister Bandaranaike was assassinated in 1959 by a Buddhist monk; Buddharakkhita was indicted as an accomplice. For more on this case, see Smith, "Political Monks," 499.

76. Interviews with Vidyalankara monks, Sept. 4–7, 1977, and with Hevanpola Ratanasara on Apr. 4, 1998.

77. *Kālaya*, June 9, 1947.

78. *Kālaya*, July 17, 1947; *Kālaya*, July 24, 1947.

79. *Kālaya*, July 31, 1947.

university in Ñanasiha's area after the elections. (After his victory, Senanayake reneged on his promise, saying that he had "bigger things to do than building a Buddhist university."[80] Distraught Nānasiha later withdrew his support for Senanayake's party).[81]

By 1947 the Vidyalankara monks had made their political affiliation public by declaring that they would "always be *samājavādihu* [socialists]."[82] This time, J. R. Jayewardene publicly branded these monks as Marxists who would "wipe out" Buddhism and the Sinhala Buddhist monastic order. He implored the Buddhists in the country to wake up and see the impending danger of Marxism to Buddhism.[83] By then, Jayewardene had published his views about Marxism in "Buddhism and Marxism," arguing that a Buddhist cannot ever be a Marxist.

> The religion of Marxism seeks to capture Sri Lanka. Though its followers have split into several sects and sub-sects . . . they all profess the same enmity to the teachings of the Buddha. . . . Let us . . . have no illusions about the challenge of Marxism to the religions we love. . . . We need not quarrel with those who have forgotten the ideals taught in these great religions, which they now seek to replace with their own interpretation of Marxism. We must, however, be vigilant and understand clearly that . . . no Buddhist can be a Marxist.[84]

As Jayewardene equated *samasamāja vādaya* (socialism) with Marxism, *Kālaya*, of the Vidyalankara Pirivena, claiming that what the Buddha taught was socialism, made a direct relation between Buddhism and Marxism:[85] the enemy of Buddhism is the wealthy. As "the Buddha taught, the path to Nirvana is one; the path to wealth another. These are not empty words . . . the wealth of the wealthy can never be an easy, just [*dhārmika*] acquisition."[86] *Kālaya* stated that the wealthy (like Jayewardene) opposed Marxism because a Marxist government wants to strip them of their unjust wealth and give it to

80. Phadnis, *Religion and Politics*, 176, n.34.

81. Ñanasiha's views that Kemper so admirably summarizes must be located in these political relations; see Kemper, *The Presence of the Past: Chronicles, Politics, and Culture in Sinhala Life* (Ithaca, N.Y.: Cornell University Press, 1991), 214–18.

82. Cited in "Yakkaduwe Nāyaka Hāmuduruwō," *Island*, May 31, 1986.

83. Paññarama, *Pävidi Vaga*, 153–54.

84. Jayewardene, "Buddhism and Marxism," in *Buddhist Essays*, 82.

85. See "Buddhāgama Saha Samasamāja Vādaya," *Kālaya*, July 24, 1947.

86. Ibid.

back those who deserve it.[87] In fact Vidyalankara monks competed to portray Jayewardene as such a politician—one who would even "sell Buddhism" to save his wealth and his electorate. They denounced Jayewardene as "a new Buddhist [*alut bauddhayā*], who lied by claiming to know Buddhism better than the monks themselves."[88]

This polemic continued as the Vidyalankara monks busied to elect their *Samasamāja* candidate, Dr. Bodhipala, as minister of Kelaniya. In July 1947, a series of articles published in the *Kālaya* newspaper questioned Jayewardene's Buddhist identity and vowed to oust him from his seat. They called him a *paragātisīliya*, "a fox who serves foreigners," and claimed that he "became a leader by using his family's name." They charged that Jayewardene was formerly a Christian but "abandoned his religion and became a Buddhist" (*pansal vūvek*) because of a dowry.[89] They castigated him as a "traitor" who was now "begging for votes" (*candaya singamin*) from Buddhist temples.[90] "Not even a hundred Jayewardenes," they stated, "possess the honesty, bravery . . . that Bodhipala does."[91] A few days later, *Kālaya* claimed that "the times when the temples, built by poor Buddhists, were exploited by the wealthy Senanayakes, Jayewardenes, and Wijewardenes are over." The newspaper portrayed the Vidyalankara monks as a "group that would not bow its head to even the demon of death" (*mārayekutavat hisa nonamana pirisak*).[92] (Incidentally, it was at this time that director Paññarama earned the popular nickname "the yakkaduwe monk who does not fear even the demon" (*yakātavat baya näti yakkaduwe hāmuduruwō.*)[93]

This terrain of polemical rhetoric generated a well-known incident of physical confrontation between the Vidyalankara monks and some Jayewardene supporters in Kelaniya. In September 1947, two prominent Vidyalankara monks, Walpola Rahula and Kalupahana Revata, were scheduled to speak at a political rally in Kelaniya, canvasing support for Dr. Bodhipala. The monks, traveling by car, could not reach the rally. On the way to Kelaniya, at

87. Ibid.
88. *Kālaya*, May 22, 1947.
89. *Kālaya*, July 4, 1947.
90. *Kālaya*, July 10, 1947.
91. *Kālaya*, July 4, 1947.
92. *Kālaya*, July 24, 1947.
93. Interviews with Kakkapalliye Anuruddha, Oct. 4, 1997, and Dewalegama Medhananda, Nov. 1, 1996.

Torana junction, a "gang of murderous thugs" (*māravara dāmarika pirisak*) stopped the car. Rahula describes the aftermath of the incident:

They were swearing and yelling at us. First, they punched the driver in the face several times. They got into the car and started beating us [*pahara dennata vūha*]. They forced us out of the car shouting angrily, "You (*topi*) criticize our ministers in public meetings? . . . If Bodhipala wins, we will kill you" [*maranavā*]. They started hitting us again with their clenched fists. Then they shoved us back into the car and continued beating us. Again they pulled us out of the car by our legs. One pulled out a knife and tried to stab Revata, saying 'we will kill you' [*topi maranavāya*]. Somebody intervened and stopped him. Then they beat me until I passed out. . . . The gang disappeared when the police and the neighbors arrived on the scene.[94]

The following day, the story made headlines in the press. Rahula stated that the "perpetrators of the crime" were innocent, uneducated people who were under the influence of arrack and money given by the wealthy. But Rahula immediately implicated Jayewardene in the attack.[95] He said that the event exemplified the kinds of "horrendous acts" that the UNP would commit in order to come to power and that the "only way to strike back is to defeat Jayewardene and elect Bodhipala," the man who represents "the poor oppressed class." "Defeating UNP candidates in forthcoming elections and removing them from power is the only just Buddhist punishment" (*yukti sahagata dharmānukūla dand14vama*).[96]

Other Vidyalankara monks depicted this event as an example of the monks' commitment to the causes of the people in Sri Lanka. Commenting on the attack, Vidyalankara monk Babarende Sirisivali said: As "citizens and national advisers, monks support the development of the country; [as the above incident indicates] monks such as Rahula are ready to sacrifice even their lives for the benefit of the suffering masses; these are virtuous and righteous [*silvat gunavat svāmin vahansēla*] monks."[97]

94. "Bhikshūn Vahanselāta Hiri Hära Kirīma: Rāhula Hāmuduruvangen Panivudayak" ("Hurting monks: A message from Rev. Rahula"), *Kālaya*, Sept. 18, 1947.

95. Rahula says that through speeches and pamphlets Jayewardene had been urging people in Kelaniya that monks supporting political parties should be "stripped of their robes and expelled [from the order]" (*sivuru kadā pannā dāmiya yutyi*); *Kālaya*, Sept. 18, 1947.

96. Ibid.

97. Bamarande Sirisivali, "Balvat Aparādayak" ("A grave crime"), editorial, *Kālaya*, Sept. 18, 1947. As far as my research indicates, there is no indication that Bodhipala ever won that election.

So far my labor has been to demonstrate some of the ways in which the discourse of Buddhism and politics emerged and became the subject of debate between different groups in the 1940s. It should be clear from the preceding discussion that in looking at the conditions of rival narratives that spurred this debate into being, I have not wanted to retell the commonplace story about the "continuing interaction between religion and politics." This notion of "interaction" is predicated upon the assumption that the link between religion and politics is a "problem" because they were originally separate domains of knowledge. This is the kind of understanding that governs the literature on the subject in Sri Lanka.

This understanding about religion and politics is not confined to Sri Lanka alone, however; it has become canonized disciplinary knowledge about the subject. By exploring the dynamics of the above debate, I have wanted to tell a different story about religion and politics. The debate, animated as it was by competing ideological arguments and counterarguments, sought to foreground authoritative claims about what and who could be seen as Buddhism and politics. I have wanted to suggest that questions about whether or not religion and politics interact are theoretically problematic because the definitions of who and what are to be included in, or excluded from, religion or politics are contingently authorized. Before I show how such definitions come to shift in different conjunctures, I will make a few more general remarks about religion and politics.

The above debate, emerging as it did in the context of the imminent departure of the British colonial rule from Sri Lanka in 1948, enables us to ask some new questions about the formations of conceptual categories like Buddhism and politics in a new light. As noted earlier, some postcolonial scholars, for example, Richard King, have argued that the separation between religion and politics as autonomous spheres is a flawed Western, Enlightenment assumption. King writes:

> I am simply wanting to acknowledge the sense in which "religious" and "political" are not separate realms in reality. The separation of the two is an Enlightenment assumption that I am not prepared to accept. . . . I am not saying that religious questions and issues should be reduced to their sociological or to their political dimensions, rather I wish to reject the enlightenment paradigm that cognitively separates these realms in the first place.[98]

98. Richard King, *Orientalism and Religion*, 14.

In light of this argument, one could conjecture if the above debate, which, among other things, sought to argue whether or not authentic Buddhism was separate from politics, can be seen as a by-product of the Western colonial heritage in Sri Lanka. After all, such preoccupations with ferreting out essential parts of religion are clearly evident in the British constructions of Buddhism in Sri Lanka.[99] But I do not want simply to reduce these opposing "native" claims about authentic Buddhist identity to colonialism. This is not because I want to undermine the dynamics of the colonial discursive economy in which conceptual labels like "Buddhism" emerged. Rather, these claims, to my mind, provide good examples of how we may see Buddhism and authenticity, politics and difference, as particular authoritative arguments emerging against the backgrounds of their own agendas, their own stakes, and their own programs. That said, I do not want to stop here. If we are to understand Buddhism, authenticity, and politics as operating within a tradition of arguments irreducible to one context, then we ought to show how those arguments, their agents, their forms, their logic, and their targets alter in other conjunctures. In the remainder of this chapter, I show some of the ways in which Buddhism and politics reemerged as the subject of public debate in the early 1980s, occupying new grounds, embodying "old" and new persons, of altered narratives and practices.

Refashioning a Debate: Discourse of Developing the Pali Language

In 1977 Jayewardene came to power by a landslide victory against Prime Minister Mrs. Bandaranaike, the wife of the late S. W. R. D. Bandaranaike. A year later, by amending the constitution, Jayewardene declared himself the first executive president of Sri Lanka.[100] A front-page newspaper article described the new political institution in these terms: "Never since the days of the monarchy has there been a greater concentration of power in a single office to administer a nation's affairs as in the office of the newly created President."[101] Jayewardene, reflecting on the executive power of his office, himself

---

99. Note the discussion of colonialism in the introduction.

100. A history of Jayewardene's complex political career is in K. M. de Silva and Howard Wriggins, *J. R. Jayewardene of Sri Lanka: A Political Biography, 1956–1989* (Hawaii: University of Hawaii Press, 1994); see vol. 2.

101. "A New Page in Sri Lanka's History," Ceylon Daily News, Feb. 4, 1978.

said once that as president the only thing he could not do was to turn a man into a woman, and vice versa.[102]

As part of his political campaign, Jayewardene promised to create a "righteous society" (*dharmista samājaya*). Claiming that no political party had ever conceived such an idea before, Jayewardene said that this righteous society included such values as living by the words of the Buddha, fostering Buddhism, and creating a free (*nivahal*) and nonviolent society, a society consisting of "real men" (*niyama minissu*).[103] Alongside this righteous society, Jayewardene said he would create a free-market economy in Sri Lanka. As Kemper informs us, "Where the Bandaranaike government had tightly controlled the economy, the UNP manifesto proposed to open it up and encourage foreign capital investment in order to create employment. If elected, Jayewardene said he would bring Sri Lanka the economic expansion and prosperity that Singapore had enjoyed in the 1960s and 1970s."[104] Once in power, the government, expanding the economy, created free-trade zones, providing employment for thousands of young people; allowed massive migration of labor to the Middle East; and developed the tourist industry. But some of Jayewardene's opponents, as we will see in greater detail in chapter 7, viewed his capitalistic economic policies as the very antithesis of a righteous society.

During the early phase of his presidency, Jayewardene tried to make clear his views on Buddhism: "My government will make every endeavor to re-establish the relations between the state and the Buddhasasana which existed in ancient times up to the advent of the imperial rulers";[105] the new government would "assist, even with money, to promote the teachings of the Buddha." Jayewardene spoke of the development of Buddhism as his government's responsibility: the "government acts according to the Buddhist teachings," he claimed.[106] He devalued certain Sinhala Buddhist rituals: "The

102. This was one of Jayewardene's popular statements.

103. J. R. Jayewardene, *"Mage Baudhha Bhaktiya Kisivekutat Venas Kala Nohäkyi"* ("No one can change my Buddhist devotion"), in *Budusasuna Saha Prajātantra Vādaya* (Colombo: Rajaye Mudrana Departumentuwa, 1982), n.p.

104. Kemper, *Presence of the Past*, 166.

105. "Ancient Ties between State and Sasana to be Restored," *Ceylon Daily News*, Feb. 8, 1978.

106. "Mē Rajaya Katayutu Karannē Bauddha Dharmaya Anukūlavayi—Janādhipatitumā" ("This government acts according to the Buddhist doctrine—president"), *Dinamina*, June 9, 1979.

teachings of the Buddha had never been confined to the offering of flowers, putting coins in a till or such other *pinkamas* [merit-generating activities]. The teachings should be practiced."[107] He saw this "practice" of Buddhism as instrumental to the creation of his righteous society and stated that "in our efforts, we seek the blessings of the Mahasangha."[108]

He often spoke at Buddhist temples and claimed that Sri Lanka was the home of "pristine" Buddhism (*nirmala bududahama*).[109] But he refused to recognize the claim that Sinhalese monks and Buddhists were the guardians of Buddhism. In 1977, speaking at the Getambe temple in Peradeniya, Kandy, Jayewardene said that the Sinhalese had played a role in "safeguarding the pristine words of the Buddha"; yet he pointed out in the same breath that "the Buddha's words prevail whether the Sinhalese exist or not"[110] and insisted that Sinhalese Buddhists remember that, as followers of the words of the Buddha, "we cannot think of a race (*jātiyak gäna hitanda bä*). The Buddha did not preach his doctrine to the Sinhalese race. At that time there was no Sinhalese race . . . the Buddha preached to the people of the entire world."[111]

Jayewardene had voiced very different views earlier in his political career. In 1944 he was one of the first politicians to lobby for Sinhala as the official language of Ceylon; he had argued that "without language a nation stands the chance of being absorbed or losing its identity. . . . It is because of our language that the Sinhalese race had existed for 2,400 years."[112] But at the Getambe temple, Jayewardene spoke of the importance of the Pali language, not Sinhala. And he reminded the audience that since the British colonized Sri Lanka, no other political party had donated as much money to the development of Buddhist temples as his government. He questioned monks rhetorically: "How can we, as a government, protect and develop the

107. "Ancient Ties."

108. Ibid.

109. J. R. Jayewardene, *"Nivan Dakitana Turu"* ("Until we attain nirvana"), in *Jayamāvataka Piya Satahan* (The footprints of a victorious path) (Colombo: Rajaye Mudranalaya, n.d.), 117.

110. Ibid.

111. Jayewardene, *"Nivan Dakitana Turu,"* 119. Here I must disagree with Walters's claim that "as had been the case for S. W. R. D. Bandaranaike, his appeal to Sinhala chauvinism ultimately proved Jayewardene's downfall": Walters, *History of Kelaniya*, 107.

112. J. R. Jayewardene, "Sinhala as the Official Language of Ceylon," in *J. R. Jayewardene: Selected Speeches and Writings, 1944–1978* (Colombo: H.W.D., n.d.).

Buddhasasana?"[113] His answer was that the Pali language should be more thoroughly studied:

> How can we develop the Pali language? Please tell me. Even if we send monks to universities they will not learn [Pali]. We have provided opportunities. We have allocated money for education. If not as a language, we must learn Pali as Buddhism, as acquiring knowledge [of Buddhism]. The Buddha taught in that language. I am not sure if the Buddha preached in Pali or the Magada language. But the texts of the Tripitaka [the Buddhist canon] are written in Pali. If we do not study this language, it will disappear from Sri Lanka. We need Pali to learn the word of the Buddha, to understand properly the meaning of Buddhism. Therefore we are now considering how to develop the language of Pali.[114]

Here Jayewardene did not envisage a Buddhism of the Sinhalese race but a Buddhism of the Pali language. Exaggerating, Jayewardene said that "there was not a single individual [monk] majoring in Pali" at any university in Sri Lanka; monks should not attend national universities, he said. At a different temple, he stated bluntly that the goal of monks should be concerned with attaining nirvana and not with trying to attend universities:

> If you want to pass SSE and HSE [university entrance examinations], if you want to join the United National Party, leave the robes [sivuru atärala yanna]. No one objects. You must be a bhikkhu [bhishūn vahanse namak venna]. That is my view [ēkayi mage adahasa]. That is the prime minister's view. No matter what happens, please remain the same. Do not change [venas venna epā]. If [you help] one person attain nirvana . . . it is greater than electing ten presidents. That is Buddhism [ēkayi buddhadharamaya]. [If you do this work], the government will give all the possible support. Do this kind of work [karanda mē väda].[115]

My point here is that the rhetoric about developing the Pali language and learning and fostering the "word" and the "meaning" of Buddhism was a different way of seeking to authorize what should count as the real relation between Buddhism and politics, the real Buddhist monk and society. The idea of the monk who does not attend national universities and seek salaried

113. Jayewardene, "Nivan Dakitana Turu," 120.
114. Ibid.
115. Jayewardene, "Mage Bauddha Bhaktiya."

employment is a euphemism for the "real" monk—one who stays away from "politics"; that is, the monk who bestows his "blessings" on the Jayewardene project of creating a righteous society.

Constructing "Apolitical" Buddhism

A few years after Jayewardene had proposed to develop the language of Pali, his government outlined the plan to create a separate Pali and Buddhist University for monks. The construction of the university can be seen as a strategic practice that enabled the Jayewardene government to communicate an authoritative idea of an apolitical Buddhism in Sri Lanka.

In the early 1980s, Jayewardene, along with Prime Minister R. Premadasa, held several meetings to discuss the proposal with leading Buddhist monks from all three monastic fraternities and premier monastic colleges (for example, Vidyodaya Pirivena). Jayewardene, perhaps still cognizant of his former antagonistic relations with Vidyalankara monks, did not invite them to the initial round of discussions, but Prime Minister Premadasa then suggested the importance of the Vidyalankara monks to the proposed project. One of the first Vidyalankara monks to take part in these early discussions about creating a separate Buddhist university was Dr. Kakkapalliye Anuruddha.[116] At one of the meetings, Anuruddha, suspicious of the proposal, questioned President Jayewardene and the monks present about the need for a separate university for monks. The answer: young monks at national universities had earned a "bad reputation" because of their public involvement in political rallies and demonstrations. Anuruddha pointed out that a clause in an early version of the proposed Buddhist University Act explicitly prohibited both student-monks and the employees of the university from taking part in any kind of "political" activity; Anuruddha objected to these clauses, arguing that they violated the rights of Buddhist monks "as citizens of the country." If the government was to create a separate university for Buddhist monks, Anuruddha went on, they should do so for the clergy of other religions in Sri Lanka— which would be impossible. Qualified Buddhist monks, he said, should be able to attend any university they wished; the government should not confine monks to one university. Anuruddha, opposing the establishment of the university, said the discussions intimated that "the government was trying to confine monks [*kotukaranda*] to one university."

116. Interview with Anuruddha, Sept. 4, 1996, and Nov. 5, 1997.

In 1981 Jayewardene appointed a new board of directors to rewrite the University Act. This time, surprisingly, Jayewardene invited his former opponent Walpola Rahula to supervise the project. By then, Rahula seemed to have changed some of his earlier views of Jayewardene, to say the least. He readily endorsed Jayewardene's plan for a separate Buddhist university, stating that "the monk should live and be educated in a Buddhist environment."[117] On the day of the inauguration of the university, Rahula spoke of Jayewardene as a "president who delivers on his promises" (*kiyapudē itu karana janādhipativarayek*).[118]

Rahula's involvement understandably generated criticism within and without the ranks of the sangha. Monks such as Labuduwe Siridhamma charged that "Rahula has fallen into Jayewardene's pocket," saying he had forgotten how Jayewardene's thugs beat him in Kelaniya.[119] As Jayewardene and Rahula planned the construction of the BPU, the president indicated to Rahula that he played no part in the 1940 attack. Rahula responded: "I do not know who engineered the attack. . . . Some claim that it was Mr. Jayewardene. I do not know that. However, it is true that I was beaten up. Now there is no use in talking about it."[120] Some lay Buddhists berated Rahula as a "traitor," saying he had been offered a house by Jayewardene for his role in the construction of the BPU.[121] Rahula's authorized biography points out that Jayewardene did indeed offer to build the Buddhist center (Ketumati) where Rahula spent the later part of his life, but Rahula refused the offer, saying the president could make "donations" toward the construction of the Buddhist center. Donations did indeed come from Jayewardene's party: Prime Minister Premadasa and ministers Gamini Disanayake and Weerasinghe Mallimarachchi provided the land, timber, and bricks for the Buddhist center.[122]

As if to include Jayewardene's concept of a Pali Buddhism, the final version of the act that Rahula supervised named the university the "Buddhist and Pali University" (*bauddha hā pāli vishvidhyālaya*). The act set forth the university's objectives as follows:

---

117. Interview with Rahula in *Kalpanā*, May 1984, 6.

118. *Dinamina*, Apr. 23, 1982.

119. Gunadasa Liyanage, *Walpola Rahula Hāmuduruwō* (Dehiwala: Bauddha Sanskrutika Madyastanaya, 1994), 140.

120. Ibid., 140–41.

121. "Drōhīhu Kavarahuda?" ("Who are the traitors?"), *Divayina*, Feb. 16, 1996.

122. Liyanage, *Walpola Rahula*, 228–32.

1. The propagation of the Buddha Dhamma
2. The promotion of Pali studies in Sri Lanka and abroad; and
3. The conduct of examinations for private students and students of affiliated colleges which have as their aims one or more of the following:

   a. The dissemination of Buddhism and the fostering of Dhammadhuta (missionary) activities in Sri Lanka and abroad
   b. The training of Bhikkhus in teaching Buddhism and Pali in pirivenas, schools, and similar institutions
   c. *The provision of necessary facilities for the maintenance and improvement of the ethical conduct and mental discipline of the Bhikkhus;* [my emphasis] and
   d. Any other matter connected with, or incidental to, any of the matters aforesaid[123]

According to the act, the president appointed the council (the executive governing body), the vice chancellor, and other staff members, from registrar to librarian. Put simply, the whole university fell under the authority of President Jayewardene, who saw himself as minister of Buddhist affairs. In 1982, on the occasion of inaugurating the BPU, attended by many senior members of the sangha, Jayewardene pronounced, "Some members of the Sangha were asking why there was no Ministry of Buddhist affairs. As the custodian of the constitution, I am the Minister of Buddhist Affairs. . . . There is no need for a separate ministry."[124]

The inauguration of the BPU provided the platform to make centrally visible the state's narrative about the importance of the president to the protection and "development of Buddhism." Newspaper front-page headlines made a particular link between Buddhism and the Jayewardene state: "The responsibility of protecting Buddhism rests directly with the president" (*Budusasuna räkīme vagakīma kelinma janādhipatita bārayi*).[125] Jayewardene outlined the centrality of the Pali language to Buddhist life and said that Buddhist monks should study Pali because Buddhists "observe five precepts, respect the three jewels, perform funeral rites, deliver sermons, and express all their ideas (*häma adahasakma prakāshakaranne*) in the Pali language." According to Jayewardene, the study of the Pali language was

123. The Buddhist and Pali University of Sri Lanka Act, no. 74 of 1981, 1–2.
124. "The Constitution Safeguards Buddhism," *Daily News*, Apr. 14, 1982.
125. *Dinamina*, Apr. 23, 1982

important because it contained the "root ideas" (*mul adahas*) of Buddhism.[126] My point here is obvious: To emphasize the state's commitment to the development of the Pali language was to authorize a particular boundary between Buddhism and politics, Buddhist monks and society. The making of the BPU enabled this authorization of this boundary in a centrally visible way.

State Constructions of Monastic "Discipline"

The internal structure of the BPU consisted of strategies that sought to oblige student-monks to embody this Jayewardene version of apolitical Buddhism. The BPU, unlike other national universities, was decentralized. It comprised four affiliated colleges (*āyatana*) located at four major pirivenas in different parts of the country: Vidyodaya Pirivena (the Siyam fraternity), in Maradana, Colombo; Vidyalankara Pirivena (the Siyam fraternity), in Peliyagoda, Kelaniya; Sadharmakara Pirivena (the Amarapura fraternity), in Panadura; and Sarasvati Pirivena (the Ramañña fraternity), in Balagalla. Jayewardene appointed the principals of the four pirivenas, who were (mostly) well-known allies of the United National Party, as heads of the four affiliated colleges (*āyatānadhipati*).[127] The government gave each head monk a handsome monthly salary and made separate annual grants to the affiliated colleges to provide room and board for its student-monks and to pay staff wages. Each affiliated college accommodated no more than fifty students, and the students lived separately from the young monks studying at the pirivenas. Vidyalankara Pirivena, given its history of sour relations with Jayewardene, never publicly associated itself with the UNP. But the discourse of the BPU, if I may call it that, was one important instance where the anti-UNP Vidyalankara Pirivena became *obliged* to support a UNP "Buddhist" project as it agreed to house and supervise a branch of the BPU on its grounds.

The new BPU act, unlike its earlier draft, did not officially prohibit its students from participating in "political" activities. One cannot, however, ignore some of the state proposals and narratives that became strikingly visible during this period. They were perhaps strategies more designed to foster

126. "Pāli Adyāpanayē Vädagatkama" ("The importance of the study of the Pali language"), in *Budusasuna Saha Prajātantravādaya*, n.p.

127. The principals were Akuratiye Amarawamsa, Welamitiyawe Dhammarakkhita, Talalle Dhammananda, and Henpitagedara Ñanavasa. Akuratiye Nanda and Welamitiyawe Kusaladhamma became the heads of the Vidyodaya and Vidyalankara affiliated colleges, respectively.

Jayewardene's vision of an apolitical Buddhist monkhood. In early 1982, for example, the Ministry of Education proposed a new university entrance (advanced-level) exam especially for monks. The move, as the ministry explained, with an added emphasis on "Buddhist" subjects, would "wean the pirivenas from a layman's education."[128] By then, some prominent monastic colleges such as Subhadrarama in Nugegoda, Vidyaratana in Horana, and Sunetradevi in Pepiliyana had begun to offer a curriculum emphasizing subjects such as economics, political science, and geography deemed by the Jayewardene state as inappropriate for monks. These pirivenas, as we will see later, attracted not only scores of young monks planning to enter national universities but many lay students as well. Some voices, supportive of the state, complained that these pirivenas had become "educational shops" and that they should be liberated from the "wave of commercialism."[129] At the same time, the state also set up scholarships and a Buddhist Endowment Fund to encourage the study of Pali and Buddhism and to "assist in the advancement of the Buddha Dhamma, the Buddha Sasana and the Sangha."[130]

What paralleled these developments in the early and mid-1980s was the emergence of a series of newspaper debates about the question "Who is a Buddhist monk?" centering on the issue of Buddhist monks attending national universities.[131] The debate alluded to the then-famous controversy about student-monks of Colombo University staging a *satyagraha* on the roof of a campus building. The newspapers carried large, colorful pictures of the monks sitting on the roof. Some Buddhists wrote to newspapers and questioned: "Will someone tell me why Buddhist monks are allowed to attend universities, lead strikes, and demonstrate and shout slogans against authority [*sic*]? This is a disgrace to Buddhism. What are our Buddhist leaders doing about it?"[132] While some monks defended the monks' right to attend national universities, saying "education is the birthright" of every individual,[133] some Buddhists tried to rebut such claims by saying that "a monk is one who had

128. "New A-level Exam for Bhikkhu Students," *Observer*, May 19, 1982.

129. *Lankādīpa*, May 10, 1987.

130. *Times*, Oct. 16, 1983.

131. For articles "Who Is a Buddhist Monk?" see *Observer*, Apr. 22 and 28, 1985; *Observer*, May 19, 1985; *Observer*, June 2, 1985; see also *Island*, Aug. 1985.

132. "A Monastic Life?" *Island*, Apr. 28, 1985.

133. "Who Is a Buddhist Monk?" *Observer*, Apr. 28, 1985.

[*sic*] renounced his rights, birthright and all, and therefore, a monk has no rights."[134] During this time, the Minister of Cultural Affairs, E. L. B. Hurulle, was campaigning to introduce a new Monastic Judiciary Act (*sanghād-hikarana panata*) that proposed to expel "those who are wearing robes and leading lives contrary to the Buddhist vinaya (discipline)."[135] Hurulle stated that "pseudo-Bhikkhus" who "bring the Sasana into disrepute will be subject to enhanced punishment which include terms of imprisonment."[136] This idea of the young monks' lack of "discipline" became an integral part of the kind of monastic image that the BPU expected its monks to cultivate.

The BPU Act, as noted before, insisted on "the maintenance and improvement of ethical conduct [*ācāra dharmānukūla pävätma*] and mental discipline [*mānasika sikshanaya*] of the Bhikkhus."[137] Each affiliated college employed a "director of the Dhamma" (*dharmādhyakshaka*) to ensure the monks' cultivation of "discipline." At all affiliated colleges, the BPU students, along with the pirivena monks, were expected to assemble daily at six in the morning and evening in a common place and walk, downcast, in procession to the Buddhist shrine room and take part in the ritual of worshipping the Buddha. They were also required to eat breakfast and lunch at specific times in a common dining room with teacher-monks and monk-students of the pirivenas. The comings and goings of the BPU students also remained under the surveillance of the Dhamma director. The violation of this discipline resulted in severe sanctions (for example, expulsion from the university). This then was part of the state's attempt at making a "disciplined monk."

Subverting State Discourses of Buddhism and Politics

In the late 1980s, the BPU monks unanimously began to protest the BPU disciplinary regulations as a way of contesting the state formation of a disciplined monk. They spoke of themselves as "university students" (*vishvavidyāla hāmuduruvaru*) and argued that the BPU university students should be

---

134. "Who Is a Buddhist Monk?" *Observer*, May 19, 1985.

135. "Sanghādikarana Panata Sammata Kalāta Pasuva Sivurata Muvāvī Sangharuvanata Nigaru Karanu Bä" ("After the Sangha Act is approved, there can be no hiding behind the robe and dishonoring the Buddhist Sangha"), *Davasa*, Jan. 3, 1986.

136. "Jail Terms for Pseudo-Bhikkhus," *Times*, Oct. 16, 1983.

137. See "1981 Anka 74 Darana Sri Lanka Bauddha Pali Vishvavidyāla Panata"; "Buddhist and Pali University of Sri Lanka," *Island*, Oct. 30, 1983.

treated differently from pirivena monks and schoolchildren.[138] The student-monks argued that the BPU rules violated the "rights of the university students" and refused to attend daily dharma activities at the pirivenas, demanding the elimination of the Dhamma director position. The monks stated that they had come to a university to do more important things than perform rituals. Some monks began to charge that the head monks of the affiliated colleges pocketed (*sākkuvalata yanavā*) the government grants by serving them "bad food."[139] They protested that their meals should be prepared separately from the fare served to the pirivena student-monks and that they should eat in a separate dining room. The affiliated colleges gave in to these demands.

The BPU monks' demand to be recognized as university monks must be seen in relation to the dominant public image of the BPU. The monastic students of other national universities did not regard the BPU monks as university monks. Public consensus was that the BPU students did not score highly enough in the advanced-level examination to enter a national university. One monk from Peradeniya University said the BPU monks were "leftover" (*ituruvecca*) students. Furthermore, the BPU degree did not carry the national and international recognition that degrees at other universities did; except in a few Commonwealth countries, the degree had no value abroad. More notably, because until 1994 the BPU remained under the special jurisdiction of the president, unlike the national universities, it was not considered part of the Ministry of Higher Education.[140]

From the viewpoint of other university monks, the BPU lacked an important component of a national university: a Bhikkhu Union (*bhikshu sanga-maya*). The decentralization of the BPU—with its students located at four different pirivenas—prevented monks from forming a Bhikkhu Union for many years. Bhikkhu Unions at national universities constitute an important aspect of the monastic life at national universities. They address economic and social problems of the student-monks, participate in community outreach programs, carry out ragging (hazing) of first-year monks, and promote student

138. Interviews with monks of the BPU at Vidyalankara and Vidyodaya affiliated colleges, Oct. 1–3, 1996.

139. Interviews with monks at Vidyodaya.

140. "Buddhist [and Pali] University under Ministry of Higher Education," *Divayina*, July 13, 1994.

awareness of national problems.[141] The BPU student-monks, despite guidelines that specifically prohibited the formation of student unions, protested
and created a "United Student Front" (the Ekābaddha Maha Sishya Sanghamaya) (they translated *sanghamaya*, which literally means *union*, as *front*).
The secretary-monk of the BPU said, "a university would not be complete
without a Bhikkhu Union."

The United Student Front publicly encouraged the monks to support any
political party in Sri Lanka that they perceived was "doing good" for the country. Many of the BPU monks became some of the most vocal supporters of the
banned Marxist JVP (People's Liberation Movement) that carried out armed
revolution in a bid to overthrow the UNP government. In 1987 many of the
key monks who assembled at Vidyalankara Pirivena to protest Jayewardene's
signing of the Indo-Lanka Accord came from the BPU. It is said that in 1989
the BPU monks were among the "most wanted" for questioning by the Premadasa government during its islandwide crackdown on the JVP. During the
height of the JVP militancy, the BPU monks took to the streets outside an
affiliated college to show their support for the JVP cause. An islandwide curfew was in effect, but they put up posters, screaming for the defeat of the UNP
government. The army and the police, patrolling the streets, had received
orders to "shoot to kill" any suspect on the street. Within hours, a truckload
of soldiers raced toward the monks in Kelaniya and started firing machine
guns. The monks took to their heels. One monk was shot and injured.[142]

Divesting an Idea of Authorized Meanings

In the early 1990s, the United Student Front of the BPU proposed a major
change in the university. In 1994—by this time Jayewardene had stepped
down and President Premadasa had been assassinated—the BPU monks
staged a massive protest in front of the Tooth Temple in Kandy. They
demanded that the government establish one national Buddhist university in
a separate location and remove the four affiliated colleges from the pirivenas.[143] The secretary of the United Student Front indicated to me that such a

141. Interviews with the secretary-monks of the Bhikkhu Unions at Kelaniya, Peradeniya, and
Vidyodaya universities in August 1996 and September 1997.

142. This account comes from my interview with a monk at Vidyalankara Pirivena, Sept. 6,
1996. That the BPU students were among the key JVP monks sought for questioning was something that I learned from my conversations with many monks in different parts of Colombo.

143. *Divayina*, Oct. 7, 1994.

move would reduce the cost of 13.7 million rupees that the government spends annually to maintain only sixty students at several colleges.

The rhetoric of "freedom" became central to the campaign for a new "united" national university. In a rally in Matara in 1995, the BPU monks accused that "in those days J. R. Jayewardene established the university as a bribe [*allasak dīme muvāven*] to silence the progressive views of the Buddhist monks and lay Buddhists; it was not for the preservation of Buddhism [*cirasti-tiya pinisa novē*]."[144] Members of other political parties such as Ariya Bulle-goda of the Sri Lanka Progressive Front and Dr. Sunil Ratnapriya of the Sri Lanka Samasamaja Party immediately rushed to support the BPU rallies.[145] Clamoring to lend "total backing for the BPU uprising," Bullegoda promised to elevate the BPU to the status of the famous Nalanda University in India. Ratnapriya urged the members of the government who earlier, in 1994, had sought the BPU students' support during elections, to endorse the demands of the student-monks.[146] These politicians' calls for support for the BPU monks' agenda show how by 1994 the BPU had become an important cause. That these calls did not go unheeded by the heads of affiliated colleges and the authorities of the government attests to the significance of the BPU monks' demand. The recognition of the demand by the (Chandrika Ban-daranaike) state meant that the Jayewardene state-authorized boundary between monks and politics was being contested.

The head monks of the BPU colleges backed the students' campaign because, they said, the affiliated colleges interfered with maintaining disci-pline among the young monks at their pirivenas.[147] Beneath this issue of discipline, there was concern about lack of "sufficient funds" to maintain the institutions. The annual grant that the government made to each BPU-affiliated college did not meet all the demands of its student-monks: some head monks spent their own money to provide the kind of food that the BPU monks demanded. The affiliated colleges had in vain asked the government to increase the annual grant.[148] Other head monks did not take kindly to the

144. "Nālandā Bauddha Vishva Vidyālayē Tatvayata Bauddha Hā Pali Vishva Vidyālaya Pat Kala Yutuyi" (The BPU should be elevated to the status of the Nalanda University"), *Divayina*, July 30, 1995.

145. Ibid.

146. Ibid.

147. *Sri Lankā Bauddha Hā Pāli Visvha Vidyālayē Vyuhaya Parīkshana Kamitu Vārtāva 1994* (Committee report of the Sri Lanka Buddhist and Pali University's service), 29.

148. Interview with Welamitiyawe Kusaladhamma, Sept. 5, 1996.

demands of the BPU monks. President Premadasa, Jayewardene's successor, had established and funded four more BPU-affiliated colleges at different pirivenas, but, owing to Premadasa's untimely death, the new affiliated colleges were not registered with the government as legal parts of the BPU.[149] In 1995 one of the unregistered affiliated colleges at the Asgiriya temple expelled all its thirty-two students. Its head monk, Palipana Chandananda, claimed that the students violated its "disciplinary standards" by participating in a rally organized by the BPU Student Front to discuss the plan for the new university,[150] but the issue of dwindling financial support by the state seemed to have played some part in the expulsion of the students. By this time, after the death of President Premadasa, these new colleges were in severe financial straits. Prior to expelling the students, they had repeatedly insisted that the government increase their financial assistance to meet the rising cost of living in Sri Lanka.[151] Whatever the reasons for the expulsions, what we see here is a falling apart of the idea of the BPU as it was authorized by the Jayewardene government. The official recognition of the crumbling of the BPU led to the construction of a new BPU university by the government of Chandrika Bandaranaike.

In the mid-1990s, removing all the affiliated colleges from the pirivenas, the Bandaranaike government planned to build a different "united" national BPU in Homagama. The Education Department proposed to write a new university act, with a view to recognizing the BPU monks as "university students"[152] entitled to all the "privileges" (*varaprasāda*) of a national university.[153] So if the decentralized Buddhist and Pali University that the Jayewardene government constructed worked strategically to authorize a particular "apolitical Buddhism" that monks should embody, the new centralized university—with a history of the monks' early protests of the BPU rules and their eventual support for the state's enemy, the JVP—symbolized the authorized contestation of the BPU. Put differently, the building of the new university

149. Premadasa established new PBU affiliated colleges at Vidyaloka Pirivena in Galle; Asgiriya temple in Kandy; Sastravinda Pirivena in Gokarella; and Sudarvasa Pirivena in Uduwara.

150. "Bauddha Hā Pāli Vishvavidyālaya Yanu Kumakda?"

151. "Asgiriya Mahānayāka Calls for the Probe on Pāli and Buddhist [sic] University," *Island*, Oct. 3, 1994.

152. *Divayina*, Nov. 11, 1995.

153. "Bauddha Pali Sarasavi Sisunata Jātika Sarasavi Adhyāpanaya" ("National university education for the BPU students"), *Divayina*, Aug. 11, 1995.

divested the Jayewardene idea of the BPU of its formerly authorized meanings. But the debate about the new BPU, about the identity of its students,
and about its relation to the state and politics, has not seen its last day. In 1995,
for example, the minister of education, Richard Patirana, announced that
though the government would rebuild a "united" BPU of national recognition, it would not be an "ordinary" (*sāmānya*) university: it would be a particular kind of "Buddhist" university.[154]

To recap, in examining these debates, locating the conjunctures of their
possibility and central visibility, I have wanted to suggest that conventional
disciplinary conceptualizations are not able to capture the altering configurations of the relation between religion and politics. Canonical disciplinary
arguments would have us believe that religion and politics are inseparably
bound or that religion plays an important role in politics. This understanding
rests on the idea that the "interaction," or interrelation, between religion and
politics is a "problem" that needs disciplinary explanation. Now some scholars make no bones about the supposed insalubrious "modern" effects of this
interaction—often put in universal terms of religious fundamentalism—and
they even lobby for a separation between religion and politics.

What animates these arguments are particular assumptions about what do
and do not constitute the identity of religion or politics. These arguments, I
have suggested, are not conceptually adequate to understand religion and
politics as concepts invested with and divested of differing meanings. I have
wanted to show the ways in which different conceptions of Buddhism and
politics, the religious and the secular, religious identity and difference,
become authorized and unauthorized, come into central sight and disappear
from sight, in contingent conjunctures of debates. It is the critical examination of these debates that should form the central focus of our endeavors constructing religion and politics as disciplinary objects of knowledge. The
failure to locate those rival narratives and the conjunctures in which they
emerge tends to reproduce the ideological meanings that inhere in them.

Take, for example, the crucial debates about religion and politics in the
1940s and the 1980s, marking very different social landscapes in Sri Lanka.
Obviously, these debates constitute particular Sinhala discourses on Buddhism and politics. However, seeking as I did to understand the dynamics of

---

154. "Bauddha Hā Pali Sarasaviya Svādhīna Āyatanayak Karanavā"("The BPU will be made
an independent institution"), *Dinamina*, Aug., 21, 1995.

these disputes, I have not wanted to determine whether or not there was some relation between the 1940s debate and that of the 1980s and to explain *how* the relationship between Buddhism and politics works in Sri Lanka; on the contrary, I suggested that the emergence and submergence of these debates should be seen in relation to the ideological contexts of particular opposing claims, agendas, and stakes. What one finds in these debates are the contingent ways in which these disputes enable different persons and practices to come into central view as defining and shaping the boundaries between religion and politics. If we arrive at the subject matter this way, we will not seek to advance more sophisticated claims about the link or the separation between religion and politics, but will investigate the ways in which altering debates make possible shifting conceptions of "religion" and "politics."

CHAPTER FOUR

A New Economy of Religious Identity

My concern in this chapter is to delineate the emergence of a "new" discursive economy of religious narratives, practices, and persons authorized by the conjunctures of the open-market policies of the Jayewardene state in "modern" Sri Lanka. What interests me are the central visibility of the new discourses and practices that came to authorize a particular relation between Buddhism and difference in this new context. Central to my task is the examination of the complex formations of the relations between Buddhism and the state in terms of the colorful careers of several monks—particularly, Pelpola Vipassi and Kananke Dhammadinna. I seek not to represent these monks as examples of what it means to be a Buddhist monk in contemporary Sri Lanka; rather, I point to the central visibility of the narratives and practices of these monks—narratives that corresponded to the Jayewardene state's prototype of an apolitical monkhood mark a "rupture" insofar as they were made possible by the new conjuncture of inaugurating the free-market economy of modern Sri Lanka.

Significant to the emergence of a new economy of Buddhism was the Jayewardene administration's initiation of new economic and "cultural" relations between Sri Lanka and Japan. These relations formed a crucial part of the state's agenda to "develop the country." The context in which such economic relations were pursued enabled the construction of a new epistemic space in which authoritative claims and debates about the relation between "pristine" Buddhism, Sri Lanka, and Japan came into central view. Some monks sponsored by the Jayewardene government—Vipassi and Dhammadinna, for example—established unprecedented "cultural" liaisons with a number of wealthy Buddhist temples in Japan and received from them millions of dollars in the form of donations to inaugurate a new brand of "social service" projects. These were readily endorsed and published as "Buddhist" projects by the Jayewardene government and some high-ranking members of the sangha. The projects placed these monks among the wealthiest elites, enabling them to occupy the "Buddhist" center of visibility in Sri Lanka.

In laying bare the epistemic and ideological conditions of a new economy of narratives about the relation between Buddhism and difference, monasticism and society, I do not labor to explain here how Buddhism has changed or to identify the emergence of a "new Buddhism" in Sri Lanka. What concerns me are the ways in which particular competing narratives about Buddhism and difference, "orthodox" identities and "unorthodox" differences, were made to come into view and fade from view, to become centered and decentered within the purview of this new context in Sri Lanka.

Pelpola Vipassi

A New Economy of "Buddhist" Discourses:
Japan and Sri Lanka, Monks and State

Pelpola Vipassi received his monastic education at Vidyodaya Pirivena, in Colombo.[1] During his tenure as a student at Vidyodaya in the late 1960s, Vipassi lived at the Mahabodhi Society in Sri Lanka, where his colleagues included monks like Banagala Upatissa and Kananke Dhammadinna, both of whom we meet below. In the 1970s, after completing his education, Vipassi traveled to India to accept a position as the supervisor of the main branch of the Mahabodhi Society in Saranath. He worked in Saranath for four years before accepting an invitation from a Japanese monk to visit Japan.

In Japan, Vipassi met the Japanese monk Nichidatsu Puji, of the Nichiren sect, the architect of the international "Peace Pagoda" movement.[2] Impressed by Vipassi's leadership skills in India, so the story goes, Puji proposed to Vipassi the plan to build a peace pagoda in Sri Lanka; he offered to supply funding. In 1975 Vipassi returned to Sri Lanka and formed a committee of several chief Buddhist monks to discuss Puji's proposal. The committee decided to build a peace pagoda near Adam's Peak (*siripāda*), the mountain where, as tradition has it, the Buddha planted his footprint during one of his visits to the island.[3] The Bandaranaike government endorsed the project by

---

1. I conducted two lengthy interviews in Sinhalese with Vipassi on Aug. 7, 1994, and Sept. 2, 1997.

2. Puji built peace pagodas in Japan, the United States, England, and Sri Lanka.

3. The Srīpādaya is a pilgrimage center visited by both Buddhists and Muslims. On some aspects of the significance of Adam's Peak as a center of Buddhist and non-Buddhist pilgrimage, see Markus Askland, *The Sacred Footprint* (Oslo: Yelti Consult, 1990).

providing land for the pagoda, which was completed in 1978, the year the Jayewardene government came to power.

Vipassi says that the peace pagoda marked an important cultural link between Sri Lanka and Japan. It also contributed to the Sri Lankan tourism industry that formed a crucial part of the Jayewardene government's new political agenda of developing the country.[4] The inauguration ceremony brought to Sri Lanka a delegation of more than six hundred Japanese monks and lay people from different Mahayana Buddhist sects in Japan. It was the first time, Vipassi claims, that so many tourists had ever visited Sri Lanka. In the years immediately following the inauguration, annually three to four hundred Japanese pilgrims arrived in Sri Lanka to celebrate the pagoda's anniversary.[5]

Significantly, the peace pagoda was ceremonially declared open by newly elected President J. R. Jayewardene.[6] The state newspapers saw it as a history-making event: "Linking the Theravada Sri Lanka [sic] with Mahayana Japan, President J. R. Jayewardene will crown the peace pagoda with an eleven-foot bronze pinnacle at the auspicious time of 10.29 on Saturday morning February 25."[7] Other newspaper accounts described it as a "great historic event and a cause of pride to the entire [Sri Lankan] Buddhist public."[8] At the opening ceremony, Jayewardene spoke about "peace" and the similarity between "Mahayana" and "Theravada" Buddhist traditions. Addressing a large audience—Japanese monks, the chief monks from all three Sri Lankan Buddhist fraternities, and several thousand Sri Lankan lay Buddhists—the president made a remarkable statement:

> We have gathered here to spread the word of peace enshrined in the teachings of the Buddha. The differences between human beings and animals largely depend on maithree [sic] [compassion] ahimsa [non-violence] and compassion. Peace remains only on these ideals which can be practiced by human beings. Buddha came to the island 2,500 years ago to propagate

4. See "Tourism: Record Earnings Last Year," and "Sri Lanka Tourism—a New Approach to Quality," *Ceylon Daily News*, Jan. 19, 1978.

5. Since Puji's death in the late 1980s, the number of Japanese pilgrims visiting the peace pagoda has decreased.

6. Jayewardene became president on Feb. 4, 1978.

7. "President to Place Pinnacle on Pagoda," *Ceylon Daily News*, Feb. 22, 1978.

8. "Peace Pagoda: Three Hundred Mahayana Bhikkhus Arrive," *Ceylon Daily News*, Feb. 25, 1978.

the ideals of peace and the same ideals of peace have now spread all over the world. Japan and Sri Lanka are bound together on these ideals. The two creeds—Mahayana and Theravada—do not have much in difference except in rituals. The Japanese follow the teachings [of the Buddha] in pristine glory.[9]

Here Jayewardene, as he would again later in his career,[10] strategically undermined the idea that "pure" Buddhism was confined to Sri Lanka alone. In arguing that the Buddha's "fundamental teaching" is about peace, and portraying the Japanese as honorable followers of the Buddha's "teachings in pristine glory,"[11] Jayewardene implied that "pristine" Buddhism exists in Japan, too.

Chief monks who spoke on the occasion described the event as one important step in the development of such economic relations between Japan and Sri Lanka. Induruwe Uttarananda, for example, said: "[The Pagoda] will promote not only harmonious cultural relations between our two countries but will also lead to cooperation in the economic development of our country." Uttarananda went on to say that "although our two countries have developed close relations in different activities in the past, of late this relationship had been developed in a wide field of activity. Our President [Jayewardene] contributed a great deal in promoting this close relation particularly because he was a champion of the cause of full freedom for Japan."[12]

The Jayewardene government was jockeying to foster new economic relations with Japan, and the significance of the development quickly became further evident. On the day the peace pagoda was opened, the government newspapers carried a report about the founding of JALANKA, an important joint venture to promote trade relations with Japan and develop Sri Lanka; it would take the form of trade, capital investment, and expertise. The report said that "as a gesture of their goodwill to Sri Lanka, the Japanese collaborators have decided to publish a monthly magazine, Shin Nosei, containing trade information about Sri Lanka so that more and more Japanese businesses would be attracted to invest in Sri Lanka. The first issue of Shin Nosei will

9. "President Crowns Peace Pagoda," *Ceylon Daily News*, Feb. 27, 1978.
10. See chapter 3.
11. "President Crowns Peace Pagoda."
12. Ibid.

carry the speech made by President J. R. Jayewardene at the San Francisco Peace Conference."[13]

In 1951, Jayewardene had delivered a speech at the Peace Treaty Conference in San Francisco, persuading other Asian countries to enter the peace pact that would later iron out the differences between Japan and the United States.[14] The Japanese government demonstrated its appreciation to Jayewardene. In 1979, following Jayewardene's first official visit to Tokyo as the first executive president of Sri Lanka, the Japanese government doubled its financial assistance to Sri Lanka, stating that its people were "profoundly moved by it [Jayewardene's speech in San Francisco] and they will never forget it."[15] Later Japan offered to build a "first-class" hospital in Jayewardenepura ("The Victorious Kingdom of Jayewardene"), the late medieval city of Kotte to which Jayewardene moved the capital of Sri Lanka. Today the hospital stands as "a monument to Japan's generosity" to Sri Lanka.[16]

The hospital was one of many "gifts" that Japan would continue to offer to the Jayewardene government. Others included financial assistance in building the Sri Lankan TV Corporation, the Samanalawewa Hydro Electric Project, the Mahaweli Irrigation Project, and the Colombo Port—all symbols of the modernity that the Jayewardene government claimed to be inaugurating.[17] Consequently, Japan became Sri Lanka's biggest trade and investment partner; in return, Sri Lanka became one of the biggest importers of Japanese products, from cookware and television sets to "reconditioned" automobiles. The early 1980s also witnessed the emergence of "cultural" exchanges between the two countries. The Japanese embassy in Sri Lanka conducted Japanese language classes, free of charge, and the Sri Lankan government

13. "Joint Venture to Boost Japan-Lanka Trade," *Ceylon Daily News,* Feb. 27, 1978.

14. "Japan's Good Will," *Ceylon Daily News,* Feb. 25, 1978.

15. *Ceylon Daily News,* Sept. 12, 1979, cited in de Silva and Wriggins, *Jayewardene of Sri Lanka,* 2:409. Even a few years later, the Japan's Prince Akihito, who visited Sri Lanka in 1983, remarked that Japan would never forget the "Jayewardene name"; see "San Francisco Vala Kala Katāva Nisā Jayewardene Nāmaya Amataka Karannä-Japan Kumaru" ("We will not forget the Jayewardene name because of the speech he delivered in San Francisco—Japanese prince"), *Dinamina,* Mar. 5, 1981.

16. "A Japanese Gift," editorial, *Daily News,* May 4, 1990. The editorial mentions that when Jayewardene was first informed of the plan to build the hospital, he asked the Japanese how many beds the largest hospital in Japan contained. Told "1,000 beds," Jayewardene said, "Then build us one with 1,001 beds."

17. "Some Lasting Symbols of Japanese Good Will and Aid," *Daily News,* May 3, 1990.

endorsed the project saying that "the languages of Sri Lanka-Japan has [sic] phonetic and grammatical similarity, making it easy for both people to learn the other language."[18] To help promote the study of Japanese, the Japanese government established a number of scholarships for various fields of graduate and postgraduate study in Japan.[19]

The new economic relations with Japan coincided with the production of a particular kind of discourse about Japan: namely, that the "Japanese" presented not only the familiar model of economic success that Sri Lanka should try to imitate, but also the model of "pristine" Buddhism.[20] It was this Japanese "pristine" Buddhism, monks like Vipassi would later argue, that would provide the model for the "reconstruction of Theravada Buddhism" in Sri Lanka. This narrative, which the Jayewardene government continued to disseminate, gained greater prominence in a seminal debate about the supposed differences between Theravada Buddhism and the Mahayana. Vipassi was at the center of this debate.

Since the inauguration of the peace pagoda in Sri Lanka, Vipassi had traveled to Japan frequently, establishing more contacts with several other Japanese temples. In the early 1980s, Vipassi allied himself with the wealthy Japanese Buddhist sect named Shingon, and this alliance turned a new chapter in his career. In 1981, assisted by the Shingon, Vipassi founded the Japan–Sri Lanka Friendship Temple in Sri Lanka. The temple proposed two objectives: "to strengthen cultural bonds between Japan and Sri Lanka and to provide 'social service' to Sri Lanka." As a symbol of the temple's commitment to social service, Vipassi founded the Japan–Sri Lanka Free Nursery School adjacent to the temple and provided free education to a handful of Buddhist children in the neighborhood. Originally constructed on only sixteen perches of land, the nursery and temple were declared open by Emperor Akihito and Empress Akihito during their official visit to Sri Lanka in 1981.[21] Proud of his achievement, Vipassi claimed to be the first monk to introduce the Japanese elementary educational system to Sri Lanka, and indeed, a Buddhist monk

18. Cited in "Long Live Sri Lanka-Japan Friendship: Japan Foundation Grant Programs," *Daily News*, May 3, 1990.

19. Ibid.

20. *Ceylon Daily News*, Feb. 27, 1978.

21. *Pelpola Vipassi Foundation: Inauguration Ceremony, 1996. Souvenir* (hereafter called *Vipassi Foundation*). This booklet contains numerous pictures depicting Vipassi positioned next to influential people such as Presidents Jayewardene, Premadasa, and Chandrika Bandaranaike.

running a nursery school was something of a novel social practice at the time. But a year earlier, Banagala Upatissa, who would later become one of Vipassi's rivals, had already started a similar Japanese nursery school in Sapugaskanda.

New Titles, New Identities

In the mid-1980s, as financial assistance continued to flow from Japan, Vipassi rebuilt the temple and the nursery school at a cost of 120 million rupees. The new temple included several buildings, one of which was a three-story luxury personal residence for Vipassi.[22] The new nursery school accommodated more than one thousand children.[23] The expansion of the temple marked an important shift in the identity of the temple. The name Japan–Sri Lanka Friendship Temple was changed to Japan–Sri Lanka Friendship Institute.[24] As the name changed, Vipassi began to represent himself as the "director-general" (*adyakshaka janarāl*)[25] of the Japan–Sri Lanka Friendship Institute. This was a new invention. Although many monks have used the title "director" (*adyakshaka*), no Sinhala Buddhist monk—as far as I am aware—had ever used the title "director-general" as part of his monastic identity. This title, later adopted by other monks—among them Upatissa and Dhammadinna—represented a new form. Vipassi defined this identity in terms of "social service" (*samāja sēvaya*). The idea of social service, of course, is hardly a novel concept among Sri Lankan monks, but Vipassi's interpretation of it is innovative.

Vipassi's definition of monastic identity in terms of social service begins with a suggestion for "refashioning" the relation between the monk and society. This refashioning must, according to Vipassi, take place at grassroots level. First the monk should be trained to be "practical" (*praktikal venda ō nā*). The monk must go to the village and inquire of the villager about his economic problems. "The monk must help to develop the village. The village will then help to develop the temple. But most monks expect support from the villagers." Vipassi asks rhetorically, "How can the villager who is poor support the monk?" The monk must evince the virtues of economic prosperity. But the problem is that "both the monk and the villager are poor"

22. Again, these are the figures given in *Vipassi Foundation*.
23. Ibid.
24. Ibid.
25. *Vipassi Foundation* uses *director-general* and *president* interchangeably.

(*hāmuduruwot higannā, dāyakayat higannā*). Arguing that poverty poses a threat to religion, Vipassi says that "a man can live without a religion; but he cannot live without food. If poverty overcomes man, his religion will disappear. A religion cannot be built on poverty." To reverse this relation between Buddhism and society, "the monk must give to the village; not the other way around." The monk who lives at a temple and relies on the village for its existence cannot ever cultivate this new role.

Vipassi claims that from the very beginning of his public monastic life, he tried to embody and exemplify this model of social service, donating more than ninety million rupees of his wealth to the "poor."[26] The irony is that the majority of these donations went to the government and to a handful of wealthy temples. Here what I want to point out is that these narratives seeking to revise the relation between religion and society in terms of the monk's giving (money) to the layman should be seen against the background of the formations of complex power relations between monks like Vipassi, the Jayewardene state, and Japan.

Social Service and Religion, Monkhood and Wealth

In the late 1980s, Vipassi donated several million rupees to various government projects: four million rupees to the president's fund; five million rupees to Prime Minister Premadasa's *sevana* fund, a program that promised to build a "million new houses for the poor"; and two million rupees to Minister Gamini Disanayake's Mahaweli Irrigation Project.[27] The "donations" were given impressive media coverage. Leading Sri Lankan newspapers and the state-owned TV ran headlines picturing Vipassi as he handed over the checks to the government.[28] These donations won Vipassi nationwide popularity as a wealthy Buddhist monk. Some began to call him the Japanese "wish-tree" (*japan kapruka*).

The Jayewardene government reciprocated Vipassi's donations in several ways. On occasion, the president met and posed for pictures with Vipassi's donors at the president's official residence.[29] On other occasions, the president, along with Prime Minister Premadasa, visited the Japan–Sri Lanka Institute

---

26. In 1998, the exchange rate for U.S. $1 was Rs.62.2. The amount Rs.90 million (almost $1.5 million) is calculated from the list of donations mentioned in *Vipassi Foundation*.

27. Ibid.

28. Personal observations from 1984 to 1988.

29. Interviews with several monks.

to "sip tea" with Vipassi's Japanese donors.[30] Sometimes such donors received gifts from the president, such as the Buddha's relics and saplings of the Sri Maha Bo Tree in Anuradhapura.[31] The government also extended Vipassi more tangible support. In 1986 it granted to Vipassi a large block of land with a three-story, dilapidated building in Haputale. He spent thirteen million rupees on renovating the building and converted it into a "higher educational institute [called Kobodaishi] for students unable to attend national universities."[32] One Sinhala Buddhist monk bluntly commented on the state's patronage to the Japanese donors: "These rich Japanese have nothing to do. Nobody cares about them [*velenavā*] in Japan, but they are treated as kings in Sri Lanka. Here they pay for what they cannot buy in Japan: prestige [*nambunāma*]."[33]

The Jayewardene government's support for Vipassi extended beyond the shores of Sri Lanka. Once Prime Minister Premadasa accompanied Vipassi to Japan as a special guest at the Shingon temple.[34] Even after his term ended, President Jayewardene flew to Japan to be the main guest of honor at the Taisoji temple, one of Vipassi's main donors.[35] Such gestures authorized Vipassi's identity as a wealthy apolitical monk who did not take part in "political" activities but assisted in the state's project of developing the country. Put differently, this kind of social service was considered to be not "political" in that it did not interfere with the government's affairs.

Vipassi also donated money to more than sixty Buddhist temples (none of them, however, received more than one hundred thousand rupees). His donations to the sangha included some unconventional gifts. In 1987 he held an alms-giving ceremony for three hundred Buddhist village monks and gave each of them a cassette radio, claiming that "the village monks cannot afford even a radio to listen to Buddhist preaching and pirit chanting." He also gave luxury automobiles to several monks whom he described as those who "live simple lives dedicating to social service even in the wake of the modern technology." These donations received wide media publicity.[36]

30. *Vipassi Foundation.*
31. Ibid.
32. *Vipassi Foundation.* Within a few years, the Kobodaishi Educational Institute was closed.
33. A conversation with a monk at the Isipatanaramaya temple, Colombo, Aug. 9, 1994.
34. A framed picture of Vipassi on an airplane seated next to Prime Minister Premadasa hangs in Vipassi's residence.
35. *Vipassi Foundation.*
36. Ibid.

The significance of the central visibility of these practices of gift-giving to the government must be located in the context of there being other, competing, Buddhist monks, practices, and narratives.

A good example of the competition is the Gangaramaya temple of Gala-boda Ñanissara (popularly known as *podi hāmuduruwō*), in Hunupitiya, Colombo.[37] A pamphlet issued by Ñanissara's temple claims that it provides seventy-seven "social and religious services."[38] Among them is the Technical Training Center, begun in 1979 to "provide free education to students unable to attend national universities due to financial difficulties"[39] (note how eerily similar this sounds to Vipassi's Kobodaishi institute). The Training Center has grown over the years, and today more than four thousand students receive education from it.[40] Other projects at Gangaramaya include a Bhikkhu Train-ing Institute and a Free Nursery School, all supported primarily by foreign nationals from countries such as Japan, Thailand, and Taiwan. Among Ñanis-sara's other "social and religious services" (again like Vipassi's) are various donations to the sangha. In 1979, Ñanissara introduced a new cultural pag-eant, "Navam Perahära." Each year, Ñanissara donated 450 robes imported from Thailand to monks who walked in the pageant, which appeared in broadcasts nationwide. Ñanissara also held massive alms-giving ceremonies for monks. Once he offered a *dāna* to five thousand Bhikkhus at his temple and gave each an "electric hair cutter." Some monks praised it: "Since Emperor Dharmashoka [who ruled India in the third century BCE] Ñanis-sara is the only individual [monk] to assemble such a large number of monks in one location and offer alms."[41]

Ñanissara, too, "donated" money to the Sri Lankan government. In 1989 he collected 1.8 million rupees from his patrons and donated it to newly

37. On some innovative aspects of Ñanissara's temple, see Richard Gombrich, "Temporary Ordination in Sri Lanka," *Journal of the International Association of Buddhist Studies* 7, no. 2 (1984): 41–65. But Gombrich thinks in the most orientalist fashion that "innovative" practices at Gangaramaya "may put the Sangha's *traditionally distinctive character* at risk" (63) (my emphasis).

38. *Gangarama Viharaya: Historical Background*, pamphlet, 1995.

39. Ibid.; *15 Vasarak Sapirena Jinaratana Kārmika Vidyālaya, 1979–1994* (Celebrating the fifteenth anniversary of the Jinaratana Vocational Training Center) (Colombo: Sri Jinaratana Karmika Vidyalaya, 1994).

40. Since 1979, a few other monks have started similar technical institutes. In 1981, Bellan-wila Wimalaratana started a similar project at his temple, as did Inamaluwe Sumangala at the Dambulla temple.

41. "Lokuväda Karana Podi Hāmuduruwō" ("The little monk who does big things"), *Lanka-dīpa*, Dec. 12, 1993.

elected President Premadasa for his Janasaviya Fund designed to help the "poor."[42] Subsequently, Premadasa offered Ñanissara four acres of state land and helped to build a luxury Pilgrims' Rest at Kataragama.[43] The resthouse, listed as one of Ñanissara's social and religious service programs, claims to provide free accommodation to both "rich and poor" pilgrims visiting the "sacred" city of the god Kataragama. Yet the rest is mostly used by the wealthy patrons of Ñanissara's temple during their vacations in Kataragama.[44] Premadasa's famous association with Ñanissara attracted many wealthy Colombo businessmen willing to pour money into the temple's social-service projects. In many cases, Prime Minister Premadasa himself organized and chaired meetings to solicit funds from these patrons[45]; in return, the donors received various state incentives such as exemption from income tax.[46]

My point is that Vipassi's impressive donations to the state and to monks must be located in the context of these competing monastic practices. In 1987, for example, Prime Minister Premadasa decided to construct a "gold canopy" (ran viyana) over the Tooth Temple of the Buddha, the "national palladium" of Sinhala Buddhists.[47] Vipassi rushed to support Premadasa's plan, donating three million rupees toward the cost of the canopy. Vipassi's gift impressed the chief monks of the Asgiriya and Malwatte Chapters, the custodians of the Tooth Temple. A few months later, as a rare gesture of appreciation, chief monks Sirimalwatte Ananda and Palipana Chandananda accepted Vipassi's invitation to fly to Japan and participate in a Buddhist ceremony held every fifty years at the headquarters of the Shingon temple in Japan.[48] In so doing, the chief monks symbolically endorsed Vipassi's relations with a Japanese Mahayana temple that became a centrally visible site of controversy and contestation in Sri Lanka.

In 1990, Vipassi announced that he would give up his "Theravada" monastic identity and become a Mahayana monk of the Shingon Buddhist tradition in Japan. The announcement, which received a spate of media

42. "New Thinking," editorial, Daily News, Mar. 25, 1989.

43. Pamphlet, Religious Rest at Kataragama; "Where the Pilgrims Rest," Sunday Leader, Jan. 1, 1996.

44. Conversations with patrons of the Gangarama temple, Nov. 1996.

45. Conversations with Ajit Serasundara, Aug. 24, 1997.

46. See pamphlet Navam Mahā Perahära: 1996 Pebaravāri 02–03 Vädasatahana (Navam Pageant: Agenda for Feb. 2–3, 1996).

47. The construction of the golden canopy is detailed in chapter 5.

48. Vipassi Foundation.

attention, generated a polemical debate between Vipassi, other monks, and lay Buddhists about Buddhism, difference, the nation, and state. The debate can be more meaningfully studied against the background of another signifi-cant event in the history of Sri Lanka–Japan relations: the visit of the Japan-ese prime minister to Sri Lanka in 1990. This event will help us see that the production of these discourses, which celebrated Japanese Mahayana Bud-dhism as "authentic" Buddhism and called into question the identity of Sri Lanka's supposed "pure" Buddhism, which the Sri Lankan state was officially obliged to safeguard, was indeed facilitated by the state's open-market policies and their relation to Japan.

On May 3, 1990, weeks before Vipassi announced his plans to convert to Shingon Buddhism, the newly elected Japanese prime minister, Toshiki Kaifu, visited Sri Lanka. The prime minister's visit was an occasion of great festivity because Kaifu was the first head of state from Tokyo to visit Sri Lanka in thirty-four years. The government of President Premadasa (who had suc-ceeded President Jayewardene) accorded the Japanese prime minister the highest possible welcome. The state newspapers ran pages greeting the prime minister's arrival. The *Daily News* ran front-page headlines: "Red Carpet for Japan's PM and First Lady." A full page inside the newspaper welcomed Kaifu, saying: "Konnichiwa, Prime Minister: Sri Lanka opens its doors to your excellency with the fragrance of her lotus & olu flowers."[49] During Kaifu's visit, the state-run *Daily News* and its Sinhala version, *Divayina*, dedicated pages to glorifying Japan's "influence" on Sri Lankan life, from television and automobiles to childhood education. At the banquet for the prime minister, Premadasa remarked that the visit marked "a time when we were emerging from a dark and dismal night into a dawn of great promise" and noted that "Sri Lanka salutes the Japanese people. We applaud your leadership."[50]

During the Kaifu festivities, Vipassi was absent, visiting Japan, and Bana-gala Upatissa stole the limelight. Upatissa, like Vipassi, had already estab-lished significant alliances with Japan. In 1979, funded by his most steadfast donor, Mrs. Tokiko Yoshida, owner of the Yoshida Private Hospital in Japan, Upatissa had founded the Yoshida Free Nursery School. Five years later Upatissa created the Japan–Sri Lanka Buddhist Center and claimed that it constituted "the headquarters of Theravada Buddhism in Japan." By 1990,

49. *Daily News*, May 3, 1990.
50. "We Are Entering a Dawn of Great Promise: President," *Daily News*, May 4, 1990.

Upatissa had established twelve more free nursery schools in various parts of the island—all funded by, and named after, Japanese philanthropists. Upatissa did not, however, enjoy Vipassi's islandwide popularity, perhaps because of the latter's impressive monetary "donations" to the government.

Upatissa used the occasion of Kaifu's visit to publicize himself and his Japanese kindergartens.[51] An entire page in the *Daily News* listed all his nursery schools and introduced Upatissa as director-general of the Yoshida Social and Educational Foundation. The page, which contained a picture of the Japanese prime minister seated with two Japanese children, further said that "every Sri Lankan is obliged to the Japanese for all what [*sic*] we have gained from them."[52] Upatissa personally met with Kaifu, the newspapers carrying pictures of the meeting at the Hilton Hotel.[53] Undoubtedly, Upatissa's involvement in Kaifu's visit to Sri Lanka helped him earn the kind of state support that he had not received before. A year later, President Premadasa awarded Mrs. Yoshida, Upatissa's premier Japanese donor, the Sri Lanka Ranjana Award, one of the most distinguished state awards and one usually reserved for the highest foreign dignitaries.[54] A few days following Kaifu's visit, newspapers reported Prime Minister D. B. Wijetunga's statement that "everybody in the country should honor Upatissa for the great service he has been rendering to the development of Japanese-style childhood education in the country."[55] It was in this context—the glorification of Japan as a great Buddhist country—that Vipassi made the public announcement of his conversion to the Mahayana Shingon sect.

The Production of a "Religious" Debate: "Authentic" Religion, Difference, and the State

A few days following Kaifu's departure from Sri Lanka, the front pages of local newspapers carried reports that on May 27, 1990, the former Theravada

---

51. Upatissa renamed Banagala, his village, as "Naritasangama" (The village of Naritasan) after the Japanese temple Naritasan Vihara, whose chief incumbent, Shojin Hashimoto, financed the building of eighty houses in the village; see the booklet *Yoshida Nursery Institute: 15 Anniversary Commemoration Souvenir* (Colombo: ANCL Commercial Printing Dept., n.d.).

52. *Daily News*, May 4, 1990.

53. *Dinamina*, May 5, 1990.

54. Yoshida Free Nursery Institute.

55. "Naritasam Ladaru Pāsal Sankranaya Ranpokunugamata Nava Ālōkayak" ("The Naritasan nursery school scheme is a new beacon of hope to the village of Ranpokunugama"), *Dinamina*, May 9, 1990.

Pelpola Vipassi would arrive in the island as a Mahayana monk.[56] Soon the report was interpreted by a number of monks as an attempt by Vipassi and Japanese temples to introduce Mahayana Buddhism to Sri Lanka and wipe out the "pure" (*nirmala*) Theravada Buddhist tradition.[57] Among the notable monks who spearheaded the intransigent opposition to Vipassi was Labugama Lankananda, the head of the monastic chapter of the Siyam Nikya in Kotte. Vipassi received his higher ordination from Lankananda's chapter and so was technically considered a member of Lankananda's Kelaniya chapter. Vipassi, however, did not associate with, much less share his wealth with, Lankananda's temple.

It is obvious that the relationship between Vipassi and Lankananda, which became quite contentious and polemical later, involved some issues of power. In the mid-1980s, Lankananda appointed Banagala Upatissa as the chief sangha *nāyaka* of Japan (*japānaye pradhāna sangha nāyaka*). The title was a symbolic act of recognizing Upatissa's authority over other (Sri Lankan) Buddhist monks living in Japan. Vipassi, as some of my monk-informants noted, became quite unhappy about Lankananda's decision to confer the title on Upatissa because Vipassi felt that he was not only senior to Upatissa but was one of the first Sri Lankan monks to develop serious cultural relations with Japan. This disagreement with Lankananda may later have caused Vipassi to ally himself with the chief monks of the Asgiriya and Malwatte chapters and eventually invite them to visit the Shingon headquarters in Japan.

Lankananda played a leading role in dramatizing the report about Vipassi's conversion to Mahayana Buddhism. He was the first monk to write to Sri Lankan newspapers, expressing "deep concern" about "a member of his monastic order [who] would soon return to the Island after becoming a Mahayana Bhikkhu in Japan." He stressed that what Vipassi had done "was in conflict with the Theravada order of Bhikkhus in Sri Lanka."[58] The front pages of the state newspapers carried a statement by Lankananda, in both Sinhala and English, describing the "conflict" between the Theravada tradition and the Mahayana in Sri Lanka:

> The history of the Theravada Buddhist tradition and its lineage of Buddhist monks in Sri Lanka is over two thousand years old. Sri Lankan history shows that some have attempted to bring Mahayana Buddhism to this

---

56. "Mahanayake Expresses Concern," *Daily News*, May 12, 1990.
57. "Sangha Stresses the Need to Preserve Theravada Tradition," *Daily News*, May 13, 1990.
58. *Daily News*, May 12, 1992.

country, but because of the vigorous opposition by educated Buddhist monks and kings, such attempts were derailed. Whenever the order of monks became weak, the committed monks have reestablished and fortified it by restoring higher ordination. Sri Lanka enjoyed the supreme place, holding the only Theravada monastic lineage that follows the early teachings of the Buddha, unaffected by other influences.[59]

In the same statement, Lankananda officially informed President Premadasa, the minister of the Buddhasasana, of the looming danger of the spread of Mahayana Buddhism in Sri Lanka. Appealing to the president to "safeguard" the Theravada tradition from the Mahayana, he wrote:

> Buddhist monks have received unstinting support from the kings of the past to protect the lineage of the Theravada Buddhist monasticism. Thus, as the present minister, bearing the responsibility for safeguarding the Buddha Sasana, you must take all appropriate measures to completely defeat Vipassi's effort to spread Mahayana Buddhism in the island. If Pelpola Vipassi arrives in Sri Lanka as a Mahayana monk, it must be condemned as an effort to distort Buddhism. It is a treacherous act that will humiliate the monks in Sri Lanka. We report to the monks of the three Nikyas, the President Premadasa, and the people of Sri Lanka that we have expelled Vipassi from our fraternity.[60]

Other influential monks joined in this appeal to the president to protect Theravada Buddhism. Kamburupitiye Wanaratana, the head of the Rohana chapter of the Siyam Nikya, put pressure on President Premadasa, stressing that "if the Theravada tradition is rescued, the president's name will be recorded in the history of Buddhism."[61] Wanaratana demanded that "when the history of this period of Lanka is written, no room be left to record that Mahayana entered this country and polluted the Theravada." He also warned that if Mahayana Buddhism "infiltrates" Sri Lanka, the president, along with monks and lay Buddhist leaders, should "bear full responsibility."[62] In a similar

59. "Pelpola Himi Nikāyen Ivatata: Janādhipatitat Danvati" ("Pelpola expelled from the Nikāya: The president is also notified"), *Dinamina*, May 13, 1990.

60. Ibid.

61. "Theravādi Bududahama Bērāgattot Janapati Nama Sāsana Itihāsaye Liyavēvi" ("If Theravāda Buddhism is rescued, the president's name will be recorded in the history of Buddhism"), *Dinamina*, May 15, 1990.

62. "President Must Ensure that Theravāda Tradition Is Not Tarnished," *Daily News*, 15, 1990.

vein, Madihe Paññasiha, the chief monk of the Amarapura fraternity, told the president that "just as the devoted kings did in the past, the president should stop this destruction (*vināsaya natarakaranna*) of Buddhism right at the airport."[63] Bellanwila Wimalaratana argued that the protection of Theravada Buddhism is a constitutional requirement.[64] Prominent Sinhalese lay Buddhists like Harischandara Wijetunga used the occasion to articulate a specific nationalist discourse: "This Sinhala Buddhist country belongs to Sinhala Buddhists. It is because Buddhism is the main religion of the country that people of other religions can live in Sri Lanka. It is our Buddhism. We will not let it be destroyed."[65]

President Premadasa seemed to remain, at best, ambivalent about this controversy. As the letters by monks calling on Premadasa to "safeguard" Theravada inundated the newspapers, the president's office issued a statement saying that the ceremony, earlier arranged to welcome Vipassi's return to the island as a Mahayana Buddhist monk, "will receive no state patronage." The statement, however, added that the "President intends to act in accordance with the advice of *the chief monks of all three Buddhist fraternities*" (my emphasis).[66] According to one Sinhalese commentator, what President Premadasa meant by the statement was to ask: "What about the chief monks of the Asgiriya and Malwatte chapters who have not yet expressed their views?"[67] And it was true that not all the chief monks shared the urgency of Lankananda's call to the government to protect Theravada Buddhism. The chief monks of Malwatte and Asgiriya refused to comment on the debate, saying that "Vipassi does not belong to our Nikāya."[68]

Premadasa let monks and lay people fight the issue in the state media for several weeks, seemingly siding with no monastic party. There was, however, more to the president's apparent neutrality than met the eye. The central visibility of the Mahayana debate enabled (and manipulated) by the state media

63. "Mē Buddha Sāsana Vināsaya Guvan Totupalen Avasan Karananna" ("Terminate this destruction of Buddhism at the airport"), *Dinamina*, May 14, 1990.

64. "[State's] Duty to Protect the Theravada Buddha Sasana," *Daily News*, May 15, 1990.

65. "Āgamika Nidahasa Labā Dī Äti Vyavastāva Rakimuda? Nätinam Bududahama Rakimuda?" ("Should we protect the constitution that has granted religious freedom? Or should we protect Buddhism?"), *Divayina*, May 23, 1990.

66. "No State Patronage to Ven. Vipassi's Reception."

67. "Mahāyāna Bhītiya," unidentified clipping, n.d.

68. "Mahasangha Ruvana Virōdhaya Pāti" ("The mahāsangha object"), *Divayina*, May 14, 1990.

overshadowed, for a while, the discursive space of other controversies revolving around Premadasa's presidency.[69] For example, at a public meeting designed to discuss the issue of Mahayana Buddhism, Lankananda spoke of Vipassi's supposed plans to convert to the Mahayana as a movement of "terror." Now this discourse of terror authorized the articulation of a particular kind of relation between Buddhism and difference. The state newspapers reported Lankananda as stating: "If the Terror of the Mahayana (*mahāyāna bhīshanaya*) is not eradicated, everybody will repent later,"[70] and within days, posters stating "Let us Terminate the Terror of the Mahayana" popped up throughout Colombo.[71]

The depiction of Mahayana Buddhism as "terror" worked to improve, somewhat, the popularity of President Premadasa. That popularity had been diminishing. During Premadasa's tenure, between 1989 and 1990, Sri Lanka had witnessed unprecedented killings, committed by both the forces of the government and the JVP movement that was attempting to unseat Premadasa.[72] Many Sri Lankans—both monks and lay people—referred to the period as "the time of terror" (*bhīshana kālaya*). Some spoke of Premadasa as a "dangerous man" (*bhayānaka minihā*) responsible for the state of the country at the time.[73] In the early 1990s, just before the Theravada/Mahayana debate, an impeachment motion was brought against Premadasa, charging his government with unleashing "a reign of terror."[74] The Theravada/Mahayana debate, in which one side portrayed Premadasa as the president who would "carve [out] a special niche in history,"[75] helped, temporarily, to derail some of the pervasive criticisms of the government.

The discursive focus of the debate about the "conflict" between Mahayana and Theravada, religious orthodoxy and unorthodoxy, came to center on

69. Ibid.

70. "Mahāyāna Bhīshanaya Pitu Nodäkkot Pasuva Hämatama Pasutävilivannat Vēvi" ("If the terror of Mahayana is not eradicated, everybody will repent later"), *Dinamina*, May 23, 1990.

71. "Mahāyānaya Prashnaya," *Divayina*, May 26, 1990.

72. Hence the reference to it as "a dark and dismal night" by Premadasa himself; *Daily News*, "We Are Entering a Dawn of Great Promise."

73. In fact, only hours after his assassination in 1993, many people in Colombo burned firecrackers in an expression of joy at his death.

74. On this controversy, see V. A. Sarat Lal Kumara, *Dōshabhiyōgaya* (Impeachment) (Wadduwa: Dinusha Mudranalaya, 1994); Joshine van der Horst, *Who Is He, What Is He Doing?* 161–63, 167, 206–9. For the ways in which "terror" was deployed as a discourse by competing political parties in the 1980s and 1990s, see chapter 7.

75. *Daily News*, "President Must Ensure."

Premadasa's identity as the head of state and minister of the Buddhasasana who would follow in the footsteps of ancient kings to rescue Sri Lanka from the "Mahayana terror."[76] It is perhaps because the debate began to revolve around the president that some nongovernment newspapers decided that they would no longer discuss the "Mahayana question." The editorial in the *Island* newspaper stated the Mahayana debate had taken on too much "political" significance.[77] The state newspapers, however, continued to place Premadasa in the center of the debate and labored to marginalize competing negative portrayals of the government. An editorial appearing in the *Daily News* stated:

> The Constitution of the Democratic Socialist Republic of Sri Lanka requires that the Republic confers the "foremost place" to Buddhism, the religion of the majority of the people of the country, and casts upon it the duty of protecting and fostering the Buddhasasana. President Premadasa, who is also the Minister for [*sic*] the Buddhasasana, has during his tenure amply demonstrated his meticulous adherence to the obligations cast upon him as Head of State and Head of Government. . . . The Buddhists of Sri Lanka are confident that he would not in any way permit any harm to be done to the Buddhasasana.[78]

The editorial added that there was no question that Sri Lanka was the "repository of the Theravada tradition" and that "no Buddhist would dispute" the expulsion of Vipassi from the Theravada tradition.

My point is that the debate authorized a particular kind of "difference"—that is, the "terror of the Mahayana"—and enabled it to come into full view. Making visible that difference, keeping the "otherness" of the Mahayana terror at the center of discourse, as a danger to the "identity" of the pure Theravada, embodied particular stakes. This, I argue, is part of the complex process that governs the constructions of the shifting relation between identity and difference, self and other.

Backed by some other monks and lay Buddhists, Vipassi jockeyed to challenge this authorized relation between Buddhism and difference, the

76. In a review article that gives insufficient attention to the complex dynamics of the controversy, John Holt, in a rather colonialist fashion, alludes to this debate as an instance of religious "fanaticism and militancy" that marks a "transition from the truly liberal attitudes of the seventeenth century"; Holt, "Protestant Buddhism?" *Religious Studies Review* 17, no. 4 (1991): 310.

77. "Mahāyāna Prashnaya," *Divayina*, May 26, 1990.

78. "Protecting the Buddha Sasana," *Daily News*, May 16, 1990.

Theravada "Self" and the Mahayana "Other," shifting the focus of the debate from the president to the economic and social "ills" of Sri Lanka. In letters to newspapers, Vipassi claimed that he decided to join the Mahayana tradition because while he was a Theravada monk he was nurtured and fostered (*pōshanaya unē*) not by Theravada monks but by Mahayana temples. He said that Theravada Buddhism could no longer address the problems of the "modern man"; the solution to them was Mahayana Buddhism.[79] The goal of Mahayana Buddhism, as Vipassi saw it, was to build a *mahāpurisa* (great human being): "It wants to turn man into a king, a powerful being. The Theravada does not do it. It talks too much about the other-worldly development; it emphasizes that everybody should attain Nirvana. Nirvana is not possible today. [But] Mahayana Buddhism talks about the development of this world."[80] The kind of Mahayana Buddhism that can respond to the problems of the contemporary world, Vipassi claimed, cannot come from just any Mahayana Buddhist country; it must come from Japan because the "Japanese have much to teach Sri Lankans."[81]

A number of monks and lay Buddhists rushed to side with Vipassi's criticisms of Theravada Buddhism in Sri Lanka. Monk Pallawela Devarakkhita wrote to *Divayina* that the Theravada tradition could no longer ignore Mahayana Buddhism because of its contribution to "economic and social development" in Japan. Dhammarakkhita claimed that when the Mazda car company in Hiroshima faced a serious economic crisis in 1973, the company's new director sent its employees for Zen training; within a few years, the company recovered and doubled its sales by improving its productivity. Zen Buddhist meditation, Devarakkhita argued, saved the Mazda company from an economic disaster.[82] Some Sinhala lay Buddhists argued along similar economic lines, undermining the discourse of the Mahayana terror by pinning the blame on Theravada Buddhism for the problem of poverty in Sri Lanka.[83]

79. "Ven. Vipassi's New Order," *Sunday Times*, Nov. 11, 1990.

80. Ibid.

81. "Japan Hapan Kam Valin Apata Gata Häki Pādam" ("The lessons we can learn from the achievements of the Japanese"), *Lankādīpa*, Feb. 6, 1994.

82. "Mahāyānaya Hīnayānaya Saha Säbä Yānaya" ("Mahayanaya, Hinayana, and the real yayana"), *Divayina*, May 23, 1990.

83. "Mahāyāna Välada Gänīme Varadak Tibēda?" ("Is it wrong to accept Mahayana Buddhism?"), *Divayina*, May 17, 1990. For similar views, see "Theravāda Sankalpaya Pirihilā" ("The Theravada concept has deteriorated"), *Lankādīpa*, May 6, 1990.

Vipassi questioned the Theravada identity of Sinhala monks; he charged that some of the monks who now criticized Mahayana Buddhism had benefited from "Mahayana money." He named his main detractor Labugama Lankananda as one such monk and said that the Sinhala Theravada monks and politicians who accepted Mahayana money "have practiced Mahayana Buddhism." He accused some Sri Lankan monks of possessing "mines of wealth" (*dhana ulpat*) and leading "more materialistic and self-indulgent [*kāmasukallikānu*] lives than the Japanese monks."[84] Less than three weeks after the debate's beginnings, Vipassi journeyed to Japan and took ordination as a Shingon (Mahayana) monk.[85] He remained in Japan for five years, disappearing from public view in Sri Lanka.[86]

This chapter so far has located some dimensions of the emergence of a new economy of narratives about "Buddhism" in the discursive site of constructing a free-market economy in modern Sri Lanka. What has interested me has been the narratives that made possible the central visibility of the relation between Buddhism and difference, orthodoxy and unorthodoxy; that is, the ways in which specific persons and practices came into view as identity and faded from view as difference. The appearing into sight and disappearing from sight of Vipassi, and his narratives and practices in the context of opening up economic relations between Japan and Sri Lanka, tell us something very complex about the discursively constituted, shifting relations between religious identity and difference. In other words, "Vipassi," as I have read this history, is a name for a complex network of narratives, practices, and persons that authorized particular forms of religious "identity" (the Theravada Buddhist "Self") while producing differences (Mahayana "unBuddhist" others) to be subordinated and marginalized in different contexts.

Earlier in his career, Vipassi corresponded to the Jayewardene state's prototype of an apolitical monk. Vipassi's narratives about social service and developing the village fit in well with the state's plans to "develop the country." His centrally visible "donations" of millions of rupees to state-sponsored organizations symbolically endorsed the ideals of a capitalist economy that had come under siege from leading opponent-monks and lay Buddhists in Sri

---

84. "Hinayānaya, Mahāyānaya Hā Hāmuduruvange [sic] Yatārta Vādaya" ("Hīnayanana, Mahayanaya, and monks' practicality"), *Divayina*, May 1990.

85. *Sunday Times*, "Vipassi's New Order."

86. Vipassi returned to Sri Lanka later and allied himself with the new government of Chandrika Bandaranaike.

Lanka. Later, the discourse of the "Mahayana terror," which was ostensibly about the innate differences between the "authentic" Theravada/Self and the "corrupt" Mahayana/other, decentered the previously authorized relations between Theravada Buddhism and the Japanese Mahayana, Vipassi's monastic identity and the state, centering other "Buddhist" persons and practices in Sri Lanka. I have argued that such shifting relations between what does and does not constitute authentic Buddhism, as against differences, are located in complex economies of competing narratives. In the next section, I examine the centering and subordinating of some other remarkable narratives about Buddhism and society.

Kananke Dhammadinna

Other Centered and Decentered New Narratives of Buddhism

Kananke Dhammadinna was one of Vipassi's and Upatissa's colleagues at the Mahabodhi Society in Colombo.[87] In the late 1960s, around the age of twelve, Dhammadinna arrived at the Mahabodhi Society and became a monk under the guidance of Hedigalle Paññatissa. Within a few years, because of a dispute with the incumbent monk of the temple, Dhammadinna left the temple. In the early 1970s, terminating his studies at the Vidyodaya Pirivena, he traveled to India, where he pursued undergraduate work at Nalanda University. Later he obtained a doctorate from Benares University for a thesis entitled "Aspects of Mahayana Buddhism in Sri Lanka."

In the mid-1980s, Dhammadinna traveled to Japan to attend the one hundredth birthday of Nichidatsu Puji. In Japan, a monk friend introduced Dhammadinna to the Venerable Shinjo Ito, the founder of the Shinnyo-en Buddhist movement that originated in early 1936.[88] The movement, headed by a family team—Shinjo Ito, his wife, and, later, their daughters—centers around the belief that the two late sons of the family reside in a distant paradise and that, by means of telepathy, the members of the family can

---

87. I conducted two lengthy interviews in English with Dhammadinna on July 23, 1994, and August 9, 1995; I have, however, known him since 1985.

88. For an account of the genesis of the Shinnyo-en in terms of its doctrines, see Jamie Hubbard, "Embarrassing Superstition, Doctrine, and the Study of New Religious Movements," *Journal of the American Academy of Religion* 66, no. 1 (1998): 59–92. I do not share Hubbard's conviction that the examination of the "doctrines" in and of themselves explains the significance of the Shinnyo-en as a "new religious movement." Hubbard fails to locate the Shinnyo-en in relation to competing religious movements in Japan.

evoke the late sons' powers and blessings on the Shinnyo-en devotees. Today, Shinyo-en, with more than one million followers, numbers among the wealthiest Japanese Buddhist organizations; it has branches in many parts of the world, including the United States.[89]

Dhammadinna considers his meeting with Ito to have been a privilege: "ordinary" lay devotees of the temple rarely see, much less converse with, the founder of the Shinnyo-en. A few months after their meeting, Ito invited Dhammadinna to become the international representative of the Shinnyo-en in Sri Lanka. Ito extended this invitation because Dhammadinna, following his initial visit to Japan, had brought to the Shinnyo-en temple a delegation of influential Sri Lankan chief monks, among them Hedigalle Paññatissa and Palipana Chandananda, who suggested that Dhammadinna be trained to propagate the Shinnyo-en Buddhist doctrine in Sri Lanka.[90]

In the mid-1980s, Dhammadinna officially became a member of the Shinnyo-en temple and traveled frequently to Japan, earning a handsome monthly salary. During this time, he wrote to Sri Lankan newspapers suggesting that "the difference between the Theravada and the Mahayana be eliminated through the Buddha's teaching." Central to this suggestion was a scathing criticism of the Sinhalese sangha and its ways of understanding and preaching Buddhism.[91] He accused the monks of distorting and misrepresenting the "original" teaching of the Buddha.[92] The Buddha "pointed out the path to the victory of life. . . . What has happened today? Monks preach to Buddhists about 'remorse' (kalakīrīma), 'afterlife' (paralova), and 'death' (maranaya). These sermons have made Buddhists depressed and "inactive" (kriyāvirahita). Today people need monks only when they die. The monk has become a "death contractor" (marana kontratkaruvā).[93] It is not Buddhism's fault; it is the fault of the monks who have preached wrong bana for a long time, without a real knowledge of Buddhism." He questioned the significance of the monks who meditate in "seclusion," saying Buddhism does not belong in a forest; if Buddhism is to survive, it must live in a world of human

89. Interview with Dhammadinna, 1995.

90. "Breach of Trust Case: Ven. Pannatissa Thera Recommended Dhammadinna Thera—Witness," *Island*, Sept. 29, 1993.

91. "Theravāda Hā Mahāyāna Atara Venasa Bududahamen Venas Kala Yutuyi," *Divayina*, Dec. 13, 1985.

92. "Jīvitayē Päradma Gäna Kiyana Väradi Bana" ("Wrong sermons [Sri Lankan monks preach] about the defeat of human life"), *Davasa*, Jan. 19, 1988.

93. "Bauddhayanta Mak Velāda" ("What happened to Buddhists?"), *Davasa*, Jan. 19, 1988.

activities and problems.[94] The new problems of Sri Lanka, he said, required a "new way of thinking" (*alut vidiyata hitanda*). "Let's talk about nirvāna and meditation after we develop the country [*rata diyunu kalāta passe*], after we solve the problems of the country. Let's meditate after we eliminate hunger."[95]

It was in the context of voicing these kinds of polemic that Dhammadinna established the Shinnyo-en free nursery school. The impressive, two-story school, constructed at a cost of more than fifteen million rupees donated by the Shinnyo-en headquarters, is located in Pamankada, a prime residential area of Colombo. It provided free education to four hundred children between the ages of three and five and employed a staff of forty teachers. The children came from various parts of Colombo and received free uniforms, snacks, and transportation to and from the school. The school's monthly maintenance cost (more than US$30,000) was provided by Shinnyo-en head-quarters.[96] Dhammadinna, appropriating Vipassi's term, became director-general of the nursery.[97]

The opening of this spectacular nursery school made headlines in news-papers and on television. In a speech, the chief guest, President J. R. Jayewar-dene,[98] recalled his famous words in San Francisco and said that the nursery school was a symbol of Japan's continuing gratitude to Sri Lanka because of Sri Lanka's involvement in gaining independence for Japan. Jayewardene, like Dhammadinna, said that Japan presented examples of economic and spiritual development from which "Sri Lanka must learn." Jayewardene promised to "extend the government's full support to Dhammadinna's Shin-nyo-en Nursery School" for carrying out social service and maintaining cul-tural relations between Japan and Sri Lanka.[99]

The Jayewardene government extended its support to Dhammadinna long before the Shinnyo-en nursery school was founded. In fact, the Shinnyo-en temple entrusted Dhammadinna with millions of dollars to build the nursery because of his "close connections" with the Sri Lankan government. In the

94. Ibid.
95. "Sinhalayāge Alasakamata."
96. From my interviews in 1995 with school staff.
97. *Dinamina*, Jan. 25, 1988.
98. Personal observations in Colombo, Jan. 1988.
99. Speech delivered by J. R. Jayewardene at the opening of the nursery school, Pamankada, Jan. 23, 1988; copy of the speech obtained from the Jayewardene Cultural Center. Also see "Japānaya Sri Lankāvata Ādāra Karnne Kelehi Guna Sälakimak Vasayen" ("Japan assists Sri Lanka to show its gratitude"), *Dinamina*, Jan. 25, 1988.

early 1980s, following Dhammadinna's proposal, a delegation of Shinnyo-en monks flew to Sri Lanka to discuss the construction of a Shinnyo-en school in Sri Lanka. At the Katunayake airport, the Japanese delegates received privileges conventionally accorded to foreign dignitaries, passing through immigration and customs without check-in and being taken to meet Jayewardene and others of Sri Lanka's elite.[100] The delegation met Prime Minister Premadasa and, at Dhammadinna's suggestion, made cash donations to Premadasa's housing project, *gam udāva*. Premadasa presented the Japanese with a sapling of the Anuradhapura Bo Tree, and today the Bo-sapling, planted at Shinnyo-en headquarters, forms an important part of the temple's definition of its identity.[101]

Supported by the government, Dhammadinna, like Vipassi, pursued significant relations with Japanese temples, and in the process he became one of Sri Lanka's wealthiest men. Documented evidence shows that by 1990 Dhammadinna possessed several bank accounts in Sri Lanka and England, with balances worth millions of U.S. dollars. He owned a number of properties: hundreds of acres of land in Sri Lanka and two private homes in England. One home was purchased in the name of Champa Patra Dhammadinna, an Indian woman alleged to be his wife.[102] The source of Dhammadinna's wealth, of course, is a subject of controversy. Dhammadinna maintained that Shinjo Ito gave him much of that money in recognition of his service to the Shinnyo-en temple. He admitted that, while director-general of the Shinnyo-en nursery school he "enjoyed an affluent life." Eventually, the controversy over his wealthy lifestyle altered his relations with the Shinnyo-en temple and the Sri Lankan state.

Webs of Rivalry, Questions of Identity

The story goes that suspicious Buddhist parents of pupils at the Shinnyo-en nursery school wrote to the Japanese headquarters about possible misappropriation of funds by Dhammadinna. They demanded an investigation into the monk's personal wealth. Following a preliminary inquiry in early 1992, the Shinnyo-en temple filed official charges of fraud against Dhammadinna

---

100. Interview with Shogo Kawabata, director of the Shinyo-en Nursery School, July, 1995; also mentioned in "Breach of Trust Case," *Island*, Sept. 29, 1993.

101. See Hubbard, "Embarrassing Superstition," 67.

102. "Alleged Misappropriation of US$26m: Suspect Bhikkhu Has Personal Accounts in London Banks—CID," *Observer* (London), Jan. 25, 1993.

and informed President Premadasa of the issue.[103] Immediately, Premadasa ordered the Criminal Investigation Department to arrest Dhammadinna and conduct an official investigation. Dhammadinna spent three months in prison. When I conducted my interviews with him in 1994 and 1995, he had just got out on bail and was battling a costly lawsuit against the Shinnyo-en. Tabloid newspapers had published pictures of the woman alleged to be Dhammadinna's wife and two children. Dhammadinna insisted that it was all a campaign by his "enemies" to tarnish his identity as a Buddhist monk doing a service for the country. Some monks indicated to me that, despite the early friendly relations between Premadasa and Dhammadinna, the president ordered Dhammadinna's arrest because the monk had done things that angered him.[104]

One particularly interesting story illustrates how the relations between Premadasa and Dhammadinna began to sour. Early in 1992, President Premadasa was chief guest at a religious ceremony organized by the Mahabodhi headquarters in Colombo. A crowd of several hundred people had gathered. Around the auspicious time that the president was scheduled to arrive, a dark Mercedes Benz with tinted windows, followed by a few more cars, entered the premises of the Mahabodhi headquarters. The Mercedes resembled the one in which President Premadasa usually traveled. The drummers started beating their tom-toms, and the crowd, assuming that Premadasa had arrived, marched toward the car to welcome him. To everyone's surprise, it was Dhammadinna who stepped out of the car, wearing a smug smile. When told of the incident, Premadasa became quite angry, and my informant felt it was no coincidence that Dhammadinna was arrested a few months later. Another monk told me that Dhammadinna could easily have spent many years behind bars had Premadasa not been assassinated in 1993.[105]

Closer scrutiny suggests that serious relations of monastic rivalry played some part in Dhammadinna's falling from favor with Premadasa. For instance, during the Japanese prime minister's visit to Sri Lanka in 1990, the Premadasa government noticeably showed favoritism to Upatissa: the state newspaper devoted an entire page to representing Upatissa as the "director-general" of the Yoshida Free Nursery Schools and as rendering a great service to the

103. Ibid.

104. A few monks suggested this, especially a monk of the Mahabodhi Society whom I interviewed Aug. 5, 1995.

105. Interview with monk of the Mahabodhi Society, Aug. 5, 1995.

nation. Later Premadasa presented Upatissa's favorite donor with a national award. Upatissa showed his gratitude to Premadasa. In 1989, when Premadasa celebrated the bicentennial of the Sucharita movement, a community-development program that Premadasa as a young man began in his own neighborhood in the ghetto of Colombo's inner city, Upatissa invited a delegation of Japanese people to visit the Sucharita and to donate several lakhs of rupees to Premadasa.[106]

It is worth noting that by the 1980s, Dhammadinna and Upatissa—both students of Hedigalle Paññatissa—had become archenemies. In the mid-1980s, a wealthy Buddhist woman named Mrs. Abeynayaka donated to Paññatissa a massive, colonial-style *valavva* bungalow built on about an acre of land in Pamandakada. When Dhammadinna learned about the bungalow, he persuaded Paññatissa to sign over the property to him. Later, Dhammadinna leased the property to the Shinnyo-en for several millions of rupees, and it was on this property that the Shinnyo-en Free Nursery School was built. Upatissa was several years senior to Dhammadinna, and, by law, monastic properties must pass to the teacher's most senior pupil. When Upatissa sought to regain the ownership of the property, it was to no avail. Over this issue, Upatissa became Dhammadinna's main detractor. Dhammadinna suspects that Upatissa or his allies wrote anonymous letters to the Shinnyo-en seeking to have Dhammadinna expelled from the Shinnyo-en.

Dhammadinna challenged Upatissa in a strikingly visible way: In 1989, Dhammadinna received the title of chief sangha nāyaka of Japan from the Rohana Sangha Sabha monastic fraternity. Here we have to recall that the same title had already been conferred on Upatissa by a different monastic fraternity. Dhammadinna's appointment directly challenged Upatissa since, in theory, there can be only one "chief sangha nāyaka of Japan."[107] Prime Minister D. B. Wijetunga, reportedly a relative of the monk, presented the new act of appointment to Dhammadinna in a ceremony attended by chief monks and government ministers. At the ceremony, Wijetunga stated that Dhammadinna's appointment honored the entire monastic community in

106. "Sucharita—How It All Began," *Daily News,* Nov. 11, 1989. Much of the content of this article was devoted to Sucharita. It carried pictures of Premadasa giving Upatissa and his Japanese donors a personal tour of the Sucharita premises.

107. "The Appointed Chief Sangha Nayaka for Japan," *Island,* Mar. 8, 1989. This rivalry perhaps explains why Dhammadinna would accept a monastic title that symbolized everything that Dhammadinna criticized.

Sri Lanka and that it helped "to further strengthen the existing bonds of friendship between Sri Lanka and Japan." The prime minister noted that Dhammadinna led an "exemplary life" and rendered "a great service" to the children of Sri Lanka.[108]

It is within this network of relationships, characterized by rivalry and competition, that the charges of fraud were brought against Dhammadinna. The charges, followed by his months of imprisonment, specifically questioned Dhammadinna's identity as a monk. The irony, of course, is, that the government contested the very identity of the "exemplary" monk rendering a great service to the country that it had helped to fashion. This questioning of Dhammadinna's identity as a monk is, then, a way of decentering a particular kind of relation between Buddhism and identity, monk and the state, that had come into central view at a specific time. In the remainder of this chapter, I consider the kinds of strategies that Dhammadinna employed to respond to the state's questioning of his monastic identity.

Central to his response was the strategic definition of what constitutes the identity of a Buddhist monk. The narratives that Dhammadinna used to define that relation between monastic identity and difference were made possible not only by the conjuncture in which he gained the image of an "exemplary" wealthy Buddhist monk but also by the controversies that later erupted concerning his alleged marriage to an Indian woman. Dhammadinna spoke candidly about these controversies, challenging what he called "institutionalized" views of Sinhala monastic identity. I contend that Dhammadinna's narratives and practices that seek to challenge the "institutionalized" monastic identity mark a rupture because their emergence is located in the economy of inaugurating new relations between Japan and Sri Lanka.

In explaining the "institutionalized" Sinhala views of monastic identity, Dhammadinna claims that, today, Sri Lankan Buddhists judge the identity of a monk on the basis of three "qualities or virtues:" (1) the yellow robe; (2) a shaven head; (3) eating only one or two meals a day, before twelve noon. These three practices form what he calls the "institutionalization of Buddhism." When a Buddhist monk fails to cultivate one of these virtues (that is, eats after noon, or wears his hair long), people suspect that he is not a "virtuous monk" (if the man no longer wears the robe, it goes without saying that he is no longer a monk). Dhammadinna says that the problem with these

---

108. "An Honor Bestowed on the Maha Sangha, Says PM," *Daily News*, June 1, 1989.

practices is that any person, "even a murderer," can put on a robe and pretend to be a monk. So Dhammadinna questions the significance of even the robe to the identity of a monk. But Dhammadinna still wears a robe, so as to strategically challenge the authority of the opposing narratives that question his identity as a monk.

Dhammadinna holds that, by institutionalizing the above "virtues," Sri Lankan Buddhists have assigned value to some "uncommon things" that determine the identity of a monk; he maintains that people have ignored the monk's "inner side." What he means by "uncommon things" is that the "normal habit of a human being is to eat three meals a day—breakfast, lunch, and dinner." If an "ordinary man" goes to a restaurant and eats the three meals, no one will come to him and say, "You are a *pāpi*, or a bad person. But if somebody dressed in a yellow robe goes to a restaurant to eat dinner, people will look at him as if he is a criminal who has killed a hundred people." "Not eating after noon," he continues, "has nothing to with the Buddha's philosophy." He asks rhetorically, "What nonsense is this?" He admits that he always eats after noon and is not afraid to tell people about it. Abstaining from eating after noon (*vikāla bhōjanā*) is one of the ten precepts that monks take during their ordinations; violation of the precept constitutes a minor offense. This does not mean, however, that some Buddhist monks do not eat at night and that Buddhists do not know that monks do so, but it is impossible to find a Buddhist monk eating dinner in a public place because such an act is considered highly offensive, if not taboo, in Sinhala Buddhist society. But Dhammadinna strategically questioned it.

Let me relate a brief anecdote to illustrate how his questioning of the "virtue of not eating after noon" is a particular practice located in the new conjuncture that fostered the new economic and cultural relations between Japan and Sri Lanka. In 1994, during his interview with me at his bungalow in Pamankada, Dhammadinna cut short our conversation to call on one of his Japanese monk-friends staying at the Taj Samudra, one of the five-star luxury hotels in Colombo. Dhammadinna asked me to accompany him to the hotel. After we met the Japanese monk, Dhammadinna offered to treat us to lunch at another five-star hotel, the Ramada Renaissance (now the Trans Asia) (Dhammadinna did not think too highly of the food or the ambiance at Taj Samudra). It was past noon, and the restaurant was swarming with the local business elite. It constituted a new experience for me: I had never been in a five-star hotel, much less dined at one in Sri Lanka with two Buddhist monks. In the restaurant, as the waiter guided us to a table, people were all eyes. Their staring at us became even more obvious when Dhammadinna refused the waiter's offer to bring food over to him. He walked over to the buffet table, inviting us to follow him, and then handed us two plates and began serving himself.[109] Other diners, still gaping at us, now began to murmur. Dhammadinna turned around and said to me: "You know they are talking about me because it is after noon. But if they say something to me, I [will] tell them off. I am not eating with their money." We returned to our table and ate lunch, and Dhammadinna later requested the waiter in English to put the bill on his account.

A distinct space of Buddhist monastic identity became visible here. Less significant than Dhammadinna's eating after noon was his doing so at a five-star luxury hotel, observed by local elites. His comportment at the restaurant— walking up to the buffet table; handing plates to his guests; serving himself; putting the bill on his tab—symbolically mocked the supposed "conventional" relation between Buddhism and society. It exemplified the idea that monks should not meditate in the forest but must participate in society. Dhammadinna's behavior questioned the identity of the monk "being served"—that is, the monk begging for alms, who depends on others for his subsistence and gives nothing back to them. This practice of taking from people, he claims, separates the monk from the world when it labels him as a "field of merit." The image of the dependent monk does not correspond to Dhammadinna's concept of the "active" monk who must "serve" society as opposed to society serving him.

These practices and narratives constitute "new" forms of being a Buddhist monk in that what made them possible was the "wealth" that Dhammadinna, like Vipassi, gained in the new economy. This wealth differs from the (hereditary) wealth of many Sri Lankan Buddhist landowner-monks.[110] How many such wealthy Sri Lankan monks dine at five-star hotels and speak to waiters in English? Dhammadinna's wealth was not "Sri Lankan Buddhist wealth" but "foreign wealth," in the sense that its acquisition was made possible by the Jayewardene state's opening up of the economy and its closer ties to Japan.

109. When monks visit a house for almsgiving (*dāna*), the laity serve them food. Monks seldom serve themselves.

110. Many Sri Lankan temples hold extensive land properties, donated by kings; see Kemper, "Wealth and Reformation."

This new wealth carried a special kind of authorization. It was not just "foreign wealth." The foreign wealth symbolized all those "authorized" Buddhist Japan–Sri Lanka relations through which it came to be acquired, relations endorsed by both influential monks and the "Buddhist" government of Jayewardene. It is this wealth that gave birth to these new "Buddhist" discourses and practices.

To conclude this section, I turn to Dhammadinna's narratives about the relation between monkhood and marriage, Buddhism and household life, a relationship that he suggests is indispensable to being a "real monk" in the new age.[111] Dhammadinna claims that wealth, family life, and social attachments—all, from a canonical standpoint, considered to be hindrances to the "ideal" Buddhist monastic life—are central to being a "good" Buddhist monk. To summarize Dhammadinna's views: Buddhism itself is a product of the "practical experience" of the Buddha; contemporary Buddhist monks do not understand Buddhism because they do not have the Buddha's experience; monks have "completely misinterpreted" Buddhism because they use the Buddha's experience to teach Buddhism to others. Monks are like "parrots," and "Buddhism is not something you can repeat like a parrot; you need practical knowledge to talk about it." This practical knowledge comes from living in the world of desires and attachments; without attachments, one cannot get rid of attachments. Dhammadinna continued:

> You need to have something to get [yourself] detached from. This is very important. [Suppose] a beggar comes to you today and says, "I have left everything I have and I am going to become a hermit hereafter, going to the jungle." But what does a beggar have to give up? He has nothing; a person who has nothing has nothing to give up. A person has to have something very valuable to say, "I got detached." But if a very rich man comes to you and says, "I have left everything and I am really tired of [the worldly life] and I want to get detached from [the worldly life]," there, you have something, something very solid to believe, and say, yes, that man is getting out of all these [worldly] things.

Dhammadinna went on to say that "unless a man is very rich at one stage of his life he cannot realize Buddhism." The Buddha's life story exemplifies how wealth and attachment can help one better understand the existential

111. The following comes from my interview with Dhammadinna, Aug. 9, 1995.

problems of human life. "Because the Buddha had all the luxuries of life," he did not have to worry about the problems that preoccupy the daily life of a poor man. All Buddhist monks should emulate the Buddha's life, and they should, as did the Buddha, go through these stages of life, fulfilling "the roles of a good child, an adult, a husband, and a saintly person."[112] These stages of life, he reasons, are thus indispensable to gaining a "practical knowledge of Buddhism." The four stages of life are interrelated: the stage of the "saintly person" is not different from that of the householder. One could not become a saint without being a householder. By the same token, the Buddhist monk ("religious man"), Dhammadinna says, is not any different from an "ordinary human being."

During our conversation, I could not resist inquiring Dhammadinna about his own "stage of life." According to rumor, Dhammadinna is married to an Indian woman and has two children by her; they were all said to be living with the monk. I asked him bluntly if the rumors were true and, if so, whether he considered himself a "married Buddhist monk." He did not deny the rumors, but said he could not go "into detail" about his personal life because of the case (since completed) that was pending in courts. In the same breath, however, he pointed out, "But let me say this: I have been known to women."

Though he did not comment explicitly on the rumors, Dhammadinna discussed the significance of the relation between love, family, attachment, and Buddhism. He pointed out that one understands the meaning of "love" when one first sees the face of a child at birth. What produces children (that is, sex) is not love but "affection." Love comes later. Without understanding love, which is the consummation of a married life, one cannot even begin to understand the Buddha's idea of *karunā*. It is out of *karunā* that one decides to renounce the world to pursue nirvana and eventually help other human beings achieve liberation. Dhammadinna emphasized, "Unless and until one is first a family man," one cannot comprehend the significance of renouncing the world and becoming a monk. The majority of monks who lack that experience are monks only by "appearance," because they wear the robe. "Appearance," he averred, "does not define a monk."

But Dhammadinna continues to define himself as a monk by the strategic reconstruction of the very "symbols" and practices he contends should not constitute the identity of a monk. In 1993, for example, he appeared in court

---

112. Interestingly, these stages correspond to the four Hindu *varnāshrama* dharmas.

to make a deposition with regard to the lawsuit against him. The charges of fraud and breach of trust formed the main agenda of the case, but as it proceeded, its focus shifted to the question of Dhammadinna's identity as a monk. The Japanese monks of the Shinnyo-en temple who testified against Dhammadinna denounced him for not being a "real monk." They informed the judge that when Dhammadinna visited Japan to join their sect, "the accused was wearing robes as a bhikkhu. [But] he later wore trousers and shirts like them." The judge quipped, "So he wanted to be a Roman while in Rome?"[113] Dhammadinna, however, maneuvered the situation to his advantage and represented himself as a "Buddhist monk" in a way that points to the complexity of the strategic, discursive productions of identity. In the midst of the court proceedings, Dhammadinna rose from his seat and informed the judge that he needed to leave the courtroom since it was time for him to have "lunch [dāna] before noon." Neither judge nor prosecution raised objections to Dhammadinna's request since he was wearing the "symbol" of the monkhood, the robe, that obviously identified him as a monk.[114]

This bringing the proceedings to a halt to allow him to eat "before noon" symbolized the court's implicit acknowledgment of Dhammadinna's monastic identity that the charges of fraud sought to question. Thus, the very practices that Dhammadinna insisted should not define monasticism enabled him to mock the state's interrogation of his monastic identity. I want to stress, however, that this is not simply because the "robe," by itself, is a symbol that embodies some unchanging essential "religious" meaning and so is a self-evident marker of monastic identity. Far from it. Rather, what the robe and its wearer mean were communicated in an authoritative manner in relation to another "Buddhist" monastic practice—taking dāna before noon. This, of course, is no guarantee that these narratives will be available for the same kind of deployment and authorization in other contexts. In 1996 the court dropped all charges against Dhammadinna on condition that he forego his claims to the ownership of the Shinnyo-en nursery, vacate his former luxury residence, and withdraw his lawsuit against the Shinnyo-en headquarters.

To sum up, let me reiterate that my exploration of the careers of Dhammadinna and Vipassi, who might at first sight seem like "extreme" cases, was

113. *Island*, "Breach of Trust Case."
114. Interview with Shogo Kawabata, director of the Shinnyo-en Free Nursery School, July, 29, 1995.

not to point out how Buddhist monasticism has changed or what is happening to Buddhism in Sri Lanka. In fact, during my research in the mid-1990s, several Buddhists themselves questioned my interest in writing about these particular monks. Some of them adjured me to look into other, "normal" monks who supposedly represented better examples of what it means to be a Buddhist monk in contemporary Sri Lanka.[115] Now, of course, I must say—and we know this as an all-too-familiar reality that confronts ethnographic research—that there was hardly a uniform consensus on who these "normal" monks were. Be that as it may, my task here has been a different one.

I examined the careers of Vipassi and Dhammadinna to delineate a conjuncture of competing and opposing narratives and debates that sought to define authoritatively the parameters of Buddhism and difference, religious orthodoxy and unorthodoxy, in the new economy of opening up those cultural and economic ties between Sri Lanka and Japan. Vipassi and Dhammadinna, as I read them, are names for a complex network of social relations between monks and the state, which authorized different narratives, persons, and practices to come into central view and fade from view as religious identity and difference. "Religious" identity, in the way I have explored it here, occupies a particular discursive relation between its supposed "self" and the difference(s) of the "other." Identity seeks to produce and authorize difference. Identity wants to make difference its centrally visible other so as to marginalize and subordinate it.

This relation between religious identity and difference, I have wanted to insist, does remain permanently authorized, but contingently positioned. Take, for example, the discourse of Mahayana Buddhism as it was deployed in different conjunctures in Sri Lanka—from the celebration of the Mahayana (and Japan) as "pristine" Buddhism worthy of emulation in the mid-1980s to the depiction of it as a movement of "terror" posing a danger to the identity of "pristine" Theravada Buddhism in Sri Lanka in the 1990s. My point here is that Vipassi and Dhammadinna, who first became centrally visible as "exemplary" monks who rendered invaluable service to the country by sustaining alliances between Sri Lanka and Japan, and who later became marginalized as agents of terror and fraud, are examples of these conjunctures of shifting debates. In the next chapter, I turn to the ways in

---

115. In particular, I recall many conversations with my landlady Mrs. Perara and her neighbors during my stay in Kohuwala in the summers of 1995 and 1996.

which the relation between religion, nation, and difference was produced and argued within the context of Premadasa's tenure as prime minister and second executive president of Sri Lanka.

CHAPTER FIVE

Religion, Nation, and Rulers

In the early 1980s, when President Jayewardene was arguing that the ideal monastic life entailed abandoning politics, his prime minister, Ranasinghe Premadasa, began to argue just the opposite. As early as 1983, Premadasa stated that the "success of the present or the future efforts of our government lies in the hands of the Maha Sangha," and he invited monks to play an active role in the affairs of the government:

> It is the Maha Sangha who in the past had the key to the success of the nation and possesses it now and will also possess it in the future. It is the Maha Sangha who can exercise the most effective influence over the people to bring about peace, unity and discipline. . . . No government can give this position of power and influence to the Maha Sangha nor can any government deprive the Maha Sangha of that position.[1]

In 1985 Premadasa pronounced that "traditionally the Maha Sangha had given its guidance to the government and its people at all times. It is in need of that guidance as never before to lead the country through the present critical period."[2] Again, two years later, the prime minister asserted that the "responsibility of directing the rulers along the right path lies with the monks";[3] he said he spent much of his time with monks because they were his "best friends" (*hodama mitrayō*).[4] Sometimes Premadasa demonstrated his "support" of the monkhood so far as to implicitly challenge the authority of President Jayewardene. In 1985, for example, despite reported warnings from his colleague-ministers, Premadasa attended the funeral of the Buddhist monk Labugama Siridhamma, who had once denounced Jayewardene as a "traitor."[5]

---

1. "Success of Govt's Effort in Hands of Maha Sangha," *Daily News*, Jan. 29, 1983.
2. "PM Calls for Maha Sangha's Guidance," *Daily News*, July 16, 1985.
3. "Pālakayan Yahamaga Yävīme Vagakīma Sangharatnayatayi" ("The monks are responsible for guiding the rulers"), *Silumina*, Mar. 8, 1987.
4. "Budu Dahama Jīvita Hädagasvana Jīvana Kramayak" ("Buddhism is a way of life that molds human lives"), *Davasa*, Jan. 8, 1987.
5. Interview with monks at the Getambe temple, Aug. 7, 1996.

Premadasa's position became even more visible during his presidency. In 1989 he remarked that "kings and ministers sought the Buddha's advice. We have to seek the advice of the Maha Sangha to the solution of the [ethnic] crisis that we are facing today."[6] Premadasa took some prominent monks to the "battlefield" in the north to inspect enemy bunkers and "bless" Sinhala Buddhist soldiers fighting the war.[7]

This chapter examines how a particular kind of relation between Buddhism and the state (and by extension Buddhism and the nation) during Premadasa's prime ministry and presidency came to be authorized. Central to my inquiry is the examination of the dynamics of several significant "Buddhist" projects—such as the construction of a so-called golden canopy for the Tooth Temple—that Premadasa undertook and completed. The significance of such practices is far from self-evident. For me, they make sense only when we look at how some authoritative Sinhala narratives made centrally visible a specific relation between Premadasa's "Buddhist" identity and the "Buddhist" nation of Sri Lanka. This relation, however, was subsequently contested by competing discourses that generated a very different kind of relation between Buddhism and the nation, focusing on Premadasa himself.

My task here is not to provide an account of "why" a decidedly complex political figure like Premadasa, unlike any other politician in the modern history of Sri Lanka (or South Asia for that matter), undertook so many costly state-sponsored "religious" projects. The "why" of his undertaking such unprecedented religious projects is precisely what governs the theoretical structure of Josine van der Horst's important book on Premadasa's religious rhetoric and performances.[8] Referring to the bloody political climate that characterized Premadasa's presidency (about this, more later), Horst argues that Premadasa's "almost frantic engagement in religious observances and performances of meritorious deeds" was a result of his "anxiety concerning the balance of his merit . . . over the excessive violence Premadasa [had] been in charge of."[9] This was Horst's own learned view: "I do not doubt that

6. *Daily News*, July 8, 1989.
7. "Rata Rakina Sebalunta Āsiri: Malwatu Maha Nāhimiyō Uturē Yudha Bimata Vaditi" ("Blessings to the soldiers protecting the country: The Malwatu chief monk visits the battlefield in the north"), *Dinamina*, Jan. 1992. This front-page newspaper story carried pctures of the chief monk inspecting bunkers of Tamil Tigers through binoculars.
8. Josine van der Horst, *Who Is He, What Is He Doing?* 131.
9. Ibid.

Premadasa was anxious over his merit status."[10] It is clear that such a claim presupposes a direct relation between the modern present and the ancient past—that is, between Premadasa's religious practices and those of the famous third-century B.C.E. Buddhist emperor Asoka, who supposedly turned to Buddhism after waging a bloody battle, Kalinga, that cost one hundred thousand lives. Horst states that Asoka's "plans of actions are discernible in Premadasa's performances."[11] For Horst, then, Premadasa's observable "religious" practices are self-evident (unlike they might be for, say, Nietzsche); that is, they are available for identification and explanation in relation to a presumed given model (the emperor Asoka). As Nietzsche argues,

> The question "why?" is always a question after the *causa finalis*, after the "what for?" . . . Here Hume was right; habit . . . makes us expect that a certain often-observed occurrence will follow another: Nothing more! That which gives extraordinary firmness to our belief in causality is not the great habit of seeing one occurrence following another but our inability to interpret events otherwise than as events caused by intentions. It [the question of "why?"] is belief . . . in will, in intention . . . it is belief that every event is a deed, that every deed presupposes a doer, it is belief in the "subject."[12]

Following Nietzsche, I avoid the question of "why" and argue that Premadasa's practices are significant within particular debates in which they are battled out and defined as Buddhism and difference. Here I examine some of those debates that authorized and contested a particular relation between religion, the state, and the nation during the Premadasa prime ministry and presidency. I want to demonstrate that the relation between religion and nation are specific discursive constructs and that it always stands within the bounds of being invested with and divested of distinct meanings in differing conjunctures.

Authorizing a Ruler, Religion, and Nation

The new constitution that made Jayewardene executive president in 1978 rendered the office of prime minister "lower in status than that of the prime minister of the fifth French Republic." Some scholars argue that, under the

10. Ibid., 130.
11. Ibid.
12. Friedrich Nietzsche, *The Will to Power*, trans. Walter Kaufmman and R. J. Hollingdale (New York: Vintage, 1968), 295.

new constitution, the prime minister (who in theory was also the "chief of the government majority") "did not have the authority to direct, supervise or command his colleagues."[13] Premadasa himself exaggerated at one point that, as prime minister, he "did not have the powers even equal to [those] of a peon."[14] However, no sooner did he become prime minister than a number of authoritative discourses began to construct a particular relation between Premadasa, his political office, Buddhism, and the nation.

In the late 1970s, the state newspapers recognized that the office of prime minister had "lost some of its power" after Jayewardene's introduction of the executive presidency; however, they went on to claim that the office had gained "enhanced importance" because of the man who then held it—Premadasa.[15] For several weeks, explaining this supposed enhanced importance of the office, the newspapers carried a flood of articles that portrayed Premadasa as a "man of the people" who had "a deep understanding of the problems of the underdog which few Sri Lankan politicians can match";[16] he was, they said, an "asset to the nation."[17] One writer observed that "the mantle of this high office sits lightly on Premadasa, who is in a sense the real man of the people to achieve the distinction of becoming the country's first prime minister. Very much unlike prime ministers before him, from D. S. Senanayake to J. R. Jayewardene, Premadasa was not born into wealth and is proud of his humble origin."[18]

Newspapers carried reports of many influential Buddhist monastic voices speaking his praises. Madihe Paññasiha celebrated Premadasa as a "great leader who has always wished for the prosperity of the motherland and the Buddha Sasana [and who] strives to follow the [Buddha's] middle path." Paññasiha said Premadasa followed "in the footsteps of Anagarika Dharmapala, a great religious leader whose worthy example Premadasa is emulating. A nonsmoker and teetotaler, [Premadasa] observes the five precepts very

---

13. A. J. Wilson, *The Gaullist System in Asia: The Constitution of Sri Lanka* (London: Macmillan, 1980), 62, cited in de Silva and Wriggins, *Jayewardene of Sri Lanka*, 385.

14. Quoted in "Groups with Vested Interests Trying to Oust President," *Island*, Sept. 21, 1991.

15. *Ceylon Daily News*, Feb. 11, 1978.

16. Ibid. In less than a year, a biography of Premadasa appeared bearing a title along these lines; see Wimal Abhayasundara, *Man of the Masses* (Colombo: Gunasena, 1979).

17. "A Friend to All—an Asset to the Nation," *Ceylon Daily News*, Feb. 11, 1978.

18. "The Prime Minister," *Ceylon Daily News*, Feb. 7, 1978.

devoutly."[19] Walegammedde Wimalajoti exalted the new prime minister as a "good Buddhist" and a "good Sinhalese patriot." "It is very rare," the monk said, "that a person who is religious, nationalistic, and patriotic is born to the world. It is a great blessing to the nation that such a person has been born. Prime Minister R. Premadasa is a person who possesses such rare qualities."[20] A day after Premadasa was sworn in as prime minister, the newspapers highlighted his Buddhist identity in front-page headlines: "The Prime Minister Attends Pooja [offering] at Temple as First Official Act."[21]

My point is that, even though the new Jayewardene constitution symbolically demoted the office of prime minister, diverse monastic and lay discourses conjoined to "enhance" the post by giving a particular "Buddhist" identity to Premadasa, making him and it key to the future of the "Buddhist" nation. These depictions of Premadasa gained prominence a few years after he came to the premiership. In 1982, at a *Bōdhi Pūja* ceremony at Kelaniya temple to invoke blessings on the prime minister, Walpola Rahula asserted that Premadasa was "devoted to Buddhism and the [Sinhalese] race" (*jāti-hitaishīāgamika bhaktiyen*). Rahula went on to claim that "if there are two or three people like Premadasa, everything in the country could be achieved, and that because of Premadasa, now ordinary Sri Lankans could have hopes unthinkable before."[22]

What interests me here is tracing the rise and fall of this relation between the prime minister, nation, and Buddhism (rather than the rise and fall of Premadasa himself). Let me first discuss some dimensions of the very publicized relation between Premadasa and one of the most popular Buddhist temples in Sri Lanka—the Tooth Temple. Of interest to my inquiry is a particular a set of practices that enabled that relation to come into public view: the construction of the golden canopy (*ran viyana*) over the Tooth Temple.[23]

---

19. "His Happiest Moments Are Spent in the Service of the People," *Ceylon Daily News*, Feb. 24, 1978.

20. "A Blessing to the Nation," *Ceylon Daily News*, Feb. 7, 1978.

21. *Ceylon Daily News*, Feb. 7, 1978.

22. "Avankakama Ätnam Ōnäma Usas Tatvayak Läbiya Häki Bava Agamätigen Oppuve-navä" ("The prime minister exemplifies that honesty can achieve any high status"), *Dinamina*, Apr. 4, 1982.

23. Mark Juergensmeyer states wrongly that the canopy was constructed by J. R. Jayewardene; see his "What the Bhikkhu Said: Reflections on the Rise of Militant Religious Nationalism," *Religion* 20, no. 1 (1990): 68.

What's in a Name? A Golden Canopy for the Tooth Temple

The Tooth Temple (dalada māligāwa), as its name suggests, is believed by many Sinhalese Buddhists to house the Buddha's tooth relic.[24] I will not retell the entire long story of how Sri Lanka came to inherit one of the Buddha's teeth, except to note that, by about the twelfth century, the tooth relic, as the conventional narrative of it goes, "became the palladium of the Sinhalese kings."[25] Over the centuries, the relic, it is said, was shifted from place to place as kings changed the capitals of Sri Lanka. In the sixteenth century, the tooth relic was moved to Kandy, where it was housed in the Tooth Temple that king Wimaladarmasuriya (1593–1603) constructed. Today the Tooth Temple is controlled by the two chief monks of the Malwatta and Asgiriya temples and by a lay Buddhist custodian (diyavadana nilame). It is frequented daily by thousands of visitors, both local and foreign.

The history of the "public" relation between Premadasa and the Tooth Temple, so far as I can gather, begins in the mid-1980s. In 1986, according to a newspaper report, the prime minister made an official visit to the Tooth Temple to "pay homage to the Sacred Tooth Relic."[26] On that day, responding to a complaint by the chief monks of the temple about water leaking from the temple's roof, Premadasa pledged to cover the roof with a bronze sheet.[27] Six months later, Premadasa announced his plans to build a "golden canopy" over the inner shrine room of the Tooth Temple. Initially, a number of people, including the then-director of the Sri Lankan Archaeology Department, objected to the plan. They argued that a canopy over the roof would not only put the safety of the building at risk but also damage the very "antiquity" of it since no additions to the building had been done since the last king of Kandy, King Kirti Sri Rajasimha.

The protests did not deter the prime minister from continuing the project: as a monk pointed out to me, "during that time Premadasa was extremely popular in Sri Lanka—even more so than President Jayewardene himself. There was almost nothing that Premadasa could not do" (karanda bäri deyak

24. For an account of the significance of the tradition of relic veneration in Buddhism, see Trainor, Relics, Ritual, and Representation.

25. Malalgoda, Buddhism in Sinhalese Society, 14; also see H. L. Seneviratne, Rituals of the Kandyan State (Cambridge: Cambridge University Press, 1978), 17.

26. "PM Promises Maligawa Repair, too, in Shelter Year," Daily News, Dec. 30, 1986.

27. Ibid.

tibunnä).[28] On December 31, 1987 (exactly a year before he would become president), the golden canopy, costing more than twenty million rupees, was ceremonially unveiled by Premadasa. The occasion made possible a public space for the articulation and authorization of a particular relation between Premadasa, Buddhism, and the nation that would later prove to be critical to his campaign for the office of president. The media portrayed the prime minister's offering of the canopy to the temple as a "historic event" that "provided shelter to the Tooth Temple, the highest lasting object of reverence [*sadā vandanīya mudun malkada*] of all Buddhists in the world."[29] The unveiling ceremony was nothing short of an "extraordinary" affair. The state newspapers carried front-page reports of eye-witness accounts testifying that immediately after the canopy was unveiled by the prime minister, the "rays of the Buddha emanated from Maligawa." It was described as a miracle (*prātihāraya*); such an event, the reports claimed, occurs only when "great people" do "great" acts of merit."[30]

Days after the construction of the golden canopy, chief monks from various Buddhist fraternities issued statements that made an explicit connection between Premadasa, the Buddha, the Sinhala nation, and its past "Buddhist" rulers. The head of the Asgiriya chapter, Palipana Chandananda, spoke of Premadasa as a "supreme individual" (*śreśta pudgalayek*) who always delivered his promises; others stated that by offering the canopy to the Maligawa, "like Ancient kings such as Bimbisara and Anata Pindika . . . [Premadasa] donated shelter to the Buddha. Premadasa's act is memorable, and all Buddhists should honor it."[31] In letters to newspapers, Madihe Paññasiha and Pottewala Paññasara praised Premadasa's leadership: he followed in the "footsteps of ancient kings"; "I have no doubt that it is the Buddha-influence which had motivated [Premadasa] to undertake this great task," wrote Paññasiha. Paññasara went so far as to predict that the merit gained from this act would help Premadasa achieve "the highest things in life" such as the

28. Interview with Warakawe Dhammaloka at the Nata Devale temple (near the Tooth Temple), Aug. 8–10, 1996.
29. "Golden Canopy for a Historic Day," *Daily News*, Jan. 1, 1998; "Sādu Nāda Mädde Ranviyana Pidē" ("The golden canopy is offered amid the cries of *Sādu*"), *Dinamina*, Jan. 1, 1988.
30. "Daladā Mädurin Buduräs" ("Buddha's rays emanate from the Tooth Temple"), *Dinamina*, Jan. 1, 1988.
31. "Daladā Vamsa Katāvata Ran Pituvak Ekkalā" ("[Premadasa] added a golden page to the history of the Daladā"), *Dinamina*, Jan. 1, 1988.

presidency of the country.[32] Lay Buddhists, too, commented on Premadasa's construction of the canopy and his "close association with monks as the sign of a noble leadership (*udāra nāyakatvayaka lakshanayak*)."[33] The lay custodian of the Tooth Temple, Neranjan Wijetunga, declared that "Premadasa's name will be written in gold in the history of Sri Lanka."[34] As if acknowledging these representations, Premadasa, in a special message, linked the construction of the canopy to the "distant" past of the Sinhala Buddhist nation: he said he decided to build the canopy because "The Sacred Tooth Relic is held in Supreme veneration by Buddhists all over the world. Our kings of old have valued and venerated the Sacred Tooth Relic of the Buddha and protected it with their very lives."[35]

Serving Temples, Saving the Nation

At the opening ceremony for the canopy, Premadasa made several important remarks about the "Buddhist" identity of himself and the nation. Addressing a massive rally of monks and lay Buddhists, Premadasa spoke of his "good knowledge of Buddhism" and acknowledged his indebtedness to monks for helping him acquire it. He stated that he honored and venerated the Buddha, the Dhamma, and the Sangha because of the "noble advice he received from monks."[36] He went on to discuss a highly contentious national issue that had taken place six months earlier: the arrival in the island of the Indian Peace Keeping Force (IPKF).

In July 1987, as part of the Indo-Sri Lanka accord, signed by President Jayewardene and Indian Prime Minister Rajiv Gandhi, forty thousand Indian troops assigned to the IPKF landed in the north of Sri Lanka to end the escalating separatist war.[37] The signing of the accord took place amid

32. "The Ceremonial Opening of Ran Viyana: More Messages," *Island*, Dec. 29, 1987.

33. "Daladā Pūjā Katāvata Tavat Alut Pituvak" ("A new page to the history of the daladā worship"), *Dinamina*, Jan. 1, 1988.

34. "Daladā Vamsa Katāvata Ran Pituvak Ekkalā" ("Golden page to the story of the tooth relic"), *Dinamina*, Jan. 1, 1988.

35. "Golden Canopy—Fulfillment of a Pledge, Says PM," *Daily News*, Dec. 30, 1987.

36. "Ran Viyana Pidīmata Häki Vūyē Ahinsaka Janatāvage Ādāra Nisayi—Mahanuvara Mahapinkamedi Agamäti Tumā Pavasayi" ("I could offer the golden canopy because of the donations of the poor people—prime minister says at the great meritorious ceremony in Great Kandy"), *Divayina*, Jan. 1, 1988.

37. The Liberation Tigers of Tamil Elam (LTTE), headed by V. Prabhakaran, are fighting for a separate state in northern Sri Lanka.

islandwide curfews because scores of young Buddhist monks and lay Buddhists, led by the JVP, rioted in Colombo against the arrival of a foreign army. The accord did not help the diminishing popularity of Jayewardene. As a Sri Lankan commentator put it, "Jayewardene, in his last five years, had been spendthrift with the unprecedentedly massive charisma that he attained at the election in 1977 and had become the lodestar of dissidence and disaffection."[38] Immediately after the accord was signed, many voices accused Jayewardene of "betraying the nation" to a foreign country; posters reading "Kill J. R." appeared overnight in several parts of the country.[39] Prime Minister Premadasa openly objected to the accord and refused to appear at its signing, an event watched live on TV by many Sri Lankans.[40] Monks, too, spoke out, among them Walpola Rahula, who later stated that Sri Lanka "lost its freedom after thirty-eight years because of the Indo-Lanka accord."[41] It is widely believed that Premadasa secretly masterminded damaging images of the accord and of Jayewardene so as to produce a picture of a nation in desperate need of a new political leadership (presumably under Premadasa).[42] On the day the accord was signed, one of Premadas's allies, the monk Galaboda Ñanissara (whom we came across in chapter 4) mobilized scores of youths to put up black flags throughout Colombo, symbolizing the death of the country.[43] The black flags, made from polythene garbage bags, were said to have come from the Colombo Municipal Council, manned by Premadasa's friends.[44]

If his opposition to the accord did not become centrally visible in July 1987, Premadasa made it glaringly public at the canopy ceremony. He pointed out that he was not afraid to say that the peace accord and having the

38. "President's [Premadasa's] 'Horoscope': He Has Not Put a Foot Wrong So Far," *Daily News*, Feb. 16, 1989.

39. Observations in Colombo and Kandy 1987; interview with Dewalegama Medhananda, Nov. 15–16, 1996.

40. Another member of the government who did not support the peace accord was Lalith Athulathmudali; many believe that he, too (like Premadasa), was a sure contender for the presidency of Sri Lanka.

41. "Indu Sri Lanka Givisuma Nisā Apata Vasara 38 Kata Pasu Nidahasa Ahimi Unā," *Divayina*, July, 2, 1990.

42. Interviews with Buddhist monks at Jayewardenapura University, July 15–17, 1995.

43. Interview with Galaboda Ñanissara, Oct. 20, 1996; "Loku Väda Karana Podi Hāmuduruwō" (The little monk who does big things), *Iridā Lankādīpa*, Dec. 12, 1993.

44. Interview with monks in Colombo, July 1996, Oct. 1997.

Indian army in Sri Lanka was a mistake: the Indian troops failed to end the "chaos" (*arbudhaya*) in the country. "It was some people's view," he added, "that only force can solve the problems of the country. If so, why can't the present problems of the country be solved with an army of 40,000 at the present. There are others who view that a political solution can be found. If so, why can't the problem be solved by the signing of the agreements [between Jayewardene and Rajiv Gandhi]."[45]

The point of all this is that Premadasa's rendering visible his opposition to the peace accord—which was an implicit form of support for the Sinhala nationalist forces who were by then seeking to remove the Jayewardene government—became possible in the context in which that particular relation between Premadasa's "Buddhist" identity, Buddhism, and the Sinhala nation came to be authorized. Take, for example, the following key statement made on the day of the canopy unveiling by the chief monk of the Tooth Temple, Sirimalwatte Ananda. Praising Premadasa as a "pious, principled Buddhist," he asserted that "as long as our great shrines such as the sacred Tooth Relic . . . exist on the soil of this Isle it will remain a Sinhala Buddhist country. The presence of non-Sinhala and non-Buddhist minorities will in no way make it a multinational or a multireligious country."[46] Such assertions, which strategically challenged the authority of Jayewardene, who argued for the importance of a multiethnic Sri Lankan society, suggested that Premadasa's support of the Tooth Temple was a form of support of Sri Lanka as a "Sinhala Buddhist country." It was in the context of depicting Sri Lanka as a Sinhala Buddhist country "betrayed" by Jayewardene to a "foreign" country that Premadasa came to construct the golden canopy for the Tooth Temple.

Exactly a year after the canopy was built, Premadasa became president, promising the immediate withdrawal of the IPKF from Sri Lanka, an idea that appealed to many Sinhala Buddhists at that time. In December 1988, a few days prior to Premadasa's inauguration, the media celebrated the anniversary of the canopy with a specific kind of rhetoric that sought to localize and nationalize the canopy: one newspaper article carried the title "The Golden Canopy Materialized by [Local] Scientific Knowledge." The text insisted that each year Sri Lanka celebrate the "miracle" of the canopy because it was cre-

45. "PM Offers Golden Canopy," *Island*, Jan. 1, 1988.
46. "Paying Homage with a Golden Canopy," *Sun*, Dec. 31, 1987.

ated by "local [Sinhala Buddhist] engineers" (*dē śī ya injinēru*) without assistance from "foreign engineers."[47] Thus the context of the canopy enabled the central visibility of Premadasa's Buddhist identity and its relation to the safeguarding of the "embattled" Sinhala Buddhist nation, an identity that became a crucial part of Premadasa's bid for the presidency.

The election of Premadasa as president became a contentious topic in Sri Lanka. Rumors circulated, as S. B. Disanayaka informs us, that Premadasa won his presidential nomination by strategically "terrorizing" the lives of Jayewardene and some of his ministers. Premadasa, according to Disanayaka, maintained secret links with the members of the JVP and eventually assisted them in creating a period of "terror" threatening the Jayewardene government.[48] Some Sri Lankans claim that although Jayewardene's first choice for the succession was Lalith Athulathmudali, one of the most popular cabinet ministers in the country, the president nominated Premadasa out of fear for his life.[49] In fact, the whole election process was considered spurious because "Premadasa's people" controlled the ballot boxes.[50] It is in this controversial context that Premadasa's continuing relations with the Tooth Temple and its chief monks should be understood.

Just days after being elected executive president, Premadasa announced that he would take his oaths on the octagon (*pattirippuva*) of the Tooth Temple. This was a novel political practice: no leader of the country had ever been sworn in on the octagon. It is said that King Kirti Sri Rajasimha built the pattirippuva in 1783 and used it to address the nation.[51] Jayewardene had been sworn in in Colombo and later went to the Tooth Temple to address the nation. Premadasa changed that convention. He not only officially became president on the octagon but also invited the temple's chief monks and others to witness the occasion.

---

47. "Vidu Nuvanin Mävunu Ranviyana" ("The canopy materialized by the [local] scientific knowledge"), *Vidunäna*, Dec. 31, 1988.

48. S. B. Disanayaka, *Mā Atsan Kala Dōshābhiyōgaya* (The impeachment I signed) (Colombo: Sirilaka, 1992), 34.

49. Conversations with people in Colombo, Kandy, Dambulla, and Sigiriya, 1994–97. The relations between Jayewardene and Premadasa became so sour by the early 1990s that the former prohibited mention of the latter's name in his home. Conversation with Mrs. Hettige, the librarian of the Jayewardene Cultural Center, Colombo. Oct. 6, 1997.

50. Disanayaka, *Mā Atsan Kala Dōshbāhiyōgaya*, 34.

51. "Hela Raja Sirita Hā Pattirippuva," ("The Sinhala royal tradition and the octagon"), *Island*, Jan. 1, 1989.

As preparations got under way for the inaugural, scheduled for January 4, 1989, the media began to depict the history of Premadasa's relation to the Tooth Temple in a particular way. For several days, the state newspapers carried elaborate pictures of the Tooth Temple showing the glittering golden canopy. One picture, encompassing a whole page, portrayed Premadasa in one of his classic postures, holding a tray of flowers, against a background of the temple with the canopy in full view.[52] It introduced Premadasa as the "president of the common people" and invited every citizen of Sri Lanka to participate in his inauguration.[53]

The media representations of the relation between Premadasa and the Tooth Temple can be explained in terms of the Sinhala concept of *älluvā*, a term that one of my main informant-monks used to characterize relations between the president and monks. The term means, among many other things, "seized" or "caught,"[54] but, as my informant used it— "*premadasa ällu-vanē daladā māligawat*," meaning "Premadasa seized the Tooth Temple, too"—points to the strategic ways in which a particular narrative came to authorize, enable, and indeed oblige monks to "show," or "exhibit," (*pen-nanna*) a particularly privileged relation between the president and the temple, Buddhism and the (Premadasa) state.[55] When Premadasa was sworn in, for instance, his wife and two children appeared beside him on the pattirip-puva. This well-known incident provoked vehement public criticism since no woman had ever appeared on the octagon, and it was believed that the violation of that tradition would bring about harmful effects (*vas*). (Some Sri Lankans attribute Premadasa's premature death at the hands of an assassin to the ill effects of his wife's presence on the pattirippuva.)[56] The two chief monks of the Tooth Temple disregarded that tradition and "permitted" Premadasa's entire family—his wife, daughter, son, and son-in-law—on the pattirip-puva because, as another informant noted, the relations between Premadasa

52. The image of Premadasa holding a tray of flowers became so popular that he came to be nicknamed "prince of flowers" (*puśpakumāra*).

53. *Dinamina*, Jan. 1, 1989; also see *Dinamina*, Jan. 2, 1989, where another full-page picture of Premadasa's whole family appeared against the background of the Tooth Temple.

54. *älluvā* is the past tense of *allanavā*, which means "catch," "touch," "seize," "arrest."

55. Interview with Medhananda, Nov. 15–16, 1996.

56. Interview with Dhammaloka and conversations with several people in Kandy in August 1996. After Premadasa's death, some monks publicly charged that he "desecrated the hallowed Pattirippuva"; see "Grandeur at Gam Udawas to Hide Own Atrocities," *Daily News*, Aug. 23, 1996.

and the chief monks had become such that "monks could not say no" (*nähä kiyanda bähä*) to him.[57]

What I want to emphasize, reminded of the final Foucauldian formulation of discourse/power, is that these kinds of relations between Buddhism, monks, and the nation cannot be conceptualized in terms of domination or coercion. Rather, they show how particular discourses enable and authorize particular forms of practices and persons to come into view as representing Buddhism and the nation. These kinds of "Buddhist" relations between Premadasa and monks became more prominent during the presidential inauguration ceremony. Delivering a speech to a "sea of people," as newspapers reported it,[58] Sirimalwatte Ananda said that Premadasa was "a real Buddhist" (*niyama bauddhayek*), a "heroic person" (*vīra puruśayek*), and "noble individual" (*śrēstayeku*), who achieved a status of "nobility" as a "great ruler":[59]

> You are a good Buddhist. We know that prior to this occasion you have come to the Tooth Temple and enjoyed worshipping the Three Jewels, the Buddha, the Dhamma, and the Sangha. Not every politician can do that. We also know how you venerated the Three Jewels, prostrating on the floor [*pasaga pihituvā*]. You are used to it. You have also donated a golden canopy for the beauty and the continuity of the Tooth Temple. Numerous are other Buddhist services you have done. A noble person [like you] will never have a bad rebirth.[60]

In a separate message, Sirimalwatte Ananda wished Premadasa "the strength to protect the Buddha Sasana and the country" and stated that "our history records that it is natural that noble [*udāra*] people appear in times of chaos in the country"; he expressed confidence that the new president would fulfill that role.[61] Palipana Chandananda supported this view and said that "monks have accepted that . . . [Premadasa is] a real Buddhist"

57. Interview with Dhammaloka, Aug. 8, 1996.

58. It is said that the government bussed thousands of people to Kandy for the ceremony. Each was given a few hundred rupees and a packet of rice. This practice continued annually.

59. "Senkadagala Yali Iyitihāsika Vū Dā" ("The day Senkadagala [Kandy] became historic again"), *Dinamina*, Jan. 3, 1993; "Nava Janādhipati Usas Dēapālakayek" ("The new president is a great ruler"), *Davasa*, Jan. 2, 1989.

60. Ibid.

61. "Budusasunat Ratat Räkumata Śaktiya Läbēvā" ("May [Premadasa] have the strength to protect the Buddha Sasana and the country"), *Dinamina*, Jan. 4, 1989.

and reminded the new president that "time has come to safeguard the Buddha Sasana and the Buddhist sacred places."[62]

These representations of Premadasa as a "real Buddhist" born to rescue the nation from a time of "chaos" are located in the context in which the golden canopy came into existence. It must be evident now that, in making this argument, I am not suggesting in any way that the canopy should be taken as a monolithic, single "event" in itself; rather, constructed during what was called a "time of chaos" in Sri Lankan history, this "Golden Canopy" is a different name for a particular conjuncture of narratives that made centrally visible a specific relation between Premadasa, Buddhism, and the nation. It was in the space of communicating this relation that more tangible gestures of monastic support for the president became possible.

For example, for three years the chief monks of the Tooth Temple permitted, and presided over, the annual celebrations of Premadasa's inauguration as president at the Tooth Temple, a practice that no previous government in Sri Lanka had cultivated.[63] Also each year the chief monks, along with other monks, accompanied the president to his *gam udāva* festivals in various parts of Sri Lanka. They appeared on stages and spoke to masses of people about the benefits of the president's project to the country. The gam udva, a project that Premadasa began as prime minister, proposed to "awaken villages" by building houses for the needy. It became a controversial project: each year's "awakening" of a given village included extravagant festivities that cost millions of rupees.[64] Some Sri Lankans considered such celebrations an abuse of government money, and in August 1991 the issue formed an important aspect of the opposition party's agenda to impeach Premadasa for "violating" the constitution.[65] The monks continued to praise the project as a "cultural renaissance" (*sanskrutika navōdayak*) and argued that it showed Premadasa's diligent following in the footsteps of Gandhi to "bring people happiness."[66]

---

62. "Obē Jayagrahanaya Nivāradi Tīnduvak" ("Your victory is a right decision [of the people]"), *Dinamina*, Jan. 4, 1989.

63. See *Dinamina*, Jan. 4, 1990–93.

64. Ibid., June 25, 1989–93.

65. See S. B. Disanayaka, *Mā Atsan Kala Dōshābhiyōgaya*, 5; for an English version of the charges presented to parliament, also see Horst, *Who Is He, What Is He Doing?* 260.

66. See, for example, "Gam Udāvata Sangaruvanē Āsiri" ("Sangha's blessings to Gam Udāva"), *Dinamina*, June 23, 1989.

This kind of authorized relation between Premadasa and monks, Buddhism and the nation, did not remain unchanged, and I now wish to examine the gradual emergence of a starkly different identity of the president in relation to Buddhism and the nation. In complex ways, competing and opposing narratives began to oust identity from its authorized domains, to turn the tables on identity, so to speak, and represent identity as difference, as the dangerous "other" to be subdued and subverted.

Identity as Difference: From Real Buddhist to Killer

In the preceding chapter, I alluded to Premadasa's alliances with the popular monk Galaboda Ñanissara, of the Gangaramaya temple. In the late 1970s, these alliances had enabled Ñanissara to solicit financial support from the business community of Colombo and inaugurate the annual Buddhist procession Navam Perahära as well as several other "social-service" projects at the temple. Even during the Jayewardene presidency—Jayewardene himself was one of the chief patrons of Ñanissara's temple—Ñanissara made no bones about his exclusive support for Prime Minister Premadasa. After Premadasa came to power, Ñanissara made his support for the new president even more public. In the midst of that "time of chaos" in July 1989, which coincided with President Premadasa's sixty-fifth birthday, Ñanissara wrote to the newspapers extolling Premadasa as a "national treasure [*jātika vastuvak*] of the Sinhalas and Buddhists." He disparaged other politicians (supposedly the former president Jayewardene and some of his ministers) and praised Premadasa as a "Sinhala Buddhist" leader who did not wear "[Western] trousers at home and the [Sri Lankan] national dress in public."[67]

In the wake of the impeachment controversy in the early 1990s, Ñanissara extended the president his unstinting support. Once he addressed a meeting of five hundred Buddhist monks gathered at the public library in Colombo and attacked the impeachment attempt as the work of "a group of people who are trying to perpetuate a system that enables an elite class to enjoy wealth and comforts which the ordinary man is deprived of." He went on to call for the immediate withdrawal of the impeachment proposal and argued that the whole "country should be eternally grateful to Premadasa" just for the fact that he got rid of the IPKF, "an invasion of our country."[68]

67. "Janapati R. Premadasa Mē Yugayata Avaśya Vunē Äyi?" ("Why was President Premadasa needed for this era?"), *Divayina*, June 23, 1989.

68. "Groups with Vested Interests Trying to Oust the President," *Island*, Sept. 21, 1991.

The relations between the president and the monk became the target of much controversy. Many of my informants in Colombo characterized Ñanissara as an aggressive monk who spoke loudly and had a quick temper, not fearing even the demon.[69] Ñanissara is said to have engaged in physical confrontations with people and have struck even police officers who failed to follow his instructions during the Navam (Perahära) procession.[70] Some held that Ñanissara committed such acts with impunity because of Premadasa's influence.[71] It is widely rumored that during the JVP insurrection Premadasa authorized Ñanissara to carry a handgun for self-defense. Some even gossiped that Premadasa and Ñanissara were in the business of printing money; one monk remarked that this was a "famous secret" (*prasiddha rahasak*). Such gossip became widespread because for three consecutive years Ñanissara held elaborate almsgiving ceremonies at his temple, offering, in addition to robes and other conventional gifts, "brand new thousand rupee bills" (*alutma dāhe kola*) to eleven thousand monks.[72] My aim here, it should be obvious by now, is not to determine the authenticity of these opposing claims or rumors, but rather to point to the context in which they began to emerge, displaying a different kind of relation between the president, Buddhism, and the nation.

Something of the significance of the emergence of such competing claims can be located by examining briefly the relation between Premadasa and one of the most prominent Buddhist monks, Kotikawatte Saddhatissa. Saddhatissa, unlike chief monks of the Tooth Temple, came from a temple of relative obscurity, in Kolonnawa, near Kelaniya. By the early 1980s, however, Saddhatissa had become one of the most popular Buddhist monks in Sri Lanka. He earned his islandwide reputation as an eloquent, "mesmerizing" (*vaśī karana*) preacher, and his Buddhist sermons (*bana*) were regularly broadcast over radio and on television. Saddhatissa, as one monk noted to me, was a popular UNP supporter, but there was a mass of people (*janagangāvak*) who disregarded the monk's political orientations and became devoted followers of his sermons. As the monk put it, "people had differentiated between

---

69. "Podihāmuduruwane Mokadda Oya Jaramarē?" ("What is this rumble?"), article in unidentified newspaper, n.d.

70. "Who Was Behind the Gangarama Clash?" clipping, unidentified newspaper, n.d.

71. Conversations with five people in Hunupitiya and several monks in Colombo, Nov. 1–4, 1997.

72. See *Jinaratana Kārmika Vidyālaya*; interviews with monks who attended the *dāna* at the Gangarama temple, Oct. 4, 1997.

his politics and his sermons [*eyāge bana saha dēshapālanaya*]." It is perhaps because of Saddhatissa's appeal to many Sinhalese Buddhists across political boundaries, my informant conjectured, that Premadasa allied himself with the monk.[73]

The history of the relationship between Saddhatissa and Premadasa, as far as I can determine, goes back to the early 1980s. In 1982, when Premadasa suffered from a minor illness, for ten days Saddhatissa conducted a massive bōdhi pūjā ceremony at his temple and rallied monks islandwide to do so in order to "invoke blessings" on the prime minister. At such events Saddhatissa, like other monks of his time, began to represent Premadasa as a "superior person" (*śresta pudgalayā*) who "won people's hearts."[74] Saddhatissa went so far as to hyperbolize that "the whole country has accepted Premadasa as a man of merit who has reaped a noble harvest through his own effort."[75]

In the early 1980s, Premadasa invited Saddhatissa to deliver the annual Vesak sermon at his official residence, Temple Trees.[76] Telecast nationwide, the sermon provided the occasion for the public depiction of Premadasa and his family as devout Buddhists listening to the words of the Buddha. This practice, which no other politician had cultivated at the official residence in modern history, continued every year for more than a decade.[77] In 1989, after he became president, Premadasa made the practice more frequent, inviting Saddhatissa to preach a sermon every Sunday at the presidential palace. These sermons, some of my informants noted, were nothing more than forms of elaborate praise (*gunavarnanāva*) of the president's virtues. By the late 1980s, Saddhatissa's relations with the Premadasa government had become so well known that he came to be called "the monk who preaches at the royal palace" (*rajagedara bana kiyana hāmuduruwō*).[78]

Other practices emerged that brought into public view this close "Buddhist" relation between the president and the monk. In 1984, with the help

73. Interviews with Medhananda, Nov. 16, 1996.

74. "Janatāva Set Pätuvē Agamäti Janahada Dinū Nisayi" ("People invoked blessings [on Premadasa] because he won people's heart"), *Lankādīpa*, Jan. 5, 1982.

75. "Agamäti Utsahayen Śresta Pala Nelgat Putāglayek" ("The prime minister is a person who has reaped noble results"), *Davasa*, June 30, 1980.

76. Vesak, a public holiday, falls in the month of May; it celebrates three major events in the life of the Buddha: birth, enlightenment, and passing away.

77. *Dinamina*, May 22, 1989.

78. Interview with monks at the Mahabodhi Society, Oct. 6–8, 1997; conversations with monks and lay people in Kolonnawa, Oct. 9–10, 1997.

of Muslim friends and businessmen, Premadasa constructed a massive preaching hall (Saddhatissa Dharma Mandiraya) at Saddhatissa's temple to mark the monk's forty-fourth birthday.[79] The preaching hall proved quite useful to a specific kind of practice that the newspapers called *pinkama* ("religious ceremony"), held annually at the temple. The pinkama, organized every year by Premadasa's Sucharita movement, was a massive meeting of monks transported to Saddhatissa's temple from different parts of the country. A newspaper report described the nature of the pinkama one year: "Over 1,500 Bhikkhus from several parts of the country along with thousands of devotees participated in the Pinkama. . . . [They] offered pirikara [gifts] to the monks. . . . [The monks] walked in a colorful procession from the Kolonnawa junction to the [temple] and Prime Minister Premadasa and Mrs. Hema Premadasa . . . also took part in the procession."[80] Notable features of this pinkama were the speeches that Premadasa and some of his close colleague-ministers delivered at the temple. Nobody quite knew the purpose of the annual meeting, but "every year [for seven years] they talked about the problem of 'terror' and 'terrorism' in the country."[81]

By then (the late 1980s), the country had already witnessed the emergence of the LTTE as a formidable guerrilla force beginning to battle for a separate state in the northeast. During this time, at Saddhatissa's temple Premadasa produced a particular narrative about this condition in the country. As it was reported in the *Island*, addressing a meeting of one thousand monks, Premadasa stated:

> The country was facing a grave threat due to the inhuman and vicious acts of a small group of people. They have resorted to the most beastly methods of killing innocent civilians and even infants and children. This showed how sick minds could disrupt the majority peace loving people. . . . It was indeed a great injustice done to Sri Lanka. . . . These terrorists with assistance from outside were bent on destroying civilization and civilized ways of living.[82]

79. "Taruna Bhikṣūn Vahansēlā Bana Kīmata Peramuna Gatayutuyi" ("The young monks must learn how to preach bana"), *Davasa*, July 23, 1984.

80. "Terrorists Fight Not to Win Ethnic Rights," *Island*, May 1987.

81. Interview with Kolonnawe Dhammika, Oct. 10, 1997. Dhammika used the words *terrorism* and *terror* interchangeably to characterize the political context in 1984; "terror" as a conceptual category, however, was constructed and deployed within a particular political context in 1989; see chapter 7.

82. *Island*, "Terrorists Fight Not to Win Ethnic Rights."

The picture painted by these words is clear: Sri Lanka, "facing a grave threat," is on the brink of losing its "civilization" (one may compare these words to the speech Premadasa gave at the canopy opening in 1987). My point here is that the possibility of voicing these warnings about the danger of terrorism to the "civilization" of Sri Lanka in front of thousands of monks, "the sentinels of the nation," was generated by the relations between Premadasa and monks like Saddhatissa. The cant about "terrorism" run amok enabled the implicit representation of himself as next president, who, if elected, could eliminate the threat.

Monks like Saddhatissa supported Premadasa because, as Saddhatissa's own student-monk put it, they "liked to be in the spotlight" (*āsayi rūpa rāmuvata*), to "appear visible" (*penī indīmata*). Saddhatissa's popularity—boosted by the president's "alliance" (*sambandatāvaya*) with the temple—attracted many Buddhist "donors" to the temple. Through the monk's influence and intervention, the donors themselves "got things done" (*väda karagattā*) by the government.[83] It was because of Saddhatissa's continuing quest for popularity, my informant continued, that the monk lost his life at the hands of an assassin. What is important about Saddhatissa's assassination is that it marked the emergence of a space that contested the formerly authorized relation between Premadasa, Buddhism, and the nation, authorized in part by monks like Saddhatissa. The context of Saddhatissa's assassination shows how competing and opposing narratives sought, on the one hand, to produce Premadasa's "Buddhist" identity as difference and, on the other, to subvert it.

As early as June 1989, Premadasa was lobbying to send the IPKF back to India, a promise he made as part of his campaign for president.[84] Here it is crucial to bear in mind some aspects of the political climate of the country. The JVP, which had begun its own "war" to overthrow the Premadasa government, also demanded the removal of the IPKF. Since January 1989, the JVP had killed, according to the government's estimate, more than seventeen hundred "police officers, politicians, and ordinary citizens" who had failed to comply with its (the JVP's) own law. For several months, this unwritten JVP law brought the country to a virtual standstill, demanding the closure of

83. Interview with Dhammika, Oct., 10, 1997. Dhammika now berates those who, after benefitting from his teacher, abandoned the temple following his death.

84. "Text of Premadasa-Gandhi Letters Tabled in House: No Mandatory Role for Indian Army in Lanka," *Daily News*, July 8, 1989.

shops, business establishments, schools, and universities, and the stoppage of work and transport.[85] In June 1989, the government imposed islandwide curfews, claiming to quell such "violent activities" (*pracanda väda*).[86]

It is in the wake of what he himself called "chaos" (*arbudaya*) that Premadasa, as president, spoke of sending back the Indian army as a "common" challenge shared by his government and the JVP opponents.[87] This he claimed was the duty of "patriotic" (*deshapremī*) Sri Lankans, which, of course, was the favored term that the JVP used to define its identity. A few weeks later, Premadasa asserted a direct correlation between this "patriotic duty" — sending back the Indian army — and Buddhism. In a public address about India's refusal to pull out its army, Premadasa warned Indian Prime Minister Rajiv Gandhi: "Keeping armed forces in a country without its consent [is] a violation of Panchasila [the five precepts of Buddhism]."[88] It is at the juncture of constructing such a strategic link between Buddhism, patriotism, and the nation that Premadasa invited Saddhatissa to support the government's cause by making a statement on television.

Issuing statements favorable to the government was seen as a dangerous practice at the time because the JVP considered any support for the government a "crime" punishable by death. Despite these visible dangers, on July 29, 1989, the anniversary of signing the accord — and this seems far from a coincidence — Saddhatissa appeared on television and commended the president's labor to send back the Indian army and invited all Sri Lankans to join in the cause. A day after his statement, Saddhatissa received a hail of anonymous calls threatening his life. The calls continued until August 3, 1989. That day, according to some "reports," at night two "unknown" men arrived at the temple. They informed the elderly temple attendant that they had

85. "Hadisi Nītiya Yalit Pänevve Akamätten Uvat Karanna Siduvelā, Ranjan" ("The curfew was imposed again because of necessity"), *Dinamina*, June 21, 1989; also see Chandraprema, "*Sri Lanka: The Years of Terror: The JVP Insurrection, 1987–1989*" (Colombo: Lake House, 1991), 265–86.

86. Ibid.; "Pracanda Kriyā Vāda Varjana Ādiyen Ārtikayatat Jana Jivītayatat Bādā" ("The violent activities and strikes are barriers to the economy and the lives of the people"), *Dinamina*, June 21, 1989.

87. "Vāda Bēda Tikakata Amataka Kara Sāma Hāmudāva Yavana Abhiyōgayata Ekāmen Muhuna Demu" ("Let us forget debates and confrontations and face the challenge of sending back the IPKF as one"), *Dinamina*, June 17, 1989.

88. "Keeping Armed Forces in a Country without Its Consent: Violation of Panchasila, President," *Sunday Observer*, July 23, 1989.

come to invite Saddhatissa to an almsgiving ceremony. As they entered Saddhatissa's reading room, one of the men greeted the monk by offering a tray
of betel and worshipping him. Then the other man pulled out a gun and fired
two shots, killing the monk on the spot.[89]

The case of Saddhatissa's assassination is still unsolved. It might be called
a mystery. No one—neither the resident monks at the temple nor the Buddhist neighbors—is said to have seen the perpetrators of the killing. There are
people who might have seen the killers, suspected to be the members of the
JVP, and who now recall sketchy details of what happened, but at the time no
one would dare identify them. Even President Premadasa, who spoke at Saddhatissa's elaborate state funeral, did not refer to the killing of Saddhatissa as
an assassination but simply as a "sudden death" (*hadisi apavatvīmak*) and "a
loss to the entire world."[90] Later the government conducted an investigation:
it lasted only a few days, and no arrests have ever been made. Even today,
some maintain that given the conditions at that time in Sri Lanka, they could
not be precise about who killed Saddhatissa. However, some of the widespread rumors linked the president to the monk's assassination, maintaining
that the government ordered it as part of a strategy to blame it on the JVP (*jvp
eka udin yanna*). Killing monks, as some hold, authorized the government to
launch an islandwide counteroffensive on the JVP, portraying them as killers
of "pious monks."[91]

Questions about the identity of the assassin are not, of course, of interest
to this study. But the assassination, marking the conjuncture discussed
above, made possible a series of competing narratives that tried to authorize
a very different kind of identity of Premadasa and his relation to Buddhism
and the nation. This new identity of Premadasa is one of a "killer" (*minī
maruvā*) who unleashed a period of "terror" that he himself claimed to have
eliminated by restoring peace in Sri Lanka.[92] Recently, the government of

89. Interview with Dhammika, Oct. 10, 1997; "Rūpavāhinī Prakaśāyen Pasuva Nādunana
Aya Durakatanayen Nāhimita Bāna Vādunā" ("After statement on TV unknown people telephoned and scolded monk"), *Rivirāsa*, Aug. 6, 1989.
90. "Saddhatissa Nāhimiyange Viyōva Mulu Lovatama Imahat Pāduvak" ("Saddhatissa's
passing away a great loss to the entire world"), *Dinamina*, Aug. 11, 1989.
91. I heard these rumors many times from a number of monks and lay Buddhists in Kolonnawa, Kelaniya, Colombo, Kadawata, Kandy, Andiambalama, and Dambulla during my research
in Sri Lanka, 1994 to 1997.
92. At the beginning of every year after 1989, the government newspapers devoted pages list-
ing various "achievements" of the Premadasa government. In 1993 two whole pages in the *Daily*

Chandrika Bandaranaike officially endorsed this identity of Premadasa as a "killer"—of not only monks but various political figures as well. It announced that special presidential commissions had uncovered "hard evidence" that pointed to Premadasa's "direct" involvement in the assassination of well-known Sri Lankans, including Premadasa's former UNP colleague Lalith Athulathmudali and his minister of defense, Kobbekaduwa.[93] These kinds of counternarratives not only contested the formerly authorized identity of Premadasa as "a real Buddhist" but also cast doubt on the "Buddhist" identities of those (monks) who helped to produce it. The counternarratives about the president became so pervasive that a few days prior to his death in 1993, Premadasa himself implored people: "Kill me by any means . . . , but do not kill my pure character (*pirisidu caritaya*)."[94]

It is in the context of the voicing of these kinds of rival narratives that I wish to locate one of President Premadasa's final "Buddhist" projects, the construction of a massive Buddha statue at a temple popularly known as the Bahirawakanda. But I must point out that Premadasa undertook and completed various other "Buddhist" projects prior to his death in 1993. Among them were the creation of a separate Ministry for Buddhist Affairs (Buddha Sasana Ministry) in 1989 and a Buddha Sasana Fund in 1990;[95] the establishment in 1990 of a Supreme Sangha Council, which would "advise the government on the measures needed to be taken to foster and develop the Buddha Sasana;"[96] and the much-contested plan in 1992 to ordain 2,300

News and *Dinamina* credited Premadasa with, among other things, the following noteworthy accomplishments: "Terror Wiped Out and Peace and Stability Ensured; A Religious Awakening"; see "Four Year Record of 'New Vision-New Ideal' for Mother Lanka," *Dinamina* and *Daily News*, Jan. 2, 1993. These were described as "immortal services." *Dinamina*, May 4, 1989.

93. "Premadasa Involved: Assassination of Lalith and Kobbekaduwa Commissions Point Finger at Ex-president," *Midweek Mirror*, Oct. 8, 1997; "Premadasa Targeted Kobbekaduwa," *Daily News*, Oct. 9, 1997.

94. "Mä Marä Dämuväta Kamak Nä; Mage Caritaya Ghätanaya Karanna Epä" ("Kill me; but do not kill my character"), *Dinamina*, May 3, 1993.

95. "Buddha Sāsana Aramudala Ärabhū Vagayi" ("The Buddha Sasana fund created"), *Dinamina*, Dec. 6, 1990.

96. "Supreme Advisory Council on the Buddha Sasana Formed," *Observer*, Sept. 30, 1990. For more on these events, see *Who Is He? What Is He Doing?* 135–45. There is more on the Ministry of the Buddha Sasana in C. R. de Silva, "State Support for Religion in Contemporary Sri Lanka: Some Ideological and Policy Issues," unpublished paper delivered at the Sixth Sri Lanka Conference, Peradeniya, Sri Lanka, 1997, 6–7.

Buddhist monks as part of celebrating the 2,300th anniversary of the introduction of Buddhism to the island.[97]

The plan to ordain monks, proposed a few months after the impeachment attempt, unlike other Premadasa projects created a hail of criticism from many members of the Sangha. One monk described it as "one of the places where Premadasa failed [to win the approval of monks]" (*eka tänakin premadasa päradunä*).[98] A few monks did express support for the proposal, but many popular monks who had endorsed earlier Premadasa projects raised severe objection to the ordination plan.[99] Walpola Rahula, a vocal advocate of Premadasa's gam udāva movement and his effort to withdraw the IPKF,[100] had praised Premadasa as the most "genuine, qualified person for the leadership of uniting all Theravada Buddhist countries";[101] but he opposed the president's plans to ordain the twenty-three hundred monks. He surprisingly stated that it was not an effort to "develop Buddhism" but a political strategy to "win votes at the next election. It is a disgrace [*nindāvak*]."[102] In the wake of the objections, the big ordination ceremony came to an abrupt halt: only a few hundred monks were ordained.[103]

These narratives about Premadasa, it is important to note, began to emerge in late 1991, when powerful antigovernment forces (for example, the impeachment attempt) charged the president with a variety of constitutional and ethical violations. By early 1992, a number of monks began to view Premadasa's projects (for example, the village reawakening celebrations and annual festivities at the Tooth Temple) as "insane activities" (*pissu väda*),[104] even though they had been authorized by monks themselves. This criticism

97. *Divayina*, Feb. 28, 1992.

98. Interview with Medhananda, Nov. 16, 1997, and Dhammaloka, Aug. 8, 1996; also conversations with monks in Kandy and Colombo, Aug. 5–8, 1996, and Oct. 5–9, 1997.

99. See the debate in the newspapers; for example, "Kula Daruvan Mahana Karavīma" ("Ordination of young boys"), *Silumina*, May 8, 1992.

100. See, *Dinamina*, Apr. 21, 1989; *Dinamina*, June 6, 1989.

101. "Theravādi Bauddha Ratavala Sandhanayaka Nāyakatvayata Niyama Sudussä Apē Janapatiyi," *Dinamina*, July 4, 1991.

102. "Rajaya 2300k Mahana Karanna Yannē Labana Pārat Balaya Labana Aramunin" ("The government plans to ordain two thousand three hundred boys with the intention of obtaining power next year"), *Divanyina*, Feb. 2, 1992.

103. Conversations with monks in Colombo and with the staff at the Ministry of the Buddha Sasana, Oct. 5, 1997.

104. Interviews with Madhananda, Nov. 16, 1996; Dhammaloka, Aug. 8, 1996; Dhammika, Oct. 10, 1997; and several other student monks at Peradeniya University, Aug. 9, 1996.

became conspicuous in regard to a particular feature of the awakenings. At each gam udāva, Premadasa built a cētiya, or pagoda, and named it after a king, a prime minister, or a political leader considered to be a "great patriot."[105] It was a novel practice since, as one monk pointed out, in the entire history of Buddhism in Sri Lanka not a single cētiya had been constructed in honor of a layman. Usually found at Buddhist temples, cētiyas enshrine relics of the Buddha and the arhats and are objects of Buddhist veneration; thus, many monks considered Premadasa's random erection of pagodas for lay people a "great shame" (maha lājjāvak) and "dishonor" (avanambuvak, tuttudekē väda) to Buddhism and the nation.[106]

The point should be obvious: a few years after he became president, a number of varying rival discourses emerged, competing to contest the formerly authorized relation between Premadasa, Buddhism, and the nation. This contestation, it is well to note, coincided with the impeachment attempt, which, among other things, depicted the president as suffering from "mental illness" (mānasika ledak).[107] It was under the heading of mental illness that the impeachment, led by Lalith Athulathmudali and others, portrayed Premadasa's construction of temples and pagodas as acts of "blind devotion" (anda visvāsayak) that conspired to "deceive the public."[108] One cannot overlook these competing narratives: the impeachment attempt became the site of debate on public platforms and in the media.[109] The power and persuasiveness of these new narratives about Premadasa grew in the context of Athulathmudali's assassination, which was widely suspected to have been ordered by Premadasa. The assassination had groups of Buddhists stoning temples and setting them on fire, among them those of monks considered to be the president's close allies.[110] It is in the context of these shifting discourses, which

105. Premadasa, for example, named cetiyas in 1990 and 1991 after Devanam Piyatissa (devana pätis mahāsäya) and Weera Keppetipola, respectively; see Dinamina, June 17, 1990; Daily News, June 19 and 22, 1992. Premadasa is said to have begun this tradition by naming the first pagoda at a gam udāva after King Dutugämunu, the archetypal hero-defender of Buddhism in the Mahāvamsa, the great chronicle of Sri Lanka.

106. Interview with Medhananda, Nov. 15, 1996.

107. The copy of the impeachment motion in Disanayaka, Mā Atsan kala Doshābhiyōgaya, 113.

108. Ibid., 115.

109. On the details of the fierce impeachment campaign led by Lalith Athulathmudali and Gamini Disanayaka, two of the most prominent cabinet ministers in the Jayewardene government, see Disanayaka, Mā Atsan kala Doshābhiyōgaya.

110. I have in mind here the case of Alle Gunawamsa, one of President Premadasa's close confidant monks. During the funeral procession of Athulathmudali, people stoned and set fire to

produced an identity of Premadasa as a killer and a danger to Buddhism and the nation, that I want to discuss his involvement in the construction of the Bahirawakanda Buddha statue at the Sri Mahabodhi Temple in Kandy.[111]

The Sri Mahabhodi Temple, or Bahirawakanda temple, is located on a hilltop, Bahirawakanda (the hill of the Bahirawa demon), that overlooks the entire city of Kandy.[112] Of relatively recent origin, the temple was built on land donated in the early 1970s to Ampitiye Dhammarama, a monk from the Amarapura Nikāya, by the minister of land in the SLFP government. Initially, the monk resided in a makeshift residence on the hill, soliciting funds for the construction of a temple. The head monks of the Tooth Temple, however, protested the plan, claiming that given its strategic location on a hill facing the Tooth Temple, a new temple from a different Buddhist fraternity would overshadow the "center" (*mulastānaya*) of the Siyam Nikāya. In the early 1980s, the monks wrote to President Jayewardene and demanded the removal of Dhammarama from Bahiravakanda, claiming that he was not a "proper monk" (*koyeda yana unnsāsē kenek*). The ownership of the land remained contested until, in the mid-1980s, a chief monk of the Amarapura Nikāya, Hinatiyana Dhammaloka, compelled Premadasa to intervene and legally grant the land to Dhammarama. This sole intervention remained Premadasa's only support for Dhammarama's temple until early 1990.

During the early phases of building the temple with the support of only a handful of businessmen from Kandy, Dhammarama extended several invitations to Premadasa to visit Bahiravakanda. Premadasa turned down such invitations, so it is said, because he did not want to be seen patronizing a temple with which the powerful monks of the Tooth Temple had sour disputes.[113] Later, all of that changed. In the late 1980s, Dhammarama began to build a Buddha statue that would stand more than eighty feet in height—a tall task that many thought would be impossible for a single monk unless he had substantial financial backing. In January 1992, a few months after

Gunawamsa's temple, forcing him to flee and live in exile for several months: interview with Alle Gunawamsa and other monks in Colombo, July 1995.

111. In chapter 7, I delineate other aspects of Premadasa's identity as a "killer," there in the context of his government-sponsored paramilitary groups' bloody battle with, and eventual elimination of, the JVP.

112. The following information about the temple's history comes from two interviews conducted with the monks at the Bahirawakanda temple, July 17–18, 1996.

113. Interviews, Bhahirawakanda temple, July 17–18, 1996.

Athulathmudali had held one of the largest impeachment rallies against the president in Kandy, the newspapers flashed front-page headlines announcing Premadasa's sudden visit to the Bahirawakanda temple "to investigate the construction work on the Buddha image" in Kandy. The newspapers portrayed Premadasa as the sole architect of the project, when in fact much work, worth almost two million rupees, had already been done on the statue.[114] During his visit, Premadasa donated a half-million rupees from the president's fund to the project; he also planned to unveil the statue ceremonially a year later, when he would be celebrating the fourth anniversary of his presidency. In January 1993, the government newspapers ran poetic front-page headlines about Premadasa's unveiling of the Buddha statue[115]—an occasion that "brings peace to the entire island of Sri Lanka." The Buddha statue at Bahirawakanda, one paper said, "brightens not only the Buddhists in Kandy but the entire Buddhist world"; it "adds a new chapter to the . . . history of Buddhism in Sri Lanka . . . it will become an object of veneration in the Buddhist world."[116]

Significantly, this event did not seem to attract the support of many monks. Despite the government's (and also Dhammarama's) attempt to portray the construction of the statue as a "historical event," there were hardly any articles about it in the newspapers, no words of praise by his former friends in the monkhood about his involvement in the project. The statue's unveiling marked that particular context in which Premadasa's image as a real Buddhist had come to be questioned by both monks and lay Buddhists. The chief monks of the Tooth Temple and many other Buddhist monks and lay people in Kandy considered that a new statue, painted gold,[117] situated on a hill facing the Tooth Temple, posed a "challenge" (abhiyōghayaka) to the Tooth Temple. It was seen as a disgrace. This intimated also that Premadasa was an accomplice to, if not the architect of, that disgrace.[118] So the "Buddhist" project of constructing the Bahirawakanda Buddha statue produced the ironic effect of contesting the "Buddhist" identity of the president.

114. "Bahirawakande Idivana Budu Pilimayē Vāda Piriksīmata Janapati Yayi" ("The president goes to investigate the construction work on the Buddha statue at Bahirawakanda"), *Dinamina*, Jan. 7, 1992.

115. One headline read, "Sambudu Piliruva Bahirawakande-Tunhelayata Sisilasayi Nibande" ("Buddha statue at Bahirawakande, always a blessing to the whole country"), *Dinamina*, Jan. 2, 1991.

116. *Dinamina*, Jan. 1, 1991.

117. After Premadasa's death, the statue was painted white.

118. Interview with Dhammaloka, Aug. 10, 1996.

It is interesting, however, that three days following the unveiling of the Bahirawakanda statue, despite implicit objections of the chief monks who had supported the president earlier, Premadasa returned to the Tooth Temple to celebrate the anniversary of his presidency and address the nation from the octagon with his family and the monks of the Tooth Temple at his side. Once again the state newspapers carried announcements with pictures of Premadasa standing with a tray of flowers against the background of the Tooth Temple. One announcement read: "May the sacred tooth relic bless his excellency the president, who ushered in a new era to our motherland, bringing solace to the poorest of the poor, dispelling the darkness in their Lives."[119] This I see as an example of the ways in which the Tooth Temple had been made a particular "Buddhist" site that enabled the Premadasa government to make centrally visible an authoritative public discourse—one that sought to attenuate the force of rival contesting narratives about the president's "true" Buddhist identity and the nation.

In providing this account of the shifting fortunes of Premadasa's "religious" identity, its rise and fall, I have wanted to argue that the configurations of questions about who and what kinds of practice do and do not define what kind of relations between religion, the state, and the nation are located in specific conjunctures of debates. The identity of Premadasa as a real Buddhist leader born to liberate the Buddhist nation came to be authorized in a particular context. Significant to making centrally visible these relations between Premadasa, Buddhism, and the nation were practices like the construction of the golden canopy for the Tooth Temple. These relations, however, were contested in a different conjuncture: competing discourses began to portray Premadasa as a man whose practices disgraced Buddhism and who had forfeited the right to rule the "Buddhist" nation. The agents of these kinds of rival narratives were the same monks who had been his former intimate allies. Premadasa himself responded to this challenge, as we saw in his completion of the Bahirawakanda statue and his official return to the Tooth Temple to celebrate his presidency. But such responses themselves produced ironic effects: they came to be seen as efforts of a beleaguered president, in the face of an ocean of controversy and contestation, desperately seeking to assert and keep in public view his formerly authorized "Buddhist" identity. The emergence

119. "A Tribute to Our Leader," *Daily News*, Jan. 2, 1993.

and submergence of this identity is a crucial instance of how identity, as Foucault has noted, is both an instrument and effect of discourse/power. A conjuncture of discourses not only produces identity but "undermines and exposes it, renders it fragile, makes it possible to thwart [and contest] it."[120]

In concluding, I want to make clear that, in using terms like *"Buddhism"* and *"nation"* frequently throughout this chapter, I have not sought to pursue an argument that informs some contemporary disciplinary studies on "religion" and "nationalism" in South Asia. Put broadly, that argument wants to show how "religion"—or "religious movements," be they Hindu, Sikh, Muslim, or Buddhist—plays an instrumental part in the processes of establishing and defining the identity of the "nation." It is this argument that comes to us in terms of "religious nationalism."[121] Now this concept, religious nationalism, it seems to me, is another disciplinary category to capture the supposed fusion of religion and politics, seeking to avoid confining nationalism to a public domain of purely "secular" modern politics.[122] This is because, as some argue, the distinction between the secular and the sacred, religion and politics—a distinction that sees such ideas as belonging to separate spheres—"is an ideological element in the Western discourse of modernity" [located in the Enlightenment and colonialism].[123] As two recent scholars, van der Veer and Lehmann, argue, this dichotomy has enabled the West to understand both its own self/identity as secular, hence nonreligious, and the non-West as embodying "a history of dangerous politicization of religious difference."[124]

---

120. Foucault, *History of Sexuality*, vol. 1, 101.

121. Here I am particularly thinking of van der Veer's *Religious Nationalism*. For others who are interested in understanding religious nationalism in terms of "religious symbols in the political field," see Thomas Blom Hansen, *The Saffron Wave: Democracy and Hindu Nationalism in Modern India* (Princeton: Princeton University Press, 1999), 148–50. In the context of Sri Lanka, see R. L. Stirrat, "Catholic Identity and Global Forces in Sinhala Sri Lanka," in *Buddhist Fundamentalism*. Stirrat, building upon van der Veer, argues, "Certainly religion has become one of the key features in the definition of the nation and national identity in Sri Lanka" (153). Similarly, speaking of the global emergence of two kinds of nationalism, ethnic and ideological, Mark Juergensmeyer writes that "if the ethnic approach to religious nationalism, *politicizes* religion by employing religious identities for political ends, an ideological approach to religious nationalism does the opposite: it *religionizes* politics"; see his "The Worldwide Rise of Religious Nationalism," *Journal of International Affairs* 50, no. 1 (1996): 5.

122. This kind of disciplinary conceptualization of religion and politics is discussed in chapter 3.

123. Van der Veer and Lehman, eds., *Nation and Religion*, 3.

124. Ibid., 3–4; see also van der Veer, *Religious Nationalism*, esp. chapter 1.

Understandably, wary of this kind of dichotomy that privileges the West an exclusive identity of rationality that the "backward" non-West supposedly lacks, Van der Veer and Lehmann want to contend that religion and nationalism are interrelated in complicated ways, not only in the East but in the West as well.

While I sympathize with this argument about the Western discourse of modernity, I am skeptical of the analytical soundness of disciplinary concepts, like that of religious nationalism, that labor to illuminate the interconnection between religion and the nation. I suspect that such labors do not yield any new insight into the discursive formations of the altering meanings of categories like "religion" and "nation" and that, instead, they participate in a set of presumptive questions about what constitute the identity of nationalism. To suggest, in other words, that nationalism should be seen as something conditioned or influenced by "religion" is to assume that religion embodies some independent autonomous "religious" identity. Here I am in agreement with Talal Asad, who has raised some serious misgivings about the supposed interrelation between religion and nationalism:

> To insist that nationalism should be seen as a religion, or even as having been shaped by religion is, in my view, to miss the nature and consequence of the revolution brought about by the Enlightenment doctrine of secularism in the structure of modern collective representations and practices. Of course modern nationalism draws on preexisting languages and practices — including those that we call, anachronistically, "religious." How could it be otherwise? Yet it does not follow that religion forms nationalism.[125]

In making this argument, what Asad wants to point out is, of course, not that nationalism should be taken as a secular matter. Rather, if I read him correctly, Asad wants to point out that categories like "religious" and "secular" are not things but efforts to identify and define elusive and opaque sets of "particular ideas, sentiments, practices, institutions, and traditions — as well as followers who instantiate, maintain, or alter them."[126]

It is the instantiation, maintenance, and alteration of the relations between religion, identity, and the nation that have preoccupied me in this chapter.

---

125. See Asad, "Religion, Nation-state, Secularism," in *Nation and Religion*, 187. Note that, surprisingly, this article is in van der Veer and Lehmann's edited volume.

126. Ibid.

I have sought to demonstrate the ways in which differing persons, practices, and narratives became authorized to come into central view and fade from view as embodying and defining what should and should not belong to the identity of religion, the nation, and difference. Approached from this perspective, one would not hurry to identify what nationalism is, whether it is religious or secular; or whether it is an "imagined community"—to use that oft-cited and oft-criticized Andersonian phrase.[127] Rather, *nationalism*—if we continue to insist on its use as a theoretical concept to identify the authoritative definitions of varying borders, features, persons, the entailments of a "nation"—can be taken, in a very broad sense, as a synonym for the relation between identity and difference. If nationalism is about (competing to authorize a particular kind of) identity, about what kinds of ("religious") persons and practices can belong to the "nation," that identity, however temporarily authorized, is produced in relation to the "difference(s)" that it (that is, identity) is not. In a brilliant discussion, Gyanendra Pandey, speaking of the "Hindu" history of famous Ayodhya, the supposed Indian birthplace of Rama, the hero of the epic *Ramayana*, makes a similar argument about the relation between identity and difference. He writes: "The recent Hindu history of Ayodhya, which also stands for the Hindu history of India, is not about the construction of the Ram Janmabhumi temple. It is about its destruction [by the 'Muslim-Others']. To that extent, it is a history, not of the temple but of the mosque built upon its ruins, not of the greatness of the 'Hindu' but of the evilness of the 'muslim.'"[128] Since this relation between identity and difference, the religious and the secular, is an altering one, located as it is in those contingent conjunctures, then the questions about whether it is religious nationalism, or whether religion influences nationalism, are theoretically faulty. In other words, what we call the "nation," like "religion," is always in the discursive making. To put it in the words of William Connolly, "[a] nation is something that has been or will be but never is at any actually existing moment."[129]

127. Benedict Anderson, *Imagined Communities: Reflections on the Origin and Spread of Nationalism* (1983; reprint, London: Verso, 1992). For a very perceptive criticism of this idea, see Partha Chatterjee, *The Nation and Its Fragments: Colonial and Postcolonial Histories* (Princeton: Princeton University Press, 1992), esp. chapter 2, "Whose Imagined Community?"

128. See Gyanendra Pandey, "The Culture of History," in *In Near Ruins: Cultural Theory at the End of the Century*, ed. Nicholas B. Dirks (Minneapolis: University of Minnesota Press, 1998), 31.

129. William Conolloy, "Liberalism, Secularism, and the Nation," in *Why I Am Not a Secularist*, 85.

In the next chapter, I seek to understand the relation between identity and difference in terms of the concept of "tradition."

CHAPTER SIX

Tradition and Difference

Since July 20, 1985, a new higher ordination (*upasampadā*)[1] movement has emerged at the Dambulla Buddhist temple in Sri Lanka. Spearheaded by the head monk of the temple, Inamaluwe Sumangala, the new ordination movement claims to "challenge" the dominant Buddhist monastic tradition of ordaining monks on the basis of caste, a practice that became institutionalized in eighteenth-century Sri Lanka. The new ordination movement provides an illustrative example of the altering formations of the relation between "tradition" and "difference." On the face of it, the movement seems to involve a debate between two groups of monks about the irrelevance of caste to monastic ordination—specifically, a debate between the Dambulla monks and the monks of the Asgiriya temple, one of several chapters of the Siyam Nikāya (fraternity) that ordains only "high-caste" Buddhist males. However, the challenge constituted by the new ordination can be seen as a complex example of the ways in which questions about tradition, identity, and difference come to be battled out in differing conjunctures. This battling is central to the authorization of Sumangala's leadership of the Dambulla temple, one of the wealthiest of its kind in Sri Lanka. I want to suggest that this new movement can be understood within a reconceptualized space of the Dambulla temple in which questions about the temple's identity, Buddhism, history, and past are authoritatively debated.[2]

As in other chapters, what concerns me are the discursive strategies that make such questions possible and important. Guided by this concern, I turn to contentious debates—between the monks of the Dambulla and other leading temples, the (Premadasa) state, and lay Buddhists—that competed to

1. There are two ordinations: the upasampada and the lower ordination (*pabbajjā*). For a discussion of the two—supposedly synonymous at the "beginning," but separated later—see Gombrich, "Temporary Ordination," 42.

2. The term *reconceptualized space* is not meant as an abstract theoretical concept; it is a name for complex conjunctures that enabled the authorization of a new identity or a representation of the Dambulla temple and its monks. Throughout the chapter, *representation* and *reconceptualized space* are used interchangeably to refer to those conjunctures.

stake out authoritative claims about Buddhism, tradition, monasticism, and difference, preempting the space of other opposing discourses. In exploring these competing narratives about tradition and difference, I do not tell that conventional story about tradition as an ensemble of practices and beliefs that existed prior to modernity, prior to our supposed rationalist, progressivist, radical ways of thinking about the "traditional past" handed down from generation to generation. We know now the failure of that story to yield the critical conceptual insights necessary to understand concepts like tradition as historically produced, contingent ideas. *Tradition*, as I pursue to understand it, with some help from David Scott and Alasdair MacIntyre, is a name for an embodied debate in which opposing moral claims about what counts as religion, orthodoxy, and truth are authoritatively, and in centrally visible ways, positioned, argued, and fought out.[3] Tradition, in other words, is a name for the ways in which identity/self is made to be *seen* authoritatively positioned against difference/other.

But this positioning, its seeming supremacy over difference, is contingently authorized. In this light we could speak of the practice of ordaining monks on the basis of caste distinctions in Sri Lanka as such a discursive tradition—animated by certain differing persons, narratives, and institutions—in which divergent truth-claims are made about its acceptability, about its virtue, about its necessity to Buddhism and monasticism, seeking to exclude countervoices and arguments as other/difference. "Necessity," of course as Nietzsche has noted, "is not a fact but an interpretation."[4] "Tradition" is constituted by such interpretations about its identity, by the stakes it engineers about what should and should not constitute the truths of its identity, and by virtue of this, tradition remains subject—vulnerable, if you will—to conflicts of interpretations, argumentation, and contestation, subject to the subversion of its identity as difference, its truth as falsehood. But the moments of a tradition's vulnerability to rival arguments and debates are never self-evident, the conditions of their possibility unknowable in advance. My effort in this chapter is to explore one moment of such a discursive tradition's vulnerability to contestation. I want to read the casteless ordination movement at Dambulla as a particular discursive site that seeks to battle out its rival tradition of caste-based ordination. This reading, I contend, has something

---

3. See David Scott's formulation in his *Refashioning Futures*, 124; again, see also MacIntyre, "The Virtues, the Unity of a Human Life, and the Concept of a Tradition," in *After Virtue*.
4. Nietzsche, *Will to Power*, 297.

crucially significant to tell us about the complex configurations of tradition, identity, and difference.

The Institutionalization of Caste as a Prerequisite to Monastic Ordination

There is documentary evidence that concerns with "caste" were present among monks as early as the medieval period of Sri Lanka, and it is well discussed in the literature.[5] However, caste as a subject of debate in the sangha became pronounced when the two renowned temples of the Siyam Nikāya, Malwatta and Asgiriya (both based in Kandy), employed a new policy of conferring the higher ordination only on those who belonged to the "highest caste" (*goyigama*). One Buddhist monk told me an oral version of it, which differs slightly from that which is found in the Sinhala text *Mandārampura-puwata*. According to the oral account I heard, the policy to ordain monks based on caste came into existence when Kirti Sri Rajasimha (1747–82) had a perplexing experience as he was riding his royal elephant into Kandy. As the king approached the city, a Buddhist novice, supposedly from a "low-caste," stood up from his seat and bowed to the king. Since a monk never bows his head to any lay person, the king was troubled and requested the chief monks of the Malwatta temple henceforth not to ordain low-caste people.[6] In the Sinhalese text *Nīthiratanāwaliya*, another version of the story has a similar

5. If we think of a phrase such as *birth* or *family name* in terms of what we today mean by *caste*, we come across references to caste considerations in the monastic order before the eighteenth century; for example, *Dambadeni Katikāvata*, an eleventh-century text, quotes a passage from the fifth-century *Samantapāsādikā*, by the Pali commentator Buddhaghosa, that says those who are ordained should be "cleansed" or "examined" (*sōdhetvā*); however, the *Katikāvata* text reinterprets the word *examine* to mean that candidates' "birth and family" should be examined (*jātigōtra vicārā*) before they are ordained; cited in A. V. Suraweera, *Sinhala Katikāvata hā Bhikshu Samājaya* (Colombo: Gunasena, 1971), 110. Buddhaghosa did not mean what the *Dambadeni Katikāvata* attributes to him; he meant that an examination should be conducted to find out if the candidate has been a debtor, slave, or soldier, which would bar him from admission into the sangha. On the "prevalence" of certain notions of caste in the medieval sangha, see Y. Dhammavisuddhi, *Polonnaru Hā Dambadeni Katikāvat* (Colombo: Karunaratna Saha Putrayo, 1995), 77–83; M. Ilangasinha, *Buddhism in Medieval Sri Lanka* (Delhi: Sri Satguru, 1992), 83–90. G. Panabokke, who maintains that caste discriminations in the sangha "gained ground from the Polonnaruwa period onwards," gives a largely complementary account; see *History of the Buddhist Sangha in India and Sri Lanka* (Kelaniya: Post-Graduate Institute of Pali and Buddhist Studies, 1993), 186–88.

6. This story is in *Mandārampura Puwata*, which is said to be an appendix to the eighteenth-century *Kīrti Sri Rājasimha Katikāvata*; cited in Suraweera, *Sinhala Katikāvata*. This

plot structure, but in that version a group of monks complained to King Kirti Sri Rajasimha that monks from low castes had received higher ordination: they requested that he issue a decree prohibiting the ordination of low-caste males into the monastic order.[7] When the king informed Velivita Saranankara, the progenitor of the eighteenth-century "Buddhist revival," about the situation, Saranankara refused even to consider it, caste differences having no place in Buddhism. However, we are told, the king later ignored Saranankara's advice and, in order to appease the high-caste monks who had threatened to leave the order, issued a decree that only "those of good birth" should be given higher ordination.[8]

In both stories, we see how the monks are portrayed as strategically using the authority of the king to authorize the practice of caste-based ordination. But in the latter story, what is striking is that the author wants to relieve Saranankara of the burden of responsibility for even thinking that the idea of caste can be part of the Buddhist monastic identity; he instead places the burden on unidentified monks and the king.

Though caste became the central qualification for (higher) ordination in the Kandyan monastic community, the monks of the Asgiriya and Malwatta temples clashed over how and where the ordinations should be performed, which led them to hold separate higher ordinations every year.[9] In this context of competing narratives about Buddhism, identity, and caste, we see the emergence of two new monastic fraternities, Amarapura and Ramañña.[10] These new fraternities broke away from the community of high-caste monks, claiming they would "reform" the caste-ridden monastic world. But they were not immune to making caste distinctions since today Amarapura and Ramanna fraternities, too, ordain monks on the basis of caste.[11] In the last hundred

---

version of the story is slightly different from the one that monks told Richard Gombrich; see his *Precept and Practice: Traditional Buddhism in the Rural Highlands of Kandy* (Oxford, U.K.: Clarendon Press, 1971), 312.

7. *Nīthiratanāwaliya*; cited in A. H. Mirando, *Buddhism in Sri Lanka in the Seventeenth and the Eighteenth Centuries* (Dehiwala: Tisara Prakashakayo, 1985), 136, 142. This incident is mentioned in K. Malalgoda, *Buddhism in Sinhalese Society*, 91; Gombrich, *Precept and Practice*, 308; however, neither Gombrich nor Malalgoda refers to the above text.

8. Cited in *Buddhism in Sri Lanka*, A. H. Mirando, ed., 142.

9. Malalgoda, *Buddhism in Sinhalese Society*, 125.

10. For an excellent discussion of the emergence of these two fraternities, see, ibid., 144–77.

11. The widespread assumption among both monks and lay people is that Rāmañña Nikāya does not discriminate on the basis of caste. But I found, as Gombrich did more than twenty years

years or so, a variety of other subfraternities, or "chapters" (*pārshava*), have come into existence in Sri Lanka, and presently approximately forty-three chapters hold separate higher ordinations.[12]

This, then, is a rough narrative about the authorization of the tradition of caste-based ordination, governed by historically produced questions and arguments about which institutions, persons, and practices can constitute or embody "proper" grounds for the ordination of monks. In other words, the tradition of caste-based ordination, since its supposed inception in the eighteenth century, has been an embodied argument. But, despite, these arguments and disagreements, a particular kind of "unity" seemingly governs that tradition; namely, the practice of caste-distinction/discrimination. My point here is that the ostensible unity of this tradition, consisting of a variety of institutions carrying out ordination, based on caste, according to a variety of procedures and standards, does not suppose that this tradition has not become subject to contention and, hence, is unchanged.[13] Rather that tradition, working through and against opposing arguments, has been able to make centrally visible a particular dimension of its identity (caste as a prerequisite for ordination) as something that has remained unchallenged, homogeneous, and coherent, as something accepted and embodied by a variety of persons and institutions. On close scrutiny what this seeming unity of tradition shows are the ways in which it has strategically used "variety" and difference to its own advantage, to confirm its position and to secure grounds of supremacy. In other words, this tradition of caste-based ordination has depended on particular differences, conflicts of arguments and interpretations, to assert its own identity. Differences have animated the unity of that tradition.

But how does the new ordination at Dambulla insert itself into this tradition of argument? What kind of "difference" does the new movement

---

ago, that certain Ramañña temples ordain only high-caste (*goyigama*) candidates; Gombrich, *Precept and Practice*, 361–63.

12. These statistics are according to the *Laṅkāve Nikāyan Pilibanda Toraturu* (Colombo: Bauddhakatayutu Departumentuwa, 1984). The number is probably higher today since it does not list Sumangala's fraternity and the most recent "chapter" that broke away from Malwatta, Ruhunu Parshavaya, which was spearheaded by Kamburupitiye Wanaratana. A report about this is in P. Hemasiri, *Ruhunu Sangha Sanvidānaya: Mäta Yugaya* (Matara: Bodhiarakshaka Sabhava, 1990).

13. The idea of the unity of tradition is MacIntyre's; see his "Concept of a Tradition," in *After Virtue*.

represent? What kinds of discursive strategies does it use to authorize its difference as "identity" in opposition to the tradition of caste-basted ordination?

The New Ordination at Dambulla: Challenging the "Center"

Sumangala explained to me that he started the new ordination movement because certain Sinhala monks, particularly those of the Asgiriya center to which he belonged, had misunderstood and misinterpreted the whole tradition of higher ordination. Central to his polemical narrative was identifying two striking "misconceptions" that govern the practice of monastic ordination in Sri Lanka. The first misconception Sumangala named was the "commercialization" of the ceremony of the higher ordination that masks the understanding of its "original" purpose. The second misconception he named was the "fallacy" of dividing monastic communities into *nikāyas*, or fraternities. He holds that there are no nikāyas as such in Sri Lanka because division of the sangha into nikāyas should be based on substantive differences between groups, and that there certainly should not be nikāyas based on caste differences in any Buddhist community. In fact, for Sumangala, nikāya and caste are interrelated features of one issue.

Higher ordination is something like what Bourdieu calls a "rite of institution" (in the sense of being instituted)—as opposed to a "rite of passage"— that a novice (*sāmanēra*) who has reached the age of at least twenty goes through in order to attain full authorized membership in the sangha.[14] "The act of institution," as Bourdiue writes, "is thus an act of communication, but of a particular kind. It signifies to someone what his identity is, but in a way that both expresses it to him and imposes it on him by expressing it in front of everyone . . . and thus informing him in an authoritative manner of what he is and what he must be."[15] In other words, it is after a novice receives higher ordination that he is authorized to be recognized as a bhikkhu, a full-fledged member of the community of monks, the mahasangha.

14. I have deliberately avoided the Van Gennepian notion of "rite of passage" and chosen Bourdieu's substitute mainly because of the active sense it embodies. Bourdieu argues that "[to] speak of rites of institution is to suggest that all rites tend to consecrate or legitimate an *arbitrary boundary*, by fostering a misrecognition of the arbitrary nature of the limit and encouraging a recognition of it as legitimate." In other words, it is like "teaching a fish to swim" or saying that "this man is a man . . . a real man, which is not always obvious"; P. Bourdieu, *Language and Symbolic Power* (Cambridge: Harvard University Press, 1991), 118–19.

15. Ibid., 121.

The process of qualifying for full membership culminates in an elaborate ceremony in which the candidate/novice, who arrives (on some occasions on an elephant) stripped of his robes, dons a dazzling royal costume, symbolic of his last journey in the mundane world on an equal footing with its highest authority, the king. He then presents himself in front of an assembly of monks gathered within a duly consecrated boundary (sīmā)[16] and undergoes an oral examination that tests his ability to memorize more than two hundred Pali verses and other passages.[17] The candidate/novice takes on a different monastic identity by putting on new robes. Before the ceremony, the candidate's teachers meet with the monks who conduct the examination and present them with gifts (pudasatkāra), which range from basic food items (rice, coconuts, etc.) to money. Some monks maintain that the more gifts the novice gives, the easier the exam will be.

Elaborating on the origin of the new movement, Sumangala recalled for me his own higher ordination examination. He had gone to the event well-prepared, accompanied by his teacher and a large retinue of lay Buddhists from Dambulla. During the examination, the monks did not test his skills of memorization; they failed to ask him to recite even one verse. It was a shameful and embarrassing experience, he maintained, because people thought that he had gotten off too easily and that his teacher had showered the examiners with too many gifts. The disappointment he felt led him to write to the newspapers from time to time suggesting that the monks should eliminate the "commercialization" of the ceremony and restore "authentic ordination" (niyama upasampadāva).[18]

---

16. It is within a marked boundary that higher ordinations and other monastic acts (sangha kamma) such as upōsata, a mutual fortnightly confession ceremony, are held. On the centrality of a sīmā to higher ordination, see Malalgoda, Buddhism in Sinhalese Society, 154–55. On the general significance of sīmā to the monastic community as found in the vinaya literature and the Sri Lankan chronicles, see K. Ariyasena, "Sīmāvan Hā Ehi Aitihāsika Samvardhanaya Pilibanda Tulanātmaka Vimansanayak," Ph.D. diss., University of Ceylon, 1967; P. Kieffer-Pülz, "Ceremonial Boundaries in the Buddhist Monastic Tradition in Sri Lanka," unpublished paper delivered at the Wilhelm Geiger conference, Sri Lanka, 1995.

17. For an account of a Kandyan upasampadā ceremony as witnessed by an Englishman in 1872, see J. F. Dickson, Ordination in Theravada Buddhism: An Early Account, ed. Piyadassi Thera (Kandy: Buddhist Publication Society, 1963). Dickson gives a brief description of the assembly hall and the kinds of questions asked of the candidates.

18. There is an instance where the Buddha himself is said to have carried out an upasampadā. It is found in the story of the little boy Sopaka whom the Buddha ordained despite his low-caste status. The Buddha is reported to have given him full membership after asking a series of

The other factor that compelled Sumangala to start the new ordination was the ordination of monastic candidates on the basis of caste. He maintains that caste in the monastic community is against the Buddha's teaching. In supporting his view, he cites from the Buddhist canon, the *Pahārāda Sutta*, where it says the Buddha compares his monastic community to the ocean and states, "Just as . . . the great rivers, the Ganges, the Yamuna, the Aciravati, the Sarabhu and the Mahi, upon reaching the great ocean, abandon their former names and *gōtras*" and come to be known as the great ocean, so do the four classes—Brahmins, Ksatriyas, Vaisyas, and Sudras—upon joining the Buddhist monastic order, abandon their former names and clans and become followers of the Buddha.[19]

What Sumangala finds astonishing is that not only have Sri Lankan monks made the doctrinally "faulty" idea of caste part of monastic higher ordination but they have confined ordination to certain central locations monopolized by a few privileged monks. He wants to deprivilege this centralized practice. He maintains that such centralization obstructs one of the purposes of the higher ordination intended by the Buddha: dispersion and decentralization. The idea of dispersion is clearly embedded within the very concept of the community of monks that is "dispersed" in different directions to carry the message of the Buddha "for the benefit and the happiness of the many," avoiding settlement within a centralized establishment. Centralization hampers that dispersion. Sumangala argues:

> The Buddha pointed out that any five monks—monks who are of ten years standing from their higher ordination—could perform the ceremony within a given marked boundary either on water [*udakukkhepakasīmā*] or on land [*baddhasī mā*] that would allow dispersion. It should not be confined to one particular geographical locality chosen by a group of individuals for some presumed notion of sacredness. By not confining the performance of the ordination ceremony to a particular place, the Buddha allowed monks the freedom to conduct an important ceremony independent of the authority

---

questions (*kumārapaññā*); cited in H. Smith, ed., *The Khuddhakapātha together with its Commentary, the Paramatthajōtikā*, vol. 1. (London: Pali Text Society, Luzac, 1959), 75–78.

19. See *Anguttara Nikāya* (IV. 197); cited in G. P. Malalasekera, *Dictionary of Pāli Proper Names* (1938; reprint, London: Pali Text Society, 1960), 175. The very structure of this sutta is similar to that of the *Upōsata Sutta* in P. Masefield, trans., *The Udāna* (Oxford, U.K.: Pali Text Society, 1994), 98.

of any particular center or group of individuals belonging to a center. There is no mention in the Buddha's doctrine that it should be done in association with a central establishment.[20]

Sumangala's strategic assertion that the ordination could be performed at any geographical location independent of a "center" blatantly contests the claim and practice of the Asgiriya monastic chapter, his main rival. The argument that the ordination can be held within any given "marked boundary" (sīmā) recognizes that such a boundary can be created anywhere without reference to any central establishment, seeking to deprive monastic chapters like Asgiriya of their exclusive right to higher ordination. These are the kinds of arguments that guided his plans to create a new ordination movement.

Sumangala formed a committee (sangha sabhā) of 170 monks from various temples in Dambulla and neighboring areas and proposed the idea of founding a new fraternity that would grant higher ordination to qualified candidates without consideration of their castes. The committee reached a collective consensus on the proposal and decided in 1985 to hold an upasampadā at Dambulla, officially terminating ties with the Siyam Nikāya of the Asgiriya chapter. The Asgiriya chief monks, enraged at the news of the new ordination, voiced strong opposition to it on at least two grounds: they argued that Sumangala could not begin a new ordination at Dambulla in that Dambulla is "one of Asgiriya's temples" (an issue to which I return shortly). And since it was a sole individual who was challenging the caste-based ordination, the Asgiriya monks questioned whether Sumangala had the "authority" to begin a new, casteless ordination just because he thought that "caste" was contrary to Buddhism.

The monks of Asgiriya whom I interviewed maintain that the majority of monks recognize and respect the "age-old tradition" (purāna sampradāya) of caste-based ordination; the new movements against tradition will not last long, they say.[21] Sumangala told me what he thinks of "age-old tradition":

[People] may have practiced tradition [sampradāya] for a hundred or two hundred or a thousand years. The number of years that a tradition has been

20. Interview with Sumangala, July 15–16, 1995.

21. Interviews with Asgiriya monks, Sept. 15, 1996. The head monk, Chandananda, refused to grant me an interview, but I spoke to the second in charge and four other monks. I had visited Asgiriya also on Aug. 10, 1996, and chatted with the second in command.

practiced is not important; what is important is that we should examine whether that tradition is correct or not. Any tradition could be maintained and continued without examination. If we should accept it on that basis, we could say that the Buddha himself might have done something wrong because he spoke against caste that had been and is an age-old tradition in Indian society. Again, in those days, there was male sovereignty in India, which enjoyed all kinds of rights and privileges to the exclusion of women. The Buddha ordained women, and it was a revolution. Did he do something wrong? That is not how it is. We should have the right to get rid of any tradition that is not proper; everybody has the power to get rid of tradition if it is wrong, improper, dangerous to any society, and particularly if it is a hindrance to the development of any organization. We should not just continue doing things because "tradition" says so.[22]

The Asgiriya's opposition to the new ordination became more visible over the issue of registering the Buddhist monks who had received the first caste-less ordination.[23] Sumangala claims that Chandananda, the chief monk of the Asgiriya temple, had instructed the Buddhist commissioner not to register the monks from the Dambulla chapter because it was not a "legitimate Buddhist organization."[24] Sumangala filed a petition with the public court, and after a prolonged period of litigation Sumangala persuaded the judge to order the Buddhist commissioner to register the "Dambulla monks" as authorized, full-fledged bhikkhus.

My recounting the origin of this movement gives a glimpse of the complex ways in which competing discourses sought to contest the supposed "authenticity" of a tradition—in this case, the caste-based ordination. Of course, Sumangala's account made it look simple, representing him as the main agent of the movement. For example, he said that when the committee of 170

22. Interview with Sumangala, July 15–16, 1995.

23. *C.A. No: 1267/90–Application for a Writ of Mandamus:* copy of court order issued Nov. 30, 1991, in the hands of Sumangala.

24. According to section 42 of the Ordinance of the Buddhist Temporalities, all monks—whether novices or full-fledged monks—should be registered at the Buddhist commission; see *Vihāra Dēvālagam Āgñā Panata* (Colombo: Bauddha Katayutu Pilibanda Departmentuwa, 1931), and *Bauddha Vihāra Dēvālagam Āgñā Panata Yatate Upanīti* (Colombo: Sri Lanka Rajaye Departumentuwe Mudranalaya, 1956). On the colonial context in which this practice came into being, see Steve Kemper, "The Buddhist Monkhood, the Law, and the State in Colonial Sri Lanka," *Comparative Studies in Society and History* 26, no. 3 (1984): 416.

monks who gathered to discuss establishing a casteless ordination questioned whether they possessed the "qualifications" (*sudusukam*) to do so, Sumangala rushed to assure them that gaining "qualifications" was as easy as memorizing a few Pali passages from the "book of discipline" (*vinayapota*) and having five senior monks recite them in any consecrated place. He bluntly contended that "qualifications" to hold a separate ordination were not derived from the authority of a group of monks but from the mere application of the "word of the Buddha." It was, he said, with this conviction that his committee of monks held the first casteless ordination at the Dambulla temple and conferred upasampadā on five novice monks, "the exact number of monks the Buddha himself had ordained when he first started the monastic order."

Beneath this easy passage to founding a new ordination, the authority for which is seemingly derived from strategic interpretations of canonical texts, and to liberating Dambulla from Asgiriya, lies a host of power relations that illustrate complex configurations of questions about Buddhism, tradition, identity, and difference in Sri Lanka. In other words, in providing this account of Sumangala's departure from the central establishment of Asgiriya and the inauguration of what he calls an "authentic ordination," I do not wish to be understood as suggesting that Sumangala is attempting to recover a "lost," historical reality of Buddhism. There is more to it than meets the eye. For example, one should not take literally Sumangala's assertion that anyone can gain the "qualifications" to hold a new ordination just by chanting a few passages from the Buddhist vinaya texts. Surely, that assertion was a rhetorical flourish. It will become evident later that these "qualifications" are authorized within the reconceptualized space of the Dambulla temple in which crucial questions about tradition, identity, the past, and history are debated.

As a way of getting at the configurations of such questions, I begin with the kind of "ambiguity" that Sumangala himself demonstrates toward caste and nikāya. This became evident in his discussion with me about the Buddhist nikāyas. Recall that there are three major fraternities in Sri Lanka. Sumangala maintains that he and his colleagues do not recognize the legitimacy of designating these three fraternities as nikāyas. For a nikāya to exist, there should be "clear differences." While Sumangala accepts that monks of the three fraternities have varying internal monastic practices, such as shaving or not shaving eyebrows, he insists that these differences are not substantive and therefore do not constitute a nikāya. He explains:

What distinguishes one "sect" from another are not just trivial matters like the caste of its members but the interpretations and perception of the ultimate reality of the teaching, to which a "given sect" collectively adheres. If we take, for example, the interpretation of Sinhalese Buddhism and that of the Korean or Japanese, we could see clear differences; while the Korean and the Japanese Buddhist monks recognize the Buddha more as a deity or a messenger of a deity than as a human being, the Sinhala monks of all three nikāyas accept indisputably that the Buddha was but human. The very same principle applies to other key concepts of the Buddha's doctrine such as "suffering," "impermanence," and "nibbāna," which all three nikāya monks accept as fundamental and preach to the laity without any difference whatsoever.

Even as he explained how he does not recognize the existence of separate fraternities among monks, I noticed that Sumangala himself had shaved his eyebrows, and I asked him why he had done so. He quickly responded: "Yes, I shaved the eyebrows because I am in the Siyam Nikāya" (*mama siyam nikāyene*). Why would Sumangala, who maintained the "fallacy" of the Buddhist fraternities, say that he is "in the Siyam Nikāya"? It certainly was not a slip of the tongue: he had not only accepted very clearly that he was "in the Siyam Nikāya" but he had also shaved his eyebrows, a practice unique to high-caste monks of the Siyam fraternity. It is worth noting that, even though he himself considers that the "external practices" do not constitute a fraternity, he is well aware that the majority of monks have adopted them as marks of distinction. Sumangala's seemingly ambiguous attitude toward caste signals that he operates within monastic relations that define his identity as a "high-caste monk" who is attempting to eliminate caste from the monkhood. If Sumangala did not shave his eyebrows, he might be identified as a "low-caste monk," an identity he apparently does not want to acquire. Were Sumangala to be categorized as a low-caste monk, his program for eliminating caste would seem to be motivated by self-interest. By maintaining the status of a high-caste monk, he more effectively removes the appearance of self-interest, but only at the expense of assuming the very identity he seeks to eliminate.[25]

25. However, Sumangala says that monks who receive higher ordination at the Dambulla temple may or may not shave their eyebrows.

Today, Sumangala is one of Sri Lanka's best-known monastic figures, among both monks and the laity. In fact, most young university monks I talked to regarded Sumangala as a "real monk" (*niyama hāmuduru kenek*) (it was from them that I learned about Sumangala during my research of Buddhist monasticism in Sri Lanka).[26] It is this identity of the "real monk" that Sumangala constructs and debates in the context of competing to authorize a new representation of Buddhism and the Dambulla temple, where the new ordination is held annually.

I want now to describe some aspects of the Dambulla temple and the context within which Sumangala and his supporters debate the relation between its identity and Buddhism, tradition and history, the new ordination and authenticity.

Construction of a Reconceptualized Space of the Dambulla Temple: The Location of the New Ordination

The Dambulla temple, or the Golden Rock Temple (Rangiri Dambulu Vihāraya), as it is sometimes (and often in formal parlance) referred to among the Sinhalese, is one of Sri Lanka's most impressive places of Buddhist pilgrimage. It sits on an enormous rock that rises to a height of more than six hundred feet, overlooking a small town. The temple, with more than seventy-three gold-painted images of the Buddha in many of its ninety-some caves, is famous for the stories associated with the "mysterious" drops of water that seep incessantly from the ceiling of rock over the image house.[27] Dambulla is also one of the wealthiest Buddhist temples in Sri Lanka, owning more than fifteen thousand acres of land donated by kings.[28] It is at this temple, of which

26. Conversations with a number of student-monks at Kelaniya University, July 10–13, 1994, and with student-monks at Jayewardenepura campus, July, 25–27, 1994.

27. *Pūjāvaliya*, which gives this account of King Nissankamalla's patronage of the temple, first uses the term *Sawarna Giri Guhā* (golden rock cave); cited in M. Ilangasinha, *Rangiri Dambulu Vihāraya* (Dehiwala: Sri Devi Printers, 1994), 22. However, there is some debate about who built the seventy-three Buddha images; see A. Seneviratna, *The Golden Rock Temple of Dambulla* (Colombo: Ministry of Cultural Affairs, 1983), 31–39.

28. On the Sinhalese royal politics of periodic land donations to Buddhist temples, see Kemper, "Wealth and Reformation," 152–58. Ilangasinha says that the popular belief is that Vattagamini Abhaya (89–77 B.C.E.) donated eighteen thousand acres of land to the temple, and today the temple owns more than fifteen thousand acres; see M. Ilangasinha, "Notes on the History of Sigiriya-Dambulla Region in the 18th and the 19th Centuries," in *Settlement Archaeology of the Sigiriya Dambulla Region*, ed. S. Bandaranayake et al. (Kelaniya: University of Kelaniya, 1990), 156.

Sumangala is the current incumbent, that the new higher ordination is held annually.

The "early" history of the Dambulla temple is a debated issue. This is because one of the most celebrated texts of Sinhala Buddhist history, the *Mahāvamsa* (literally, the great chronicle of Sri Lanka), does not have any mention of the temple until about the tenth century.[29] However, Sumangala, with a well-respected historian on his side, challenges the *Mahāvamsa* and claims that the Dambulla temple not only existed "long before" the *Mahāvamsa* account of Sinhala Buddhist history began but was an important center of Theravada Buddhism as well. On the basis of inscriptions that excavation works unearthed in 1988, they argue that the area of Dambulla was "among the earliest Aryan settlements in the Island"[30] and trace the origin of the temple to King Devanampiyatissa himself (3rd century B.C.E.), under whose leadership Buddhism is said to have been introduced to Sri Lanka.[31] Implicit in this claim is that the Dambulla temple is as "ancient" as both Buddhism in Sri Lanka and the "Aryan" Sinhalese race itself. It is within the context of this debate about the "earliest" existence of the Dambulla temple that a new identity of the temple begins to emerge.

The debate about the antiquity of the Dambulla temple—and the discursive embellishments of the "ancient past" associated with it today—has been in the making since the late 1970s. The debate came about in the wake of at least two important projects by the UNP government.[32] The first project took place in 1979, when the UNP government of Sri Lanka designated and "developed" the city of Dambulla as a "sacred site" (*pūjā bhūmiyak*). The previous SLFP government had proposed to undertake this project in the early 1970s, but abandoned it because of a "lack of funding"[33]; however, when the newly elected UNP government financed the project, it did not single out Dambulla; rather, as Steven Kemper observes, Dambulla was one of many

29. Cited in Ilangasinha, *Rangiri Dambulu Vihāraya*, 69–70.

30. M. Ilangasinha, "Dambulla Rock Temple: Its Name and History," in *Dambulla Project: First Archaeological and Excavation Project*, ed. H. T. Basnayake (Colombo: Ministry of Kelaniya, 1988), 59–70.

31. Ilangasinha claims that it was king Devanampiyatissa's brother, Suratisa, who donated the temple to its "early Buddhist monks"; see Ilangasina, "Dambulla Rock Temple," 61.

32. It is probable that there were other state projects. These two are the most visible to me from my interviews and archival research in Sri Lanka.

33. *Divayina*, June 20, 1982.

Buddhist areas that the government undertook to develop (at a cost of more than 1,000 million rupees) and designate as "sacred."[34] Moreover, Dambulla is located at the center of the triangle constituted by three "ancient," "sacred" capitals, Anuradhapura, Polonnaruwa, and Kandy.

The second state project began when the UNP government sponsored an archaeological excavation program — the "Dambulla project." The purpose, as the project director put it, was to "excavate and expose, as far as possible, the 'ancient' monuments belonging to Dambulla" and "develop and elevate Dambulla as a center of pilgrimage and visitor interest."[35] In the ambitious words of W. Lokubandara, the minister of cultural affairs, it was to "reveal the hitherto unknown past" of the Dambulla temple.[36] This was part of a larger program that the government's Cultural Triangle had undertaken to excavate and develop six other "sacred places."[37] In 1985, the chairman of the Triangle program, Prime Minister Premadasa, inaugurated the "Dambulla project." Significant about his involvement is his published estimate of the project: in the foreword to the "Project Report" in 1988, Premadasa endorsed its findings as "scientific and authoritative."[38] My point here is obvious: these state programs and the high opinions of them represented by the prime minister contributed significantly to the conditions that made possible the authorization of this particular ancient, sacred identity of the Dambulla temple. The new ordination is located in this new representation of the Dambulla temple.

Already, during the early phase of these state programs, certain discourses about the antiquity of the Dambulla temple had begun to surface. For example, an article published in a Sinhala newspaper in 1982 carried the captivating title "Dambulla, the Golden Rock: the Oasis of the Sinhala Heroes."[39] After racing through the "ancient history," the very beginning of the Dambulla temple, the article abruptly highlights the seventeenth-century Sri Lankan political climate. It refers to past Dambulla monks in the context of a peasant revolution that took place against the British in 1848, turning the "Dambulla monks" into "heroic monks" who had "counseled and helped

34. See Kemper, *Presence of the Past*, 179.
35. Basnayake, introduction to *Dambulla Project*.
36. Lokubandara, preface to *Dambulla Project*.
37. Roland Silva, "Note on the Project," in *Dambulla Project*.
38. Premadasa, foreword to *Dambulla Project*.
39. "Sinhala Vīrayangē Kśma Bhūmiyak Vū Rangiri Dambulla," *Divayina*, June 20, 1982.

Sinhala leaders like Virapuran Appu launch the last Sinhala freedom struggle even at the expense of risking their own lives."[40]

In a similar way, Sumangala today speaks of Mahatissa, a monk from a different period (29 B.C.E.), who occupies a controversial place in the history of Buddhism in Sri Lanka. Mahatissa, as Rahula points out, belonged to one of the early schools of Buddhism, Mahavihara. But he was later expelled from the Mahavihara as he had accepted the rival monastery Abhayagiri from King Vattagamini, to whom he is said to have given shelter at his monastery during the king's fourteen-year period of exile.[41] So far as I know, there is no documented "evidence" to suggest that Mahatissa had ever lived at the Dambulla temple and had given King Vattagamini shelter there, but Sumangala argues otherwise. He claims that "heroic monks" (*vīra hāmuduruwaru*) like Mahatissa lived at the Dambulla temple and "counseled kings who saved the Sinhalese nation." Sumangala claims that the *Mahāvamsa* chronicle did not mention the Dambulla temple because its authors, who were monks of the hegemonic tradition of the Mahavihara school, considered Mahatissa an unorthodox monk who did unorthodox things.[42] These narratives about the temple and its "past heroic monks" were communicated in relation to a hallmark debate that took place in 1992, to which I will return shortly.

The early phases of representing the Dambulla temple as an "oasis" in which heroic monks lived in the ancient past were accompanied by another very important shift within the Dambulla temple. The shift took place in the administrative leadership of the temple. Sometime in the early 1980s, Udugama Buddharakkhita, the previous incumbent of the temple, who was Sumangala's teacher, fell ill; in accordance with convention (the "tradition of the pupillary succession," in which the eldest pupil assumes the leadership of the temple following the death or illness of the teacher/incumbent— a convention that has now become law) his office passed to Sumangala.[43]

40. Ibid.

41. W. Rahula, *History of Buddhism in Ceylon*, 3rd ed. (1956; reprint, Dehiwala: Buddhist Cultural Center, 1994), 83.

42. Interview, 1996. The *Mahāvamsa* mentions this episode between Mahatissa and Vattagamini, but it says Mahatissa was from Accagala; cited in A. Seneviratna, *Dambulla Rock Temple*, 14–15. However, Ilangasinha holds that Accagala was Dambulla; Ilangasinha, "Dambulla Rock Temple," 65.

43. Regarding pupillary succession, see U. Phadnis, *Religion and Politics in Sri Lanka*, 99. For a discussion of the process by which this "tradition" became legal, in 1924, see Kemper, "Buddhist Monkhood," 416–21.

As early as 1984, Sumangala's emerging leadership of the temple had generated unease among the Asgiriya monks: he did not seem to conform to the
known relationship between the Asgiriya chapter and the Dambulla temple.[44]
Dambulla was considered one of seven temples that were under the jurisdiction of the Asgiriya.[45] This is because, as Ilangasinha points out, *Potuhära
Tudapata*, an eighteenth-century "letter patent," records that King Kirti Sri
Rajasimha, who had renovated the temple, had entrusted the Asgiriya monks
with the administration of the Dambulla temple on the grounds that its resident Lenavala monks had not executed the "rituals of the temple satisfacto-
rily"[46] (King Kirti Sri Rajasimha is the king said to have issued the royal decree
prohibiting the ordination of "low-caste" candidates into the Siyam Nikāya).
Over time, as Ilangasinha further shows, the Asgiriya monks oversaw the task
of appointing the head of the Dambulla temple, who was usually a monk
selected from the Asgiriya temple itself.[47] There is evidence that as late as
1835 the Asgiriya monks had appointed one of their own monks as the head
of the Dambulla temple and had justified doing so because, they claimed, the
"priests resident at Dambulla were ignorant of Pali" and therefore unqualified
for the office.[48]

It is important to note that the head monk that the Asgiriya temple
appointed did not reside at the Dambulla temple: he played a mainly symbolic role in administering the temple, paying perfunctory annual visits. However, it is in the context of the head monk's annual visits that the Asgiriya
monks made visible the authority of their claim to the ownership of the
Dambulla temple. During the head monk's visits to Dambulla, the resident
monks would pay respect to him by handing over keys not only to the
Dambulla temple but also to five other temples that belong to Dambulla.
Ilangasinha points out the unique aspect of this practice: once the Asgiriya

44. "*Sāmpradāya Rāka Gänīma Api Agē Karamu*" ("We must admire the safeguarding of tradition"), *Lankādīpa*, Oct. 9, 1984; the author of the article is an Asgiriya monk.45. Ibid.; the article clearly identifies Dambulla as a property of the Asgiriya temple. Malalgoda, too, says it is one
of seven temples that fall under the Asgiriya jurisdiction: Malalgoda, *Buddhism in Sinhalese Society*, 68.

46. Ilangasinha, "Notes on the History," 157; idem, *Rangiri Dambulu Vihāraya*, 71.

47. Ilangasinha, "Notes on the History," 157; elsewhere, Ilangasinha points out that there
were two heads at the Dambulla temple because the Lenavala monks who continued to live
there claimed that they, too, were heir to it; see Ilangasinha, *Rangiri Dambulu Vihāraya*, 72.

48. This is found in A. C. Lawrie, "A Gazetteer of the Central Province of Ceylon," in S.
Bandaranayake et al., *Settlement Archaeology*, 169–93.

head monk received the keys he could refuse to return them to the Dambulla monks or could even hand them over to some other monks.[49] Thus the ritual gesture of handing over the keys clearly enforced the Asgiriya's authoritative claim that Dambulla is "one of its temples" and that the monks who maintain it are its temporary custodians. In fact, as Ilangasinha notes, this practice of handing over the keys had given rise to sporadic confrontations between the Asgiriya's head monk and the resident monks of the Dambulla temple. This created eventually what Ilangasinha calls a "dual control system" in which there were two heads of the Dambulla temple at the same time, one at Dambulla and the other at Asgiriya.[50]

With Sumangala's emerging leadership of the temple in the mid-1980s, supported by more than 170 Buddhist monks from Dambulla and its neighboring areas, the Dambulla temple entered a new phase of administration. It was during this time (a year before Sumangala started the new ordination) that the secretary-monk of the Asgiriya temple wrote to a Sinhala newspaper an open letter entitled "We must protect proudly the long-standing [*cirāgata*] tradition." The substance of the letter indicated clearly that by "long-standing tradition" the Asgiriya monk meant that the Dambulla monks should recognize Asgiriya's long line of monastic leadership of the Dambulla temple.[51]

However, following Sumangala's leadership, the Dambulla temple's representations of itself as "an oasis," an "independent temple" with its "ancient" lineage of "heroic monks," implicitly contested the authority of the Asgiriya's claim. Moreover, the new ordination at Dambulla explicitly questioned the Asgiriya's caste-based ordination, which had worked to link the two temples for many years and to authorize the Asgiriya monks' claim to the "long-standing" leadership of the Dambulla temple. It was through the Asgiriya's caste-based ordination, which they received, that the Dambulla monks had defined themselves as bhikkhus, full-fledged monks. By obviating the Dambulla monks' long-maintained necessity of receiving ordination from the Asgiriya temple, the new ordination created a gulf between the two temples: the Asgiriya monks could no longer be part of the Dambulla temple since they did not now participate in the same tradition of the higher ordination.

---

49. Ilangasinha, *Rangiri Dambulu Vihāraya*, 76–77. Ilangasinha does not mention when this practice originated or ended.

50. Ilangasinha, "Notes on the History," 157; idem, *Rangiri Dambulu Vihāraya*, 72.

51. *Divayina*, June 20, 1984.

Before I discuss the ways in which the narratives about the relation between the temple, history, and the past became the site of public debate, I want to point out a few practices that render these ideas about the antiquity of the Dambulla temple centrally visible within the space of the Dambulla temple. Today, the Dambulla temple presents itself as an "ancient," "sacred," "independent" Buddhist temple, in every sense of those terms. The practices that communicate these adjectives as meaningful are made strikingly visible to visitors. One such practice is the dress code ("dressing properly"), to which all visitors—both local and foreign—are expected to conform when entering the "sacred" grounds of the temple on the rock. Until the early 1990s, as far as my research indicates, there was no formal injunction against wearing "short frocks" or "short-trousers" within the "sacred" premises at Dambulla.[52] It is, of course, customary that when Buddhists enter the "image house" (buduge) at any Buddhist temple, they do so dressed—as a mark of reverence for the Buddha—in attire that covers almost completely both the upper and lower parts of the body. However, there is no "guard" at the entrance to most temples to bar those "dressed improperly" (the only religious establishment where there are such "guards" is the Temple of the Tooth,[53] a center of pil-grimage frequented daily by thousands of visitors, local and foreign). Visitors needing to rent sarongs may do so at the main entrance. Sumangala has imposed the same practice at the Dambulla temple: no visitor dressed improperly can enter the image house, and a dozen guards are stationed at the entrance to enforce this practice. Those who need to rent a sarong (as I did; I was dressed in shorts) may do so from flower shops at the base of the rock.

Among other injunctions against headgear and footwear, which are observed at all Buddhist temples, the most conspicuous is the ban on cameras in the temple. This ban is rendered visible by a display of "confiscated" film rolls, hanging behind the security desk near the temple entrance. The injunction was introduced after a much publicized scandal: a foreign tourist was photographed seated in the lap of a statue of the Buddha.[54] An article in a Sri Lankan English newspaper, the Daily News, in 1994 alluded to the episode and characterized taking pictures at Dambulla as "taboo." The episode

52. "Footwear, Headgear, Cameras Taboo at Dambulla Viharaya," Daily News, Feb. 8, 1994.
53. The temple is so named because it is believed to house one of the Buddha's tooth relics.
54. Daily News, Feb. 8, 1994.

received wide publicity because it was the first time a "desecrated" statue of the Buddha, as the article pointed out, was "washed with fragrant water and re-painted" so as to "reconsecrate" it.[55] The ideas of the antiquity of the Dambulla temple played right into this process of repainting the statue of the Buddha: Sumangala hired a painter who was a "descendent of a guild of people who had come from India during ancient times."[56] This claim implies that a "modern" painter could not paint an "ancient" statue of the Buddha situated in an "ancient Buddhist temple" and restore it to its "original purity."

These practices, or "rules," are new constructions; they are strategic attempts at making visible those discourses about the temple, Buddhism, tradition, and the past. These practices attempt to communicate the new identity of the Dambulla temple as an oasis, an ancient temple with an "ancient history" that is independent of all other Buddhist temples, including the Asgiriya temple, which claims to hold authority over Dambulla. It is in these narratives that we can locate the new ordination. My point is that the existence of Dambulla from the "very beginning" of Buddhism in Sri Lanka that Sumangala and others claim for this temple is as old as those discourses.[57] In other words, the antiquity of the Dambulla temple that these discourses construct is as old as the new ordination.[58] The representation of this new image of the Dambulla temple gained central visibility in the context of a hallmark debate that took place in Dambulla in 1992. It is in the context of this debate that claims about "real" Buddhism, tradition, and past are fought out. Since this debate involves the issue of building a tourist hotel in Kandalama, an area

55. Ibid.

56. Ibid.

57. Here I am aided by a similar argument that Jeganathan has made recently with regard to Anuradhapura, one of the "ancient" capitals of Sri Lanka. Jeganathan questions its antiquity, arguing that Anuradhapura is only as old as the nineteenth century because the forms of authoritative knowledge about its antiquity came to be produced in the nineteenth-century colonial rupture. He writes that "the 'very beginning,' or point of origin of contemporary authoritative forms of knowledge about Anuradhapura is recent. The 'very beginning' was only 'the day before yesterday'"; see P. Jeganathan, "Authorizing History, Ordering Land: The Conquest of Anuradhapura," in *Unmaking the Nation: The Politics of Identity and History in Modern Sri Lanka*, ed. P. Jeganathan and Qadri Ismail (Colombo: Social Scientists' Association, 1995), 107. I want to suggest, however, that the antiquity of Anuradhapura does not remain permanently located in the nineteenth century; it may be constructed anew in other conjunctures.

58. For a very different account of the temple's history from mine, see D. G. A. Perera, "King Valagamba's Role in the Uncharted History of the Dambulla Temple," *Sri Lanka Journal of the Humanities* 22, nos. 1–2 (1996): 83–142.

of Dambulla, I will call it the Kandalama debate. This was a seminal debate. It was following Sumangala's controversial involvement in it in 1992 that the new ordination movement at the Dambulla temple gained publicity and Sumangala himself became one of the best-known monastic figures in Sri Lanka. What this debate, like the debate about Mahayana Buddhism (chapter 4), illustrates are the ways in which particular conjunctures of competing narratives conjoined to define and contest, authoritatively, the relation between Buddhism, tradition, and difference in centrally visible ways.

The Possibility of the Central Visibility: The Kandalama Debate

The Kandalama debate revolved around a private corporation's plan to build a massive four-story luxury hotel in Kandalama, a village near the Dambulla temple. The government of President Premadasa endorsed this plan to boost tourism in the country. (During this time tourism had become, in terms of the state rhetoric, almost synonymous with Buddhism itself. The government of Premadasa claimed that any "campaign against tourism" was a "conspiracy against Buddhism" because a "tourist was a pilgrim.")[59] Sumangala and the Dambulla people requested the government to revoke the plan, arguing that, as Bond observes, "a large hotel would adversely affect the cultural and moral environment of the community, disrupt the ecological balance of the semi-wilderness area, pollute the water supply and infringe on the sanctity of the ancient, sacred [Dambulla] Buddhist shrine."[60] As the government ignored the request and continued with its plan, Sumangala staged a massive, "peaceful demonstration" (a satyagraha) at the Dambulla temple, in which more than fifty thousand people—monks and lay people—participated, in opposition to the government's decision.[61] Among those joined in this opposition effort were prominent lay Buddhist leaders such as A. T. Ariyaratna.[62]

According to one Sinhalese commentator, the government confronted Sumangala's challenge head-on by mobilizing more than three thousand

59. "Lokubandara [minister of cultural affairs and information] Describes a Tourist as a Pilgrim," *Daily News*, June 15, 1992.
60. The movement in relation to Ariyaratne's participation in this event has been examined by G. Bond, "Conflicts of Identity and Interpretation in Buddhism," in *Buddhist Fundamentalism and Minority Identities*, 36–52.
61. See L. Piyasena, *Väve Bända Hōtalaya* (Ratmalana: Sarvodaya Vishvaleka, 1994), 69; Piyasena is an ally of the Dambulla temple.
62. Bond, "Conflicts of Identity," 47.

official and undercover police officers. These officers marched into the houses of the Dambulla people, threatening them and saying they should not attend the demonstration at the temple.[63] The government, after attempting to impose a curfew and designate Dambulla a "restricted area" on the day of the demonstration at the temple, then staged a progovernment counter-demonstration. The progovernment event was poorly attended; the government did, however, have the support of some high-ranking monks (*mahānāyaka*), who argued that the hotel would advance the development scheme that President Premadasa had launched to usher the country into a new era of prosperity.[64] As these monks began to voice views supporting the government, a number of debates took place centering on questions about Buddhism, the leadership of the Dambulla temple, the new ordination, and the past.

The Kandalama debate served as a platform for making centrally visible the reconceptualized space of the Dambulla temple. This was facilitated at the most fundamental level by the argument that the construction of the hotel would "infringe upon the sanctity of the ancient, sacred [Dambulla temple]." That argument made Sumangala a leading player in the Kandalama debate since he was now the head of that "ancient temple" on which the hotel would infringe. During this period, the nongovernment newspapers carried a flood of articles that dramatized the debate. Some of the articles had large, provocative captions like "The Dambulla rock is waging a cold war" and "The Dambulla temple has been set on fire by villains"—an incident that never happened.[65] One newspaper ran a story of how Sumangala had received death threats, sent by unidentified people, demanding that he withdraw the satyagraha.[66] While these newspaper articles explained how the Dambulla

---

63. Piyasena, *Vāvē Bända Hōtalaya*, 68.

64. *Daily News*, July 23, 1992; cited in Bond, "Conflicts of Identity," 52. It must be evident that we are not interested in questions of who "won" this debate though it must be noted that the hotel was built later.

65. "Dambulu Gale Sītala Satana" ("The cold war of the Dambulla Rock"), *Lankādīpa*, May 17, 1992; "Dambulu Mahāvihārayata Märavarayō Gini Tabati" ("The Dambulla royal temple has been set on fire by villains"), *Ätta*, Apr. 30, 1992; "Dambulu Rajamahāvihārayē Potgulata Gini Tabati" ("The Dambulla temple's library is set on fire"), *Divayina*, Apr. 29, 1992. Many of these statements were polemical. Piyasena says that only the temple library—not the whole temple—was set on fire; Piyasena, *Vāvē Bända Hōtalaya*, 45.

66. "Ināmaluwe Nāhimiyanta Marana Tarjana" ("Death threats to Inamaluwe Sumangala"), *Lankādīpa*, May 8, 1992.

temple was involved in the debate, they introduced (and popularized) Sumangala not only as the head of the Dambulla temple but also as the architect of a new ordination held at that "ancient temple." One such article ostensibly discussing the Kandalama debate devoted much of its content to describing the new ordination and its significance to Buddhist identity in the country.[67]

The meteoric rise of Sumangala and the new ordination in the public consciousness witnessed a climate in which the questions about Buddhism, the ownership of the temple, and what it means to be a "real" monk came to be debated in centrally visible ways. In the wake of Sumangala's popularity, one chief (Asgiriya) monk, Aruvala Somaratana, supportive of the government, appeared live on state-owned television and accused Sumangala of misleading the public by pretending to be the head of the Dambulla temple. He charged that Sumangala had been falsely representing himself as the head of the Dambulla temple: the real head of the Dambulla temple, he said, was in fact at Asgiriya. Since the new ordination is held under Sumangala's leadership, implicit in this accusation was the question of the ordination's validity.[68]

In responding to this accusation, Sumangala criticized monks such as Somaratana as "state monastic tools" whom the government was using to distract the public from the Kandalama debate.[69] Leading Sinhalese newspapers carried reports of Sumangala's speaking to professional lay and monastic audiences at Sri Lankan universities and accusing progovernment chief monks of having become "pliable as rubber [rabar patipanna velā], when the Buddha had said that they should be firm and upright [ujupatipanna]."[70] Other newspapers reported his addressing large audiences at Buddhist temples in Colombo: "Some monks have thrown to the winds the dignity of the sangha because of greed for high office and other [political] material benefits," he was reported as saying.[71] In my interview with him, Sumangala insisted that some monks had "lost their autonomy and power [balaya] and become like puppets because they seek political benefits." Sumangala has also made such criticisms at meetings where chief monks who had supported

67. Lankādīpa, May 17, 1992.
68. Cited in Piyasena, Vävē Bända Hōtalaya, 63–66.
69. Lankādīpa, July 10, 1992.
70. Lankādīpa, Aug. 12, 1992.
71. Divayina, Oct. 12, 1993.

the construction of the Kandalama hotel were present.[72] From Sumangala's perspective, as he stated it, the "real monk" is the "firm monk" who is "apolitical" and does not seek political benefits. He claims to embody this identity of the "real monk," and he does so, as he stated in our interview, at the Dambulla temple—a place "where heroic monks lived in the past and worked to help the nation without seeking political benefits."

The competing narratives about what it means to be a "real monk" gained greater visibility in relation to a different aspect of the Kandalama debate. Sumangala met with his sangha committee, consisting of 170 monks, and they decided that they would boycott every "political" meeting taking place in the area and that no politician would be invited to a Buddhist event until the government had withdrawn its plan to build the hotel.[73] An author who is a known supporter of Sumangala claims that after the newspapers carried the report of this decision, President Premadasa called Sumangala at 5 A.M. one day and warned him to persuade other monks in the Dambulla area to reverse their decision:[74] Sumangala refused to do so, saying the decision was a collective one.[75] Today, some Sinhalese writers, viewing this episode in retrospect, portray Sumangala as the heroic, real monk who did not accede to the president's "threat" to gain "political benefits" but moved ahead with his decision even at the risk of his life;[76] some refer to the Dambulla monks' "path of independence" and assert in hyperbolic phrases that "those cardboard political leaders [like Premadasa] who had threatened the Dambulla monks on the phone crumbled to pieces."[77] A famous Buddhist Sinhala monk, Maduluwawe Sobhita, congratulating Sumangala on his leadership in the Kandalama debate, writes that "a Buddhist priest exercises an unlimited sovereignty of free thought, expression, and writing. . . . No one possess[es] this privilege other than a Buddhist monk. Ven. Sumangala is fully conscious of [this] role of the bhikkhu [monk]."[78] My point is that these claims about

72. *Island,* Oct. 18, 1993.

73. *Lankādīpa,* May 8, 1992.

74. Piyasena, *Vävē Bända Hōtalaya,* 42–43.

75. Piyasena records the entire content of the conversation; Piyasena, *Vävē Bända Hōtalaya,* 42–43.

76. Ibid., 43.

77. See "Dambulu Vihārayē Svādīna Gaman Maga" ("Independent path of the Dambulla temple"), *Divayina,* July 30, 1995.

78. See D. Ananda, ed., *Abhivandana: Felicitations* (n.p.).

Buddhism, heroism, and Dambulla monks are located in the conjunctures in which questions about the new ordination, the Dambulla temple, and the "ancient past" came to be authoritatively debated.

I began this inquiry into the formation of the new ordination movement at Dambulla not because it claims—taking it at face value—to challenge the tradition of caste-based ordination in Sri Lanka. This does not mean, of course, that I want either to deny or to affirm the "validity" of the stated purpose of this new movement: to do so, I hold—as must be clear from the preceding pages—is not a privileged position that disciplinary enterprises can arrogate to themselves: such adjudication participates in some unquestioned ideological assumptions about concepts like religion and culture. Rather, in the way I have read the dynamics that made its emergence possible, the new ordination movement represents an important example of the ways in which particular conjunctures of narratives authorize opposing definitions of the relations between religion, tradition, and difference.

Now the movement, as it claims, seeks to "challenge" the dominant Sri Lankan monastic tradition of ordaining candidates on the basis of castes. This tradition, I have noted, is itself an embodied argument, consisting of a variety of competing claims, persons, and institutional practices that have, over the years, come into being to argue and question its authoritative stance on ordination and monastic identity in Sri Lanka. So one can safely say that it is hardly a homogenous, seamless tradition that has endured without differences of interpretation, debate, and indeed dissension. But it is also a particular kind of tradition governed by a particular practice; namely, the ordination of monks on the basis of "caste." This practice defines the seeming "unity" of that tradition supposedly accepted (or made to be seen as accepted) by the very differences (that is, different fraternities) that seek to contest it. In other words, this kind of tradition, as David Scott points out, "presupposes 'common possession' but it does not presuppose uniformity or plain consensus. Rather it depends upon a play of conflict and contention" to secure the grounds of supremacy and authority.[79]

It is precisely because of its location in such a play of conflicts that it remains vulnerable to differing representations, to the possibility of being divested of its authoritative identity. In that sense, there can be no tradition that is not contingently and discursively produced. But this does not mean

79. David Scott, *Refashioning Futures*, 124.

that tradition, its supposed identity, and its supposed truth remain available for any person/subject to contest it at any moment. Identity is not simply a fluid, always "open" site of contention. (Critics like Dana R. Villa have raised important misgivings about the "incessant contestation" of identity that informs some postmodern and postcolonial conceptualizations about culture.)[80] The possibility of what subject can make what kinds authoritative moral statements about that site occurs only in particular conjunctures. The new monastic movement at Dambulla constitutes such a conjuncture generating new possibilities. It is into this site, into this tradition of embodied moral arguments about ordaining monks on the basis of caste, that the new ordination movement seeks to insert itself, with particular claims and complaints about its unacceptability, about the supposed "untruth" of its values and virtues. It competes to represent that "tradition" as the "other/difference" so as to dismantle its authority and deny the unity that it presupposes for itself. But how is the new ordination movement at Dambulla able to "open" that site of caste-based ordination for contention?

We saw that the making of the new ordination in the 1980s centered around a field of diverse narratives about the relation between the identity of the Dambulla temple, Buddhism, the past, history, and heroism in Sri Lanka. These narratives—enabled as they were by complex power relations between the temple, the state, and its excavation projects—sought to authorize not only the new ordination but also an "independent identity" of the Dambulla temple, contesting and breaking away from the "center" of Siyam Nikāya of the Asgiriya chapter. But those narratives and their "challenge" to the center and the tradition of caste-based ordination did not occupy the center of visibility until they entered the space of the "public" debate about Kandalama, Buddhism, tourism, and the state. Prior to the Kandalama debate, the (discourse of) the new casteless ordination occupied an "arbitrary boundary," particularly from the standpoint of the hegemonic tradition of caste-based ordination. The "Kandalama debate" was the authorized site in which the arbitrariness of the Dambulla discourse, of its contention of the Asgiriya

---

80. Dana R. Villa, "Democratizing the Agon: Nietzsche, Arendt, and the Agonistic Tendency in Political Theory," in *Politics, Philosophy, Terror: Essays on the Thought of Hannah Arendt* (Princeton: Princeton University Press, 1999), 110. Villa takes this phrase from Seyla Benhabib, introduction to *Democracy and Difference*, ed. Seyla Benhabib (Princeton: Princeton University Press, 1996), 9.

center's caste-based ordination, was enabled to be *misrecognized* (to evoke Bourdieu again).[81] Put alternatively, the Kadalama debate was the site in which the "difference" of the Dambulla discourse became a "sight," so to speak—became a centrally visible adversary that could not easily be dismissed or marginalized as a mere "other," but demanded to be battled out, to be reckoned with.

So, one may ask, what does this battling for the misrecognition of the difference of the new movement, the competition for the authorization of it as "identity," as embodying "Buddhism," mean? Has the new movement, in its supposed struggle to contest a dominant religious tradition, made a "dent" in it, changed the way in which monastic ordination is carried out? Since the practice of caste-based ordination still takes place in Sri Lanka, does the new monastic ordination simply constitute a "failed" attempt? Is it, at most, a "marginal" movement?

Instructive though these questions are from a sociological point of view, they are not central to the way in which I have proposed to conceive the relation between tradition and difference. What has concerned me are the contingent conjunctures of debates that make possible the relation between tradition and difference to be authoritatively argued in centrally visible ways. The very possibilities of the central visibility of who can and cannot stake out what kinds of claims about that relation, of what should and should be arbitrary, render irrelevant questions about who 'won" or "lost" such debates. Surely, the central visibility of the new movement enabled by the Kandalama debate marked a particular discursive shift from its "arbitrary" grounds to an authorized space in which it sought to make the moral claims it did. But whether the new movement does—today, as I write, or will, tomorrow— occupy that authorized space and sustain those moral claims about Buddhism and difference can never be guaranteed. The exploration of such contingent sites of possibility, I have argued, provide critical instances of understanding tradition and difference as embodied arguments.

81. Bourdieu, *Language and Symbolic Power,* 118–19.

CHAPTER SEVEN

Violence and Religion, Terror(ism) and Identity

Today "violence"—like "religion," "ritual," "culture," and "nationalism"—has become another canonical category that scholars use to produce authoritative knowledges about the universe of South Asia.[1] For example, in a major work that tries to explain the "culture of nationalism" ("violence") in Sri Lanka, a work that provoked strong criticism, anthropologist Bruce Kapferer, ventured a thesis that there exists an ontological relation between Sinhalese "violence" and Sinhalese "demonic" practices of sorcery. "There is," says Kapferer, "a relation between the passion of sorcery and the furious passion of ethnic violence."[2] In other words, from Kapferer's perspective, to understand violence in Sri Lanka is to know a specific quality ("the culture of nationalism") of the Sinhalese Buddhists.[3] Such is the importance of the category of violence to the continuing disciplinary studies of the Sri Lankan Buddhist universe.[4]

1. For an excellent study that shows, among other things, how "violence" in Sri Lanka achieved a "canonical status" as a problem needing anthropological explanations, see Pradeep Jeganathan, "After a Riot: Anthropological Locations of Violence in an Urban Community of Sri Lanka," Ph.D. diss., University of Chicago, 1997; see also his "Violence as an Analytical Problem: Sri Lankanist Anthropology after July 1983." Nethra 4, no. 2 (1998): 7–47. I owe my critical thinking on the category of "violence" to Jeganathan's groundbreaking work.

2. See Bruce Kapferer, Legends of People, Myths of State, 32. For Kapferer, Sinhalese Buddhist culture is characterized by a "cosmic logic," "a logic within which the modern Sri Lankan state and a personal identity within the state can take form" (78).

3. For a brilliant criticism of Kapferer's attempt at explaining the supposed culture of violence in terms of an ontology, see David Scott, "The Demonology of Nationalism: On the Anthropology of Ethnicity and Violence in Sri Lanka," Economy and Society 19, no. 4 (1992): 492–510. For further incisive comments on the category of violence, see also David Scott, "'Culture of Violence' Fallacy," Small Axe: A Journal of Criticism 2 (1997): 140–47. Disciplinary theories about the "cultures of violence" are, however, unceasing; for example, see Juergensmeyer, Terror in the Mind of God, 10–13.

4. For other examples of disciplinary attempts to construct violence, nationalism, and ethnic conflict as objects of knowledge from a variety of perspectives, see Jonathan Spencer, ed., Sri Lanka: History and the Roots of Conflict (London: Routledge, 1990); Jonathan Spencer, "Writing Within: Anthropology, Nationalism, and Culture in Sri Lanka," Current Anthropology 31, no. 3 (1990): 283–300; Michael Roberts, Exploring Confrontation, Sri Lanka: Politics, Culture, and History (New York: Hardwood Academic, 1994); Ananda Wickremaratne, The Roots

Like Kapferer's, many scholarly writings that discuss the relation between "violence" and "Buddhism" in Sri Lanka are dominated by a particular assumption—namely, that violence is the antithesis of a supposedly *authentic* Buddhism that specifically teaches nonviolence. Hence, for some leading anthropologists and other scholars of Buddhism, violence is a "dark underside"[5] of Buddhism, and the very relation between the two represents "ethical dilemmas" for Buddhists.[6] As Kapferer puts it, violence stands for the "nonreason" (which is associated with the "demonic" practice of sorcery) as opposed to "the reason, the teaching and way of the Buddha."[7]

This supposed contradiction of violence to Buddhism led Stanley Tambiah, followed by several others, to pose a question that decisively (and more explicitly) intervenes in rethinking the relation between Buddhism and violence. Pointing particularly to the "participation" (Tambiah's word) of monks in recent events of "violence," Tambiah asks (in his *Buddhism Betrayed?*) if Buddhism is "betrayed" by those "who are ideally dedicated to nonviolence and required by disciplinary rules to abstain from killing and to be nowhere near the marching armies and traffic in arms."[8] It is not hard to see that the

---

of Nationalism: Sri Lanka (Colombo: Karunaratne & Sons, 1995); K. N. O. Dharmadasa, *Language, Religion, and Ethnic Assertiveness: The Growth of Sinhalese Nationalism in Sri Lanka* (Ann Arbor: University of Michigan Press, 1992).

5. Obeyesekere argues that it is not Buddhism but Buddhist history that justifies violence. It is this Buddhist history that he calls a "dark underside"; see Obeyesekere, "Buddhism, Nationhood, and Cultural Identity: A Question of Fundamentals," in *Fundamentalism Comprehended*, ed. Martin E. Marty and R. Scott Appleby (Chicago: University of Chicago Press, 1995), 233–34, 254. For a critical reflection on Obeyesekere's paper, see Jeganathan, "In the Shadow of Violence: Tamilness and the Anthropology of Identity in Southern Sri Lanka," in *Buddhist Fundamentalism*. For Obeyesekere's other concerns with violence as something opposed to the Buddhist doctrine of "nonviolence," see his "Origins and Institutionalization of Political Violence," in *Sri Lanka in Change and Crisis*, ed. James Manor (New York: St. Martin's Press, 1984). For scholarly preoccupations with trying to make sense of how Buddhists "legitimate their ethical stance" on violence and war in Sri Lanka, see Tessa Bartholomeusz, "In Defense of Dharma: Just-War Ideology in Buddhist Sri Lanka," *Journal of Buddhist Ethics* 1999. A similar concern is found in Juergensmeyer, *Terror in the Mind of God*, 112–16, 242.

6. Sarath Amunugama, "Buddhaputra or Bhumiputra?" For Similar concerns with "unsettling images . . . of monks swept up in the mobs of anti-government Sinhalese rebels," see Juergensmeyer, "What the Bhikkhu Said," 53, 68.

7. Thus violence as a "dark underside" of Buddhism is implied; see *Legends of People*, 11.

8. Tambiah, *Buddhism Betrayed?* 95–96. Others advance similar arguments; see Bruce Kapferer, "Remythologizing Discourses: State and Insurrectionary Violence in Sri Lanka," in *The Legitimation of Violence*, ed. David E. Apter (New York: New York University Press, 1998), 175; Holt, *Religious World*, 99, 133n. 3. Holt's essentialist claim that "Most truly religious

very question of his book title presupposes an authentic, nonviolent Buddhism as opposed to a "political Buddhism" (Tambiah's term) that advocates violence. Based on such an assumption, Tambiah goes on to state that "the increasing participation of monks, specially young monks . . . in violence, whether directly or indirectly, is a disturbing experience."[9] Note that Tambiah's essentialist understanding of the relation between monks and violence is made possible by, among other things, (some) monks' participation in the proscribed JVP movement, a practice that, as we will see later, became possible and centrally visible in the late 1980s. For Tambiah, this participation constitutes violence because the JVP stands for "militant politics" that the "central normative [Buddhist monastic] rules" forbid.[10]

My complaint is that this argument takes both categories of "violence" and "Buddhism" to be self-evident. That is to say, it assumes that what gets defined as "Buddhism" and "violence" in differing contexts always remains the same. In this chapter, I argue against these assumptions by critically rethinking the formations and deformations of the relations between Buddhism and violence. This exploration, I submit, is crucial to understanding religion and violence as "historical" concepts whose meanings shift; that is, the ways in which specific persons and practices are authorized, enabled, and indeed obliged to come into central view and fade from view as Buddhism and non-Buddhism,

---

Buddhists are peace-loving people, as are most truly religious Hindus and Christians" is part of the continuing disciplinary normalization, and indeed moralization, of the relation between religion and violence (108). Likewise, Jonathan Spencer, who has produced a considerable body of literature on violence and nationalism in Sri Lanka, writes, "I found myself desperately trying to make sense of that familiar paradox—the perpetration of evil by apparently nice, decent people"; see his "Popular Perceptions of Violence: A Provincial View," in *Sri Lanka in Change and Crisis*, 187; quoted in Jeganathan, "Shadow of Violence," 106. In a more recent work, Spencer correctly suggests that violence is not endemic to "Sinhala culture" (123). But surprisingly he claims that "violence has been a part of political life since the beginning of mass electoral politics in 1931." This violence, he says, is "steadily growing" (123); in other words, what makes (supposedly political) "violence" possible is "mass electoral politics"; see his, "On Not Becoming a 'Terrorist:' Problems of Memory, Agency, and Community in the Sri Lankan Conflict," in *Violence and Subjectivity*, ed. Veena Das et al. (Berkeley: University of California Press, 2000).

9. Tambiah, *Buddhism Betrayed?* 100. It must be noted here that for Tambiah the late 1940s and the early 1950s represent the "political activism" of monks, while the 1980s represent the "militant politics" of young monks. For other aspects of his understanding of violence as "dehumanization," "nonhuman," and "demonization," see Tambiah, "Entering a Dark Continent: Political Psychology of Crowds," in his *Leveling Crowds: Ethnonationalist Conflicts and Collective Violence in South Asia* (Berkeley: University of California Press, 1996), 284–86.

10. Tambiah, *Leveling Crowds*, 101.

religion and violence, civilization and terror, identity and difference, in fleeting domains of opposing debates.

To do so, I will show some ways in which since the early 1980s a variety of Buddhist discourses began to authorize a particular Buddhist image of a "fearless" young monk who would march to the "battlefront" and lay down his life to rescue and lead the Buddhist nation facing the threat of "terrorism." These authoritative discourses became possible and centrally visible within a period of a few years in which some prominent members of the sangha and lay Buddhists began vociferously to contest the "Buddhist" identity of the UNP (Jayewardene) government and its mandate to rule the Buddhist country and the nation "safeguarded by monks for centuries." In the mid- and late 1980s, the JVP strategically drew upon these "Buddhist" discourses and appealed to young monks to join forces with its movement. To join the JVP was to support an urgent "sacred," Buddhist task because the JVP claimed to liberate the Sinhala Buddhist (monks') country and nation. In such a context, the discourse, "country or death," became an authorized "Buddhist" practice for the JVP monks seen as the true patriots of the country. Yet, this patriotic image of fearless monkhood came to be contested and invested with a different kind of meaning as the Premadasa government crushed the JVP, portraying it as a "criminal," "un-Buddhist" movement threatening the "great Buddhist civilization" of Sri Lanka. To depict the JVP as an un-Buddhist movement was to depict the monks of the JVP as criminal and un-Buddhist. The government of Premadasa tortured these JVP monks and made them "Buddhist monks" again.

In light of this ethnographic terrain, I argue that conceptualizations of violence as a contradiction to Buddhism do not help us understand how certain ideas and practices that became centrally visible as "Buddhism" yesterday came to count as "violence" today. The notion of the contradiction of violence to Buddhist identity presupposes a nonviolent, humanistic concept of Buddhism. As anthropologist Jeganathan has convincingly argued, "humanism" cannot be the "residual, default category that is somehow politically known or safe. Humanism, as it is invoked, carries with it a complex, contextually located politics that cannot be known or assumed a priori."[11] In other words, to suppose that violence represents the opposite of humanism (that is, Buddhism) is to take the category of violence itself at face value. My account

11. Jeganathan, "After a Riot," 223–24. Part of Jeganathan's telling argument is that after the famous July 1983 riots, scholarly texts that sought to constitute violence as an anthropological object of knowledge employed "horror" as an abstract category to describe that event. "Horror,"

will avoid the trap of essentialism by demonstrating that what does and does not count as religion or violence is authorized within varying bounds of discourses and debates.

In problematizing the dominant disciplinary narratives about violence as the "dark underside" of religion, I do not, however, seek to advance the influential Girardian argument that "violence and the sacred are inseparable."[12] Nor am I interested in claiming, as does van der Veer, following Marcel Mauss, that violence is a "total social phenomenon," embodying "those phenomena at once legal, economic, religious, aesthetic, morphological, and so on."[13] Put alternatively, what preoccupies me is not questions about "religious violence" or "religious terrorism" that have now become key hermeneutical concepts in scholarly texts seeking to make available the supposed interrelation between religion and violence as objects of knowledge;[14] such concepts are grounded in assumptions about whether religion can or cannot be *justifiably* violent;[15] they fail to understand, in my view, that

---

he argues, is "the initial name given to the political incomprehensibility of '1983.' This name is then transformed into an analytic, which is called violence." It is through this constitution that the equation "violence=horror" becomes possible for anthropology (6). But the equation does not end here. As Jeganathan goes on to state, if horror is another name for the "destruction of the human, which cannot be apprehended politically and violence its analytic, a return to horror by way of violence will also return to the problem of the human." The equation then becomes: Horror=>violence=>horror=>humanism (223). For Jeganathan, the anthropological constitution of violence as a category rests on these "twin legs of horror and humanism" (221–23). One of the first scholars to try to explain violence in terms of horror was S. J. Tambiah; see "Horror Story," in his 1986 *Sri Lanka: Ethnic Fratricide.*

12. Rene Girard, *Violence and the Sacred* (Baltimore: Johns Hopkins University Press, 1971), 19. Girard later writes that *"religion,* in its broadest sense, then, must be another term for that obscurity that surrounds man's efforts to defend himself by curative or preventative means against his own violence" (23).

13. Peter van der Veer, "Writing Violence," in *Contesting the Nation: Religion, Community, and the Politics of Democracy in India,* ed. David Ludden (Philadelphia: University of Pennsylvania Press, 1996), 268–69.

14. See Juergensmeyer, *Terror in the Mind of God,* esp. 4–10; Brian K. Smith, "Monotheism and Its Discontents: Religious Violence and the Bible," *Journal of the American Academy of Religion* 66, no. 2 (1998). Smith writes that "religious violence, in all of its many forms, must be accounted for *as religious* and not merely wished away as external to some self-proclaimed ideal form of the true nature of religion" (404). Smith's is a review essay of Regina Schwartz's *The Curse of Cain: The Violent Legacy of Monotheism* (Chicago: University of Chicago Press, 1997). For Schwartz, "[all religious] acts of identity formation [particularly linked to biblical monotheism] are themselves acts of violence" (5).

15. Questions about the *religious* "justification for violence" govern Juergensmeyer's entire book. For example, he writes, "This is one of history's ironies, that although religion has been

different conjunctures of debates render the terms and parameters of what persons, practices, and knowledges can count as religion or violence contingent, and hence unavailable, for disciplinary canonization as transparent objects of knowledge.

The Making of a "Fearless" Monk

In the early 1980s, numerous Sri Lankan newspapers headlined statements by Buddhist monks defining the role of a monk in Sri Lankan society in a particular way. Among the monks quoted, the prominent monk Maduluwawe Sobhita, the incumbent of Nagavihara temple in Kotte, stands out. A popular preacher and steadfast supporter of the former SLFP—his picture appeared on the cover of Tambiah's *Buddhism Betrayed?*—Sobhita became a formidable critic of the Jayewardene government. In March 1983, addressing the twelfth anniversary of the sangha council held at Visuddharamaya temple in Colombo, Sobhita stated: "We can not do anything except through politics." He elaborated:

> Some say that monks do not need politics; but we cannot do anything except through politics. Even if we do not endorse party politics, we have to take certain decisions in important situations. We should have the right to comment on good and bad things that the government does . . . if a government engages in things that are against the religion [Buddhism] and the nation [*jātika virōdhi āgam virōdhi*] it becomes necessary for Buddhist monks to appoint a new government.[16]

---

used to justify violence, violence can also empower religion"; *Terror in the Mind of God*, 242. In a set of deeply flawed arguments, without any critical awareness of the problematic of Western (colonial and orientalist) constructions of categories like "religion," Juergensmeyer suggests that one "scenario for peace" is "separating religion from politics," which he claims is to be found in "the noble rhetoric of . . . Enlightenment thinkers" (235–39). For an instructive account of the problems of the Enlightenment assumptions about violence, society, and politics, see Pierre Saint-Amand, *The Laws of Hostility: Politics, Violence, and the Enlightenment*, trans. Jennifer Curtiss Gage (Minneapolis: University of Minnesota Press, 1996). For other concerns with conceptualizing the relation between religion and violence in terms of justification, see also Sudhir Kakar, *The Colors of Violence: Cultural Identities, Religion, and Conflict* (Chicago: University of Chicago Press, 1996), 192–94. Kakar contends that "religious justification of a conflict involves fundamental values and releases some of our most violent passions. . . . Every religion has a vision of divinely legitimized violence" (193).

16. "Dēshapālanayen Torava Apata Kala Häki Deyak Nä" ("There is nothing we can do apart from politics"), *Divayina*, Mar. 10, 1983.

Again in 1983, speaking at a Buddhist monk's funeral, Sobhita insisted that "monks cannot be separated from common public issues"; providing people with knowledge about solutions to life's problems is a monk's "duty" (*yutukamak*), he said.[17] Elsewhere, he pointed out that in order to fulfill this duty, the monk must reverse his role. On a different occasion, Sobhita quite ironically stated that "there is no point in preaching sermons when people are suffering"[18]—when the country is reaching an abyss of decadence, corruption, bribery, and injustice. In such a society, he claimed, "Buddhism cannot be followed."[19]

Sobhita argued that today lay Buddhists assume that Buddhist monks live in luxury and do nothing but sleep; in fact, "after visiting a temple, most people immediately ask, 'Is the monk sleeping?' [This deception] is a product of the open market economy."[20] Sobhita emphasized elsewhere that "monks are not a race that sleeps" and said that "if they had done so the religion and the nation [*jātiya āgama*] would not exist today."[21] Well-known Buddhist newspapers like *Budusarana* readily endorsed Sobhita's views:

> We must accept that there would be no Buddha Sasana, the Sinhaleseness [*sinhalatvaya*], and ancient temples and pagodas if the venerable Maha Sangha had been sleeping. Our venerable monks have achieved such an elevated status [*shrēsta tatvayata patva äta*]. Yet some [people] have not realized the monks' importance. The monks are a noble group that never 'sleeps through' the issues of the nation, religion, and language. Monks are the custodians of the nation. . . . They must be given the highest respect.[22]

This rhetoric in the early 1980s about the recognition of the role and place of the monks who safeguarded the religious and national values of the country, now threatened by the vices of the open-market economy, was a debate with the government of President Jayewardene. The debate, which continued well into the late 1980s, must be located in the context in which President

17. "Podu Janatā Prashanavalin Bhikshūn Ät Karannna Bä" ("Monks cannot be separated from common public issues"), *Dinakara*, Feb. 1, 1983.

18. "Janatāva Asahanayen Inna Yugayaka Bana Dēshanā Kirīmen Vädak Nä" ("There is no point in preaching *bana* when people are unhappy"), *Divayina*, Jan. 4, 1984.

19. Ibid.

20. Ibid.

21. "Hāmuduruwaru Nidāganna Jātiyak Novē" ("Monks are not a race that sleeps"), editorial, *Budusarana*, Nov. 22, 1984.

22. "Hāmuduruwaru Sätapīma" ("Monks' sleeping"), *Budusarana*, Nov. 30, 1984.

Jayewardene came to portray a particular "Buddhist" image of himself and his administration.

An important part of the Jayewardene government's political discourse was the establishment of a *dharmista* ("righteous") society. In such a society, Jayewardene argued, people would lead, free (*nivahal*), moral lives that accorded with the "pristine" (*nirmala*) words of the Buddha. Jayewardene presented himself as an example of the ideal Buddhist. In 1981, as the chief guest speaker at a Buddhist temple, Jayewardene claimed that "people know my strong devotion [*vishāla bhaktiya*] and my strong acceptance [*vishāla piligānī ma*] with regard to Buddhism." Jayewardene averred that he "undertook the office of presidency and would leave it without any craving" because he followed the "pristine" words of the Buddha. He exhorted others to emulate his example and said, "That is how we should all live."[23] For Jayewardene, contrary to many of his monk critics, this pristine Buddhism was not confined to any particular nationality but transcended all ethnic boundaries. Once, he stated that "in keeping with [Buddhist] principles" he did not "differentiate between people saying that this is a Sinhalese, this is a Tamil."[24] (Jayewardene claimed that Buddhaghosa, one of the best-known Buddhist commentators, who lived and worked at the historic Mahavihara temple in early fifth-century C.E. Sri Lanka, was a Tamil.)[25] Equally significant, Jayewardene insisted that in a dharmista society in which this multiethnic, pristine Buddhism exists, monks remove themselves from "politics" and lead "pure," exemplary monastic lives. Jayewardene supporters hailed

23. Speech delivered by Jayewardene at Sirimalwatte temple in Ganegoda, Mihirigama, May 16, 1981.

24. Speech delivered by President Jayewardene at Hindu College in Ratmalana, Apr. 1979; quoted in "Hätta Hatveni Vasarata Pā Tabana Bauddha Nāyaka Janapati" ("The Buddhist leader-president who turns seventy-seven"), *Budusarana*, Oct. 16, 1982.

25. "Bududahama Anuva Gätalu Visadamu" ("Let's solve problems according to Buddhism"), speech delivered by Jayewardene at Hambuluwa Rajama Temple, article in unidentified newspaper, n.d. In a recent imaginative reading of Jayewardene's slim text *Golden Threads* (Colombo: Govt. Printing, 1984), Sankaran Krishna claims that President Jayewardene yielded no political space for the recognition of Tamil "minority"-identities in Sri Lanka; see Krishna, "Producing Sri Lanka from Ceylon," in his *Postcolonial Insecurities: India, Sri Lanka, and the Question of Nationhood* (Minneapolis: University of Minnesota Press, 1999). Now I do not want to contest this claim empirically since I think that Jayewardene does not remain available for a monolithic interpretation. But Krishna's analysis of *Golden threads* hardly captures the complexity that animated the shifting configurations of the Jayewardene state; for more on Jayewardene, see chapters 3 and 5.

him as the "best national symbol that Sri Lanka could present to the world" because "he practices Buddhism to the letter" (*akuratama pilipadinavā*).[26] This "Buddhist" image of the Jayewardene government, with its rhetoric of an "apolitical" monkhood practicing pristine Buddhism, became the subject of fierce criticism from both monks and lay Buddhists, a criticism that came into central view in the early 1980s. It is in the context of such a debate that we must locate the emerging monastic demands for the recognition of the role and place of the monk in society.

One of the vocal critics of the Jayewardene regime was Ediriweera Sarachchandra, a well-known lay Buddhist intellectual and playwright in Sri Lanka. In early 1982, Sarachchandra published a book titled *Dharmista Samājaya* (Righteous Society). He argued that in the name of "development" (*samvardhanaya*), far from creating a righteous society, the open-market, capitalistic policies of the Jayewardene government introduced various vices—from tourism to the emigration of Buddhist women as domestic servants to the Middle East—that brought about a complete moral downfall of society. In short, Sarachchandra's book is a story about a society in which inequality, craving, selfishness, and indignity abound, and the rich and the powerful dominate the poor and the weak. In such a society, the difference between the human and the beast disappeared and "the law of the jungle" reigned supreme.[27] Other criticisms of the Jayewardene administration followed. In 1982, Buddhist monk Labuduwe Siridhamma, a staunch supporter of the SLFP, called Jayewardene a "traitor," a term that formed an important part of the JVP's anti-UNP government rhetoric (more on this below). Siridhamma, like Sobhita and Sarachchandra, accused Jayewardene of creating an "unrighteous society"[28] and demanded that Jayewardene be

26. *Budusarana*, Oct. 16, 1982.

27. Ediriweera Sarachchandra, *Dharmista Samājaya* (Colombo: Elko Industries, 1982), 144–45. His criticisms of the state provoked opposition. It is alleged that in 1982, at a Sinhala Bala Mandalaya meeting in Colombo to discuss the theme of (the Jayewardene government's) "Destruction of the Sinhala Civilization," a mob of UNP supporters attacked Sobhita and Sarachchandra with bicycle chains and chairs; see "Adō Saracchandra Tōda Jātiya Bēraganna Avē Kiyalā Pahara Dunnā" ("They beat us saying, 'Yo, Saracchandra, did you come to save the nation?'"), *Divayina*, June 84, 1984.

28. "Ada Sri Lankādvīpaya Adarmatdvīpayak" ("Today the island of Sri Lanka is an island of unrighteousness"), *Ätta*, Sept. 2, 1982; see also *Dinakara*, May 22, 1984; "Dharmista Samājaya Kō?" ("Where is the righteous society?"), *Dinakara*, June 27, 1985.

removed from office.[29] In fact, Siridhamma was one of the first monks in the 1980s to call on monks to "march forward and protect the country and the nation" from the government. Such monks who opposed Jayewardene became "heroes." After his death in 1985, Siridhamma came to be portrayed as a "heroic" and "brave"[30] (nirbhīta) monk, a "fearless lion" (kēsara sinhayek).[31] Some argued that Siridhamma should be held as an "example to the Buddhist monk" (bhikshuvata ādarshayak) living in a country ruled by "beastly" (mruga) and "unfortunate" (mūsala) policies of the Jayewardene government.[32]

Such discourses about the brave monk who must protect the threatened nation gained momentum. In 1985, Sobhita stated that "it was the primary duty of the sangha to come forward bravely against injustice."[33] He demanded that monks stop "eating and sleeping" and "march forward":

Since the introduction of Buddhism to Sri Lanka, the Bhikkhus have played an important role in the government by fulfilling the duty of advising the king. Monks became important advisers to . . . [various kings]. On occasion some kings lived on the food collected by monks on their alms round. Therefore, when the Sinhala race is facing a decisive situation, monks must march forward [peramuna gata yutuyi]. It does not befit a monk to continue the daily schedule of eating and sleeping. [We must remember that] in the wake of foreign threats to the country, monks such as Variyapola, Kudapola and Miggettuwatte acted fearlessly. Some of these monks happily confronted the bullet![34]

Sobhita continued to evoke this image of the monk who, like past Sinhala heroes, is fearless—who braves death to protect the country. He linked that image to the "Sinhala race and nation" and said, "Monks have no families to protect, no homes, no properties, no cattle. But they must guard with their lives [pana men räka gata yutuyi] the country in which the [Sinhalase

29. Ätta, Jan. 31, 1985.

30. Dinakara, Sept. 18, 1985.

31. Divayina, June 1, 1985.

32. Dinakara, May 31, 1985; see also "Oba Apagen Samugatte Ratata Oba Vännan Dahas Gananak Avashyava Äti Yugayakayi" ("You passed away in an era in which the country needs thousands of monks like you"), Divayina, June 1, 1985.

33. "Thero Deplores Bhikkhus Dabbling in Politics," Island, July 3, 1985.

34. "Väladīmat Sätapīmat Pamanak Bhiskhu Jīvitayata Taram Nove" ("Only eating and sleeping do not befit a monk"), Divayina, Feb. 11, 1985.

Buddhist] race exists, the race that fed them for two thousand years. The monks must not bow their heads to any person."[35]

Other, similar discourses became visible. At a Buddhist ceremony held to transfer merit to the soldiers killed in the war, a Buddhist monk named Mahapallegama Dhammalankara clamored that "monks should march to the battle front [*satan peramunata*] without practicing the monastic image of silence [*muni vata noräka*]."[36] He claimed that "there is no Buddhist sangha where there is no Sinhalese race and there is no Sinhalese race where there is no Buddhist sangha"; he implored the "educated and virtuous [*silvat*] monks" to march forward to protect the Sinhalese race. If monks "isolate themselves [*pättakata visitiyot*] practicing meditation in times of national crisis," they would jeopardize the future of the country.[37]

More influential members of the sangha such as Walpola Rahula joined forces with these discourses. At a meeting of five hundred monks convened to protest the proposed legislation by the All-Party Conference to "solve the ethnic problem" in Sri Lanka, Rahula went so far as to say that the "Sangha is ready to lay down their lives" to prevent the government from implementing the proposals. Claiming that the proposals would lead to the division of the country, Rahula said that if "peaceful avenues" do not work, the sangha has a "weapon," and "using that weapon [we] will wage a battle all over the country. The police, the armed forces or any other force will not stop us."[38] Rahula did not explain what the weapon was, but Sobhita, who was present on the occasion, pointed out that if these proposals are implemented "the Sangha will be willing to sacrifice the lives of ten theros [*sic*] for every clause [in the proposals]. We have no families nor any wealth. If one [monk] can die before you grow old, that is a comfort. We are ready to sacrifice our lives for the sake of country, race and religion. [Otherwise] future generations will ask whether we were sleeping."[39]

35. "Bhikhūn Vahansēlā Kisivekuta Hisa Nonamā Ratat Jātiyat Rāka Gata Yutuyi" ("Without bowing their heads to any one, Buddhist monks must protect the country and the nation"), *Davasa*, July 9, 1985.

36. "Maha Sagaruvana Munivata Norāka Satan Peramunata Vädiya Yutuyi" ("Monks should march to the battlefront without practicing the monastic image of silence"), *Divayina*, Feb. 11, 1985.

37. Ibid.

38. "Sangha Is Ready to Lay Down Their Lives," *Island*, Dec. 24, [1984?].

39. *Divayina*, Dec. 24, [1984?].

Such rhetoric continued to make headlines.[40] Among published articles, one in particular stands out. In 1986, Bengamuwe Nalaka, joint secretary of Mavbima Surakime Vyaparaya (MSV—the Movement for the Protection of the Motherland),[41] wrote a piece with a famous line in Pali, "Mā Nivatta Abhikkama" ("Do not stop; come forward")—words that the Buddha is supposed to have uttered in encouraging his disciples to tread the path from samsara to nirvana. Nalaka, however, used the words to mean something else. Recalling the history of "brave" Sinhala monks who "fostered and protected the heritage of the Buddha Sasana" by "facing the bullet and fearing no death," he argued:

> Buddhists must recall these words of the Buddha. This is exactly how the Buddha used these words addressing the monks. As those dedicated to travel the path of the Dhamma, especially monks should always recollect these words. This is no recollection of God. . . . These words of the Buddha did and do bring solace to the monk who never cowardly runs away [*bayen noduvana*] and hides in the face of threats [*tādana pādana*] and physical blows [*pahara*]. We must record that today the occasion has arrived to think about this precious saying and act on it.[42]

It is easy to see that these dominant narratives begin to make centrally visible a particular image of the Buddhist monk—the monk who does not sleep, who abandons bana preaching and meditation and marches forward, who is fearless and ready to sacrifice his life to protect the Buddha Sasana and the

---

40. See "Maha Sangharuvanata Ārayumak: Nihadava Nosita Peramunata Vadinna" ("An invitation to the monks: Do not be silent; march forward"), *Dinaräsa*, Mar. 13, 1986; "Rata Jātiya Räka Gänīmata Bhikshuva Peramunata ĀYutuyi" ("Buddhists monks must come forward to protect the country and the nation"), *Divayina*, 1986 [?]; "Vatman Arbudaya Hā Bhikshun Vahanse" ("Contemporary crisis and the Buddhist monk"), *Divayina*, Sept. 19, 1986.

41. The MSV was founded in 1986, as its secretary, Bengamuwe Nalaka, explains, to "generate opposition . . . to any . . . political division of the country along communal or racial lines." Its administrative body consisted of both monks and prominent lay members such as Prime Minister Mrs. Bandaranaike. Nalaka claims that since some early monk-members of the movement like Sobhita and Wilegoda Ariyadeva issued "misleading and harmful" statements that violated the movement's objective, the name Vyāpāraya (movement) was changed to Sanvidānaya (organization); see "A Reply from the Mavbima Suräkīme Sanvidhānaya," *Divayina*, May 24, 1989; and I interviewed Nalaka on Oct. 8, 1997. On the organizational structure of the MSV, see Peter Schalk, "'Unity' and 'Sovereignty': Key Concepts of a Militant Buddhist Organization in the Present Conflict in Sri Lanka," *Temonos* 24 (1988): 55–82.

42. "Mā Nivatta Abhikkhama" ("Do not stop, come forward"), *Divayina*, Sept. 6, 1986.

Sinhala nation. My argument is that this image of the monk is construed as "Buddhist" not simply because the agents of these discourses are Buddhist monks; that image is authorized by a context in which the very same monks contested the "Buddhist" image of the Jayewardene government.

The Emergence of the Discourse of "Terrorism": Contestation of "Buddhist Nonviolence"

By the early 1980s, the force of the Tamil LTTE claim for a separate state in northern Sri Lanka became a visible reality. On July 23, 1983, the Tamil Tigers ambushed and killed eighteen soldiers of the Sri Lankan army. A few days later, a massive riot broke out in central Colombo, a riot in which the Sinhalese attacked and killed Tamil citizens: they looted and set fire to Tamil businesses and properties worth billions of rupees. After the riot, the LTTE continued to massacre Sinhalese civilians in the north and in the capital periodically detonated bombs. In the wake of the LTTE demand for a separate state, a ferocious public debate arose between Jayewardene and some influential Buddhist monks, focusing on questions about violence, Buddhist (monastic) identity, and the "country and the nation."

In early 1984, several Buddhist monks and monastic committees insisted that Jayewardene wage a full-scale war to eradicate the "problem of terrorism." Identifying the Tamil Tigers as a "terrorist" group threatening the "unity of the country," Labuduwe Siridhammma demanded that the government hold "no peace talks [with the Tamil Tigers] before [achieving] a victory by war."[43] Similar monastic voices insisting on war against the Tigers flashed across the newspapers,[44] and one statement in particular generated controversy. In January 1984, Walpola Rahula told Jayewardene in a public meeting that the government should eradicate terrorism militarily.[45] Two years before, Rahula had worked with Jayewardene in creating the Buddhist and Pali University (see chapter 3), but in this context he turned against the president because he did not heed the monk's advice to "curb terrorism" in the north.[46]

---

43. "Yuddhayen Jayagannā Turu Sākaccā Pävätvīma Natara Karanu" ("Suspend [peace] talks until victory by war"), *Divayina*, Jan. 12, 1984.

44. "Curb Terrorism First, then Consider [a] Solution," *Island*, Dec. 29, 1984.

45. Cited in "Rahula Hāmuduruwō Hā Janādhipati Tumā" ("Rahula and the president"), *Ätta*, Jan. 30, 1984.

46. "Monk Blames Jayewardene," clipping from unidentified newspaper, Jan. 29, 1984.

Jayewardene stated bluntly that he was not ready to "kill innocent people" in the name of eradicating terrorism. He would not, he said, act like Idi Amin or Hitler; nor like Sinhalese King Sirisaga Bo, who cut off and handed his own head to a bounty hunter. He questioned the Buddhist identity of those monks who endorsed war by saying that "Buddhists would never ask him to [kill and] act inhumanely" (*amānushika andamin katayutu karannäyi bauddhayō nam kavadāvat kiyannä*).[47] Jayewardene repeatedly expressed his opposition to "the use of violence in Sri Lanka"[48] and challenged monks advocating a military solution to the problem of terrorism: speaking specifically about monks who had picketed to "inform the president about the danger of terrorism" in the north, Jayewardene on one occasion said that monks did not understand the gravity of violence because "monks are not the ones who die" in a war; berating the monks' picketing as "false activities" (*boru väda*), Jayewardene said that if monks "want to go to war we can send them to war."[49]

As Jayewardene refused a military solution to the problem of terrorism, claiming that it contravened Buddhism, vociferous monastic voices contested his position. In 1985, Uduwawalle Chandananda issued a statement that made front-page news. Chandananda argued that by failing to "handle terrorism" successfully the government "made it impossible for the Sinhala people to live in dignity in their own country."[50] Chandananda questioned why a powerful government like the UNP could not "tackle terrorism" when kings [in the past] "consulted monks on all matters" and fought invaders to unify "the country under one flag." He demanded that if the government could not "stop the terrorists, it hand over the country's ruling powers to the Mahasangha."[51]

---

47. "Ahinsakayan Marā Dāmā Trastavādaya Madinu Bä" ("Killing innocent people cannot eradicate terrorism"), *Dinamina*, Jan. 31, 1984.

48. See also *Weekend*, Jan. 8. 1984.

49. "Satya KriyāYanu Kumakda?" ("What is Satya Kriyā?"), speech by President Jayewardene at Sri Piyaratane Pirivena in Galle, Sept. 9, 1985; printed in J. R. Jayewardene, *Apē Jātika Urumaya* (Our national heritage), speeches by Jayewardene (Colombo: Rajaye Mudranalaya, 1986).

50. Cited in "Lalith Counters Monk Who Said, 'Give Us the Country to Rule.'" *Daily News*, July 31, 1985.

51. *Daily News*, July 31, 1985. In response to Chandananda, the then minister of defense, Lalith Athulathmudali, argued that contemporary problems were different from those faced by King Parakrama Bahu, but he assured the monks that "Buddhists had nothing to fear so long as the government was in power." Another minister, U. B. Wijekoon, said monks should not blame the government when "the Sangha had failed in taking the Dhamma to Tamil People"; *Daily News*, July 31, 1985; see also "An Amazing Proposal," editorial, *Daily News*, Aug. 1, 1985.

Rahula (whom we have encountered earlier), too, spoke of the monk as an ideally qualified individual for the leadership of the country.[52]

Such narratives that envisioned monks both as political advisers and capable leaders of the country who would advocate war to defend the "dignity" of Sinhala Buddhists challenged the government's position as a "Buddhist" regime because it did not seek a military solution to terrorism. Implicit in the argument is that, by failing to combat terrorism by war, the government lost not only its Buddhist identity but also its mandate to rule. And over time, such monastic voices became more vocal. Following the LTTE's shooting and killing of Buddhist devotees worshipping at the Bo Tree in Anuradhapura in the mid-1980s, a newspaper reported Sobhita's clamoring that "the government must resign without destroying [*kābāsiniya nokara*] the country and the nation."[53] Holding Jayewardene responsible for the "river of blood [*lē vilak*] that terrorists created in Anuradhapura," Sobhita said, "If the government continues to rule Sri Lanka, the country, religion, and nation will be over [*ivarayi*]. I demand [*balakaranava*] that President J. R. Jayewardene resign, handing over the country, which Buddhists have protected for two thousand five hundred years, to a better qualified [Buddhist] person."

Sobhita went on to argue that as individuals "who are dedicated to protecting the future of the country on behalf of the younger generation," the monks "must awaken" (*avadikaraviya yutuyi*) the nation.[54] Another well-known monk, Hedigalle Paññatissa (like Rahula, an early Jayewardene ally), stating that the ruler of the country should be "righteous" and "virtuous" (*silvat*), warned that if monks did not oppose Jayewardene's leadership, future generations would see them as "traitors."[55] (These concerns about the threat

52. "'Nāyaktvayata Bhikshuva Taram Sudusu An Kisi Kenek Nä'—Walpola Rahula" ("There is no other individual more qualified for leadership than a Buddhist monk"), *Divayina*, Mar. 19, 1985; see also "Sagaruvanē Anusāsanā Notakā Kriyākalot Anāgataya Andurē—Bellanwila Wimalaratana" ("If Buddhist monks' advice is ignored, the future [of the country] will be in the dark"), *Davasa*, Aug. 19, 1986.

53. "Ratat Jātiyat Kābāsiniya Nokara Ānduva Illā Asviya Yutuyi" ("The government must resign without destroying the country and the nation"), *Dinarāsa*, May 15, 1986.

54. *Dinarāsa*, May 15, 1986. Such demands for Jayewardene's resignation became unceasing; see "Bäri Magula Damā Gedara Palayan: Ānduvata Erehiva Mahajana Hada Nägeyi" ("Go home if you cannot do the job: The public voice rises against the government"), *Dinarāsa*, June 2, 1986.

55. See "Budu Sasunata Kala Nigāvak" ("A dishonor to the Buddha Sasana"), *Divayina*, June 16, 1987; "Himivaru Gātanaya Kalat Budu Sasuna Nasanna Bä" ("Even if monks are killed, the Buddha Sasana cannot be destroyed"), *Divayina*, Aug. 3, 1987.

of "terrorism" to Buddhism in general and to monks in particular were rendered more visible in mid-1987, after the LTTE decapitated thirty-two monks on Buddhist pilgrimage in Arantalawa, Ampara.)[56]

These discourses depict the Jayewardene government as unrighteous and as having lost its right to rule the country because it failed to listen to the sangha and "curb terrorism." In other words, for Jayewardene to be "righteous" and "virtuous"—that is, to be truly Sinhala Buddhist at this particular time—he should protect the Buddha Sasana even at the cost of human lives. This critiquing of Jayewardene's inability to deal with the problem of terrorism became prominent within the UNP party itself. In late 1987, Gamini Jayasuriya, a reputable Buddhist who was both minister of agriculture and secretary of the Mahabodhi Society in Sri Lanka, resigned from the cabinet when the government proposed a bill to give greater autonomy to Tamils in the north. Jayasuriya, whom some prominent members of the sangha later honored as a man "born to save the country and Buddhism" because he resigned from his ministerial post, claimed that the bill would destroy the unity of Buddhist Lanka.[57]

Questioning the Jayewardene government's Buddhist identity also inevitably involved questioning the identity of monks who were Jayewardene allies. On President Jayewardene's eightieth birthday, in September 1986, for example, the government newspapers published statements by several chief monks—Talalle Dhammananda, Pahamune Gunananda, Dompe Dammaratana, and others—praising Jayewardene's leadership.[58] Days later, a newspaper editorial berated this support for Jayewardene as "utterly shameless behavior," questioning bluntly: "Are these monks?"[59] On some occasions, chief monks who expressed support for the government were physically assaulted in public by younger monks.[60]

---

56. *Divayina*, Aug. 3, 1987. The Arantalawa incident did not take place, as Tambiah says, in 1986; *Buddhism Betrayed?* 75.

57. Cited in Akuretiye Nanda and Premasiri Abeysinha, eds., *Gāmini Jayasuriya Abhinandana* (Colombo: Samayavardhana, 1996); see also *Sunday Times*, May 10, 1998, SLnet. In recognition of Jayasuriya's "eternal" service to Buddhists in Sri Lanka, the Malwatta and Asgiriya monastic chapters conferred on him two honorary Buddhist titles, "Lankābhimāni" and "Sāsanabandhu Janaranjana Kīrti Srī Dhara"; see *Gāmini Jayasuriya Abhinandana*.

58. See *Dinamina*, Sept. 24, 25, 29, 1986.

59. "Mahā Sangha Ratnayada Mē?" ("Is this the mahasangha?"), *Ätta*, Sept. 30, 1986.

60. I have detailed accounts of a popular incident in which a group of supposed JVP monks attacked and threatened the life of a staunch UPN supporter, Akuretiye Amarawamsa, the

Such acts of opposition must be seen in a context in which chief monks who expressed support for the government came to be branded by the JVP as "traitors to the country" while monks—mostly young monks—who opposed the government (*rājatdrōhi*) came to be praised as "patriotic" (*dēshaprēmī*).[61] The Jayewardene government was being deemed the biggest "traitor" to the country by the discourses that continued to appear in the mid- and late 1980s, calling on monks to "get off the old couch"[62] and "get down from the balcony [of the mansion]"[63] and save the country and the nation, and they targeted a specific audience of monks.[64] Many such hegemonic discourses depicted young monks (*taruna himivaru*) as "unselfish" (*parahitakāmi*)[65] and "patriotic" heroes[66] who should be guided not to be the "tools" (*atakolu*) of the government;[67] the chief monks (*nāyaka hāmuduruwaru*), on the other hand, were portrayed as dishonoring the sangha by supporting the government.[68]

During this time some monks wrote, for example, that "the Buddha Sasana and monks are helpless like a ship without a captain"[69]; other monks expressed confidence that young monks would, however, protect the sasana. In the late 1980s, at the Sri Lanka National Sangha Council (at the Mahabodhi Society in Maradana), Sobhita said, "Young monks should be safeguarded. If young monks are molded correctly, the whole Buddha Sasana will

---

principal of the Vidyodaya Pirivena, who was one of the guest speakers at Yakkaduwe Paññarama's funeral in 1985. The monks demanded that Amarawamsa not mention in his speech the name of President Jayewardene, the chief guest at the funeral; interview with Kakkapalliye Anuruddha at Vidyalankara Pirivena, Nov. 4, 1997.

61. This, he says, is precisely why in 1984 Nalaka founded the Deshapremi Bhikshu Peramuna (Patriotic Bhikkhu Front); interview with Nalaka, Oct. 8, 1997.

62. "Parana Kavicciyen Bimata Bahimu Api" ("Let us get off the old couch"), *Divayina*, June 14, 1987.

63. "Samiduni Sadällen Bäsa Midulata Vadinna" ("Venerable monk! Get down from the balcony and march to the field"), *Divayina*, Feb. 22, 1987.

64. "Nāyakatvayata Bhikshuva Taram Sudusu An Kenek Nä."

65. "Parahitakāmi Taruna Himivaru" ("Unselfish young monks"), *Dinamina*, Oct. 1, 1987.

66. "Vatman Taruna Bhikshuva Samājayata Väda Dāyaka Viya Yutuyi" ("The contemporary young Buddhist monk must serve society"), *Divayina*, Dec. 29, 1986.

67. "Parana Kavicciyen Bimata Bahimu Api."

68. See "Mahanāhimivarunta Sinhala Akäpada?" ("Are the chief monks against the Sinhala?"), *Divayina*, Oct. 29, 1986; "Mahasagaruvanata Nāhima Saranaya" ("May the chief monks bless the mahasangha"), *Dinaräsa*, Sept. 11, 1987.

69. "Parana Kavicciyen Bimata Bahimu Api."

be protected."[70] Another monk, Bellanwila Wimalaratana, argued that the "power" of young monks (balavēgaya) and the leadership that they give when the country is facing a national problem are noble (vishistayi). Other influential monks at the council (among them Welamitiyawe Kusaladhamma, Muruttetuwe Ananda, and Kamburupitiye Wanaratana) made statements such as: "Young monks should act with foresight" when the government "denigrates" and "suppresses" (avamānayata hā mardanayata) monks; "The young monks can create a righteous society within a united Sri Lanka. The time has come to take action."[71]

Such portrayals of young monks as the future engineers of a righteous society in an "unrighteous" country that was suppressing the sangha preceded an important event: the signing of the Indo-Sri Lanka Peace Accord on July 28, 1987. When President Jayewardene and the Indian prime minister signed the accord to bring Indian troops to help Sri Lanka disarm the LTTE, thousands of young monks, headed by, among others, Maduluwawe Sobhita and Muruttetuwe Ananda, took to the streets and joined Sinhalese mobs rioting against the accord.[72] Later, the police took hundreds of monks into custody, charging them with the violation of law and order in the country. A few weeks after the arrest of the monks, the government announced its plan to issue special identity cards to all Sri Lankan monks because of its concern about the "unattractive" [aprasanna] behavior of monks during the signing of the accord.[73] The government suggested that many monks who took part in the riots were not "real monks" but "rebels disguised as monks" (bhikshu ves gena). It warned the public against such robed "men," claiming that the sale of saffron robes had recently increased in the city.[74]

Many monks and lay Buddhists challenged the government's charges against the monks and questioned the government's own Buddhist image. Newspapers carried sarcastic reports of how "Jayewardene's righteous government" locked up the "monks who are engaged in a noble task of claiming the

70. "Sangaruvanata Abhibavā Yämata Kisivekuta Ida Tabannē Nä" ("We will not allow anyone to supersede monks"), Davasa, n.d. [late 1980s].

71. Davasa, n.d. (late 1980s).

72. "Bhikkus Protest," Daily News, July 28, 1987.

73. Bhikshūn Vahansēta Jātika Hädunum Patak" ("A national identity card for the Buddhist monk"), editorial, Dinamina, Sept. 1, 1987.

74. "Kaha Sivuru Vikinīma Vädivē" ("The sale of yellow robes increases"), Divayina, Aug. 10, 1987.

rights of people."[75] Influential monks like Palipana Chandananda demanded the immediate release of monks from prisons.[76] Later, other monks (among them Sobhita, who was arrested for inciting monks) clamored at rallies that all Sri Lankan Buddhists "should be grateful [*nayagäti*] to young monks who ate prison food to solve a national problem."[77]

Some monks decried the government plan to issue identity cards to Buddhist monks, asking if the government was demanding that people worship monks after inspecting their identity cards.[78] Others claimed that monks do not need special forms of identification because they already carry national identity cards as citizens of Sri Lanka.[79] Though the plan to issue bhikkhu identity cards never went into effect, many voices charged that the state was trying to destroy young monks and urged them to "rally and defeat the suppression of monks."[80] This image of young monks being subjected to suppression became more public after President Jayewardene personally ordered the suspension of state grants to many monastic educational pirivenas whose students the government claimed were "engaging in harmful activities that obstruct peace" in Sri Lanka.[81] One newspaper editorial characterized the Jayewardene decision as an attack not only on the sangha but on Buddhism itself, claiming that it violated the constitution that promises to safeguard the Buddha Sasana in Sri Lanka. "It is the biggest treason [*lokuma drōhikama*] the government committed against Buddhism."[82] Several monks portrayed it as a

75. "Dharmista Jayewardene Rajaya Bhikshūn Tunsiyak At Adanguvata Aran" ("Jayewardene righteous government has taken three hundred monks into custody"), *Ätta*, Sept. 5, 1987.

76. "Cōdanā Näti Himivarun Vahāma Nidahas Karanna" ("Release innocent monks immediately"), *Divayina*, Sept. 1, 1987.

77. "Sangha Ruvanata Abhibavā Yämata Kisivekuta Ida Tabannē Nä."

78. "Hädunum Pata Balā Namaskāra Kirīma?" ("Paying respect after inspecting the identity card?"), *Davasa*, Sept. 4, 1987.

79. See "Bhikshūnta Hädunum Pata Avashya Nä" ("Monks do not need identity cards"), *Dinamina*, Oct. 14; "Bhikshūnta Hädunum Pata Nisā Matuvana Prashna" ("The questions that monks face because of the identity cards for monks"), *Davasa*, Oct 15, 1987.

80. "Bhikshu Mardanayata Ida Denna Epä" ("Do not allow the suppression of monks"), *Ätta*, Aug., 28, 1987.

81. "Piriven Valata Ādāra Athituvē Janapati Niyamayen" ("Funds for the pirivenas stopped on president's order"), *Ätta*, Sept. 10, 1987. Some of the pirivenas, said to have been badly affected by the grant cuts, were Vidyaratana Pirivena in Horana, Sunetra Devi Pirivena in Pepiliyana, and Subhadrarama Pirivena in Nugegoda; *Divayina*, Oct. 29, 1987.

82. "Piriven Adyāpanayata Pahara Gävve Äyi" ("Why did the government attack the pirivena education?"), *Dinaräsa*, Sept. 9, 1987.

"revenge on monks"[83] and questioned if it was the way that a "righteous government" treated the "guardians of the nation" (jātiyē muradēvatāvan).[84]

It is in the context of authorizing the above "Buddhist" image of young monks that we must examine the relation between Buddhist monks and the JVP.[85] One could argue that if young monks came to be portrayed as "a ship without a captain," the JVP became its captain who would later navigate the sangha to the battlefront to save the country. To do so, the JVP drew upon a particular kind of "Buddhist" language that remarkably paralleled the language in which the above image of young monks was constructed. Below I examine what kinds of discourse made possible what kinds of "Buddhist" practices for young monks within the umbrella of the JVP, particularly in the late 1980s. Then I look at the ways in which such practices came to be contested and construed as "un-Buddhist" and "violent" in the context of the Premadasa administration.

Monks, the JVP, and "Sacred Religious Duty"

The Janata Vimukti Peramuna, or JVP, founded in the late 1960s by Rohana Wijeweera, is predominantly a youth movement that tried to unseat two governments by armed revolt. On both occasions, the JVP failed. In 1971 the SLFP government of Mrs. Sirimavo Bandaranaike subdued the JVP by killing at least three thousand of the movement's supporters. Then in a bloody battle that lasted from August 1989 to January 1990, the Premadasa government crushed the movement, eliminating more than twenty thousand JVP members.[86] Though exact figures are unknown, it is said that thousands of them were young Buddhists monks.

83. *Ätta*, Sept. 25, 1987.

84. *Dinarāsa*, Sept. 17, 1987.

85. For a historical overview of the JVP, see Mick Moore, "Thoroughly Modern Revolutionaries," *Modern Asian Studies* 27, no. 3 (1993): 593–642. For an account of the JVP during the late 1980s, see Chandraprema, *Sri Lanka: Years of Terror*; Rohan Gunaratna, *Sri Lanka: A Lost Revolution? The Inside Story of the JVP* (1990; reprint, Sri Lanka: Institute of Fundamental Studies, 1995); A. C. Alles, *The JVP, 1969–1989* (Colombo: Lake House, 1990).

86. Some estimate the total number of JVP members killed by the security forces at about twenty-two thousand (eight thousand from August 1987 to July 1989 and about fifteen thousand from August 1989 to January 1990). Over a period of three years, the JVP is said to have claimed more than seventeen thousand lives; see Gunaratana, *Sri Lanka: A Lost Revolution?* 269.

Since Jayewardene banned the movement in 1983, claiming that it insti-
gated anti-Tamil sentiments during that year's July riots,[87] the JVP functioned
as an underground movement with the support of many rural-based young
people drawn from all parts of the island. In the early 1980s, Buddhist monks,
primarily university students, began to join the JVP. In fact, D. M. Ananda, a
Buddhist monk-student at Peradeniya University, who later gave up the robes
to devote his entire time to the JVP, was considered to be number three in the
organization.[88] It was only in the mid- and late 1980s, however, that the JVP
concertedly recruited young monks, particularly from pirivenas; hence,
before examining the tactics of recruiting monks, this chapter discusses the
kinds of rhetorical strategies that the JVP deployed to authorize a "Buddhist"
definition of the movement.

According to some of the JVP leaflets and handwritten documents from
the 1980s—documents that, at one time, to have in one's possession meant
possible interrogation, abduction, or even death—the JVP urged all patriots,
including monks, to join the movement. Following its attack on two army
camps to obtain weapons in 1987, for example, in one particular leaflet the
Deshapremi Janata Vyaparaya (People's Patriotic Organization—DJV),
which was considered to be the armed branch of the JVP, spelled out its
objective:

> We are always ready to liberate our motherland from all enemies; to pave
> the path for a free [*nivahal*], peaceful society; to follow in the footsteps of
> our former heroic brothers. We will use the weapons we obtained from the
> two army camps to defeat the enemies of the motherland. We will safe-
> guard the motherland. We will liberate our brothers from the suffering they
> are facing. The doors of our movement are open to every fearless [*nirbhīta*]
> citizen.[89]

The word *enemies* pointed to the government of President Jayewardene.
What is remarkable is that this leaflet—written, like many others I have col-
lected, just a few weeks before the Indo–Sri Lanka Peace Accord—refers to
Jayewardene as *dēshadrōhī* (traitor)—a term that monks had been the first to

---

87. On this, see "The Proscription July 1983," in Chandraprema, *Sri Lanka: Years of Terror*,
59–63.

88. Chandraprema, *Sri Lanka: Years of Terror*, 144.

89. A leaflet issued by the DJV, June 10, 1987. I thank Ajit Serasundara for providing me
with these valuable leaflets.

use in blaming Jayewardene:[90] the leaflet announced that the DJV was ready to liberate the country from the "traitor Jayewardene," the LTTE "terrorists," and the "Indian invaders" (referring to Rajiv Gandhi)—all concerns that monks had taken up. Promising that they will be "victorious" (*api dinan-nemu*), the DJV concluded the message with the slogan "Motherland or death" (*mavbima nätnam maranaya*).

The Saffron Army: "Motherland or Death"

The JVP sought to authorize the choice of "motherland or death" as an "authentic Buddhist" practice for monks by adopting particular discursive strategies. The JVP leaflets, addressing monks as "Venerable Sir" (*garu svāmin vahansa*), called upon monks to "rally" (*pela gähev*), "lead" (*peramuna-ganiv*), and "fight" (*satan karav*) against the government. They spoke of monks as the greatest "patriots" who had "fought and sacrificed their lives" (*bhiksūna divi pudamin satan keruvōya*) for the motherland in the past.[91] In one leaflet, "The venerable [*gauravanīya*] monks" were "implored with patri-otic devotion [*bhaktiyen*] to fight."[92] This call carried a particular "Buddhist" ring because, as we saw above, Rahula, Sobhita, and other influential monks had already declared that monks were ready to lay down their lives for the unity of the country. The JVP reinforced this claim and authorized a space for monks to discharge their "Buddhist" duty. Put differently, for monks to join the JVP "army of patriots" (*dēshaprēmi hamudāva*) was to support a Buddhist movement that tried to reclaim the glory of their Buddhist country and the nation "betrayed" by the "unlawful" Jayewardene government.[93] To be a "patriotic [JVP] soldier" (*dēshaprēmi sebalā*) was to oppose the "unrighteous" ("un-Buddhist") government.

---

90. My research indicates that in 1982, Yakkaduwe Paññarama first used this specific term to criticize the tenure of Jayewardene as Kelaniya's minister; see "Kelaniyē Mantrīvarayāgē Dēshadrōhī Vāypāraya" ("Traitorous movement of the [former] minister of Kelaniya"), *Dinakara*, June 17, 1982. Later, Labuduwe Siridhamma called him just *drōhiyā*.

91. "Jīvita Bilidīma Nävatiya Yutuyi" ("We must stop the sacrifice of human lives [to the LTTE]"), JVP leaflet, Apr. 4, 1987; "Āchārya Molē Arshas Hevat Nalin Silva Saha Gōla Bālayō Sisu Balaya Bidīmata Dangalati" ("Nalin Silva and his pupils are trying to destroy the power of students"), JVP leaflet, 1987.

92. "Api Hamudā Kandavaru Valata Kadā Vädunē Äyi?" ("Why did we attack army camps?"), JVP leaflet, July 27, 1987.

93. Ibid.

In calling on "patriotic soldiers" to riot against the government of Jayewardene, whose [nonviolent] policies made "murderer Prabhakaran" [the leader of the LTTE] the "king" in the northeast,[94] the JVP, like some of the above-mentioned monks, questioned not only the Buddhist identity of Jayewardene but also the Buddhist identities of the "senior monks" who supported Jayewardene and his successor Premadasa. Seven months after Premadasa came to power (on the second anniversary of the accord), for example, the JVP berated some chief monks as "traitors of the country," "men disguised as monks" (*shramana vēshadāri*) uttering "false words" in support of the government.[95] Such monks were marked for death because the JVP policy dictated that every traitor to the country should meet the punishment of death (*mavbimata drōhivannanta maranaya*). Thus, at this particular time, from the standpoint of the JVP, the monk—that is to say, the undisguised, true monk—was one who did not support the government but who would wage war against it to protect the country.

To authorize this definition of the monk, the JVP employed a specific kind of "Buddhist" rhetoric. In a handwritten document entitled "Ranabima" ("Battlefield"), for example, it quoted one of the provocative poems of S. Mahinda, a famous Buddhist monk who, earlier in the twentieth century, though Tibetan by nationality, lived and composed Sinhalese poetry in Sri Lanka:

> Ätot ratata ādarayak sitin papā
> Atat payat oluvat venkalat kapā
> Katat kalat näta editara gatiya papā
> Ayuktiyata atdeka osavanna epā

> If you love your country with your heart,
> Even though they sever your hands, legs, and head,
> Even though you cannot speak, be fearless;
> To injustice, do not surrender.[96]

Circulated in the immediate wake of the battle between the Premadasa government and the JVP, "Ranabima" went on to invite all patriots to come

---

94. Ibid.

95. "Dēshaprēmi Sanhāraya Nävatvīmata, Janatā Mardanaya Välakvīmata Satan Vadiv!" ("Fight against the suppression of the patriotic movement and the public"), JVP leaflet, 1989 (late August?).

96. "Ranabima," Dēshaprēmī Janatā Vyāpāraya, handwritten JVP newsletter, 1989 (late August?).

forward "without fear" and protect the country. It explained the urgency of that duty by use of a specific kind of canonical "Buddhist" imagery. First, it portrayed Premadasa as an "executioner" (*alugōsu janādhipati*) who was trying to wipe out the JVP movement by "raiding Buddhist temples and firing on sacred Buddhist books . . . and killing and kidnapping innocent people [in the state search for the JVP]." It then portrayed the whole country as a "Visala Mahanuwara," a popular ancient Indian city, which, according a Buddhist commentary (the *khuddaka Pāta*), once ravaged by famine and death and haunted by nonhuman beings, was restored to normalcy by the Buddha and his enlightened disciples. "Ranabima" pointed out that rescuing and making Sri Lanka into Visala was a "sacred [Buddhist] task" (*pūjanīya katayutta*).[97] To accomplish this sacred task, the JVP—perhaps in the absence of the Buddha and his arhats who restored Visala city by sprinkling protective water (*pirit vatura*) on it—instructed its members to "shed sweat and blood, and even sacrifice life [*dādiya lē väl helalā- jīvitiyama vuva pudalā*]" to rebuild the country. The JVP promised to kill anyone who opposed it.[98]

Since the mid-1980s, as though demonstrating the seriousness of its purpose, the JVP assassinated many Sinhalese—politicians, security personnel, intellectuals, supporters of political parties, and other citizens—who opposed the JVP and who, by its definition, had become traitors. In 1987 it tried—though unsuccessfully—to assassinate President Jayewardene and members of his cabinet.[99] In the midst of such practices, young Buddhist monks came to form a crucial part of the JVP cadre.

A good example of monks' support for the JVP is *Vinivida*, the only magazine run by monks of the Manava Hitavadi Bhikkshu Sanvidanaya (Bhikkhu Organization for Humanity). During its initial phase in 1984, the magazine claimed that it had no connection to any political party,[100] but later the JVP took control of it.[101] In fact, its editor in the late 1980s, Kongasdeniye Ananda, was considered to be a key member of the JVP.[102] *Vinivida* proved to be a

97. "Premadasat Jayewardene Adipārēma Yayi" ("Premadasa, too, follows in the footsteps of Jayewardene"), leaflet issued by Wijeweera and Upatissa Gamanayaka, second in command, Aug. 9, 1989.

98. Leaflet issued by Wijeweera, Mar. 28, 1989.

99. For more on JVP assassinations and JVP destruction of state properties, see Gunaratna, *Sri Lanka: A Lost Revolution?* 237.

100. *Vinivida*, no. 10 (Nov.–Dec. 1986).

101. Communication with Ajit Serasundara, Oct. 26, 1996.

102. Interview with Sorata, lecturer at Peradeniya University, Dec. 11, 1996.

crucial conduit for the dissemination of the JVP "Buddhist" ideas among monks and lay Buddhists in Sri Lanka. It carried articles, poems, and short stories, focusing on many issues (for example, the problem of "terrorism," the open market economy, and the Indo-Lanka Peace Accord). It reinforced the idea that the monk should play a particular role in politics and encouraged them to abandon "Buddhist meditation on death and the three marks of existence"—suffering, impermanence, and no-soul—and join the fight.[103] It said that the Buddha himself dictated such a role for monks when he said, "O monks, behave for the benefit of the people."[104] Inviting all monks to be "united" against the government, *Vinivida* urged them to exercise the "power" of the "saffron army" (*kaha hamudāva*). As examples of the power of the monks, *Vinivida* told the stories of monks such as Udakendewala Saranankara, who suppposedly went to jail for rebelling against the colonial government. In an article entitled "The Showdown in the House of Punishment" (*dagageyi raga*), it recounted how Saranankara stood up to prison guards, refusing to take off his robe and wear the prison uniform. The article—a tribute to monks in prison at the time (from July 1987)—said that going to prison for the protection of the nation from "spurious Buddhists [*ī niyā bauddhayō*], who call themselves Sinhala and serve imperialists," an obvious reference to the government, was a noble act.[105]

Such views of what a monk should be were rendered accessible to monks in a variety of ways, and many translated them into action. By the late 1980s, a majority of monk-students at all universities had joined the JVP.[106] They performed various tasks for the JVP: they drew posters and wrote flyers (which the government called "subversive literature"), organized rallies and demonstrations, and even hid weapons in their temples.[107] In July 1987, the university monks formed the majority of the sangha that took to the streets to protest the Indo-Lanka Peace Accord (more on this below).

103. "Mē Satana: Ratē Muradēvatāvantayi" ("This battle: For the guardians of the nation"), *Vinivida*, no. 9 (July-Aug. 1986).

104. *Vinivida*, no. 9 (July-Aug. 1986); *Vinivida*, no. 12 (Apr. 1988).

105. "Sukhā Sanghassa Sāmagghi" ("The unity of the sangha brings about happiness"), *Vinivida*, no. 12 (1988). The title of this article is part of a verse from the *Dhammapada*.

106. Interviews with monks at Kelaniya, Jayewardenepura, Peradeniya, and Colombo Universities, 1995–98.

107. "Monks Held Along with Automatic Weapon," *Sun*, Aug. 11, 1987; Gunaratna, *Sri Lanka: A Lost Revolution?* 235.

Notably, in the late 1980s, the JVP received the support of many younger monks—those between the ages of fifteen and twenty. In interviews, several monks indicated to me that many of the pirivena monks came to believe that they were invincible because they belonged to the JVP. In the midst of mounting demands for Jayewardene's resignation in late September 1988, for example, several hundred young monks from Colombo gathered on the Maligakanda road to demonstrate against the government; they were then joined by several hundred students from Ananda Balika and Ananda College, Buddhist schools in the area. Despite the presence of the army and police monitoring the scene, these monks shouted provocative "fighting slogans" (satan pāta). A monk who observed the event recalled two of these popular slogans, which are chanted rhythmically:

> yamav, yamav, perata yamav
> JRva panna damav

> March, March, March forward!
> Chase away JR

> JRva genallā, vangediyē damālā,
> mōlgahen kotālā, maduvaligen talālā
> hadanawa api ānduvak

> Having brought JR, put him in a mortar
> pounded him with a pestle, beaten him with the Madu tail,
> we will form a government.[108]

Some monks went further than shouting slogans. Incidents described to me by my informants illustrate how some monks came to demonstrate the "fearless" monastic image. In one JVP demonstration in Matara, where several hundred Buddhist monks had gathered, police arrived within minutes. As officers got out of their jeep and walked toward the crowd, the monk in charge of the demonstration flashed a razor (dälipihiya), threatening to cut the police if they dared come nearer.[109] The officers pulled back. Later they fired

108. Interview with a monk at a temple in Maradana, Oct. 23, 1996.

109. A razor is part of the atapirikara (the eight requisites of a monk), which is one of the most meritorious gifts Buddhists can donate to the sangha. Monks use a razor to shave both face and head. I am told that in late 1989 many JVP monks carried razors as weapons to defend themselves against the "enemy."

teargas, dispersing the crowd.[110] In late 1989, as part of islandwide JVP strikes, student monks at a pirivena in Matara demanded that the school's principal cancel all classes and close the pirivena indefinitely. When the principal objected, the group's leader kicked him in the face and stomach. When the police arrived, the young monks, along with other men from the neighborhood, stoned and wrecked the police vehicle. My informant, who took part in this riot but now denounces the leader's conduct, said that at the time he "felt I liked him beating up [the principal] [*gävvata kämatiyi vage*] because I was in such a state of mind [*ehema manusikatvayak tibuene*]."[111]

Atureliye Indaratana, a senior Buddhist monk from Matara who in 1997(at the time of my interview with him) was an adviser to the Ministry of the Buddha Sasana, told me of an incident unlike any other. In late 1989, an unidentified person telephoned Indraratana one morning to inform him that three monks from the Bhikhsu Balakaya (the Monastic Power Front) would visit him at his temple in Matara. The caller warned that if he failed to keep the appointment, he should be prepared to die on the road. Immediately, the phone line was cut. Indaratana told me he knew he surely faced death that day. Minutes later, three "monks" carrying handguns arrived at the temple. Only one of them, Indaratana says, was a "real monk"; the other ("robed men") wore their robes incorrectly. They ordered Indaratana to sit down. Pointing a gun to his head, one said, "If you betray the people, you must be prepared to face the punishment that the people give." They questioned him as to why he had written to newspapers supporting Jayewardene's decision to bring the Indian army to Sri Lanka. Indaratana said that he no longer held such views, and the trio demanded that he publish a letter to that effect in the newspapers. Indaratana acquiesced (he later wrote the letter). Following hours of interrogation, the visitors treated themselves to breakfast and left the temple, saying they would return the following week after reporting to "head office"; head office would examine the facts and judge if Indaratana should be killed. Indaratana was spared: the "monks" did not return.[112]

My point is that such practices by young Buddhist monks became possible in the context of the 1980s, when that definition of the monk was authorized by both monks and the JVP. This definition came to be contested, however;

---

110. Interviews with five monks at Kelaniya University, July 10–13, 1995, 1996.
111. Interviews with ten monks at Jayewardenepura University, Oct. 20–22, 1997.
112. Interviews with Atureliye Indaratana, Oct. 5, 1997.

it was construed as "violent," and therefore "un-Buddhist," in the context of the Premadasa government.

"Sacred Duty" as "Violence"

In late 1988, about a month before Jayewardene stepped down from office, the JVP brought the country to a virtual standstill. It was as if it was another government. Rohan Gunaratna, a Sri Lankan commentator on the saga of the JVP, writes that "in November 1988, it was the order of the JVP—the unseen government— which ran the country":

> A state of near anarchy prevailed. People were threatened and kept away from work. No transport was available as several bus drivers who defied orders of the JVP were killed. The stoppage of work at the petroleum refinery resulted in long queues in front of gas stations. . . . People from the lower middle class queued to buy kerosene for lighting and cooking. Shops were closed for weeks and food shortage grew acute. Prison riots resulted in several deaths. Many were injured in prisons of Colombo, Mahara, Anuradhapura, Negombo and Pelwatte. Several prisoners escaped from the jails too. From Velikada 221 prisoners including Ragama Somae, a central committee member of the JVP and other high ranking members escaped. Bank, postal, and telecommunication facilities came to a virtual halt. Trees were cut and placed across the roads. Power pylons and transformers were damaged and telephone exchanges sabotaged. Even hospitals were not functioning.[113]

Such was the state of affairs in Sri Lanka in December 1988 when Premadasa became president. Well into mid-1989, the JVP continued seeking to unseat the Premadasa "illegal" government—one they claimed had come to power by "false votes" and was following in Jayewardene's footsteps.[114] The JVP simultaneously began to portray itself as a movement enjoying mass support. And sometimes it did receive such support: rallies were attended by thousands (in some cases, however, it coerced participation).[115] A Buddhist monk told me that the JVP "did some good things, too" (*honda vädat kalā*): it prohibited the sale and drinking of illicit liquor (*kasippua*) and in parts of

---

113. Gunaratna, *Sri Lanka: Lost Revolution?* 293–94.
114. "Premadasa Jayewardene Adipārēma Yayi."
115. Gunaratna, *Sri Lanka: Lost Revolution?* 294.

the island ordered groceries to lower food prices: "People, particularly the villagers, liked [*pähädunä*] these kinds of things," the monk told me. But after the JVP started to "destroy public properties" in its effort to debilitate the government, people began to "intensely dislike" the JVP because events such as prolonged transport strikes and work stoppages affected the poor. The monk quickly added, however, that a widespread rumor had it that many of the acts of sabotage—such as setting fire to buses, post offices, and train stations—were in fact the work of the Premadasa government, aimed at undermining the JVP. Such rumors, the monk said, were "unclear" because the situation at that time was so complex.[116]

In the face of the JVP's many supposed killings and acts of sabotage, it must be noted, Premadasa did not publicly accuse the JVP of wrongdoing—at least, not until November 1989. It is no secret that during the presidential election both Premadasa and the JVP presented an explosive political agenda; namely, the "urgent" task of sending back to India the Indian Peace Keeping Force. In July 1989, Premadasa requested the JVP to join in his "Buddhist patriotic" quest to get rid of the IPKF, but the JVP refused, claiming the idea was theirs.[117] One informant noted, perceptively, that by campaigning to remove the IPKF from Sri Lanka, Premadasa "wrested the flag from the JVP"—that is, he grabbed its patriotic image. Shorn of that image, the JVP simply became an "armed man" (*tuvakkukārayek*) that the "patriotic Buddhist" government could and had to kill.[118] It did just that.

Discovering "Buddhist Identity" in the "Criminal" of the JVP: Torture and "Rehabilitation" of Monks

As early as August 1989, the government defense ministry, headed by Ranjan Wijeratne, a Buddhist, began a nationwide crackdown on the JVP by mobilizing a number of "paramilitary groups," or "death squads." (Wijeratne, believed to be the mastermind behind the invention of these death squads, later revealed that he was able to stand up and stamp out the JVP not because he was a Premadasa man but because he followed "the master's [Buddha's]

116. Interview with Medhananda, Oct. 1996. Gunaratna, too, says that "many Sri Lankans have been sympathetic to the views of the JVP but not to their methods"; Gunaratna, *Sri Lanka: Lost Revolution?* 336.

117. "Premadasa Jayewardene Adipārēma Yayi."

118. Interview with Sorata, lecturer at Peradeniya University, Dec. 11, 1996.

teaching that there is nothing permanent.")[119] Mostly operating by night, these death squads largely consisted of army or security personnel whose families the JVP had threatened or killed. They went on a spree of kidnapping, torturing, and killing, not only of those suspected to be the JVP members but also their families.[120] They raided houses, villages, towns, Buddhist temples, and pirivenas. Given the history of the monks' support for the JVP, temples and pirivenas became a major target.

The arresting of monks was an explicit form of questioning the "Buddhist" identity of the JVP monks. According to several eyewitness accounts, when the members of a death squad raided a temple, they kicked down doors and ransacked rooms for JVP flyers and leaflets, "evidence" that would link the monks to the JVP. If suspicious monks were found, before being "arrested" they were ordered to strip naked and wear bedsheets (taken from their temples) in front of their teachers or other monks, an act that symbolized the monks' return to lay status. If other resident monks at the temple intervened, they, too, were attacked.[121] Some monks were even shot dead in their temples.[122] On other occasions, monks were stripped naked and kicked into vehicles (vehicles that did not have license plates) in broad daylight, in full public view.[123] To be a monk and a member of the JVP at this time was to face the possibility of losing one's identity as a monk.

The arrested monks were detained and questioned for months at camps in various undisclosed locations—questioning that entailed subjecting suspects to physical punishment. One punishment technique, called "hitting the dhammacakka" (*dhammacakke gahanavā*), is worth noting because of its

119. Cited in Gunaratna, *Sri Lanka: Lost Revolution?* 336.

120. For more on this, see, ibid., 295, 339–40.

121. Interviews and conversations with monks at universities and pirivenas in Colombo. In 1996, a newspaper carried an account of a monk's near-death encounter with one of the paramilitary groups at a temple; see "Tisek Denek Maladāmu Walpita Minīvala" ("The grave in which thirty-one people were buried"), *Divayina*, Nov. 24, 1996. Even during the height of the confrontation between the JVP and the government, other newspapers pointed out similar concerns; they did so rarely, however; see "Sivuru Adanakada Galavā Mēsaredi Andana Yugayak" ("This is an era in which monks are stripped of their robes and forced to wear table cloths"), *Dinarāsa*, Sept. 26, 1989.

122. I have located a list of about one hundred names, addresses, dates, and places of kidnapping and killings of monks. This list was prepared by Students for Human Rights in Colombo 8.

123. Interviews with three monks at Peradeniya University and five monks at Jayewardenepura University, cited above. Such narratives were also related to me in informal conversations by many other monks and lay people.

"Buddhist" connotation. *Dhammacakka* is a Pali canonical term that stands for the "the wheel of the Dhamma," a symbol of the early Buddhist doctrine about life as suffering, and the way out of it (the Buddha is said to have set this wheel in motion in his first sermon). The monk who was given this punishment was made to resemble this wheel. A monk who spent two months in a camp described the details of the punishment to me: the monk was ordered to squat on the ground, elbows encircling the knees; a pole was pushed under the knees and over the elbows; with the body hanging from it, the pole was lifted and supported by the arms of two chairs; the body was then spun like a wheel in the space between the chairs and beaten with a bat until the victim passed out or bled to death. It is as if the state invented a specific kind of "Buddhist" punishment for a specific kind of "Buddhist" subject. That is to say, if the punishment of torturing the JVP monks was part of questioning their Buddhist monastic identities, the punishment must necessarily be rendered "Buddhist."[124]

It was in the midst of arresting and punishing the JVP monks that the government publicly contested the "patriotic" (Buddhist) identity of the JVP. In November 1989, immediately after the security forces captured and killed Wijeweera, the leader of the JVP who many had considered to be invincible, President Premadasa addressed the parliament. In a lengthy speech describing the details of Wijeweera's death, Premadasa contrasted his "peaceful" government with the "violent" JVP. Stating that "from the time [his] government came to power, it worked for peace," the president questioned the JVP's image of itself as a "patriot" movement that tried to liberate the country. He characterized the JVP as a "terrorist," "criminal" organization whose "violence" posed a threat to "Buddhist" Sri Lanka (a Sri Lanka that he took pains to describe):

> The People of Sri Lanka are heirs to a great civilization. We are also heirs to a culture that values even the lives of very humble creatures like insects and ants and even of beings such as poisonous snakes. That is why our people condemn the destruction of any kind of life. That is why we condemn violence.[125]

124. It is important to note that I understand this concept of "torture" to have a particular history. For an excellent discussion of the uses of the idea of torture in modern history, see Asad, "On Torture, or Cruel, Inhuman, and Degrading Treatment," in *Social Suffering*.

125. "President Tells Government Parliamentary Group, 'If Wijeweera Heeded My Call None Need Have Suffered,'" *Daily News*, Nov. 17, 1989.

As if to further demonstrate the danger of the JVP "violence" to this "great civilization," Premadasa specifically pointed to the JVP killings of monks. Stating how "so many . . . ven. members of the Mahasangha have been killed," who "have loved our country and our religion," the president read out more than twenty names of monks killed by the JVP. The "killing of venerable monks," he said, attested to the "seriousness" of JVP violence. Reminding people of his election pledge to "reestablish peace in the country" and to "put an end to the suffering of the people," Premadasa said he would not "allow the country and the people to be subverted" by JVP violence. He concluded by appealing to all people of Sri Lanka to "fearlessly . . . come forward" and help the government "wipe out JVP terrorism and violence."

Premadasa portrayed his government as the true "patriot" who would liberate the country from the JVP "terrorists." The government tried to depict this image of itself in other ways, too. A few days before Premadasa's speech to parliament, government newspapers published a statement by, along with a mugshot of, the monk Thalakolawewe Chandaratana, a prominent member of the JVP. Chandaratana's statement, believed to have been obtained through torture, was a confession and atonement that clearly supported the government's representation of the JVP as an un-Buddhist movement that betrayed its objective by resorting to violence. Chandaratana castigated JVP killings of monks as "terrorist" acts; they were "ignoble," he said: the JVP "failed to understand the [Buddhist] culture of the country." He appealed to members of the JVP to "rally around [the government] to restore peace and unity."[126]

Having authorized an image of the JVP as a terrorist, criminal movement that must be eliminated, the government intensified its nationwide search for JVP cadres, a search that cost more than a hundred lives a day. After the search ended in mid-1990, several hundred "monks" were left in detention camps. Given its depiction of the JVP as a "criminal" organization, the government could not simply release the monks, who now remained symbolically stripped of their former patriotic Buddhist monastic identities. In order to deal with this problem, the government invented a particular strategy: it gave the "JVP monks" new "non-JVP" Buddhist identities by subjecting them to a disciplinary process of "rehabilitation" (*punaruttāpanaya*).

---

126. "A Bhikkhu, Once a JVP Activist, Blows the Lid off the Movement," *Daily News*, Nov. 14, 1989.

I met one monk who first spent several months at a detention camp and later underwent a program called "redisciplining (the undisciplined) [*āyati samvara*]" at a rehabilitation center in Maharagama.[127] The government invited popular monks to give these former JVP monks supervised training in meditation, preaching bana, chanting pirit, practicing vegetarianism, alms begging, and abstaining from eating at night—all practices that the government deemed should constitute the identity of a monk. It was a strategy of not only making former JVP monks "Buddhist" monks again, but making them specific kinds of monks; namely, monks who are "non-JVP" and hence "non-violent" and "disciplined." The state symbolically inscribed this identity by issuing to each monk a certificate testifying to the successful completion of the rehabilitation program. The state required that during travel the rehabilitated monks carry the certificate so as to avoid the future possibility of being arrested. The certificate, symbolizing the discipline of rehabilitation, identified the Buddhist monk "discovered in the criminal" of the JVP.[128]

The contestation—criminalization—of the JVP as a "terrorist" movement threatening the great Sri Lankan Buddhist civilization and its elimination authorized Premadasa to represent himself as the Buddhist president who destroyed "terror" and delivered his election promise to restore peace in Sri Lanka. But, as we saw in chapter 5, various other competing narratives in this context began to contest the "Buddhist" image of Premadasa, eventually depicting him as the agent of terror who had come to dishonor the Buddhist country. Other political parties came to employ the discourse of terror; for instance, during the presidential campaign in 1994, a year after the death of Premadasa, Chandrika Bandaranaike made an election pledge to eliminate the Premadasa "era of terror."

After assuming office, Bandaranaike set up commissions to inquire into the disappearances during the Premadasa period of government, including those of Buddhist monks. One of her ministers, Mangala Samaraweera, read to parliament a list of (JVP) monks said to have been killed by the death

---

127. Interview with a Buddhist monk (who wished to remain anonymous), Maharagama, Nov. 6, 1997. I thank Ajit Serasundara for making possible this important interview.

128. I am borrowing this phrase from Michel Foucault's discussion of the ways in which the "[hu]man" was "discovered in the criminal" in the context of "punishment without torture" in nineteenth-century Europe. Foucault, of course, has in mind a broader epistemological space than the minute conjunctures of knowledge production that concern me here; see Foucault, *Discipline and Punish: The Birth of the Prison* (1977; reprint, New York: Vintage, 1995), 74.

squads in 1989.[129] Later, the government published the names of more than one hundred such "victim" monks. It is noteworthy that the representation of these monks directly challenged the kind of image of terror that the Premadasa government produced of the JVP monks. Introducing the list of names, the government said: "The fact that they tortured and killed young noble monks who gave up all life's luxury to liberate the whole human kind from the wheel of samsara, is true [*satyavādīya*], real [*sābāya*]. This is part of a list of such monks who became prey to the curse of a seventeen-year murderous [UNP] rule [*minimaru pālanaya*]."[130] Thus continues the debate about what is and is not Buddhism or violence.

My preoccupation in this chapter has been to propose alternative approaches to the conceptualization of the discursive formations of the relation between religion and violence, religious identity and difference. Conventional disciplinary narratives that tend to view religion and violence in terms of their difference or interrelation are governed by assumptions about the self-evidently defined nature of such categories. Such categories, I have insisted, are not available as transparent objects of disciplinary knowledge: the meanings of "religion" and "violence" are discursively produced, and hence shift within the conjunctures of different debates. Central to my argument is delineating some of the complex ways in which competing and rival discourses and debates authorized diverse persons and practices to come into (central) view and fade from view as religion or violence, civilization or terror, and so on in contingent conjunctures—in this case, the specific ethnographic landscape between the early 1980s and the 1990s in Sri Lanka.

In exploring this narrative terrain, working though those specific details, I have not, however, wanted to invoke some supposed authority of "ethnographic evidence" that would guarantee us a privileged epistemological purchase on religion and violence. Rather, I wish to read the content of this chapter, as I do this entire book, as a modest example of the contingency of the "native" ethnographic field. So one of my points is that our claims, which we stake on that ethnographic terrain, and which, more often than not, stand authorized as universally applicable knowledges about categories like religion, violence, culture, and identity in archives of disciplinary texts, must be

---

129. Interview with Atureliye Indaratana, Nov. 5, 1997.

130. "Sārā Sankhya Kalpa Lakshayak Purā" ("Having aspired [to become monks] for infinite lifetimes"), *Dinamina*, Feb. 25, 1997.

contingently positioned. (Today the esteemed canonical status that these categories occupy is such that it is common to see the supposed culture of religious violence or religious nationalism in Sri Lanka mentioned right along with other places like Punjab, Iran, Egypt, Israel, Bosnia, Ireland, and so on.)[131]

My stress on the recognition of contingently authorized native knowledges about discursive concepts such as violence, however, is not simply to advance the well-rehearsed postcolonial, postmodern argument about the nonessential, hybrid nature of religion and culture. On the contrary, I have labored to demonstrate some of the strategic ways in which terms and parameters of what and who can and cannot be Buddhism or violence (non-Buddhism) have been authorized to appear and disappear in those microconjunctures. If we are to understand religion, violence, and culture as nonessential, "historical" ideas—that is, as discursive traditions or as embodied arguments—we must explore those conjunctures of competing debates in which such categories come to be invested with, and divested of, fleeting authoritative meanings. Failure to do so, in my view, leads to the uncritical reproduction of native knowledges about such categories. Take, for example, the concept of so-called terror(ism): I have tried to demonstrate that questions of who and what could and could not count as "terror" are located within the bounds of those authoritative debates between different political parties. My point is that, without a critical genealogical awareness of the authorization of its deployment by rival discourses, it would be impossible to employ "terror" as a disciplinary synonym for, as another way of making sense of, the dynamics of that particular context and not reproduce its ideological meanings.[132]

This is not to say—to repeat a point worth repeating—that there is no "terror" as opposed to "religion"; rather, fleeting knowledges of what is and is not terror are not available for canonization as they are conventionally understood in terms of "Buddhism betrayed," "religious violence," and "religious terrorism," but must be located in those specific conjunctures of debates.

131. See, for example, Juergensmeyer, "Worldwide Rise"; see also his *Terror in the Mind of God* and "What the Bhikkhu Said"; also Ian Reader, *Religious Violence in Contemporary Japan: The Case of Aum Shinrikyō* (Reader is indebted to Juergensmeyer's work).

132. On increasing disciplinary representations of violence in terms of "terror," see, for example, P. Lawrence, "Work of Oracles, Silence of Terror: Notes on the Injury of War in Eastern Sri Lanka," Ph.D. diss., University of Colorado, 1997; see also Valentine Daniel, "Embodied Terror," in his *Charred Lullabies*. For a critical engagement with Daniel's text, see Jeganathan's "Violence as an Analytical Problem."

What I have sought to argue here bears a subtle relevance to a provocative question that Joseba Zulaika and William Douglass posed in their 1996 book on the Western discourses of terrorism: "What can we say about the fact that terrorism has become such a shifty category that yesterday's terrorists are today's Nobel Prize winners?"[133]

Concluding Remarks

This book has attempted to develop a critical reflection on the discursive productions of the altering relation between religion, identity, and difference. These categories are usually taken by many scholars of religion as transparent objects of disciplinary knowledge waiting in the ethnographic field— "anthropologyland," to use Bernard Cohn's term[134]—to be apprehended, analyzed, and explained. Such categories, I have insisted, are far from self-evident since they are located in specific conjunctures of debates that authorize differing persons, practices, and institutions to come into central view and fade from view, defining and contesting the terms of what does and does not count as religion or politics, identity or difference, civilization or terror.

So what I have urged here is the recognition and appreciation of concepts such as Buddhism, tradition, politics, nation(alism), violence, terror(ism), identity, and difference as embodied arguments, or as concepts whose meanings are produced, battled out, and contested in altering conjunctures of discourses and debates. That is, in (final) Foucauldian terms, identity is not only an effect but also an instrument of discourse/power.[135] Authoritative discourses and debates not only fashion identity/self in opposition to difference/other but also make it possible to contest it and sanction it as difference. It is important to note, however, that my insistence upon the contingency of the relation between identity and difference, religion and violence, is not the same as the now-popular postmodern argument that religion and culture are nonessential and unbounded. What I have sought to demonstrate is that such concepts are not simply "open" discursive sites easily available for *any* subject or discourse to define and contest at any moment. Rather, the questions of who can and

---

133. Joseba Zulaika and William A. Douglass, *Terror and Taboo: The Follies, Fables, and Faces of Terrorism* (London: Routledge, 1996), x.

134. I borrow this term from Bernard S. Cohn's groundbreaking essay "History and Anthropology: The State of Play," in Cohn, *An Anthropologist among the Historians.*

135. Foucault, *History of Sexuality*, vol. 1.

cannot make what kinds of moral claims about what constitutes religion or difference in *centrally visible ways* are authorized by specific conjunctures of opposing debates.

The examination of such debates enables us to ask new questions about the complex configurations of the nexus between discourse, knowledge, and identity that cannot be understood by mapping those large discursive fields discussed earlier. This, as far I can see, is the critical task that should preoccupy the disciplinary enterprises seeking to understand the *historical* forms of religion, and it is a far more fundamental task than simply making claims about the supposed "truth" of it. I quarrel with many sophisticated studies that continue to posit truth-claims about religion, culture, and difference in South Asia because of the theoretical unsoundness of such exercises: it is, indeed, impossible to posit such claims—in that the meanings of what persons and practices constitute Buddhism or violence, civilization or terror, are authorized by fleeting conjunctures of debates that do not remain available for disciplinary canonization.

What has governed the theoretical space of this study is an examination of the emergence and submergence of competing moral debates and arguments about Buddhism. If, as MacIntyre and Scott suggest,[136] concepts like religion and difference should be taken as traditions of embodied arguments and debates, the discourses that constitute and alter their meanings are, as Hayden White informs us, "running to and fro," moving "back and forth," "between alternate ways," defying all "logic, 'tactical' rules . . . including those originally governing [their] own formation."[137] In this light, I view this entire work as a story of differing, socially embodied arguments that make possible the moving—that is, authorizing, negotiating, and shifting—to and fro, back and forth, of those boundaries, relations, and parameters between religion and difference, Buddhism and politics, civilization and terror. It is this moving of discourses between alternate ways that I have sought to understand in terms of the emergence and submergence of the central visibility of authoritative debates about religion and difference. Part of my argument is that the differing relation between these concepts, who and what they are supposed to embody, cannot be theorized in terms of the now available hermeneutical

---

136. See MacIntyre, *After Virtue*; Scott, *Refashioning Futures*.

137. I owe this formulation to Hayden White's seminal *Tropics of Discourse: Essays in Cultural Criticism* (Baltimore: Johns Hopkins University Press, 1978), 3–4.

registers like "religious fundamentalism," "religious violence," and "religious nationalism," all of which are meant to convey, in different ways, the supposed fusion or interaction between religion and politics. Let me shed more light on this point by returning to the subject of religion and violence.

In late 1997, I was back in the "ethnographic field" in Sri Lanka, conducting interviews and archival research and gathering "more data" on the dynamics of the relation between Buddhism, monkhood, the JVP, and violence in the 1980s. Three years had passed since the election of the government of Chandrika Bandaranike, and it had been several more years since the "wiping out" of the JVP leadership and the eventual assassination of that complex figure behind it all, President Ranasinghe Premadasa. In 1997, the JVP no longer remained a proscribed underground movement. The JVP, at the time a "legalized" political party, was out and about, so to speak, making its presence visible with posters on the bulletin boards of major universities, on the "stick-no-bills" parapet walls of private and public properties, at bus stations, and on the sidewalks of main roads. Television and radio stations and newspapers and magazines periodically featured interviews with the new secretary of the JVP, Tilvin Silva, debating the history of the movement's past identity and practices and its future visions of one day offering a new Marxist leadership for Sri Lanka—this time without the bloodshed that drenched the body of Sri Lanka in the early 1990s. So a movement submerged a few years earlier as difference, subverted as the violent and uncivilized other, was coming into view again, with *altered* visions, persons, and practices, competing to stake out new moral claims about the future political identity of Sri Lanka.

The members of the JVP, both young Buddhist monks and lay students, held meetings at various locations and sought to rally loyal supporters. On occasion, these meetings encountered fierce (and feared) opposition from some parties. A year earlier, in 1996, a number of anti-JVP students had disrupted a JVP meeting and threatened its organizers and attendants at Kelaniya University, where it once enjoyed a large following of loyal monks and lay students. In 1997, despite its "legal" status and continuing attempt to make its new identity/self visible, the image of the JVP as a movement (perhaps partly) responsible for a period of "terror" remained the subject of discussion in some corners of Sri Lanka. The movement still retained a particular image of difference/terror that opposed civilization/peace.

In late September 1997, as the JVP sought to rally support for its new leadership, perhaps seeking to divest it of its otherness and difference, a particular "event" rendered centrally visible the contested identity of the movement in a way that pointed to the impossibility of the disciplinary canonizing of the altering relation between religion and violence. The JVP held a meeting at the public library in Town Hall, Colombo, and among its audience were two dozen or so young Buddhist monks. The meeting attracted much press coverage and was highlighted on the evening TV news bulletin. Central to the media coverage was a specific portrayal of the participant monks ardently heeding the words of the speakers. As the TV cameras zoomed in on the audience, the monks quickly covered their faces with their hands.

The monks' presence at a public JVP meeting—a virtual impossibility not so long before—was a visible expression of "Buddhist" support for a movement that had been submerged as an un-Buddhist organization of "terror." The monks' concealing their faces, however, hints at the possibility that "Buddhist" support remains within the constraints of an ongoing moral debate about the "identity" of the JVP. The possibility that those covered faces may or may not become visible is located in future conjunctures of debates. If we are to understand the historical forms of religion or violence as embodied arguments, the conjunctures that we must try to investigate are those that make possible and centrally visible the altering relation between religion and difference, that transcend not only their own tactical rules and logic of formation but also disciplinary attempts at canonizing them as universal categories.

BIBLIOGRAPHY

Abeysekara, Ananda. Review of *The Work of Kings: The New Buddhism in Sri Lanka*, by H. L. Seneviratne. *American Ethnologist* 28, no. 2 (2001): 499–501.

Abhayasundara, Wimal. *Man of the Masses*. Colombo: Gunasena, 1979.

Abu-Lughod, Lila. "Writing against Culture." In *Recapturing Anthropology*, ed. Richard Fox. Santa Fe, N.M: School of American Research Press, 1991.

Alles, A. C. *The JVP, 1969–1989*. Colombo: Lake House, 1990.

Almond, Philip. *The British Discovery of Buddhism*. New York: Cambridge University Press, 1988.

Ames, Michael. "Magical Animism and Buddhism: A Structural Analysis of Sinhalese Buddhism." *Journal of Asian Studies* 23 (1964): 21–52.

Amunugama, Sarath. "Buddhaputra or Bhumiputra? Dilemmas of Modern Sinhala Buddhist Monks in Relation to Ethnic and Political Conflict." *Religion* 21 (1990): 115–39.

Anderson, Benedict. *Imagined Communities: Reflections on the Origin and Spread of Nationalism*. 1983. Reprint, London: Verso, 1992.

Appadurai, Arjun. *Modernity at Large: Cultural Dimensions of Globalization*. Minneapolis: University of Minnesota Press, 1996.

Ariyasena, K. *Sīmāvan Hā Ehi Aitihāsika Samvardhanaya Pilibanda Tulantāmaka Vimansanayak*. Ph.D. dissertation, University of Ceylon, 1967.

Asad, Talal. "Reading a Modern Classic: W. C. Smith's *The Meaning and End of Religion*." *History of Religions* 1 (2001): 205–22.

———. "Religion, Nation-state, Secularism." In *Nation and Religion: Perspectives on Europe and Asia*, ed. Peter van der Veer and Hartmut Lehman. Princeton: Princeton University Press, 1999.

———. "On Torture, or Cruel, Inhuman, and Degrading Treatment." In *Social Suffering*, ed. Arthur Kleinman, Vena Das, and Margaret Lock. Berkeley: University of California Press, 1997.

———. *Genealogies of Religion: Discipline and Reasons of Power in Christianity and Islam*. Baltimore: Johns Hopkins University Press, 1993.

———. "Conscripts of Western Civilization." In *Dialectical Anthropology: Essays in Honor of Stanley Diamond*, ed. Christine Ward Gailey. Gainesville: University Press of Florida, 1992.

Askland, Markus. *The Sacred Footprint*. Oslo: Yelti Consult, 1990.

Bakhtin, Mikhail. *The Dialogic Imagination,* ed. Michael Holquist, trans. Caryl Emerson and Michael Holquist. Austin: University of Texas Press, 1981.

Bartholomeusz, Tessa. "In Defense of Dharma: Just-War Ideology in Buddhist Sri Lanka." *Journal of Buddhist Ethics* (1999).

———. "Buddhist Burghers and Sinhala-Buddhist Fundamentalism." In *Buddhist Fundamentalism and Minority Identities in Sri Lanka,* ed. Tessa Bartholomeusz and C. R. de Silva. New York: State University of New York Press, 1998.

———. *Women under the Bō Tree: Buddhist Nuns in Sri Lanka.* Cambridge: Cambridge University Press, 1994.

Bechert, Heinz. "Contradictions in Sinhalese Buddhism." In *Religion and Legitimation of Power in Sri Lanka,* ed. Bardwell Smith. Chambersburg, Pa.: Anima, 1978.

———. "Sangha, State, Society, 'Nation': Persistence of Traditions in 'Post-Traditional' Societies." *Daedalus* 102, no. 1 (1973): 85–95.

———. "Therāvada Buddhist Sangha: Some General Observations on Historical and Political Factors in Its Development." *Journal of Asian Studies* 29, no. 4 (1970): 761–78.

———. *Buddhismus, Staat und Gesellschaft in den Ländern des Theravāda-Buddhismus.* 3 vols. Frankfurt: A. Metzner; Wiesbaden, O. Harrossowitz; 1960, 1967, 1973.

Benhabib, Seyla. Introduction to *Democracy and Difference,* ed. Seyla Benhabib. Princeton: Princeton University Press, 1996.

Bhabha, Homi. "Of Mimicry and Man: The Ambivalence of Colonial Discourse." In *The Location of Culture.* 1994. Reprint, New York: Routledge, 1997.

Bond, George, D. "Conflicts of Identity and Interpretation in Buddhism: The Clash between the Sarvodaya Shramadana Movement and the Government of President Premadasa." In *Buddhist Fundamentalism and Minority Identities in Sri Lanka,* ed. Tessa Bartholomeusz and C. R. de Silva. New York: State University of New York Press, 1998.

———. *The Buddhist Revival: Religious Tradition, Reinterpretation, and Response.* Columbia: University of South Carolina Press, 1988.

Bourdieu, Pierre. *Language and Symbolic Power.* Cambridge: Harvard University Press, 1991.

———. *Outline of a Theory of Practice.* Cambridge: Cambridge University Press, 1977.

Breckenridge, Carol, and Peter van der Veer, eds. *Orientalism and the Postcolonial Predicament.* Philadelphia: University of Pennsylvania Press, 1993.

Butler, Judith. "Restaging the Universal: Hegemony and the Limits of For-malism." In *Contingency, Hegemony, Universality: Contemporary Dia-logue on the Left,* by Judith Butler, Ernesto Laclau, and Slavoj Zizek, New York: Verso, 2000.

Carrithers, Michael. "Is Anthropology Art or Science?" *Current Anthropology* 3 (1990): 263–81.

——. "The Domestication of the Sangha." *Man* 19, no. 2 (1984): 321–22.

——. *The Forest Monks of Sri Lanka: An Anthropological and Historical Study.* New Delhi: Oxford University Press, 1983.

——. [Response to Steven Kemper]. *Man* 15, no. 1 (1980): 195–97.

——. "The Modern Ascetics of Lanka and the Pattern of Change in Bud-dhism." *Man* 14, no. 2 (1979): 294–310.

——. "The Social Organization of the Sinhalese Sangha in an Historical Perspective." In *Contributions to South Asian Studies,* vol. 1, ed. Gopal Krishna. Delhi: Oxford University Press, 1979.

Chakrabarty, Dipesh. "Modernity and Ethnicity in India." In *Multicultural States: Rethinking Difference and Identity,* ed. David Bennett. New York: Routledge, 1998.

Chandana, Orukmankulame. *Buddhaputrayekugē Dēshanāva.* Ratmalana: Petikada, 1995.

Chandraprema, C. A. *Sri Lanka: The Years of Terror: The JVP Insurrection, 1987–1989.* Colombo: Lake House, 1991.

Chatterjee, Partha. *The Nation and Its Fragments: Colonial and Postcolonial Histories.* Princeton: Princeton University Press, 1992.

——. *Nationalist Thought and the Colonial World: A Derivative Discourse?* 1983. Reprint, Minneapolis: University of Minnesota Press, 1998.

Clifford, James. *Routes: Travel and Translation in the Late Twentieth Century.* Cambridge: Harvard University Press, 1997.

——. "Introduction: Partial Truths." In *Writing Culture: The Poetics and Politics of Ethnography,* ed. James Clifford and George Marcus. Berkeley: University of California Press, 1986.

Cohn, Bernard S. *Colonialism and Its Forms of Knowledge: The British in India.* Princeton: Princeton University Press, 1996.

——. *An Anthropologist among the Historians and Other Essays.* Delhi: Oxford University Press, 1985.

Connolly, William. *Why I Am Not a Secularist.* Minneapolis: University of Minnesota Press, 1999.

——. *The Augustinian Imperative: A Reflection on the Politics of Morality.* London: Sage, 1993.

——. *Identity/Difference: Democratic Negotiations of Political Paradox.* Ithaca: Cornell University Press, 1991.

Daniel, Valentine. *Charred Lullabies: Chapters in an Anthropography of Violence*. Princeton: Princeton University Press, 1996.

Das, Veena. "Language and Body: Transactions in the Construction of Pain." In *Social Suffering*, ed. Arthur Kleinman, Vena Das, and Margaret Lock. Berkeley: University of California Press, 1997.

de Silva, C. R. "The Plurality of Buddhist Fundamentalism." In *Buddhist Fundamentalism and Minority Identities in Sri Lanka*, ed. Tessa Bartholomeusz and C. R. de Silva. New York: State University of New York Press, 1998.

————. "The Monks and the Pontiff: Reflections on Religious Tensions in Contemporary Politics in Sri Lanka." *South Asia* 19 (1996): 233–44.

de Silva, K. M., and Howard Wriggins. *J. R. Jayewardene of Sri Lanka: A Political Biography, 1956–1989*, vol. 2. Hawaii: University of Hawaii Press, 1994.

Dhammarakkhita, Velamitiyave, and Kakkapalliye Anuruddha eds. *Vidyalankāra Pirivena: Satasanvassaraya, 1875–1975*. Colombo: Sri Lanka Rajaye Departumentuwa, 1975.

Dhammavisuddhi, Y. *Polonnaru Hā Dambadeni Katikāvat*. Colombo: Karunaratna Saha Putrayo, 1995.

Dharmadasa, K. N. O. *Language, Religion, and Ethnic Assertiveness: The Growth of Sinhalese Nationalism in Sri Lanka*. Ann Arbor: University of Michigan Press, 1992.

Dickson, J. F. *Ordination in Theravada Buddhism: An Early Account*, ed. Piyadassi Thera. Kandy: Buddhist Publication Society, 1963.

Dirks, Nicholas. Foreword to *Colonialism and Its Forms of Knowledge*. Princeton: Princeton University Press, 1996.

Disanayaka, S. B. *Mā Atsan Kala Dōshābhiyōgaya*. Colombo: Sirilaka, 1992.

Embree, A. T., ed. *Alberuni's India*. New York: Norton, 1971.

Ernst, Carl W. *Eternal Garden: Mysticism, History, and Politics at a South Asian Sufi Center*. New York: State University of New York Press, 1992.

Evers, Hans-Dieter. *Monks, Priests, and Peasants*. Leiden: E. J. Brill, 1972.

————. "Monastic Landlordism in Ceylon." *Journal of Asian Studies* 28, no. 4 (1969): 685–92.

Flood, Gavin. "Limits of Phenomenology." In *Beyond Phenomenology: Rethinking the Study of Religion*. New York: Cassell, 1999.

Foucault, Michel. *Religion and Culture*, selected and ed. Jeremy R. Carrette. New York: Routledge, 1999.

————. "Technologies of the Self." In *Ethics, Subjectivity, and Truth*, ed. Paul Rabinow, trans. Robert Hurley et al. New York: New Press, 1994.

————. "Nietzsche, Genealogy, History," In *Aesthetics, Method, and Epistemology*, ed. Paul Rabinow, trans. Robert Hurley et al. New York: New Press, 1988.

―――. *The Care of the Self: The History of Sexuality*, vol. 3. Trans. Robert Hurley. 1986. Reprint, New York: Vintage, 1988.

―――. *The Use of Pleasure: The History of Sexuality*, vol. 2. Trans. Robert Hurley. 1985. Reprint, New York: Vintage, 1990.

―――. "Subject and Power." Afterword to Herbert L. Dreyfus and Paul Rabinow, *Michel Foucault: Beyond Structuralism and Hermeneutics*. Chicago: University of Chicago Press, 1983.

―――. *Power/Knowledge: Selected Interviews and Other Writings, 1972–1977*. New York: Pantheon, 1980.

―――. *Discipline and Punish: The Birth of the Prison*. Trans. Alan Sheridan. 1977. Reprint, New York: Vintage, 1995.

―――. *The History of Sexuality*, vol. 1. Trans. Robert Hurley. 1976. Reprint, New York: Vintage, 1990.

―――. *The Archaeology of Knowledge and the Discourse on Language*. Trans. A. M. Sheridan Smith. 1969. Reprint, New York: Pantheon, 1972.

―――. *The Order of Things: An archaeology of Human Sciences*. 1966. Reprint, New York: Vintage, 1990.

Gard, Richard. "Buddhism and Political Authority." In *The Ethic of Power: The Interplay of Religion, Philosophy, and Politics*, ed. Harold Lasswell and Harlan Cleveland. New York: Harper & Brothers, 1962.

Geddess, Jennifer L., ed. *Evil after Postmodernism: Histories, Narratives, and Ethics*. New York: Routledge, 2001.

Geertz, Clifford. *Islam Observed: Religious Development in Morocco and Indonesia*. Chicago: University of Chicago Press, 1973.

―――. "Religion as a Cultural System." In *The Interpretation of Cultures*. New York: Basic, 1973.

Girard, Rene. *Violence and the Sacred*. Baltimore: Johns Hopkins University Press, 1971.

Gombrich, Richard. *Theravada Buddhism: A Social History from Ancient Benares to Modern Colombo*. London: Routledge, 1988.

―――. "Temporary Ordination in Sri Lanka." *Journal of the International Association of Buddhist Studies* 7, no. 2 (1984): 41–65.

―――. *Precept and Practice: Traditional Buddhism in the Rural Highlands of Kandy*. Oxford: Clarendon Press, 1971.

Gombrich, Richard, and Gananath Obeyesekere. *Buddhism Transformed*. Princeton: Princeton University Press, 1988.

Gowans, Christopher W., ed. *Moral Disagreements: Classic and Contemporary Readings*. New York: Routledge, 2000.

Gray, John. "Agonistic Liberalism." In *Isaiah Berlin*. Princeton: Princeton University Press, 1996.

Gunaratna, Rohan. *Sri Lanka: A Lost Revolution? The Inside Story of the JVP*. 1990. Reprint, Sri Lanka: Institute of Fundamental Studies, 1995.

Gunasinghe, Newton. "The Symbolic Role of the Sangha." *Lanka Guardian*, October 1, 1986.

Gupta, Akhil, and James Ferguson. "Beyond 'Culture': Space, Identity, and the Politics of Difference." In *Culture, Power, Place: Explorations in Critical Anthropology*, ed. Akhil Gupta and James Ferguson. 1997. Reprint, Durham, N.C.: Duke University Press, 1999.

Hallisey, Charles. "Roads Taken and Not Taken in the Study of Theravada Buddhism." In *Curators of the Buddha: The Study of Buddhism Under Colonialism*, ed. S. Donald Lopez Jr. Chicago: University of Chicago Press, 1995.

Hansen, Thomas Blom. *The Saffron Wave: Democracy and Hindu Nationalism in Modern India*. Princeton: Princeton University Press, 1999.

Hanssen, Beatrice. "Power/Force/War." In *Critique of Violence: Between Poststructuralism and Critical Theory*. New York: Routledge, 2000.

Harrison, Peter. *"Religion" and Religions in the English Enlightenment*. New York: Cambridge University Press, 1990.

Hemasiri, P. *Ruhunu Sangha Sanvidānaya: Mäta Yugaya*. Matara: Bodhiarakshaka Sabhava, 1990.

Holt, John. *The Religious World of Kīrti Śri: Religion, Arts, and Politics in Late Medieval Sri Lanka*. New York: Oxford University Press, 1996.

———. *Buddha in the Crown: Avalōkiteśvara in the Buddhist Traditions of Sri Lanka*. Oxford: Oxford University Press, 1991.

———. "Protestant Buddhism?" *Religious Studies Review* 17, no. 4 (1991): 307–12.

———. "The Persistence of Political Buddhism." In *Buddhist Fundamentalism and Minority Identities in Sri Lanka*, ed. Tessa Bartholomeusz and C. R. de Silva. New York: State University of New York Press, 1998.

Hubbard, Jamie. "Embarrassing Superstition, Doctrine, and the Study of New Religious Movements." *Journal of the American Academy of Religion* 66, no.1 (1998): 59–92.

Hubel, Teresa. *Whose India? The Independence Struggle in British and Indian Fiction and History*. Durham, N.C.: Duke University Press, 1996.

Ilangasinha, M. *Rangiri Dambulu Vihāraya*. Dehiwala: Sri Devi Printers, 1994.

———. *Buddhism in Medieval Sri Lanka*. Delhi: Sri Satguru, 1992.

———. "Notes on the History of Sigiriya-Dambulla Region in the Eighteenth and the Nineteenth Centuries." In *Settlement Archaeology of the Sigiriya Dambulla Region*, ed. S. Bandaranayake et al. Kelaniya: University of Kelaniya, 1990.

————. "Dambulla Rock Temple: Its Name and History." In *Dambulla Project: First Archaeological and Excavation Project,* ed. H. T. Basnayake. Colombo: Ministry of Kelaniya, 1988.

Inden, Ronald. *Imagining India.* London: Basil Blackwell, 1990.

Jayewardene, J. R. *Apē Jātika Urumaya.* Colombo: Rajaye Mudranalaya, 1986.

————. *Golden Threads.* Colombo: Govt. Printing, 1984.

————. *Budusasuna Saha Prajātantra Vādaya.* Colombo: Rajaye Mudrana Departumentuwa, 1982.

————. *Buddhist Essays.* 1942. Reprint, Colombo: Government Press, 1982.

————. "Buddhism and Politics." *Daily News Wesak Number,* May 19, 1934.

————. *Jayamāvataka Piya Satahan.* Colombo: Rajaye Mudranalaya, n.d.

————. *J. R. Jayewardene: Selected Speeches and Writings, 1944–1978.* Colombo: H.W.D., n.d.

Jeffery, Patricia, and Amrita Basu, eds. *Appropriating Gender: Women's Activism and Politicized Religion in South Asia.* New York: Routledge, 1998.

Jeganathan, Pradeep. "Violence as an Analytical Problem: Sri Lankanist Anthropology after July 1983." *Nethra* 4, no. 2 (1998): 7–47.

————. "In the Shadow of Violence: Tamilness and the Anthropology of Identity in Southern Sri Lanka." In *Buddhist Fundamentalism and Minority Identities in Sri Lanka,* ed. Tessa Bartholomeusz and C. R. De Silva. New York: State University of New York Press, 1998.

————. "After a Riot: Anthropological Locations of Violence in an Urban Community of Sri Lanka." Ph.D. dissertation, University of Chicago, 1997.

————. "Authorizing History, Ordering Land: The Conquest of Anuradhapura." In *Unmaking the Nation: The Politics of Identity and History in Modern Sri Lanka,* ed. Pradeep Jeganathan and Q. Ismail. Colombo: Social Scientists' Association, 1996.

————. "Sri Lanka as a Curative Project: Ordering and Authorizing a Post-Colonial Scholarship." Forthcoming.

Juergensmeyer, Mark. *Terror in the Mind of God: The Global Rise of Religious Violence.* California: University of California Press, 2000.

————. "The Worldwide Rise of Religious Nationalism." *Journal of International Affairs* 50, no. 1 (1996): 1–20.

————. "What the Bhikkhu Said: Reflections on the Rise of Militant Religious Nationalism." *Religion* 20, no. 1 (1990): 53–75.

Kakar, Sudhir. *The Colors of Violence: Cultural Identities, Religion, and Conflict.* Chicago: University of Chicago Press, 1996.

Kapferer, Bruce. "Remythologizing Discourses: State and Insurrectionary Violence in Sri Lanka." In *The Legitimation of Violence,* ed. David E. Apter. New York: New York University Press, 1998.

————. *Legends of People, Myths of State: Violence, Intolerance, and Political Culture in Sri Lanka and Australia*. Washington: Smithsonian Institution Press, 1988.

Kemper, Steven. *The Presence of the Past: Chronicles, Politics, and Culture in Sinhala Life*. Ithaca, N.Y.: Cornell University Press, 1991.

————. "Wealth and Reformation in Sinhalese Buddhist Monasticism." In *Ethics, Wealth, and Salvation*, ed. Russell Sizemore and Donald Swearer. Columbia: University of South Carolina Press, 1990.

————. "The Buddhist Monkhood, the Law, and the State in Colonial Sri Lanka." *Comparative Studies in Society and History* 26, no. 3 (1984): 401–21.

————. "Buddhism without Bhikkhus: The Sri Lanka Vinaya Vardhana Society," in *Religion and Legitimation of Power in Sri Lanka*, ed. Bardwell Smith. Chambersburg, Pa.: Anima, 1978.

————. "Radical Asceticism and the Sinhalese Case." *Man* 15, no. 1 (1980): 195–95.

————. The Social Order of the Sinhalese Buddhist Sangha. Ph. D. dissertation, University of Chicago, 1973.

Kieffer-Pülz, P. "Ceremonial Boundaries in the Buddhist Monastic Tradition in Sri Lanka." Unpublished paper delivered at the Wilhelm Geiger conference, Sri Lanka, 1995.

King, Richard. *Orientalism and Religion: Postcolonial Theory, India, and 'The Mystic East.'* New York: Routledge, 1999.

Kitagawa, Joseph. "Buddhism and Asian Politics." *Asian Survey* 2, no. 5 (1962): 1–11.

Kopf, David. Review of *Imagining India*, by Ronald Inden. *Journal of the American Oriental Society* 112, no. 4 (1992): 674–77.

Krishna, Sankaran. *Postcolonial Insecurities: India, Sri Lanka, and the Question of Nationhood*. Minneapolis: University of Minnesota Press, 1999.

Laclau, Ernesto. "Identity and Hegemony." In *Contingency, Hegemony, Universality: Contemporary Dialogue on the Left*, by Judith Butler, Ernesto Laclau, and Slavoj Zizek, New York: Verso, 2000.

Lal Kumara, V. A. Sarat. *Dōshabhiyōgaya*. Wadduwa: Dinusha Mudranalaya, 1994.

Lawrence, P. *Work of Oracles, Silence of Terror: Notes on the Injury of War in Eastern Sri Lanka*. Ph.D. dissertation, University of Colorado, 1997.

Liyanage, Gunadasa. *Walpola Rahula Hāmuduruwō*. Dehiwala: Bauddha Sanskrutika Madyastanaya, 1994.

Lorenzen, David N. "Who Invented Hinduism?" *Comparative Studies in Society and History* 41, no. 4 (1999): 630–59.

MacIntyre, Alasdair. *Whose Justice? Which Rationality?* Notre Dame, Ind.: University of Notre Dame Press, 1988.

————. *After Virtue: A Study in Moral Theory.* 1981. Reprint, Notre Dame, Ind.: University of Notre Dame Press, 1984.

Malalasekera, G. P. *Dictionary of Pāli Proper Names.* 1938. Reprint, London: Pali Text Society, 1960.

Malalgoda, Kitsiri. *Buddhism in Sinhalese Society.* Berkeley: University of California Press, 1976.

Manor, James. *The Expedient Utopian: Bandaranaike and Ceylon.* Cambridge: Cambridge University Press, 1989.

Marty, Martin E., and Scott Appleby, eds. *Fundamentalisms Observed.* Chicago: University of Chicago Press, 1991.

Masefield, P., trans. *The Udāna.* Oxford: Pali Text Society, 1994.

Mirando, A. H. *Buddhism in Sri Lanka in the 17th and the 18th Centuries.* Dehiwala: Tisara Prakashakayo, 1985.

Moore, Mick. "Thoroughly Modern Revolutionaries." *Modern Asian Studies* 27, no. 3 (1993): 593–642.

Mouffe, Chantal. *The Democratic Paradox.* London: Verso, 2000.

————. *The Return of the Political.* London: Verso, 1993.

Nietzsche, Friedrich. *The Will to Power.* Trans. Walter Kaufmman and R. J. Hollingdale. New York: Vintage, 1968.

Obeyesekere, Gananath. "Buddhism, Nationhood, and Cultural Identity: A Question of Fundamentals." In *Fundamentalism Comprehended,* ed. Martin E. Marty and R. Scott Appleby. Chicago: University of Chicago Press, 1995.

————. Review of *The Forest Monks of Sri Lanka,* by Michael Carrithers, and *The Buddhist Saints of the Forest and the Cult of the Amulets,* by S. J. Tambiah. *American Ethnologist* 12, no. 4 (1985): 791–94.

————. "Origins and Institutionalization of Political Violence." In *Sri Lanka in Change and Crisis,* ed. James Manor. New York: St. Martin's Press, 1984.

————. "Religious Symbolism and Political Change in Ceylon." In *The Two Wheels of the Dhamma,* ed. Bardwell Smith. Chambersburg, Pa.: American Academy of Religion, 1972.

————. "Great Tradition and the Little in the Perspective of Sinhalese Buddhism." *Journal of Asian Studies* 22, no. 2 (1963): 139–53.

Panabokke, Gunaratne. *History of the Buddhist Sangha in India and Sri Lanka.* Kelaniya: Post-Graduate Institute of Pali and Buddhist Studies, 1993.

Pandey, Gyanendra. "The Culture of History." In *In Near Ruins: Cultural Theory at the End of the Century,* ed. Nicholas B. Dirks. Minneapolis: University of Minnesota Press, 1998.

————. *The Construction of Communalism in Colonial North India.* Delhi: Oxford University Press, 1990.

Paññarama, Yakkaduwe, ed. *Pävid Vaga Hā Sasun Maga: Kotahēnē Paññākitti Upahāraya, Apē Gaman Maga.* Kelaniya, Sri Lanka: Vidyalankara Sabhava, 1970.

———. *Vanakatā: Mituran Ketavīma.* Kelaniya, Sri Lanka: Sirisena Saha Mitrayo, 1947.

Perera, D. G. A. "King Valagamba's Role in the Uncharted History of the Dambulla Temple." *The Sri Lanka Journal of the Humanities* 22, nos. 1–2 (1996): 83–142.

Perera, Sasanka. "Some Comments on Tambiah's Response." *American Ethnologist* 24, no. 3 (1999): 492–94.

———. Review of *Buddhism Betrayed? Religion, Politics, and Violence in Sri Lanka*, by S. J. Tambiah. *American Ethnologist* 23, no. 4 (1996): 905–6.

Phadnis, Urmila. *Religion and Politics in Sri Lanka.* New Delhi: Monohar, 1976.

Piyasena, *L.Vävē Bända Hōtalaya.* Ratmalana: Sarvodaya Vishvaleka, 1994.

Rahula, Walpola. *The Heritage of the Bhikkhu: A Short History of the Bhikkhu in Educational, Cultural, Social, and Political Life.* New York: Grove Press, 1974.

———. *What the Buddha Taught.* Bedford: Gorden Fraser, 1959.

———. *The History of Buddhism in Ceylon.* Colombo: Gunasena, 1956.

Reynolds, Frank E. "Coming of Age: Buddhist Studies in the United States from 1972–1997." *Journal of the International Association of Buddhist Studies* 22, no. 2 (1999): 459–83.

Roberts, Michael. *Exploring Confrontation, Sri Lanka: Politics, Culture, and History.* New York: Hardwood Academic, 1994.

Said, Edward W. *Orientalism.* New York: Vintage, 1978.

Saint-Amand, Pierre. *The Laws of Hostility: Politics, Violence, and the Enlightenment.* Trans. Jennifer Curtiss Gage. Minneapolis: University of Minnesota Press, 1996.

Sarachchandra, Ediriweera. *Dharmista Samājaya.* Colombo: Elko Industries, 1982.

Schalk, Peter. Review of *Buddhism Betrayed? Religion, Politics, and Violence in Sri Lanka*, by S. J. Tambiah. *Temenos* 29 (1993): 183–89.

———. "'Unity' and 'Sovereignty': Key Concepts of a Militant Buddhist Organization in the Present Conflict in Sri Lanka." *Temonos* 24 (1988): 55–82.

Schwartz, Regina. *The Curse of Cain: The Violent Legacy of Monotheism.* Chicago: University of Chicago Press, 1997.

Scott, David. "The Permanence of Pluralism." In *Without Guarantees: In Honor of Stuart Hall*, ed. Paul Gilroy et al. New York: Verso, 2000.

———. "Fanonian Futures?" In *Refashioning Futures: Criticism after Postcoloniality*, ed. David Scott. Princeton: Princeton University Press, 1999.

————. *Refashioning Futures: Criticism after Postcoloniality.* Princeton: Princeton University Press, 1999.

————. "Colonialism." *International Social Science Journal* 49, no. 4 (1997): 517–27.

————. "'Culture of Violence' Fallacy." *Small Axe: A Journal of Criticism* 2 (1997): 140–47.

————. "The Aftermaths of Sovereignty: Postcolonial Criticism and the Claims of Political Modernity." *Social Text* 48, no. 3 (1996): 1–26.

————. "Religion in Colonial Civil Society." *Cultural Dynamics* 8, no. 1 (1996): 7–23.

————. "Colonial Governmentality." *Social Text* 43 (summer 1995): 191–220.

————. "A Note on the Demand of Criticism." *Public Culture* 8 (fall 1995): 41–50.

————. *Formations of Ritual: Colonial and Anthropological Discourses on the Sinhala Yaktovil.* Minneapolis: University of Minnesota Press, 1994.

————. "The Demonology of Nationalism: On the Anthropology of Ethnicity and Violence in Sri Lanka." *Economy and Society* 19, no. 4 (1992): 492–510.

————. "Criticism and Culture: Theory and Post-colonial Claims on Anthropological Disciplinarity." *Critique of Anthropology* 12, no. 4 (1992): 283–300.

Senaviratna, Jayakodi. *Podi Hāmuduruwō.* Colombo: Dayawamsa Jayakody, 1995.

Seneviratna, Anuradha. *The Golden Rock Temple of Dambulla.* Colombo: Ministry of Cultural Affairs, 1983.

Seneviratne, H. L. *The Work of Kings: The New Buddhism in Sri Lanka.* Chicago: University of Chicago Press, 1999.

————. "The Sangha's Role Reassessed." *Lanka Guardian,* March 15, 1997, 11–12.

————. "The Buddhist Monkhood and Social Concern." *Lanka Guardian,* September 19, 1996, 17–19.

————. "A Critique of Religion and Power in the Sociological Sciences." *Social Compass* 32, no. 1 (1985): 31–44.

————. *Rituals of the Kandyan State.* Cambridge: Cambridge University Press, 1978.

Silawamsa, Talpwala. *Vāda Dekak: Mahana Rävulu Vādaya, Pävidi Kula Vādaya.* Colombo: Ratna Mudranalaya, 1960.

Siriwardene, C. D. S. "Buddhist Reorganization in Ceylon." In *South Asian Politics and Religion,* ed. Donald Smith. Princeton: Princeton University Press, 1966.

Smith, Bardwell, ed. *Religion and Legitimation of Power in Sri Lanka.* Chambersburg, Pa.: Anima, 1978.

Smith, Brian K. "Monotheism and Its Discontents: Religious Violence and the Bible." *Journal of the American Academy of Religion* 66, no. 2 (1998): 403–11.

Smith, Donald Eugene, ed. *South Asian Politics and Religion.* Princeton: Princeton University Press, 1966.

———. "Sinhalese Buddhist Revolution." In *South Asian Politics and Religion,* ed. Donald Smith. Princeton: Princeton University Press, 1966.

———. "Political Monks and Monastic Reform." In *South Asian Politics and Religion,* ed. Donald Smith. Princeton: Princeton University Press, 1966.

Smith, H. ed. *The Khuddhakapātha together with Its Commentary, the Paramatthajōtikā,* vol. 1. London: Pali Text Society, Luzac, 1959.

Smith, Wilfred Cantwell. *The Meaning and End of Religion: A New Approach to the Religious Traditions of Mankind.* 1962. Reprint, New York: Macmillan, 1963.

Southwold, Martin. "True Buddhism and Village Buddhism in Sri Lanka." In *Religious Organization and Religious Experience,* ed. J. Davis. London: Academic Press, 1984.

———. *Buddhism in Life: The Anthropological Study of Religion and the Sinhalese Practice of Buddhism.* Manchester, U.K.: Manchester University Press, 1983.

Spencer, Jonathan. "On Not Becoming a 'Terrorist': Problems of Memory, Agency, and Community in the Sri Lankan Conflict." In *Violence and Subjectivity,* ed. Veena Das, Arthur Kleinman, Mamphela Ramphele, and Pamela Reynolds. Berkeley: University of California Press, 2000.

———. "Tradition and Transformation: Recent Writings on the Anthropology of Buddhism in Sri Lanka." *Journal of the Anthropological Society of Oxford* 21, no. 2 (1990): 129–40.

———. "Writing Within: Anthropology, Nationalism, and Culture in Sri Lanka." *Current Anthropology* 31, no. 3 (1990): 283–300.

———. "Popular Perceptions of Violence: A Provincial View." In *Sri Lanka in Change and Crisis,* ed. James Manor. New York: St. Martin's Press, 1984.

Spencer, Jonathan, ed. *Sri Lanka: History and the Roots of Conflict.* London: Routledge, 1990.

Spivak, Gayatri. "Can the Subaltern Speak?" In *Marxism and the Interpretation of Culture,* ed. Gary Nelson and Lawrence Grossberg. Urbana: University of Illinois Press, 1988.

———. "Rani of Sirmur." *History and Theory* 24, no. 3 (1985): 128–51.

Stirrat, R. L. "Catholic Identity and Global Forces in Sinhala Sri Lanka." In *Buddhist Fundamentalism and Minority Identities in Sri Lanka,* ed. Tessa Bartholomeusz and C. R. de Silva. New York: State University of New York Press, 1998.

Strathern, Marilyn. "Out of Context: The Persuasive Fictions of Anthropology." *Current Anthropology* 28, no. 3 (1987): 251–82.

Strenski, Ivan. "Religion, Power, and Final Foucault." *Journal of the American Academy of Religion* 66, no. 2 (1998): 345–67.

———. "On Generalized Exchange and the Domestication of the Sangha." *Man* 18, no. 3: 463–77.

Strong, John. *The Experience of Buddhism: Sources and Interpretation.* Belmont, Calif.: Wadsworth, 1995.

Suraweera, A. V. *Sinhala Katikāvata hā Bhikshu Samājaya.* Colombo: Gunasena, 1971.

Swearer, Donald. "Fundamentalistic Movements in Theravāda Buddhism." In *Fundamentalisms Observed,* ed. Martin E. Marty and R. Scott Appleby. Chicago: University of Chicago Press, 1991.

———. "Lay Buddhism and Buddhist Revival in Ceylon." *Journal of the American Academy of Religion* 68, no. 3 (1970): 255–75.

Tambiah, S. J. "On the Subject of Buddhism Betrayed?" *American Ethnologist* 24, no. 2 (1997): 457–59.

———. "Entering a Dark Continent: Political Psychology of Crowds." In *Leveling Crowds: Ethnonationalist Conflicts and Collective Violence in South Asia.* Berkeley: University of California Press, 1996.

———. *Buddhism Betrayed? Religion, Politics, and Violence in Sri Lanka.* Chicago: University of Chicago Press, 1992.

———. "Horror Story." In *Sri Lanka: Ethnic Fratricide and the Dismantling of Democracy.* Chicago: University of Chicago Press, 1986.

———. *World Conqueror and World Renouncer: A Study of Buddhism and Polity in Thailand against a Historical Background.* Cambridge: Cambridge University Press, 1976.

Trainor, Kevin. *Relics, Ritual, and Representation in Buddhism: Rematerializing the Theravada Tradition.* Cambridge: Cambridge University Press, 1997.

van der Horst, Josine. *Who Is He, What Is He Doing? The Religious Rhetoric and Performances in Sri Lanka during R. Premadasa's Presidency.* Amsterdam: VU University Press, 1995.

van der Veer, Peter. "Writing Violence." In *Contesting the Nation: Religion, Community, and the Politics of Democracy in India,* ed. David Ludden. Philadelphia: University of Pennsylvania Press, 1996.

———. *Religious Nationalism: Hindus and Muslims in India.* Berkeley: University of California Press, 1994.

———. "The Foreign Hand: Orientalist Discourse in Sociology and Communalism." In *Orientalism and the Postcolonial Predicament,* ed. Carol Breckenridge and Peter van der Veer. Philadelphia: University of Pennsylvania Press, 1993.

van der Veer, Peter, and Hartmut Lehmann, eds. *Nation and Religion: Perspective on Europe and Asia*. Princeton: Princeton University Press, 1999.

Villa, Dana R. *Politics, Philosophy, Terror: Essays on the Thought of Hannah Arendt*. Princeton: Princeton University Press, 1999.

Walters, Jonathan. *The History of Kelaniya*. Colombo: Social Scientists' Association, 1996.

Walzer, Michael. *Interpretation and Social Criticism*. Cambridge: Cambridge University Press, 1987.

White, Hayden. *Tropics of Discourse: Essays in Cultural Criticism*. Baltimore: Johns Hopkins University Press, 1978.

Wickremaratne, Ananda. *Buddhism and Ethnicity in Sri Lanka: A Historical Analysis*. New Delhi: Vikas, 1995.

———. *The Roots of Nationalism: Sri Lanka*. Colombo: Karunaratne, 1995.

Wilson, Jeyaratnam. "Buddhism in Ceylon Politics, 1960–1965." In *South Asian Politics and Religion*, ed. Donald Smith. Princeton: Princeton University Press, 1966.

———. *The Gaullist System in Asia: The Constitution of Sri Lanka*. London: Macmillan, 1980.

Wriggins, Howard. *Ceylon: The Dilemmas of a New Nation*. Princeton: Princeton University Press, 1960.

Wuthnow, Robert, ed. *The Encyclopedia of Politics and Religion*. Washington, D.C.: Congressional Quarterly, 1998.

Yalman, Nur. "Dual Organization in Central Ceylon." In *Anthropological Studies of Theravada Buddhism*, ed. Manning Nash. New Haven: Yale University South Asian Studies, 1966.

———. "The Structure of Sinhalese Healing Rituals." *Journal of Asian Studies* 23 (1964): 115–50.

Zizek, Slavoj. *The Fragile Absolute—or, Why Is the Christian Legacy Worth Fighting For?* New York: Verso, 2000.

Zulaika, Joseba, and William A. Douglass. *Terror and Taboo: The Follies, Fables, and Faces of Terrorism*. London: Routledge, 1996.

INDEX